Spectacular Logic in Hegel and Debord

Critical Theory and the Critique of Society Series

In a time marked by crises and the rise of right-wing authoritarian populism, **Critical Theory and the Critique of Society** intends to renew the critical theory of capitalist society exemplified by the Frankfurt School and critical Marxism's critiques of social domination, authoritarianism and social regression by expounding the development of such a notion of critical theory, from its founding thinkers, through its subterranean and parallel strands of development, to its contemporary formulations.

Series editors: **Werner Bonefield**, University of York, UK and **Chris O'Kane**, John Jay College of Criminal Justice, City University of New York, USA

Editorial Board:
Bev Best, Sociology, Concordia University
John Abromeit, History, SUNY, Buffalo State, USA
Samir Gandesha, Humanities, Simon Fraser University
Christian Lotz, Philosophy, Michigan State University
Patrick Murray, Philosophy, Creighton University
José Antonio Zamora Zaragoza, Philosophy, Spain
Dirk Braunstein, Institute of Social Research, Frankfurt
Matthias Rothe, German, University of Minnesota
Marina Vishmidt, Cultural Studies, Goldsmiths University
Verena Erlenbusch, Philosophy, University of Memphis
Elena Louisa Lange, Japanese Studies/Philology and Philosophy, University of Zurich
Marcel Stoetzler, Sociology, University of Bangor
Moishe Postone†, History, University of Chicago
Matthias Nilges, Literature, St Xavier University

Available titles:
Adorno and Neoliberalism, Charles Andrew Prusik
Right-wing Culture in Contemporary Capitalism, Mathias Nilges
Towards a Critical Theory of Nature, Carl Cassegård

Spectacular Logic in Hegel and Debord

Why Everything is as it Seems

Eric-John Russell
With a Foreword by Étienne Balibar

BLOOMSBURY ACADEMIC
LONDON • NEW YORK • OXFORD • NEW DELHI • SYDNEY

BLOOMSBURY ACADEMIC
Bloomsbury Publishing Plc
50 Bedford Square, London, WC1B 3DP, UK
1385 Broadway, New York, NY 10018, USA
29 Earlsfort Terrace, Dublin 2, Ireland

BLOOMSBURY, BLOOMSBURY ACADEMIC and the Diana logo are trademarks of Bloomsbury Publishing Plc

First published in Great Britain 2021
This paperback edition first published in 2022

Copyright © Eric-John Russell, 2021

Eric-John Russell has asserted his right under the Copyright, Designs and Patents Act, 1988, to be identified as Author of this work.

Foreword © Étienne Balibar, 2021

For legal purposes the Acknowledgements on p. xi constitute an extension of this copyright page.

Series cover design: Ben Anslow

All rights reserved. No part of this publication may be reproduced or transmitted in any form or by any means, electronic or mechanical, including photocopying, recording, or any information storage or retrieval system, without prior permission in writing from the publishers.

Bloomsbury Publishing Plc does not have any control over, or responsibility for, any third-party websites referred to or in this book. All internet addresses given in this book were correct at the time of going to press. The author and publisher regret any inconvenience caused if addresses have changed or sites have ceased to exist, but can accept no responsibility for any such changes.

A catalogue record for this book is available from the British Library.

Library of Congress Cataloging-in-Publication Data
Names: Russell, Eric-John, author.
Title: Spectacular logic in Hegel and Debord : why everything is as it seems / Eric-John Russell.
Description: London ; New York : Bloomsbury Academic, 2021. | Series: Critical theory and the critique of society |
Identifiers: LCCN 2020049446 (print) | LCCN 2020049447 (ebook) | ISBN 9781350157637 (hardback) | ISBN 9781350157651 (ebook) | ISBN 9781350157644 (epub)
Subjects: LCSH: Debord, Guy, 1931-1994. Société du spectacle. | Hegel, Georg Wilhelm Friedrich, 1770–1831–Influence. | Critical theory. | Social psychology. | Logic. | Spectacular, The. Classification: LCC HM480 .R875 2021 (print) | LCC HM480 (ebook) | DDC 302—dc23
LC record available at https://lccn.loc.gov/2020049446
LC ebook record available at https://lccn.loc.gov/2020049447

ISBN: HB: 978-1-3501-5763-7
PB: 978-1-3502-1736-2
ePDF: 978-1-3501-5765-1
eBook: 978-1-3501-5764-4

Series: Critical Theory and the Critique of Society

Typeset by RefineCatch Limited, Bungay, Suffolk

To find out more about our authors and books visit www.bloomsbury.com and sign up for our newsletters.

It is only shallow people who do not judge by appearances.

Oscar Wilde

Contents

List of Illustrations	x
Acknowledgements	xi
Note on Translation	xiii
Foreword	xiv
Introduction	1
The spectacle as a critical theory of society	4
Against nominalist interpretations	5
A fairly amiable taunting	8
Avoiding the eyes of a blameworthy world	13
An *a priori* engagement	16
Structure of the book	19
1 The Truth of the Spectacle	23
The true is the whole	24
The whole is the untrue	30
In a world which really is *topsy-turvy*, the true is a moment of the false	34
The materialization of ideology	42
Conclusion	46
2 The Speculative of the Spectacle	49
Speculative identity	51
Force and the understanding	54
The interiority of things	56
The structure of solicitation	57
The inverted world	60
The interiority, solicitation and inversion of the spectacle	61
Unity and division of appearances	66
The speculative in Feuerbach and Marx	73
Conclusion	81
3 The Value of the Spectacle	83
The spectacle as a category of the critique of political economy	86

	Value and its spectacular forms of appearance	89
	The spectacular nature of money	90
	Money as the visualization of value	92
	Money as the monopoly on use-value	93
	Hunger is never simply hunger	97
	Money as *Gemeinwesen*	101
	Capital as spectacle	103
	Conclusion	107
4	The Reflection of the Spectacle	109
	Philosophies of reflection	111
	An antinomic theory of reification	113
	An untarnished reflection	115
	A unitary theory of reification	117
	Conclusion	125
5	The Essence of the Spectacle	127
	The problem of indifference	129
	The relational world of the spectacle	130
	The spectacle as a reign of commensurability	137
	The optical actuality of the spectacle	144
6	The Concept of the Spectacle	153
	The spectacle as automatic subject	154
	The concreteness of the concept	158
	The syllogistic structure of the spectacle as concept	160
	The spectacle as self-differentiation	162
	Unity of work and leisure	166
	Unity of state and economy	170
	Unity of town and country	175
	Unity of diffuse and concentrated spectacle	178
	The coherence of the spectacle	183
	The idea of the spectacle	184
	The life of the spectacle	186
	The spirit of the spectacle	188

Conclusion: A Nightmarish Baroque	191
Appendix: *The Society of the Spectacle* and Its Time	197
The fear of integration	197

Beneath the 'French fiddlededeee', Parisian socialists are all liars and rascals	200
The *Trente glorieuses* years	202
Notes	205
Bibliography	229
Index	239

List of Illustrations

2.1	The Concentrated Spectacle, *Internationale situationniste* 10 (1966).	70
2.2	The Diffuse Spectacle, *Internationale situationniste* 10 (1966).	71
4.1	The Independence of the Commodity, *Internationale situationniste* 10 (1966).	123
6.1	The Domination of the Spectacle over Life, *Internationale situationniste* 11 (1967).	168

Acknowledgements

This book is the revision of a doctoral dissertation. Chapters 3 and 4 are expanded versions of essays published elsewhere: the former appeared as 'From the Commodity to the Spectacle: Debord's Marx', published in the collected volume *Capitalism: Concept and Idea – 150 Years of Marx's* Capital: *The Philosophy and Politics of Capital Today*, edited Peter Osborne, Éric Alliez and Eric-John Russell (2019); the latter appeared as 'The Eyes of Narcissus: the Province of Reflection in Georg Lukács and Guy Debord', published in the 2017/2018 *Jahrbuch der Internationalen Georg-Lukács-Gesellschaft*, edited by Rüdiger Dannemann.

It is with gracious esteem that I acknowledge the support of the Centre for Research in Modern European Philosophy. Particularly valuable have been the encouragement and guidance of its faculty, with noteworthy assistance from Peter Osborne. His support, beyond the fruitful instruction that can be garnered from a supervisor of tact and prowess, gave traction to the reservations of Chateaubriand for whom, it is said, contempt ought to be dispensed sparingly, since there are such a great number of those who deserve it.

I am also indebted to Laurence Le Bras at the Bibliothèque nationale de France, Département des manuscrits, whose assistance not only procured several worthwhile discoveries within Guy Debord's archival material, but also reignited the fading experience of intimacy still to be had when perusing the posthumously temperamental scribbles of an author.

My gratitude is also extended to Robert Hullot-Kentor whose guidance, knowingly or not, set me on the path of this investigation and taught me that sensibility need not relinquish the instinct to disparage; they in fact make for fine bedfellows.

Further acknowledgement goes to Jade Grogan and Liza Thompson at Bloomsbury, Étienne Balibar, Chris O'Kane, Werner Bonefeld, Howard Caygill, John McHale, Elena Louisa Lange, Frank Engster, Christopher J. Arthur, Tom Bunyard and Anselm Jappe, all of whom, through various discussions over the years, have assisted in bringing this monograph to light.

A debt I owe to few others has the distinction of traversing, all at once, ungodly indulgences, maniacal laughter and an almost insatiable appetite for critique which, as memory serves, cannot be quelled by either promises of popularity or the prevailing criteria of success. For this I name Jonathan Harvey, Zac Dempster, John Clegg and Jacob Blumenfeld, all of whom, through various guises but on the whole, have, in the words of Michèle Bernstein, 'confirmed the correctness of our reproaches and the irredeemability of the people who have not proved capable of remaining with us'.

Finally, it is with an exclusive sincerity that I single out Veronika Zhizhchenko, who, besides partaking in the aforementioned exploits, has given me so much more. It would be banal to simply concede that this book would not exist without my wife. Her consultation, gaze and breadth saturate every word. For what she has endured, only multiple lifetimes can restore.

Note on Translation

When the original French sources of the writings of Guy Debord and the Situationist International are cited, English translations, when available, were consulted through the following digital archives: www.notbored.org; www.cddc.vt.edu/sionline; and isinenglish.com.

Foreword

Heretic Hegelianism

Étienne Balibar

As an introduction to Eric-John Russell's beautiful book on Debord and his *Society of the Spectacle*, I will offer some spontaneous reactions inspired by my excitement at the idea that his analyses, which I had found quite illuminating when they existed in the form of a philosophical dissertation, are now available for a broad intellectual public in a more polished, incisive and concentrated version.

Guy Debord (1931–94), a French philosopher who was also an artist, moviemaker, poet and radical activist, remained an outsider with respect to the established intellectual world and the academia, but he played a crucial role in the underground and the birth of a new counter-culture confronting the society of mass consumption He had a wide influence in the fields of art criticism, urban and media sociology and strategic gaming, notwithstanding his continuous prestige in the circles of the ultra-revolutionary left, where he is perceived as the first theorist of what is now called 'destituent power'. In the post-1968 period, he acquired for some a heroic, and for others a quasi-mythical figure. He also provoked many controversies linking his life and actions to his ideas. His name remains mainly attached to a short book, made of 221 aphorisms in Nietzschean or Wittgensteinian fashion, both abstract and eloquent, *The Society of the Spectacle* (1967), which no 'history of ideas' can neglect. With the passing of the century, however, the question inevitably arises as to which side of the great divide imposed by time he would fall, a divide separating the many works with a mere antiquarian interest from the few whose importance for our life and thought has increased. Despite the evidence that he keeps being commented upon emotionally, or strategically invoked, but also pointedly 'refuted' by major contemporary thinkers (think of Agamben and Rancière respectively), this is a question that cannot be brushed away without a closer examination, especially because our image of his political activism and theoretical practice evokes 'paradigms' widely supposed to belong to the culture of the twentieth century rather than the twenty-first: 'break-away' avant-gardism and a 'Hegelian Marxist' philosophy of history (a paradoxical combination in many respects).

The steady flow of recent commentaries (in part prompted by the opening of Debord's archive and the new edition of his 'collected writings', in part by the perception that his words might resonate again strongly in our 'apocalyptic' times) would testify for the second hypothesis. Books and essays with remarkable erudition and lucidity have appeared (Eric-John Russell knows them and refers to them), or they are about to appear (notably in French). I believe that the present book will feature prominently in the list, and in fact could redirect our interpretation of Debord in a manner that is both original and philosophically very productive. This derives, in my view, from the fact that the author is taking up a rather risky 'hermeneutic' challenge: while proposing a systematic interpretation of Debord's theory (mainly in the *The Society of the Spectacle*), with the help of its preparatory material revealed by the newly accessible archive, he identifies a 'secret' key to the construction of the book, namely its continuous inspiration drawn from Hegel's *Science of Logic* (particularly the 'Logic of Essence' and the 'Logic of Concept'): not in the sense of a simple 'model' of dialectical reasoning, but in the sense of a genuine *translation* of its categories and progressions into a new idiom (that of the critique of 'mature' or 'absolute' capitalism). And, from there, he moves towards a veritable *transformation* of Debord's text into *another text*, which happens to be a 'materialist' version of Hegel's Logic itself (that very transformation that Marx and later Marxists had always 'promised' but never achieved in a convincing manner). Here of course lies the paradox: by performing this transformation (which requires an intimate knowledge of both texts), Russell is not betraying any one of them, but he is extracting and realizing a *theoretical surplus-value*, setting creative thinking in motion. I am speaking of his own thinking as much as ours, provided we play by the rules of this game: which, I am sure, will be a strong temptation for many readers.

Russell's argument relies on one of those essential *wordplays* which, not uncommonly but always specifically, reveal the origin of a great philosophical idea: the 'spectacle' (therefore the *spectacular*) and the 'speculative' (which always retains a relationship to the *specular* and the question of *specularity*) are but two sides of the same idiomatic and theoretical coin, but they are also indicative of the two opposite directions arising from its original ambivalence. Philosophy (already calling itself 'dialectics') started with a *choice* between these two sides, with Plato rejecting the spectacle and its *mimetic* (specular) principle outside rationality and isolating the speculative autonomy of the *intelligible essences*, a demarcation still (perhaps more than ever) haunting the 'Marxist' critique of *ideologies* (*qua* 'reflections' of social interests and mystification of their goals). Then it was reinvented by Hegel through a paradoxical use of the category 'appearance' (*Erscheinung*, which forms the core of what is at stake in this book), whereby the most 'speculative' enunciations and syllogisms are supposed to express the *immanent truth* (or rationality) of the real itself (*die Sache selbst*, or the Thing *qua* ultimate Reality).[1] In a sense (I don't say that this is the *only* aspect of Russell's interpretation, but I submit that it is a *central* line of argument), the idea would be that, through a Marxian and anthropological detour, we can read in Debord's 'spectacle' a final step towards the reunification of both lineages, the incorporation of the 'spectacular' into the 'speculative' movement itself. This would be a dialectical synthesis which unexpectedly produces a *materialist* and *critical* effect in theory, and a possibility of reducing to zero the distance between theory and *praxis*. The crux of the discussion will therefore reside in rigorously articulating the two categories of the 'spectacle' (within which the whole critique of capitalist forms is condensed) and the 'appearance' (whose *mediating* function in the Hegelian process leading to the absolute 'idea' will now be seen as its most determining aspect).

Let me cut short at this point, since I am not trying to summarize in advance Russell's carefully crafted demonstration, which follows a dialectical progression itself: I just want to express what I retained from it at its most general level, that made it so exciting to me. I shall propose two observations, on each side of the equation.

My first observation regards the category of the 'spectacle' itself and its articulation with a renewed critique of capitalism. Every reader of Debord's treatise knows that he was using this category in an extremely broad and, in fact, unusual sense, which lent itself at the same time to confusion and extrapolation. The relationship to contemporary analyses of mass media, mass consumption and the pervasive function of advertising in the creation of 'artificial needs' and the subjection of the daily life of individuals from the middle class (or even the poor) to the dictatorship of the commodity form (which seemed to challenge a 'classical' Marxist view of class relations) was at the same time quite obvious and enigmatic, given Debord's propensity to draw conclusions thereof which were antithetic to the new 'sociological' and 'semiotic' paradigm (as illustrated by Barthes or Baudrillard). Russell's book will discuss and clarify this at length. What I want to emphasize is the fact that, in his interpretation, it is not the case that 'spectacle' is just an additional element inscribed in the development of the *value-form*, but rather the opposite. To describe capitalist relations of production and consumption as a continuous generalization of the 'spectacle', that is, the *representation of the use* which is immanent *in the exchange value itself*, does certainly expand the concept of 'commodity fetishism' (albeit in a direction that is not exactly that of a Lukácsian 'reification', even if Debord knew *History and Class Consciousness* very well, but rather approaches some aspects of Benjamin's 'capitalist religion'). But above all it makes the value-form itself *secondary* with respect to a more general process of alienation that *separates* life from its own conditions in time and space, or alienates the world itself. In that sense, Russell's insistence on the originality of the category 'spectacle' goes in a direction opposed to other interpretations which have dominated the reading of Debord in the last period (e.g. Anselm Jappe): although quite brilliant, they were more faithful to a standard Marxist reading, and tended to measure Debord's contribution to the analysis of capitalism against pre-established models taken from political economy and its critique. This new interpretation instead does full justice to the Debordian philosophy of history, in which the *world market* is identified with a *global spectacle* (or system of representation), which includes or incorporates 'existing socialism' itself as its mirror image. At the time, of course, this was a crucial political issue, linked to a radical critique of the 'Leninist' notion of a proletarian revolution as the capture of state power, and an affirmation that the overthrowing of capitalism is possible only in the form of a *break with every form of representation*; an idea which already elicits uncanny resonances with the Hegelian *Aufhebung* of representation into 'absolute knowing' (in the final chapter of the *Phenomenology of Spirit*).

Hence my second observation. As I said, in this 'fusion' of Debord's phenomenology of the 'world of capital' which has become historically an absolute with the internal movement of the Hegelian speculation in the *Logic*, the strategic category has to be *appearance*. Any reader of the 'Logic of Essence' in Hegel knows that this notion paradoxically 'merges' the two opposite meanings of *Schein* (illusion, false appearance) and *Erscheinung* (phenomenon, necessary appearance as a condition of experience), overcoming the old philosophical divide and making it possible to understand that the illusion (or the fetishism) is not external to the 'essential relation' which it represents, but, rather, constitutes its very *form of manifestation*. As Hegel famously writes, 'the essence must appear' (*das Wesen muss erscheinen*). This is still classical Hegelianism, but a mutation begins to take place when Russell reads the internal articulation of appearance, essence and constitutive relationality as a blueprint for a *social ontology* (again, of course, a point of close vicinity and bifurcation with the later Lukács, whose social ontology is based on *labour relations*, not representation and communication: featuring almost opposite understandings of 'materialism'). The range of this social ontology in Debord is mapped by successive analyses of *Money*, the *State*, monotheistic *Religion*, *Art* as bourgeois institution, *Urban* environment and planning, all of them originating at different moments of history and illustrating in a specific manner the principle of *separation of life from its own meaning*, or 'world', which Debord calls *materialized ideology*. Spectacle becomes then identified with what, in a striking passage quoted from Hegel's *Realphilosophy* (1805), he calls 'the life of what is dead endowed with self-motion'.[2]

I am now hopefully in a position to justify the title I gave to this preface, which is also a tribute to the originality of Eric-John Russell's work: 'Heretic Hegelianism'. It means that Debord must be read (and understood) as a 'heretic Hegelian' (which, of course, was already the case with Marx himself and some of the best Marxists), who derives revolutionary consequences from a philosophical system apparently intent on granting legitimacy to the *present* institutions of society, under the motto 'rational is real, and real is rational'. As Russell convincingly argues, Debord's work on Hegel was even more intrinsic and deep ranging than his (arguably intense, but circumscribed) work on Marx. This, however, leads to a more surprising discovery: that of *Hegelianism as its own heresy*, therefore Hegel as his own heretic, or the presence of a 'counter-Hegel' within Hegel. This, perhaps, is not an absolutely unique endeavour: one thinks, of course, of Adorno's idea of the 'negative dialectics' (which is also linked to a thorough examination of the question of appearances and 'objectivity' in Hegel). I find it extremely interesting that Russell, beside the inevitable comparisons with Lukács or Lefebvre, so frequently proposes correspondences between Debord's project and the critical reformulation of Hegel attempted by Adorno. Beyond a short essay on "Music and Technique" translated in 1960 in the journal *Arguments*, Debord had not read Adorno (hardly introduced in France at the time), but the comparison is illuminating.[3] From the point of view of this book, however, Adorno's project of a 'negative dialectic' might remain caught in the attempt at *dissociating* a 'pure' negativity in Hegel from its 'reified' negation of the negation in the 'system', where all determinations of history and practice are incorporated into a single totality. As I understand it, the 'heretic Hegel' invented by Debord by means of Russell does not rely on this kind of dissociation. Rather, it is the product of an internal *subversion*, a reversal in the meaning of the 'logical speculation' itself, arising from the very development of its idea. In this perverted and perverse Hegel, which we cannot reject because its existence is based on literal and accurate reading (so accurate, in fact, that Russell's book might very well become one of the best *critical introductions* to the reading of the *Subjective Logic*), it is the movement of *appearances* (called 'spectacle') that provides the truth of the totality which is always in contradiction with itself, separated from itself, and not the reverse. Hence the spectacular (itself speculative) reversal of the famous motto in the Preface to the *Phenomenology of Spirit*: no longer 'the true is the whole' (*das Wahre ist das Ganze*), but conversely, 'the whole is the untrue' (another meaningful encounter with Adorno), and *the true is a moment of the false*. Let's play here for a minute with another philosophical tradition: *falsum index sui et veri* … This primacy of the false or the untrue in the conceptualization of the present world is uncompromising, but not nihilistic. Philosophically it means that Debord's objective (our objective, if we decide to follow him) is not to return to a 'Hegelian' Marx, but rather to produce a 'post-Marxian' Hegel. But it also means, politically, that Hegel, or perhaps the subverted Hegel invented through this 'spectacular' reading, is a direct critic of the 'absolute' capitalist society, inasmuch as he deduces the 'falsity' of its economic totality, or the *impossibility of its social and political reality*. Revolutionary practice is rooted in this impossibility, or it is its own manifestation. It requires of no mediation.

Let me stop here. I am not claiming that what I have presented is exactly what Eric-John Russell wanted to assert: he doesn't need a translation, and he is much more sophisticated. Having the privilege of reading the book in advance, before its readers, I am only offering this as my reaction to his provocative interpretations. Above all, I hope that a reader who followed me until this point has not been deterred from reading further by the abstraction of my formulas. The present book is animated by a continuous passion for the speculative dimension of philosophy which includes the capacity to make it accessible and elicit resonances in our own experience of an impossible world. Let the author now speak for himself.

Introduction

Fortune and the drapery with which it is surrounded
present life as a spectacle in the midst of which any man,
however honest, ends by play-acting in spite of himself.

Nicolas Chamfort

Guy Debord's *The Society of the Spectacle* is a book whose reputation tends to eclipse its actual content. Since its 1967 publication, the work has bitterly contended with its interpreters and the society that its 221 short theses critically diagnose.[1] Accordingly, it has become a ubiquitous observation to say that we live in a society of 'spectacles', whether with reference to television, advertising or social media. The omnipotence of the category is at once its trivialization. Herein, Debord is at a loss to appear as more than a theorist of media distraction or excessive consumerism, as a bitter pill of the postwar avant-garde or as simply a precursor to punk rock sensibility. Elsewhere, Debord is often situated within the discursive parameters set by postmodernism, existentialism and media or cultural studies, and the content of his book therewith frequently emerges as, for example, indistinguishable from the simulacra of Baudrillard or merely as an aphoristic exercise into problems of communication, semiotics or virtualization.

Setting aside such myriad approaches, this book instead offers a sustained examination of the concept of the society of the spectacle through the two pillars upon which Debord understood his own work as a critical theory of society: Marx's critique of political economy and Hegel's speculative philosophy. As Debord elucidates in a December 1971 letter to Juvenal Quillet, 'I will affirm to you straight away: I understand *perfectly* what I have written. Obviously one cannot fully comprehend it without Marx, and especially Hegel' (2004a: 454). The point is contextualized in another correspondence, this time to Giorgio Agamben in 1990:

> I was happy to have attempted – in 1967 and wholly at variance with that absolute lunatic Althusser – a kind of 'salvage by transfer' of the Marxist method by putting a large dose of Hegel back into it accompanied by a resumption of the

critique of political economy, a critique wide-ranging enough to take into account and verify those developments in our unfortunate century that were foreseeable in the eyes of the previous one.

2008a: 212

The investigation to follow unfolds these brief comments with a sustained examination of Debord's concept of the spectacle, that is, to determinately ground its content generally within what might be cursorily referred to as the critical tradition of Hegelian Marxism. This book will argue that the spectacle is a category that derives from both Marx's critique of political economy and the dynamic of Hegel's speculative philosophy. However, more specifically, the category of the spectacle will be cast as a critical theory of society precisely through a conceptual reconstruction built through elements of Hegelian and Marxian logic.

The majority of interpretations of the spectacle both in the French and Anglophone discourse either simply ignore this lineage or at best render it anecdotal, wherein Debord is regarded as simply 'popularizing' Hegel or that *The Society of the Spectacle* contains 'Hegelian motifs' (Merrifield 2005: 31, 50).[2] At best, acknowledgement of Debord's debt to Hegel is more frequently eclipsed by the latter's adherence to Marx. As is well known, *The Society of the Spectacle* begins with a line appropriated from the opening of *Capital*, Volume I: 'In societies where modern conditions of production prevail, all of life presents itself as an immense accumulation of *spectacles*' (1970: §1).[3] However, completely absent from the literature is recognition that the sentence which follows is itself directly taken from the preface to Hegel's *Phenomenology of Spirit*: 'Everything that was directly lived has moved away into a representation' (1970: §1).[4]

The Society of the Spectacle – whose real contribution to critique was in naming its adversary – outlines the extent to which the commodity economy under the capitalist mode of production has, throughout the twentieth century, developed its fetish-character into a social form mediated by appearances. The book follows the intellectual line of modern dialectical thought from Hegel, Marx, Feuerbach, Georg Lukács and Karl Korsch, while tracing the theoretical and practical ventures of the twentieth-century workers' movement. Debord follows in this tradition, placing central emphasis on the fetish-character of the commodity social form, and therewith, on the phenomena of reification [*Verdinglichung*] – elements of Marx's critical project that will receive attention and clarification within our analysis. The society of the spectacle consists in a peculiar form of domination developed through the autonomy of the commodity economy in which human activity becomes structured by objective forms of appearance. Its spectacular logic gives credence to the manifold social phenomena that Debord describes with critical and conceptual continuity under the multivalent category of the spectacle as a form of social domination that has developed in accordance with twentieth-century capitalism.

The spectacle refers to the nature of capitalist society as a totality: the total result of social objectification, including both the social process of human activity and the immediate appearance of that objectified social reality. With the increasing fragmentation of human experience through the capitalist division of labour and the structuring of social relations through the form of the commodity, the spectacle is for Debord the reconstitution of a unitary social life from its separated and disjointed moments *at the level of the appearances*. It is what Debord could possibly mean by the category of appearance that is the subject of this book, appearances that somehow result in a social reality held together with 'positive cohesiveness' (Debord 1970: §8).[5] Yet for Debord, this social cohesion achieved within the society of the spectacle adheres through the principle of separation. It is a social separation of human beings from their own activity falsified into appearances operating outside of their control.

It is the argument of this book that in order for such a diagnosis to acquire full coherence, both the logical dynamics of Marx's theory of the forms of value within the capitalist mode of production, as well as the notion of unity we find in Hegel's speculative philosophy, must be made explicit. Each of these resources will be treated extensively through this book, via a logical reconstruction, in order to fully elucidate the society of the spectacle as a unified social totality that reproduces itself through a movement of appearances. However, our investigation does not simply rest content on highlighting the Marxian and Hegelian sources of Debord's thought. Rather, it will be argued that Debord did not simply find within Hegel's philosophy the language necessary to speak to the problems of contemporary capitalism, but that Hegel's speculative logic, while articulating the basic categories of thought, is sardonically actualized within the spectacle. Its spectacular logic emerges as a really existing rationality, an active force in the world that gives structural coherence to the organization of appearances within capitalist society. We name this rationality as *spectacular logic*.

At its core, Debord's concept of the spectacle adheres through a spectacular logic of commensurability, an identity of and within difference historically grounded within the principle of commodity exchange which reproduces without extinguishing qualitative distinctions in a relation of equivalence. For this, the spectacle is a social structure of unity-in-separation modelled on elements of Hegel's *Phenomenology of Spirit* and *Science of Logic* that gives speculative identity to seeming dualities and antinomies. This is the *spectacular logic* of the spectacle. It is our argument that it is the *speculative* aspect of Hegel's dialectic which constitutes the spectacular logic of the society of the spectacle. Indeed, there is something about the very concept of the spectacle that contains a distinctly Hegelian structure, that is, more specifically, a *speculative* structure which overcomes division in a positive unity that at once both differentiates and reconciles ourselves to the world through a dialectic of appearance. Here, as will become clear, Hegelian logic is given historical actuality within Debord's concept of the spectacle, not as a purveyor of thought or *demiurgos* of the real, but in truth, as a really existing *demiurgos*.

The spectacle as a critical theory of society

This book approaches Debord by questioning the merit of theorizing capitalism in terms of its modality of appearing [*Erscheinungsformen*] or in the phenomenality of *a world that cannot be seen otherwise*. Asking as much suggests that the concept of the spectacle constitutes a fruitful resource for both contemporary Marxian and Frankfurt School critical theory. It isn't sufficiently recognized that for the latter, Debord ought to reside in that same tradition of working out a critical theory of society based on the dynamics of commodity exchange. Therefore, throughout this book, connections will be frequently made that draw Debord's concept of the spectacle closer to certain dimensions of Frankfurt School critical theory.

In order to best conceive Debord's concept of a society of the spectacle as a critical theory of society however, it is first important however to give clarification to what is meant by the latter. Here we understand critical theory as a particular social theory that grasps society as an organic whole, reproducing itself precisely through inherent social antagonisms. This critical theory of society, articulated by the early generation of the Institut für Sozialforschung, examines the *essential* nature of society – itself a concept of the third estate – 'by what it purports itself to be, in order to detect in this contradiction the potential, the possibilities for changing society's whole constitution' (Adorno 2000: 15). More specifically, and most notably for Theodor W. Adorno, the objective and essential law of society – that is, what makes society *social* – consists in the relationship of exchange. Exchange is, to borrow a formulation from Alfred Sohn-Rethel, the predominant mode of social synthesis,[6] that which binds together the social whole and which nevertheless exudes immanent antagonism through the inequality internal to exchange equivalence (Marx 1994: 233–4), and therein reproduces, through exploitation, the class relationship between the buyer and seller of labour-power as the source of surplus value. In addition, the abstract equivalence realized in exchange necessarily occasions the fetish-character of commodities within the capitalist mode of production, an inversion by which the objective forces of economy assert themselves in their absurdity [*verrückten Form*] over and against the social relations comprising society. Here, for the inner nature of capital, social relations necessarily and objectively assume the form of a relation between things.

If a critical theory of society thereby refers to the way in which society, as a totality, reproduces itself by means of its reified character outside the control of those who comprise it, then already Debord's theory of the society of the spectacle finds company. Fundamental to the society of the spectacle is indeed the fetish-character of the commodity, that is, a social form mediated by abstractions having attained an autonomous objectivity that in turn give concreteness to the world through the self-expanding process of capital valorization and that, as a result, comes to dominate human beings as mere personifications or character-masks of that process (Marx 1989: 514). The spectacle as a form of domination by the autonomy of abstraction is a characterization repeatedly found throughout *The Society of the Spectacle*, most notably within chapters one and two.[7] Debord in fact opens the second chapter with a discussion on how the fetish-character of the commodity is 'absolutely fulfilled' (1995: §36) in the self-movement of the spectacle.

Against nominalist interpretations

It can be said without controversy that theories of society are today increasingly characterized by radical nominalism and particularism. With great relativity, individual aspects of the world are made to sit alongside a multiplicity of worlds with varying epistemic standpoints and contending perspectives on the truth of social reality. Most deadly is when it is accompanied by an avaricious philistinism that always wants to touch and taste, to participate under a fuming ideology of praxis. Its correlate is a weak labour market. Never before has there been such an intense need to excise ambiguity from a critical theory of society. What Henri Lefebvre called 'the great pleonasm' in which '[v]ulgar encyclopedism is all the rage' (2002: 76–7) has procured open-ended flights of fancy saturated by whimsical interpretations, gorged with imposters and failing on the whole to adequately grasp the internal necessity that grounds seemingly disparate phenomena. However, necessity remains blind only insofar as it not conceptualized and at a time of so much change, not all in equal measure, the need for determinate conceptuality with internal coherence in a critical theory of society is all the more pressing so as not relinquish critique to that uncouth and half-educated behaviour which finds recourse in 'the noisy clamour of current affairs and the deafening chatter of a conceit which prides itself on confining itself to such matters' (Hegel 1969: 42).

There is a rationality according to which the irrationality of the present unfurls. Faced with such exigency, it is crucial to comprehend the composite and seemingly heterogeneous content of social life, a task gifted to the Hegelian dialectic in order to make explicit the perverted social order and rationality of society. The 'randomness of a [W]eltanschauung' (Adorno 2007: 7) and its formalism would do well to consider the logic of its own impoverishment. It is in this sense that this book will seek to return to the Hegelian system that which Debord took to be its greatest fault: a lack of strategy for combating any 'nebulous indeterminacy' (Hegel 2010: 24) that characterizes social critique in the present moment.[8]

Yet the history of interpreting *The Society of the Spectacle* is a history of rehearsing the same tired story of a masquerade through what Werner Bonefeld, in another context, refers to as 'register[s] of blame' (2016: 7). Here the isolated particularities of an excess in advertising, mass media or consumerism, corporate ascendancy, political misrepresentation, entertainment industries or simply the technological proliferation of images are all, in turn, through different forms of manipulation, said to index the critical theory of *The Society of the Spectacle*. These interpretations of the spectacle, as well as the visual culture readings which place primacy on the categories of 'image' or 'representation', often result in a certain dualist framework for which the spectacle emerges merely as a 'false' representation that conceals a 'true' reality (Rancière 2009: 7; Nancy 2000: 49–52). However, Debord makes clear at the outset of *The Society of the Spectacle* that a focus on imagery per se, along with an association of inauthentic illusion, could not be further from the concept of the spectacle (Debord 1995: §§4–6).[9]

Literal interpretations of Debord's vernacular persist in their obsessive identification with single elements of the society of the spectacle without paying heed to any underlying determinate structure of totality. The nominalism of these approaches, for which questions of form are neglected, reduces the essential structure of the spectacle to its individual component parts and particulars while abandoning any necessary connection between observed phenomena. The difficulty here can be illustrated by giving an account of what Debord describes as the tripartite mechanism or sectors [*la secteur*] of the spectacle. Here, within the book's opening provocations, one finds the following division:

> The spectacle presents itself simultaneously as all of society, as part of society, and as instrument of unification. As a part of society it is specifically the sector which concentrates all gazing and all consciousness. Due to the very fact that this sector is separate, it is the common ground of the deceived gaze and of false consciousness, and the unification it achieves is nothing but an official language of generalized separation.
>
> Debord 1970: §3

The society of the spectacle can be analytically divided into a syllogism that is at once *all of society*, a *part of society* and a *means of unifying society*.[10] However, as merely *part of society* – exemplified with propaganda or rudimentary deception and misinformation – the spectacle appears at its most immediate or phenomenal level. It is here that the spectacle is understood 'in the limited sense of those "mass media" that are its most stultifying superficial manifestation' (Debord 1995: §24). The empirical thought of what this book terms the nominalist interpretations of *The Society of the Spectacle* cannot rise to the totality of the spectacle since its categories are already presupposed so as to reaffirm the immediately given. It is characterized by an affixation to those *parts of society* that correspond only to the most apparent and what appears most starkly is erroneously designated as the most false. Similarly, this approach tends to set the spectacle in abstract opposition to concrete social activity, at base an antinomy between image and reality. However, while Debord himself forewarned against such interpretations early on in the book (Debord 1995: §8), it is his adjourned critical discussion of certain themes in American postwar sociology (1970: §§197–200) that calls attention to the specific deficiencies of these nominalist readings.

Exemplified by the 1962 work of Daniel J. Boorstin, *The Image: A Guide to Pseudo-Events in America*, Debord reproaches the condemnation of mass culture accelerating in the 1950s as myopic critical analyses that fail at surmising more than irrational parasitic infestations on the general decency of this world. The discourse is symptomatic of a reformist morality which places blame on what it apprehends as mere excess, unreality, illusion or simply an elite nefariously manipulating the masses. As Debord writes, '[b]ut while this approach has been able to gather much empirical data, it is quite unable to grasp the true nature of its chosen object' (1995: §197). Therewith, the spectacle is the 'immeasurable abbreviation of the multitudes of particular things which are [only] vaguely present to ... pictorial thought [*Vorstellen*]' (Hegel 1969: 39).

A failure to grasp the *essence* of the spectacle as an organization of appearances coupled with myopic attention towards particularistic malevolence in an otherwise prudent society together forms the nominalism which characterizes these interpretations of the society of the spectacle.[11] They are short-sighted towards any internal relations beyond the most immediate appearances. The spectacle as the organized unity of appearances is ignored while its individual phenomenon is held with cynical esteem, at best comparing the particulars of excessive consumerism and advertising while never posing the question of the universal and essential determinations of its individual instances.

There is nothing accidental or contingent about social satisfaction under the society of the spectacle. As will become clear in accordance with Hegelian thought, differences are subsumed within a unifying concept, giving rational coherence to empirical reality in all of its singularity, diversity and indeterminacy. As Debord writes, '[s]o far from realizing philosophy, the spectacle philosophizes reality, and turns the material life of everyone into a universe of speculation' (1995: §19). Debord's characterization here of the spectacle as the inverted *philosophizing of reality* – specifically in accordance not simply with the discovery of 'intersectional' connections or reciprocal implications in social life, but in the *unitary* critique of capitalist social relations in their totality – can be translated into a concept of the spectacle as the *Hegelianization of reality*. In this way, this book seeks to *Germanicize* Debord against the complaints he himself made for which the theoretical concepts of *The Society of the Spectacle*, 'almost all of which have a German origin', have gone 'quietly unnoticed' (Debord 2005: 61).

A fairly amiable taunting

Remarkably, as his archival materials can attest, Debord took more notes on the work of Hegel than he did on Marx's *Capital*. His lifelong acquaintance with Hegel derives firstly from Hegel himself, most notably from Hyppolite's translation of *Phenomenology of Spirit*, but also from *Elements of the Philosophy of Right*, the *Encyclopaedia Logic*, the *Science of Logic*, the *Philosophical Propaedeutic*, the early theological writings and elements from his philosophy of history. However, beyond Hegel himself, Debord learned much of Hegel through the Marxist tradition, including Marx himself in his early writings. The contours of Debord's Hegelian education acquire even greater definition with the works of Ludwig Feuerbach, the Polish young Hegelian August Cieszkowski, Georg Lukács, Karl Korsch, Kostas Papaïoannou and Henri Lefebvre. Lefebvre's *Logique Formelle, Logique Dialectique* provided Debord with immense instruction on, for example, Hegel's *Wesenslogik*, as did Hyppolite's *Studies on Marx and Hegel* and the latter's spring 1967 seminar at the Collège de France on Hegel's logic, which Debord attended and took ample notes on.[12] At this time, *The Society of the Spectacle* had yet to go to print and the seminar notes are sprinkled with the signposts of 'pour SdS [society of the spectacle]'.

Yet it is not easy to surmise precisely what version of Hegel can be found in Debord's thought. In a 1973 letter, he describes his engagement with Hegel as 'a fairly amiable taunting [*une raillerie assez gentile*]' (2005: 89). Hegel is both lauded as a 'friend of the International' (Debord 2005: 42) and yet also someone who merely glorifies 'what exists' (Debord 1970: §76). Here we find a tension best sustained by an appreciation of two separate versions of Hegel found within Debord's ideas.

The first version of Hegel found within Debord's thought has been captured by Tom Bunyard, who does a great service to the fidelity with which Debord understood his own critical project as an extension of the work of Hegel, the young Marx and Lukács. There, Debord is convincingly cast as 'a twentieth-century Young Hegelian' and as a thinker of historical praxis. Such a portrayal, in which self-determinate human activity is grasped as a unity of subject and object, is argued as having incorporated and reformulated elements of Hegel's philosophy within Debord's entire works, most notably with the concepts of time and history as his central preoccupations. As Bunyard makes clear from the outset, *The Society of the Spectacle* is 'best understood as ... a book that describes a society that has become detached from its capacity to consciously shape and determine its own future' (2018: 4). Debord's Hegelianism becomes, for Bunyard, a 're-figuration of Hegel's claims, in which subject–object unity ceases to be a state of final resolution, and instead becomes the ground of a self-determinate future' (2018: 158). This interpretation adheres to Debord's own explicit comments regarding Hegel and the way in which the latter 'developed a mode of thought capable of thinking change, conflict and historical movement' (2018: 10). Indeed as Debord writes, '[f]or Hegel it was no longer a matter of interpreting the world, but rather of interpreting the world's transformation' (1995: §76). For Bunyard, it is a specific interpretation of Hegel, laying great emphasis on the *Phenomenology of Spirit*, which informs Debord's thinking about historically developing social relations more generally. In this way, Hegelian thought is important less for the way in which it illustrates a logic of the spectacle but for the way in which it allows Debord to conceive human practice as self-directed, transitory and free. Despite the way in which, for Debord, Hegel's philosophy becomes instructive for grasping both the historical significance of social forms and their alienation, Bunyard's reading is left with little to say about how that philosophy *specifically* inheres within the logic of the spectacle; in fact, one almost gets the impression that Hegel's philosophy is everything the spectacle *isn't*.

And yet Debord also is critical of Hegel's thought. Here we find in large part, as a second version of Hegel, a rehearsal of the criticisms wielded by the young Marx. As Debord continues:

> Inasmuch as he did *no more* than interpret that transformation, however, Hegel was merely the philosophical culmination of philosophy. He sought to understand a world that *made itself*. Such historical thought was still part of that consciousness which comes on the scene too late and supplies a justification after the fact. It thus transcended separation – but it did so *in thought only*.
>
> 1995: §76; see also 2004a: 94–5

As with Marx, these comments reflect Debord's subscription to what appears as the idealist limits of Hegel's philosophy, beyond which beckons the realization of philosophy in human praxis. Debord follows here the work of Karl Korsch in his reading of Hegelian philosophy which, with the rise of bourgeois society, reaches the impasse of its own revolutionary and historical present and is left merely glorifying 'what exists'. For this, as Debord writes, 'the only court capable of ruling on truth and falsehood [Hegelian philosophy] has been adjourned' (1995: §76).

This is the manner by which Hegel is explicitly invoked by Debord within *The Society of the Spectacle*. He is at once venerated as a thinker of free and self-conscious historical praxis and yet repudiated as an apologist for the existing state of things. Our investigation will however pivot this latter trope of Hegel as an idealist and argue that there is something about the very concept of the spectacle that contains a distinctly Hegelian structure, that is, more specifically, a speculative structure that overcomes separated antinomies in which a positive unity at once both differentiates and reconciles its individual moments in a dialectic of appearances. Again, the central thesis of this book is that this logic acquires practical dominance within the society of the spectacle. It is from this perspective that we can fully do justice to Debord's remark that '[a]ll the theoretical strands of the *revolutionary* workers' movement stem from critical confrontation with Hegel's thought' (Ibid: §78).

If it is the *method* of the dialectic that registers the venerated Hegel within Debord's writing, it will be argued that it is Hegel's speculative – as the *systematic* unfolding of determinate relations within the dialectic that comprehends the unity of opposites – that inscribes the society of the spectacle with rational coherence. That Debord implicitly conceived speculation, 'the most important aspect of dialectic' (Hegel 2010: 35), as *undialectical* need bear little consequence for the way in which its immanently determinate and autonomous structure nevertheless coheres within the logic of the spectacle. As Debord writes:

> [T]he contemplation of the movement of the economy in the dominant thought of present-day society is indeed a *non-inverted* legacy of the *undialectical* aspect of the Hegelian attempt to create a circular system; this thought is an approbatory one which no longer has the dimension of the concept, which no longer has any need of Hegelianism to justify it, because the movement that it is designed to laud is a sector of the world where thought no longer has any place – a sector whose mechanical development in effect dominates the world's development overall.
>
> 1970: §80

Problematic though this passage may initially appear for our analysis, as will be seen, it will be the extent to which Hegel's *Begriffslogik*, and the described circularity of his speculative system, outpaces the negative moment of the dialectic that the following book will examine. Here it is the *actuality* of Hegelian speculation in and through the social organization of appearances bereft of negation – that is, without what Lenin described as 'the salt of the dialectic'[13] – that will be argued as the logic of the society of the spectacle: the sealed and tasteless thought of separation. As Debord writes, '[n]egation has been so thoroughly deprived of its thought that it was dispersed long ago' (1998: 84).

It is important to acknowledge those few instances in the literature that do however stand above the rest and take seriously the Hegelian thought at work within Debord's writings. The work of Anselm Jappe and Tom Bunyard stand out for the uncustomary manner in which Debord is examined specifically and with sustenance within the tradition of Hegelian Marxism. Jappe's work, which Debord himself considered to be 'the best-informed book about me' (Debord 2008a: 453), is unmatched in grounding Debord's theory of the spectacle within Marx's critique of the fetish-character of commodities and therewith in Lukács' theory of reification. It remains the authoritative account of the ways in which the spectacle develops out of the autonomy of the capitalist economy. However, aside from some Hegelian – or more accurately Feuerbachian – genitive reversals (Jappe 1999a: 7, 12) and terminological appropriations (Jappe 1999a: 21), it is really only a *categorial lineage* that is drawn between Hegel and Debord rather than any substantive engagement. More important becomes the way in which both Marx and Lukács filter Debord's commitment to Hegelian thought. It is an approach not altogether inaccurate – and desperately needed against the dominant literature – although the way in which Hegel is given a back seat to Lukács' interpretation becomes problematic for any efforts to give qualitative distinction between the theory of reification and spectacle, a point which will receive greater attention in our fourth chapter. In the absence of engaging with Hegel himself, Jappe forfeits the capacity to generate a nuanced approach to the Hegelian thought of Debord beyond its mere canonization.

While the work of Bunyard has already been mentioned, it needs to be remarked how his emphasis on Hegelian *separation* which, it is said, Debord utilizes in his concept of the spectacle, presents certain problems. Here, inattention to the way in which Hegelian *unity* might wield pertinence for the logic of the society of the spectacle renders Bunyard's interpretation partial at best and almost indistinguishable from the Young Hegelians at worst. When, for Bunyard, the spectacle does constitute a unitary structure, it is simply a unity within content and not in form. Potentially lost in this reading is the reason for which Debord titled his opening chapter 'Separation Perfected [*La séparation achevée*]'. As will become clear, it is the self-moving form-determinations as a *unifying force* that constitutes the social reality of the spectacle. While accurate that separation remains pivotal for the spectacle as its 'alpha and omega' (Debord 1970: §25), single recourse to the framework of division risks failing to grasp the spectacle as 'the social organization of appearances' (1970: §10). It is in fact a self-mediating totality, but one which is determinately structured through a unity-in-separation. In contrast, for Bunyard, the Hegelian unity of subject and object is only incorporated in Debord's theory of social praxis, not in the concept of spectacle, one which, following the young Marx, has failed to actualize itself beyond thought (Bunyard 2018: 31, 34).

Despite the important scholarship of Jappe and Bunyard, and in contrast to the prevailing literature on *The Society of the Spectacle*, this book will neither read the Hegelian influence on Debord exclusively through Lukács and therewith preclude an analysis on the strong Hegelian distinctions between reification and spectacle, nor will focus be placed strictly on the negativity of the dialectic for invoking Debord's ideas on history and praxis. In a word, this book is less an evaluation of the role of Hegel for Debord's thought in general than it is of the importance of Hegel for the social ontology and logical structure of the spectacle *as a mode of social cohesion*.

Avoiding the eyes of a blameworthy world

The existing scholarship around Debord all too frequently sidelines the lineage between the concept of the spectacle and together the critical theory of the Frankfurt School, Marx's critique of political economy and, most crucially for our purposes, Hegel's speculative philosophy. This book will as such pull Debord away from the discourses in which he is normally situated, such as media and cultural studies and avant-garde art history, and instead examine his work within the lineage of German Idealism, Left Hegelianism, Hegelian Marxism, Marxist Hegelianism and Frankfurt School critical theory.

It can however be said that Debord's popularity outside of these traditions has much to do with his opaque writing style and the prose through which he formulated his critical theory of society. Indeed, as 'a remarkable example of what this era did not want' (Debord 2004b: 68), Debord's notion of a society of the spectacle remains a largely misunderstood critical analysis of the reified social relations of a society dominated by the capitalist mode of production. However, the myriad approaches to his work are an index of Debord's own allegedly cryptic formulations, which foment arbitrary interpretations. His writing is by no means as straightforward as one may find in a classical formal mode of logical or philosophical argumentation. Nevertheless, and matched possibly by Karl Kraus, Debord weighed his words more carefully than most. As an author who once professed to 'never give explanations' (2006f: 70), Debord rarely employs his categories in a technical capacity and his work is often littered with seemingly contradictory ideas. Attention is thereby required when investigating his categories, which are, as the author himself admits, often 'provisional [*occasionnel*]' (2004a: 457).[14]

Debord's writing has always proceeded with the caution and meticulous precision of a war strategist.[15] For example, in introducing his 1988 *Comments on the Society of the Spectacle*, Debord forewarns his reader that

> I obviously cannot speak with complete freedom. Above all, I must take care not to give too much information to just anybody. Our unfortunate times thus compel me, once again, to write in a new way. Some elements will be intentionally omitted; and the plan will have to remain rather unclear. Readers will encounter certain decoys, like the very hallmark of the era.
>
> Debord 1998: 1–2

Debord finds himself maneuvering inside a 'social reign of appearances where no "central question" can any longer be posed "openly and honestly"' (Debord

1970: §101). This puts any cogent analysis of his work into the curious position of having to evaluate less a lucid argument developing elements of Hegel's thought or Marx's critique of political economy than something more closely resembling a puzzle whose author provocatively flatters himself for 'never engaging in any activity that could pass for socially honest' (Debord 2006b: 1834). And yet it remains the case that Debord is not without the strength to write about the predicament he finds himself, one that is thoroughly binding.

Debord's unapologetic and fragmentary writing yields no systematic approach to his concept of a society of the spectacle. In an almost rhapsodic spirit, *The Society of the Spectacle* exhibits clauses insolent to any sound logic or pedantic fidelity, with the cunning to decide between a swift gash or a concentrated incision and yet all the while seeming to capriciously drift upon the wind. New pivoting axles appear around each corner and further extend into allusions that unfurl out into spirals. It is thinking insubordinate to the commanding conjunctions of a logical structure, hardly resembling the arm wrestling of a peremptory argument or a simple stream of assertions. In this way, and despite Debord's skill for speaking in the noble voice of a Tacitus, a certain humility emerges in the writing as a composition that completely turns itself over to its own object. The reader finds there neither an additive approach in which the conjunctions are modes of subjugating one moment to the next, nor a collection of mere juxtapositions. It is difficult to discern a centre of gravity within *The Society of the Spectacle*. Scarcely deductive, every proposition is equally close to its truth without abandoning their authoritative overture.

The Society of the Spectacle resembles less the systematic structure of Marx's *Capital* than it does, on account of its scope and purview, Adorno's *Minima Moralia*.[16] Nevertheless, despite the strategic ambiguity that might be said to characterize *The Society of the Spectacle*, the conceptual contours and theoretical lineage that make up the book are not altogether impalpable, or even unverifiable; hence the justification for the logical reconstruction that is to follow. However, if one importance of this book concerns the manner of rectifying Debord's intentionally obscure locutions and thereby cauterize his work against the dominant interpretations, another concerns how we might help elucidate the pertinence of his diagnosis beyond the historical moment in which it was initially written.[17]

A reconstruction of spectacular logic is required for distinguishing the essential determinations of the society of the spectacle in order to evaluate its lasting significance beyond postwar prosperity, that is, to determine its explanatory power beyond the period of postwar abundance. This can be accomplished through a meticulous exposition of the spectacle's logic and conceptual objectivity, so that any ambiguity or contingency of Debord's diagnosis can be exorcized. As a result, this book offers a theory of the society of the spectacle as an eminently logical system, ultimately justified by the prerogative to expel from the critical theory of society any of the indeterminate or capricious orientation so prevalent within contemporary dissatisfaction. This is the second importance of our investigation. If the need within a critical theory of society for determinate conceptuality and rational coherence is all the more pressing at times of unbridled irrationality, to adequately grasp internal necessity within the spectacle as a form of domination becomes paramount. Our approach thereby attempts to purify the terms of Debord's critical diagnosis beyond mere contingency. We argue that to give the concept of the spectacle its greatest explanatory power is to emphasize its logical structure as the rational actuality of Hegel's speculative. It is the contention of this analysis that only through a logical reconstruction of Debord's concept of the spectacle can the society of the spectacle as a distinctly critical theory of society be brought to bear beyond the historical moment in which it was initial formulated.

The central importance of this book is thus twofold: on the one hand, there is the scholarly importance of recasting Debord's diagnosis within the critical traditions in which it is predominantly neglected, but also, on the other hand, of advancing Debord's diagnosis as a critical theory of society pertinent to the present moment. We might add here that this book will not be an evaluation of whether Debord *correctly* interpreted Hegel's philosophy or whether he relinquished any fidelity to Marx himself. Further, this book will not be a biographical history of Debord's intellectual development. To paraphrase Fontenelle, in the memory of a rose, no one has ever seen a gardener die. We aim to avoid reducing the critical concept of the society of the spectacle as *a total critique of a structured totality* to mere historical circumstance, one saturated with sociologisms and psychologisms. Additionally, by no means is what follows a holistic analysis of Debord's work. For this, aspects of Debord's thinking on, for example, history, temporality, aesthetics or revolution, and the project of the Situationist International more generally, are left to others. These themes, while important, subsist within the literature upon excessively trodden paths. Further, if readers find within our investigation a divergence from elements of Debord's thought, or that lines of inquiry run counter to the 'spirit' of his thinking, it ought to be emphasized that this book is not an attempt to unearth or decipher what Debord *really* meant, but what he *should have* meant. This book retains fidelity to Debord's thought only to the extent that his diagnosis helps advance and make explicit the speculative logic of the society of the spectacle. The particular perimeters and contours have been set to examine his theory of a society of the spectacle as consisting in a very specific logical structure grounded in Hegelian thought and Marx's critique of political economy, a reading that aspires to open Debord up as a diagnostician pertinent to the critical theory of the Frankfurt School. The aim as such is to provide a logical reconstruction of the spectacle as a distinctly speculative concept, devoid of capricious arbitrariness, and, seeing through the relatively aphoristic language of Debord, grasp the actual weight and give full logical determinacy to its concept, which on the surface can admittedly appear quite fickle.

An *a priori* engagement

While Debord invoked the category of spectacle as early as 1955,[18] it is only through the 1960s and finally within *The Society of the Spectacle* that it emerges as a critical concept for a structured totality. Nevertheless, the book's fragmentary form lacks systematic regularity. Therefore, in the most rigorous sense of the term, this book shall examine the *concept* [*Begriff*] of the society of the spectacle in and through its structure of appearance. If capital has 'reached a magnitude and acquired a weight of its own that enables [it] to present itself ... as the expression of society as a whole' (Adorno 2003a: 99), the logic of that mode of expression or appearance-form elicits dialectical and necessary moments of determination for its reproduction. Indeed, although Debord's book does not bear on its sleeve any systematicity for which an immanent development of the categories yields an exposition of a totality, there is a way in which its dialectical thinking of a totality is nevertheless operative, despite the absence of a dialectical sequencing of exposition [*Darstellung*] as we might find in Hegel or Marx.

The nature and specific essence of the spectacle, as well as the complexity and contingency of its appearances and seemingly capricious phenomena, is its *Begriff*, an indispensible unity which renders its internal differences manifest. Therefore, it will be in accordance with Hegel's approach for comprehending the '*pure essentialities*' (Hegel 2010: 10) of thought within the *Science of Logic* – in which logical categories are in fact determinations of objective relations that permeate the whole of life (2010: 14–15) – that the spectacle will be investigated. To raise the spectacle to its highest universality is to make explicit its logical determinations. Here it is discovered that the cohesion of its concept, and the determinations of its immanent appearance-forms through the critique of political economy, together gives the spectacle its independence and self-subsistence. 'To focus attention on this *logical* nature which animates [*Geist*], moves and works in it, this is the task' (Hegel 1969: 37).

Only through a rational reconstruction and exposition of the essential and necessary determinations of the spectacle as a totality can its prescience beyond postwar prosperity become explicit. Here is discovered the importance of going beyond the immediacies of bare facticity and historical contingency in order to establish the logical necessities for the reproduction of a totality, a level of abstract analysis fundamental for gauging that totality's appearance and transformation within history. If it is conceded that the modern spectacle is a development of the commodity economy and so long as exchange relations remain the predominant mode of social synthesis, then heedless of the historical transformations of capitalist society, an idealization on the manner in which the spectacle as a totality reproduces itself, that is, a comprehension of its rational core and necessary lines of determination, remains a fundamental component of the category of the spectacle as a critical theory of society.

Yet it has been a frequent judgement that *The Society of the Spectacle* fails at providing any coherent concept of spectacle. For example, within the article 'How Not to Understood Situationist Books', which appeared in the final twelfth issue of *Internationale situationniste* (*IS*) in 1969, a series of responses were composed prompted by *Nouvel Observateur* journalist François Châtelet and his accusation that the writing of Debord and the SI fails to exceed 'the empirical' and is altogether 'without concepts'. Further, in a publishing atmosphere when 'a hundred mediocre books are quickly saluted as highly conceptual', the article identifies Claude Lefort's criticism that *The Society of the Spectacle* has failed 'to notice its debt to Hegel'. As the SI responded:

> The fact that 'this idea is reflected in all the others' is precisely what we consider the characteristic of a *dialectical book*. Such a book does not have to 'advance,' like some doctoral dissertation on Machiavelli, toward the approval of a board of examiners and the attainment of a diploma. (And as Marx put it in the Afterword to the second German edition of *Capital*, regarding the way the dialectical 'method of presentation' may he viewed, 'This reflecting may make it seem as if we had before us a mere *a priori* construction.') *The Society of the Spectacle* does not hide its *a priori* engagement, nor does it attempt to derive its conclusions from academic argumentation. It is written only to show the *concrete* coherent field of application of a thesis that already exists at the outset, a thesis deriving from the investigations that revolutionary criticism has made of modern capitalism.
>
> Knabb 2006: 340

It will be the argument of this book that the way in which *The Society of the Spectacle* consists in an '*a priori* engagement' with society is precisely because of 'its debt to Hegel'. The spectacle's spectacular logic, as 'spirit's consciousness of its own pure essence' (Hegel 1969: 51), is accordingly as *actual* as it is *rational*. Indeed, the rationality of the spectacle is its actuality, an admittedly complex Hegelian insight that will gain greater lucidity as this book proceeds. The point is nevertheless important to annunciate at the outset in order to forestall any pedestrian understandings of conceptuality which subsists externally to that rational 'unity which is not abstract but living and concrete' (Hegel 2010: 38–9); or with a colourless concept of the spectacle as somehow independent from its actual existence within history. Generally, as will become clear, the identity of actuality and reason is internal to Hegel's *Begriffslogik*, a relation that endures within the concept of the spectacle. Indeed, for Hegel 'it is the *concept* alone ... which has *actuality*, and in such a way that it gives actuality to itself' (1991a: 25). Further, while the Hegelian concept of reason (*Vernunft*) will receive greater attention in chapters 2 and 4, it can briefly be noted that for Hegel, *Vernunft* is spirit actualizing itself or making itself material in the world; it is the *grammar* of *Geist* (Hegel 2010: 36) reconciling the ideal to the real and making itself objective in the world. As Hegel writes, 'To recognize reason as the rose in the cross of the present and thereby to delight in the present – this rational insight is the *reconciliation* with actuality' (1991a: 22). With these comments it should be anticipated that Hegel's famous adage from the preface to *Elements of the Philosophy of Right* will acquire considerable purchase within the conceptuality of the spectacle: 'What is rational is actual; and what is actual is rational' (1991a: 20).[19]

The society of the spectacle as a critical theory of society cannot simply offer a laundry list of contingent 'spectacles' exemplified through various social phenomena. If it is to elucidate a social totality, it must expound the necessary relations between differentiated spectacles, their heterogeneous content alongside formal reconciliation. The spectacle as a critical theory of society must as such offer logical coherence on spectacular social organization despite the apparent discontinuity between various spectacles. It is the argument of this book that only a Hegelian logic of appearances in their actuality can give credence to such spectacular organization. To highlight the essential logic of the spectacle is therefore to elevate it above those historical contingencies, such as postwar consumerism, to which commentators erroneously anchor Debord's diagnosis. Its implications beyond postwar prosperity, by which social structures of appearance have as much to say about periods of immiseration and austerity as they do about periods of strong welfare expenditure and greater proletarian purchasing power, can only be grasped by distilling its essential and speculative logic of accommodating differentiated appearances. This amounts to a dimension of the society of the spectacle that subsists irrespective of the ebb and flow of capital accumulation. The spectacle as a critical theory of society poses the question of what is the unifying logic by which, for example, new means of consumption are adequate for productive levels as much as for the urban environment, statecraft, ideological attitudes, experiences of time and dynamics of entertainment. In a word, it is a logic that must offer a coherent account of a dialectic between homogeneity and heterogeneity, a task exclusively endowed to Hegel's notion of speculative identity. Only through the logic of the spectacle can a reconciliation of differences – whether as phenomena of entertainment, politics, economy, culture, material environment and so on – be rendered as a coherent feature of capitalism as a totality.

Structure of the book

This book will proceed along two axes, both traversing Debord's theory of the society of the spectacle while also offering nuanced engagement with particular elements of Hegel's philosophy. For both, it will be aspects of both the *Phenomenology of Spirit* and *Science of Logic* that will be of the utmost importance, namely incorporating the *method* and *system* of Hegel's thought for evaluating the spectacular logic of the society of the spectacle. It is speculative identity and commensurability that will be traced in Debord's concept of the spectacle and upon which the arc of this book will develop, specifically through majors works of Hegel's philosophy, beginning with the *Phenomenology of Spirit*, moving subsequently to *Faith and Knowledge* and finally to the second and third doctrines of the *Science of Logic*. It will be the speculative logic of Hegel's *Science of Logic* that will be of increasing importance as the chapters proceed.

While each chapter can to a degree be read as separate essays, the golden thread tying each together will be Hegel's distinctively speculative notion of identity. As we will see, it is this concept of identity that will be what, in the logical reconstruction of the spectacle, mediates truth and falsehood (chapter 1), unity and division (chapter 2), use-value and exchange-value (chapter 3), reflection and separation (chapter 4), appearance and essence (chapter 5) and universal and particular (chapter 6). Each of these categorial pairs will be demonstrated as crucial determinations of the spectacular logic of the society of the spectacle, through which an insidiously persistent social form of identification and commensurability structures the movement of appearances.

If the reader finds frustration with the reluctance of this book to define at the outset what can appear as quite complex philosophical terminology and proceed accordingly, we ask only that some patience find its way into the reading. It is a wholly intentional approach to avoid what would become unsatisfying preliminary appeasements. We have instead elected that the categories themselves acquire greater and greater specificity and determination as the chapters unfold. In this way, the concepts employed will indeed come into themselves as the investigation deepens, rather than from without. It is a methodological insight only dialectical categories deserve and therewith brings us closer to the spirit and importance of Hegelian thought and Frankfurt School critical theory, the two pillars between which Debord's theory of the spectacle ought to gain entry.

Chapter 1 begins by simply asking what is false about the society of the spectacle. There it will be argued that Debord's distinct rendition of truth and falsehood derives directly from Hegel's philosophy, albeit mediated by Adorno's criticism of Hegel's thought. Hegel's thought on the relation between truth and falsehood will in turn allow us to assess Debord's relation to Adorno's critical theory, insofar as the latter's critique of Hegelian philosophy will be argued to be an unacknowledged critique of the society of the spectacle. Here, a critical theory of society is not simply enriched by Hegelian philosophy but rather both speak volumes about a form of domination whose characteristic features evince modes of identification, affirmation and reconcilement. The chapter will close with a comparative account between the spectacle and the notion of ideology, thereby highlighting the peculiar nature of the spectacle's falsehood.

Equipped with a distinct notion of falsehood characteristic of the society of the spectacle, chapter 2 will then examine the precise meaning of the category of appearance optimal for such falsehood. With commentary first on precisely how our investigation understands Hegel's concept of speculation, it is the concept of appearance found within the third chapter of Hegel's *Phenomenology of Spirit*, 'Force and the Understanding', that will be of service. This section is in the distinctive position of offering a portrait of the spectacle as a society organized by way of appearances in and through a speculative identity of identity and non-identity. It will be argued that the structure of solicitation found therein can be interpreted as a relation of exchange which, through a dialectic of appearances, yields a 'sensuous supersensible' inverted world. Hegel's 'Force and the Understanding' will thereby emerge, through its speculative logic of unity and division, as a vignette of the logical movement of the spectacle, exemplified in an analysis of chapter 3 of *The Society of the Spectacle*.

Yet if we can find in Hegel a categorial model of exchange through a dialectic of appearances, the extent to which this dynamic encapsulates the domination of appearances characteristic of the spectacle remains incomplete without integrating how Marx inherits this concept of appearance in his critique of political economy. Chapter 3 therefore explores the manner in which the spectacle relates to Marx's forms of value. While having its conceptual basis within them, the category of spectacle, it will be argued, exceeds the specific determinations of value as a broader model of social organization. Particular attention is given to the role of money and how select functions of this particular form of value is directly inherited by the spectacle which helps to evaluate Debord's concept of use-value and exchange-value.

Chapter 4 functions as an interlude of sorts and seeks to evaluate Debord's relation to Georg Lukács, or more specifically, how it might be said that the spectacle differs from the latter's concept of reification. While many commentators have emphasized the way in which Debord's theory of the spectacle is the direct inheritor of Lukács' theory of reification, this chapter will assess such affinity with conceptual resources provided by Hegel's *Faith and Knowledge*. In a word, the chapter aims to demonstrate that the *historical* transition between Lukács' reification and Debord's spectacle is a *conceptual* transition between Hegel's early critique of philosophies of reflection and the *Wesenslogik* of the *Science of Logic*. By deploying a distinctly speculative concept of unity from Hegel's notion of reflection, it will be demonstrated that Lukács and Debord aren't simply in the same tradition but wield substantively different concepts of reification.

Having reconstructed the society of the spectacle with the central tenets of falsehood, appearance, money, use-value and the unity of reflective identification, chapters 5 and 6 will cap our investigation with an in-depth engagement with Hegel's *Science of Logic*. It is here that the *essence* and *concept* of the spectacle will be given consideration. The argument here is that the spectacle requires a *Wesenslogik* and *Begriffslogik* for determinate coherence as a social totality, first as a unitary structure amidst a changing multiplicity of appearances-forms and, second, as a self-differentiating unity or conceptual structure, an 'automatic subject' whose internal differences are but the self-movement of its own universality that subsists precisely through its particulars. It is argued that only through these categorial determinations of Hegel's speculative philosophy can the spectacular logic of the society of the spectacle emerge as an internally coherent form of social domination, that is, as encompassing a dialectic of appearances that carries with it the kernel for its own actuality as a social totality.

We will conclude with comments on how a meticulous exposition of the spectacle's rationality does not by itself warrant prescriptions for the overcoming of the society of the spectacle. Instead, we will have provided a diagnostic for examining a rationality whose purpose, for Hegel as much as for Debord, is to reconcile us with the positivity of its historical moment in a 'manner of only conceiving of a positive adhesion to *all that exists*' (Debord 2006c: 339). This book aims as such to pull Debord away from the discourses in which he is normally situated and instead examine his work within the traditions of Hegel's speculative philosophy, Marx's critique of political economy and Frankfurt School critical theory. Tracing Debord's diagnosis out of this lineage makes explicit the merit of theorizing capitalism in terms of its modality of appearing, or put another way, in the difficulty in seeing the world *not as it really is*.

1

The Truth of the Spectacle

Some things are so wrong that not even their opposite is true.

Karl Kraus

A month after *The Society of the Spectacle* was published, Guy Debord wrote to Robert Chase, member of the American section of the Situationist International (SI), claiming that the primary task of their organization 'is to produce the most adequate critical theory' (2010: 329). It would not be the only time Debord would characterize the critique of the society of the spectacle as a critical theory: 'In 1967 I wanted the Situationist International to have a book of theory ... impos[ing] its victory on the terrain of critical theory' (2006h: 1463; see also 1995: §7, §§204–11). Despite these references, his own direct relation to the critical theory coming out of Frankfurt via the Institut für Sozialforschung, despite the similarities to be examined, are few and far between. It is known that Debord's personal library contained copies of Adorno and Horkheimer's *Dialectic of Enlightenment* and Marcuse's *One-Dimensional Man* and *Eros and Civilization*.[1] Additionally, Debord's archive notes include comments on Adorno's 'Music and Technique', whose French translation appeared in issue 19 of *Arguments* in 1960.[2]

It is part of the argument of this book that Debord's analysis, knowingly or not, carries the tradition of Frankfurt School critical theory. To elucidate the connection, let us first outline precisely what is *false* about the society of the spectacle. Indeed, throughout *The Society of the Spectacle*, a social world is portrayed that is not just saturated by '[e]ach new lie of the advertising industry' (1995: §70), or for which one finds 'a lie that can no longer be challenged' (1995: §105), but more ominously the spectacle appears as 'the social organisation of the absolute lie' (1995: §106) and as 'the new potentiality of fraud [*la tromperie*]' (1995: §215). Moreover, Debord frequently attaches a 'pseudo' prefix to various social phenomena and the book is littered with instances of 'false consciousness', 'false models', 'false choices', 'false conflicts' or 'alternatives', 'false cohesion', 'false promises', 'false memory', 'false ideas' and 'false way[s] out'. The problem of deciphering exactly what qualifies this *reign of falsehood* characteristic of the spectacle is perhaps most perplexingly thrust upon the reader within §9: 'In a world which really is *topsy-turvy* [*réellement renversé*], the true is a moment of the false' (Debord 1970: §9).

This last thesis – and its intermingling of both truth and falsehood – offers the opportunity not only of expounding what makes the spectacle characteristically false, but also of reconstructing the affinity between Debord's critical theory of society and the critical theory of Adorno[3] while illustrating the continuity between Debord's thought and Hegelian philosophy. Indeed, Debord's ninth thesis is itself an appropriation of a line from the preface to Hegel's *Phenomenology of Spirit* and, as will be argued, amounts to a variation on Adorno's own inversion of the same line found within *Minima Moralia*. We therefore find a lineage of critical thought on the true and the false with the following three formulations:

1. 'The true is the whole' (Hegel).
2. 'The whole is the untrue' (Adorno).
3. 'In a world which really is *topsy-turvy*, the true is a moment of the false' (Debord).

This chapter will proceed through these three quotations on the true and false as registers for explicating a theory of the society of the spectacle. More specifically, it is through these three signposts that what is *precisely false* about the society of the spectacle will become clear. We will begin by unfolding the constitutive relation between the true and false of Hegel's philosophy. Adorno's criticisms of this philosophy as a critique of identity will proceed as a critique of the exchange relation. How it is that Debord then poses his own rendition of the relation between the true and the false in order to illuminate the social reality of the spectacle will follow, with a final section on how Debord adopts a peculiar concept of ideology to elucidate his notion of falsehood. In a word, the chapter will evaluate the conceptual identity of the true and the false through Hegelian thought and assess its implications for a society dominated by forms of appearance. The aim in this chapter is to demonstrate why within the spectacle there is no truth hidden behind the false and that Debord does not contrast the spectacle with any concealed depth of displaced authenticity or true reality.

The true is the whole

Strictly speaking, there is nothing *wholly* false in Hegel's philosophy. Everywhere its immanent movement, if followed, exhibits an ontological priority of the whole over its parts. However, the whole as a totality or the dynamically developing relations between parts cannot be assumed from the outset but is the unity of its own self-development. For Hegel, truth as the absolute is both the result and the process through which the result is generated. Beginnings, so apparently fickle in Hegel's thought, are but the immediate prompt for the movement of the dialectic whose essential truth can be garnered only from its entire process. In a passage within the preface to the *Phenomenology of Spirit*, Hegel shows his cards: 'The True is the whole. But the whole is nothing other than the essence consummating itself through its development. Of the Absolute it must be said that it is essentially a *result*, that only in the *end* is it what it truly is; and that precisely in this consists its nature, viz. to be actual, subject, the spontaneous becoming of itself' (1977c: 11).

While for Hegel it is the whole alone that is ultimately true, this is not to say that truth is merely an aggregation of finite parts or the sum total collection of immediacies. Importantly, the parts or individual moments of Hegel's philosophy are not simply accorded subordinate status to the truthful whole. It is the mediation between parts, the necessary and immanent movement of particular moments that allows conceptual thinking to acquire its essential and universal meaning. Mediation is here conceived as the relational structure of content in and through the determinate negation of immediate appearance. The absolute emerges through the interrelationship of its moments and it is only through the whole that individual aspects can be understood in their full significance. Without stopping short or taking portions of his philosophy in their isolation do immediate phenomena acquire full determination, as moments of a totality, the systematic presentation of a whole that refuses to sit still.

Hegel's *Phenomenology of Spirit* imparts the journey of natural or naive (*natürliche*) consciousness as it proceeds towards true knowledge (*Wissenschaft*), charting the ways in which it takes different shapes (*Gestalten*), developing through its own immanent movement. Through this process, Hegel offers a critique of immediacy in which the mediated determinations of immediate appearance unfold. Any authoritative claim of immediacy will, for consciousness through its voyage, lose its justification and disclose an abundance of determinations of which no immediacy is itself unmediated. Although ultimately disclosing a unity for which 'everything turns on grasping and expressing the True, not only as *Substance*, but equally as *Subject*' (1977c: 10), for the naive consciousness undertaking the trials and tribulations of the phenomenological movement, the knowing subject initially appears upon a precipice for which its object is seemingly set interminably apart. However, within both the preface and introduction to the *Phenomenology of Spirit*, Hegel elucidates how it is that this mode of exposition will ultimately render such a separation of subject and object to be a momentary *Vorstellung*.[4] Within these opening passages and unbeknownst to the protagonist of the book, Hegel outlines its central idea: an exposition or presentation (*Darstellung*) of phenomenal knowledge in its modes of appearing. For Hegel, the *Darstellung* stands in contrast to momentary *Vorstellungen* insofar as the latter are designated as initial and unrefined representations, presuppositions or that which is simply taken for granted and apprehended without reflection, as characteristic of the immediacies of phenomenal knowledge. The *Darstellung* of the *Phenomenology of Spirit* thereby follows the journey of experience as 'the conscious insight into the untruth of appearing [*erscheinenden*] knowledge' (1977c: 50).

In addition to these two divergent categories of appearing found within Hegel's philosophy – *Vorstellung* and *Darstellung* – two further categories are worth registering here in order to account for a full topography of the modality of appearances within Hegel's thought. First there is *Schein*, commonly translated as 'semblance'. As a verb, *scheinen* means to seem, shine or even glow. Its usage usually denotes a deception; it is what *seems* to be, but is not really so. Further, from the appearance of *Schein* we arrive at its usual correlative: *Wesen* or 'essence'. Essence shows or appears but remains hidden under a veil of *Schein*. As such, *Schein* is dependent on something else, an essence not fully manifest. Related but not synonymous, and a concept which will play a larger role in the subsequent chapters of this book, is the category of *Erscheinung* which is usually given the translation of 'appearance', although 'manifestation' is also a helpful rendition. Unlike *Schein*, *Erscheinung* is also used for the appearance or the coming into existence of something. However, for Hegel, *Erscheinung* differs from *Schein* in two crucial respects.

Firstly, with *Erscheinung*, the essence fully discloses itself and tends to keep nothing hidden. It is the *necessary* manifestation of an essence. Thus, through the category and dynamic of *Erscheinung* we find Hegel rejecting any attempts at setting up a rigid dichotomy between appearance and essential reality. The two are understood as internally related. *Erscheinung* is the showing forth or the display of an essence that must appear.

Secondly, *Erscheinung* is transient and dependent. However, what it depends on and succumbs to is not, immediately at least, an essence, but through Hegel's dialectic, *another Erscheinung*. Such an understanding draws heavily from the *Phenomenology of Spirit* and will indeed be given greater explication in our next chapter. Nevertheless, it is worth noting here that *Erscheinung*, in contrast to

Schein, unfolds a world or *totality of appearing*. For example, with the *Phenomenology of Spirit*, consciousness, in coming to know the world, posits a supersensible world beyond the phenomenality of appearances in order to establish unity within the objectivity of the world. *Schein*, the immediate surface show of empirical reality, becomes the manifestation (*Erscheinung*) of an inner unity. For this, *Erscheinung* is a higher development and contains or expresses the truth of *Schein* in fuller measure. The development of *Schein* to *Erscheinung* is the explanatory movement of identifying the immediacies of sensual appearance to be governed by *a totality of appearance* that registers an existent objective realm beyond sensible apprehension.

How the truth of the whole is to be rendered explicit must proceed through the false, as an immanent critique of appearance-forms. Hegel's *Darstellung* is a movement of appearance-forms in which appearances of the false (*Schein, Erscheinung, Vorstellung*) appear as moments in the unfolding of the true. Said another way, *Darstellung* is the transitoriness of a totality as the revelation of the movement of the false becoming true. As a result, the distance initially set between the knowing subject of the *Phenomenology of Spirit* and its object is only the way in which an immediate truth *appears*. This *Vorstellung* will thereby turn into a phenomenology for which Hegel, in allowing immediacies to be what they are, show themselves to be both an illusion (*Schein*) and a necessary manifestation (*Erscheinung*). The movement of appearing is not passive but produces its own truth. Appearance negates itself, which is how it can appear as what it truthfully is.

The object of the *Phenomenology of Spirit* in its entirety is *apparent knowing*, or that which appears and is speciously self-evident. Hegel's phenomenological standpoint is an organizational principle of the relationship between knowledge and social life. This relationship is exposed through the development of consciousness and in its constant confusion of itself with its own conceiving. There is as such a double movement in both the experience of thinking the truth and the movement of a developing reality. This phenomenological approach establishes that we can know the meaning of an object only in its relation to a knowing subject. Hegel's phenomenology treats the separate thing-like appearance of subject and object as a problem undertaken by experience. He begins with such a positivist or empiricist approach to phenomena that nevertheless overcomes such deficiencies by revealing an inherent tension: a tension between the object and its concept, between truth and certainty, between substance and subject. The phenomenology is possible for relationships in which a subject fails to recognize itself in its object or fails to recognize that its object is implicated in itself.

The dialectic undermines the immediacy of appearances, best articulated in a passage from the *Science of Logic*: '*there is* nothing in heaven or nature or spirit or anywhere else that does not contain just as much immediacy as mediation, so that both these determinations prove to be *unseparated* and *inseparable* and the opposition between them nothing real' (Hegel 2010: 46). Here determination refers to identity, difference and individuation and specifically entails how any content is distinguished from another. Determination is what gives objects their exclusiveness: how they are *this* and *not that*. Its essence is therefore negation. As Hegel writes, 'it is through its determinateness that the thing excludes others' (1977c: 73). The movement of the *Phenomenology of Spirit* demonstrates the precarious status of immediacy as a standard of knowledge, appearances which always implicitly carry more determination than they directly disclose. However, immediacy itself is not simply reduced to an inferior status that merely withdraws from the development of substance into subject. It returns at every moment in the *Phenomenology of Spirit*.

Integral to recognize for our purposes is that the untruth of immediacy is constitutive of the experience of consciousness. While immediate knowledge discloses mediated conceptualizations, new immediacies arise with every new shape of consciousness, only to thereby further deepen both its consciousness of the world and of itself. As such, Hegel does not make any effort to venerate any 'true reality' hidden underneath appearances, nor will he deny the deceptive significance of appearances themselves. Hegel seeks to repudiate the authority of respective appearances in their claims of a legitimate and robust explication of subjective consciousness and its relation to the world. Through this process, *the reality of appearances is in fact affirmed*. However, it is through the activity of consciousness that this reality reveals certain deficiencies that negatively prompt consciousness, a disruption which emerges at every moment in the *Phenomenology of Spirit*, into calling into question the mode by which the appearance of reality is apprehended.

The dialectical process by which this revelation takes place consists in natural consciousness demonstrating itself not to possess true knowledge, but rather within the coming-to-be explicit inadequacy of its own concept. However, this disparity between certainty (*Geweißheit*) and truth (*Wahrheit*) is only revealed retrospectively. In its varying moments, consciousness apprehends its immediate object *to be* true knowledge, a certainty which propels consciousness into a loss of itself; a loss of its truth and, as such, a path of despair (1977c: 49) against its own apprehended naturalisms. It is thereby through the conscious insight into the untruth of phenomenal knowledge that consciousness experiences a progressive maturation retrospectively attained from the standpoint of truth or absolute knowing. The object of knowledge gained by consciousness will not be something that externally acts upon consciousness, but instead eventually disclosed to be structured by an *acting* self-consciousness through the development of spirit, that objective structure of sociality that has developed various institutional, cultural and intellectual practices for reflecting on what it takes to be authoritative for itself in terms of whether such practices live up to its own claims and achieve the aims set for itself.

The *Phenomenology of Spirit* proceeds to come to terms with different modes of what appears to be the activity of knowing, progressively negating the inadequacy of the appearing, and thus going beyond that inadequacy. Apparent knowing therefore, while partial in its grounding of consciousness' awareness of itself and the world, nonetheless points beyond itself. As a result, for Hegel truth is inherently processual, a development of necessary moments of the untrue. In it is this way that Hegel fully repudiates any dichotomous relation between the true and the false. As he writes in the preface to the *Phenomenology of Spirit*:

> 'True' and 'false' belong among those determinate notions which are held to be inert and wholly separate essences, one here and one there, each standing fixed and isolated from the other, with which it has nothing in common. Against this view it must be maintained that truth is not a minted coin that can be given and pocketed ready-made. Nor *is* there such a thing as the false, any more than there *is* something evil ... One can, of course, know something falsely. To know something falsely means that there is a disparity between knowledge and its Substance. But this very disparity is the process of distinguishing in general, which is an essential moment [in knowing]. Out of this distinguishing, of course, comes their identity, and this resultant identity is the truth.
>
> 1977c: 22–3

For Hegel, no finite judgement can ever acquire such an accord and as such truth exceeds the perimeters of predicative logic and only subsists at the level of the whole. Further, divested of epistemological subjectivism, Hegel inaugurates the overcoming of truth as *adaequatio rei atque cogitationis*, as a correspondence between the concept produced by the intellect and the thing known, as holding timeless and immutable validity – the scam of *prima philosophia*. Instead, the objectivity of truth emerges from the self-movement of subject and substance in their essential unity.

Just as truth is no mere relation between a judgements and its object, the false is not something arbitrary or contingent error subjectively made, but emerges necessarily through the movement of the concept through its individual and finite moments. While the *Phenomenology of Spirit* proceeds through particular forms of experience whose claims to truth are revealed in their falsity, all untrue modes of knowing can only be grasped as necessarily emerging from that which it is the result. In this way, the necessary appearances of the untrue consciousness derive from what was true in the preceding knowledge. *The truth of the lie is that which came before.* It is a retrospective necessity that makes the appearance false. What as a whole guides the patterns of consciousness is therefore not only the progressive development of the true, but also *the apparently true becoming false*. It is a phenomenology of *the experience of the true becoming false* just as much as the reverse: how the truth of the whole is to be acquired must proceed through the false, as an immanent critique of appearance forms through their inadequacy. For this, throughout the *Phenomenology of Spirit*, natural consciousness constantly tastes dissatisfaction while nevertheless restoring immediacy at every moment.

It is only the false that gets you somewhere. This is what Adorno calls Hegel's 'doctrine of universally self-restored immediacy' (2007: 313; see also 1993: 7 and 2008: 159). For Hegel, philosophical truth as such contains both the true and the untrue at the same time, a process by which the true is brought to light by the deficiencies of the untrue, not through an abstract negation, or simple rejection of the false, but rather through a determinate negation of which the implicit truth contained within the untrue is made explicit. In fact, 'the truth is actually nothing but the path that leads precisely through the falseness' (Adorno 2017: 155). The perspective of the whole exhibits the false to always be a moment of the true. At the initial level of appearances, there is only superficial truth. With the further development of distinctions, the initial appearances become false. However, continuing, the false becomes true as moments of a self-developing concrete totality for which all previous determinations have been sublated. Dialectical thought is driven not simply *to* its own falsehood, but *by* its falsehood. It is not simply a vindication of the false that is found within Hegel's philosophy, but, at least for the *Phenomenology of Spirit*, a vindication of the *spiritual experience of the false*.

The whole is the untrue

For what reason, within *Minima Moralia*, does Adorno invert Hegel's dictum and write: 'The whole is the untrue [Das *Ganze* ist das Unwahre]' (2005a: 50)? As will become clear, the whole as untrue refers for Adorno to an antagonistic social totality that, through its concept, is optimally captured by Hegel's systematic philosophy, or more specifically, by the way in which Hegel's philosophy relinquishes itself to 'the untrue affirmative' (Adorno 2007: 65; translation amended). As Adorno writes, 'this untruth is none other than the untruth of the system of the society that constitutes the substratum of his philosophy' (1993: 32). As we will see, it is precisely this inversion of truth and falsehood in Hegel that bespeaks to the notion of falsehood found in Debord's diagnosis.

As we have seen in the previous section, for Adorno, Hegelian philosophy 'proves its worth only as a totality, in the concrete interconnections of all its moments ... incompatible with any kind of tendency to harmony' (1993: 2, 4). And yet at the same time, Adorno reproaches Hegel for the way in which the system does in fact strive for a harmonious reconcilement. For this, Adorno's chiding of Hegel concerns the failure to give the particular its due. Nowhere does this conflicted relation with Hegel receive its attention as much as within Adorno's *Hegel: Three Studies*. The three essays, arguably Adorno's most intimate engagement with Hegel, offer explicit analyses on the extent to which a critical theory of society is not simply enriched by Hegelian philosophy but that both speak volumes about a form of domination whose characteristic features evince modes of identification, unification, affirmation and reconcilement.[5] It is Adorno's unrelenting concern for the possibility of an experience which isn't reducible to the identity of the concept given actuality within the administered world of capitalist society and its omnipotent principle of exchange that Hegel is, within the essays, both venerated for first articulating a dialectic of negativity beyond what is simply the case and admonished for that same philosophy's positive envelopment of the real by the rational without remainder.

Adorno ventures to salvage the immanently determinate character of the Hegelian dialectic by placing emphasis on its negativity over the affirmative supremacy of the concept. However, the stakes of a dialectic that pronounces objects to conform to their concepts without remainder are the stakes of a dialectic hardly resembling a cognitive law, but an existent principle of a reality dominated by the social form of exchange. As such, for Adorno and following Hegel, the dialectic is not simply a method of thought but a particular structure belonging to the objectivity of reality itself, to *die Sache selbst*. For both Hegel and Adorno, the dialectic concerns the conceptual determinations of objectivity. Moving in accord with its own concept, it is a dialectic of reality and not simply a cognitive structure most appropriate for phenomena eliciting a contradictory character. Indeed, thought 'finds its measure in and as objectivity' (Adorno 2017: 31) and concepts themselves are 'moments of the reality that requires their formation' (2007: 11).

Adorno finds in part both the truth and untruth of Hegel in the question of 'whether the conceptual order we bestow upon objects is also the order which the objects themselves possess' (Adorno 2017: 2). In the service of reconcilement, it is a dialectic that has inaugurated a form of reification as the insulation from the non-conceptual whole, a fortification against the heterogeneity of unregimented experience and less a static petrification than the affirmation of the enveloping movement of the concept. In a word, reification is found in the speculative proposition of the identity of identity and non-identity, as an objective law of exchange, the socially constitutive category. Adorno, in 'reopening the case of dialectics' (Adorno 2007: 7), is therefore oriented towards a critical theory of society based on the principle of exchange. We are dealing with a conceptuality that 'holds sway in reality (*Sache*) itself' (Adorno 1976: 80), one which is indeed 'preformed by class relations' (Adorno 2018: 5). The process of abstraction through the identity of exchange is the objectivity of the concept rather than the concept as the 'subjective unity of features [*Merkmalseinheit*] of the object comprehended under it' (2018: 4).

Pivotal for Adorno's *Negative Dialectics* is the way in which the identity of identity and non-identity is critically said to consummate Hegel's idealism. For Adorno, Hegel's philosophy is positively conclusive and ceases the movement of the negative. However, whether Adorno's criticism of Hegel is accurate is secondary to what the latter's philosophy means historically.[6] As Adorno writes, '[t]he impoverishment of experience through dialectics, which infuriates mainstream opinion, proves itself however to be entirely appropriate to the abstract monotony of the administered world. What is painful about it is the pain of such, raised to a concept' (2007: 6; translation amended). For Adorno, Hegel's *Begriff* attempts to cope with everything heterogeneous to it and its untruth is found within that all-encompassing breadth of identification. Its autocratic reign derives from an excessively affirmative dialectic that is given verification in and through society. Here, the movement of Hegel's philosophy relinquishes itself to the untrue affirmative, one for which the 'strains and toils of the concept are not metaphorical' (Adorno 1993: 21). The identity of concept and its object is precisely untruth. It is not simply that thought and its object coincide but that the totality of determinations procures an absolute identity with itself. Accordingly, Adorno reads Hegelian spirit as social labour, as society dominated by the principle of exchange (1993: 18–32). As he writes, 'The principle of the equivalence of social labor makes society in its modern bourgeois sense both something abstract and the most real thing of all, just what Hegel says of the emphatic notion of the concept' (1993: 20). Hegel's dialectic – as an objective universal compulsion for adjustment and reconcilement – thereby acquires verification within history. 'Hegel should be defended against the old slur on "the strait-jacket of dialectics". It is the strait-jacket of the world' (Adorno 2008: 122). In a passage echoing the observations of Lukács in *The Young Hegel*, Adorno remarks:

> Satanically, the world as grasped by the Hegelian system has only now, a hundred and fifty years later, proved itself to be a system in the literal sense, namely that of a radically societalized society. One of the most remarkable aspects of Hegel's accomplishment is that he inferred that systematic character of society from the concept long before it could gain ascendancy in the sphere of Hegel's own experience, that of a Germany far behind in its bourgeois development. A world integrated through 'production,' through the exchange relationship, depends in all its moments on the social conditions of its production, and in that sense actually realizes the primacy of the whole over its parts; in this regard the desperate impotence of every single individual now verifies Hegel's extravagant conception of the system.
>
> 1993: 27

Post-Kantian idealism, in its integrative capacity for unifying difference within subjectivity, acquires an historical ontology through the determinative logic of capitalist society as the subject of society itself. The principle of identity constituted through the exchange relation – for which use-value and concrete labour are mere moments of abstraction commensurable through the objectivity of the money-form – stands as the actualization of Hegel's speculative philosophy. Here we arrive at *'philosophy's uncritical complicity with civilization'* (Adorno 2008: 159). It is a verdict for which the logic of commensurability found in the exchange relation between commodities finds expression within a philosophical system of equivalence.

For Adorno, exchange is as such 'the key to society' (2018: 7) and bears an unwavering relation (*urverwandt*) to the principle of identification, subsuming 'the entire world to the identical, to totality' (2007: 146; translation amended). The axiom of identity raised to a system and its criterion of universal equivalence debases all qualitative distinction, a tendency to level all differences to moments of its own totality. It is a circle of rationality identical to itself which, as an organizing principle of society, leaves less and less outside of itself. Here, the implications of identity and, as will be more explicitly examined within chapters 3 and 5, its dialectical relation to difference are not a simple liquidation of distinction into a colourless homogeneity. Indeed it remains the case that the unity imposed by socially necessary abstract labour-time is one for which use-values and human needs are made coherent and actual in and through the abstraction of exchange. Such is the case that the principle of identity germinating within what will become clear as a speculative concept is the sinister handler of difference in its 'suppressed and damaged form' (2007: 318). The exchange abstraction of selfsameness is but the system for accommodating qualitative distinction as a condition for its actualization.

For Adorno, Hegelian idealism and its dialectic is the programme for a totality that has acquired actuality within society itself. It is in this regard that Adorno reverses Hegel's dictum and pronounces the whole as untrue:

> 'The whole is the untrue,' not merely because the thesis of totality is itself untruth, being the principle of domination inflated to the absolute; the idea of a positivity that can master everything that opposes it through the superior power of a comprehending spirit is the mirror image of the experience of the superior coercive force inherent in everything that exists by virtue of its consolidation under domination. This is the truth in Hegel's untruth. The force of the whole, which it mobilizes, is not a mere fantasy on the part of spirit; it is the force of the real web of illusion in which all individual existence remains trapped.
>
> 1993: 87

The mediating concept of society is exchange, the essence of a totality that is at once the truth of the objectivity of social relations as well as untrue as a form of domination. Both the comprehension and objectivity of the world proceed through the axiom of identity. It will be the concept of the society of the spectacle that lets us examine the full accord by which concept and thing, the genesis of a false totality, refuses disassociation and whose identity, vegetating within the speculative concept, is, again, the baleful vendor of difference in its 'suppressed and damaged form' – a harmonious totality which, in the end, subdues its antagonisms and resigns individuation to be an inferior and yet gaspingly existent moment within itself.

In a world which really is *topsy-turvy*, the true is a moment of the false

There are two distinct threads derived from the aforementioned comments on Hegel and Adorno that are central for examining Debord's ninth thesis of *The Society of the Spectacle*: 'In a world which really is *topsy-turvy*, the true is a moment of the false' (1970: §9). First, Hegel's dialectic of appearance-forms, through which the truth of the whole emerges, repudiates not simply any dichotomous and absolute opposition between the true and the false but that, most notably within the *Phenomenology of Spirit*, the false is generative of the true and the latter is the retrospective vindication of the spiritual experience of the false. Second, with Adorno's reversal of Hegel's adage that the whole is on the contrary *untrue*, we find that the whole of Hegel's philosophy, itself given social actuality by the domination of exchange raised to a system, is a false totality whose individual moments are but the subordinated results of its own envelopment. As will become clear, both of these insights are implicitly contained in Debord's ninth thesis and assist in explaining the extent to which the society of the spectacle refers to a false social totality.

To anticipate these points of inheritance, we can first remark that the spectator of the society of the spectacle is partly situated in the same dilemma as Hegel's natural consciousness, in which immediate appearance elicits the falsity that such an appearance is the most endowed, when in fact, it couldn't be more impoverished, or as Hegel writes, 'it is always at its poorest where it fancies itself to be the richest' (1977c: 77). As Debord writes in a 1966 letter to Mustapha Khayati, 'The spectator always considers himself enriched by what he has seen. This is the principal property that remains his, and the exact essence of modern property is the display of it' (Debord 2003b: 169).

Secondly, it can be said that Debord always conceived dialectics as moving towards a unified accord with 'the reality that seeks it' (Debord 2006i: 1536)[7] and that the 'dialectician' wields, as he remarks in a 1972 letter, 'intelligence of the real' (2004a: 609). For Debord, dialectical logic exhibits itself within society itself, a perspective reaffirmed within Debord's notes on the work of Joseph Gabel, particularly with the following fragment: 'the paradoxes of appearance in the S of S is [sic] the dialectic of reality'.[8] Despite this shared understanding of dialectics, similarities between Debord and Adorno are however often directed towards the structure and aphoristic style of *Minima Moralia* as an indication of an affinity. For instance, Adorno begins *Minima Moralia* with formulations that strongly accord with ideas found in *The Society of the Spectacle*, most notably with an observation that the relation between the economy and life proceeds by debasing the latter to a form of appearance of the former. It is a development for Adorno in which 'life has become appearance [*Erscheinung*]' (Adorno 2005a: 15). As Adorno continues later on, 'people cling to what mocks them confirming the mutilation of their essence by the smoothness of its own appearance [*Erscheinung*]' (2005a: 147)

However, let us not get ahead of ourselves but take a step back by asking first what, based on his own archival notes, Debord garnered from Hegel's *Phenomenology of Spirit*, or more specifically, what elements stood out to him as they relate to ideas on the true and the false. Indeed, his own annotations on both the *Phenomenology of Spirit* and Hegel's 1808–11 lecture notes on *Philosophical Propadeutic* illustrate an attention to the role of the true and false. As might be expected, Debord followed Hyppolite's reading of the *Phenomenology of Spirit* in terms of general strides (Debord 2004a: 65). However, in terms of the book's preface, specifically in the lead-up to Hegel's remark that '[t]he true is the whole' (1977c: 11), one finds within Debord's notes the idea that the whole, in its actual and self-moving development through various forms and moments, has a greater meaning than immediate appearances. For Hegel, the false is retrospectively revealed to be a moment of the true. For Debord, on the other hand, because objectively social reality is constituted as a *false social totality*, the true can only ever be a moment of the false. The spectacle is the false in its mode of exposition whose individual moments are as such and in truth moments of that totality. For Hegel, apparent knowing, while partial in its grounding of consciousness' awareness of itself and the world, nonetheless is capable of pointing beyond itself, an *experience* for which essential truth is acquired at the level of the whole. For Debord, the essence by which the spectacle falsifies through its fragmented moments also points beyond itself, however only into a depth of greater fragmentation affirmed as a unity. Continuous with Adorno's own position, Debord thereby reverses Hegel's formulation by which the truth of particular moments subsists only within a universal falsehood.[9]

Debord refers to the spectacle as 'the general falsification of society' (1970: §101) whose individual moments are *truthfully authentic* moments of a *false totality*. The criterion of truth within the society of the spectacle has become the false as the social whole, thereby inverting Spinoza's proposition *verum index sui et falsi* and inaugurating a schema for which falsehood becomes a standard of itself. The relation between the true and the false under the society of the spectacle is not a relation of opposition but one in which truth appears only in synchronicity with the false. As Debord writes, '[t]he spectacle subjugates living men to itself to the extent that the economy has totally subjugated them. It is no more than the economy developing for itself. It is the *faithful* reflection of the production of things, and the *unfaithful* objectification of the producers' (1970: §16; translation amended and emphasis added). Under the spectacle, the false has become *so false* that even its direct opposite appears as a moment sustained only in and through the social whole. The totality of its *Schlechtigkeit* is therefore at pains for *particular* relief.

Irreducible to any of its particular appearances, there is here the more difficult philosophical problem – one inherited by German Idealism – in which the whole is never directly given. And yet, the spectacle is fundamentally, as the first sentence of *The Society of the Spectacle* announces, a social experience for which '[t]*he whole life* of those societies in which modern conditions of production prevail *presents itself* as an immense accumulation of spectacles' (1995: §1; emphasis added); further, 'in the spectacle the totality of the commodity world is *visible in one piece*, as the general equivalent of whatever society as a whole can be and do' (1995: §49; emphasis added). For Debord, the society of the spectacle is not directly perceived or tangible and is yet manifested in all individual phenomena. How then to reconcile this point with the notion that the whole can never appear *as a whole* but only in its individual moments?

The omnipotence of the society of the spectacle's verification renders any effort to isolate and scrutinize particular aspects of its dominance partial and, as was remarked in our introduction, nominalistic. For unless the spectacle is conceived at the level of the social totality, it cannot be empirically substantiated. But a whole cannot be reducible to perceptual apprehension. The whole is never wholly at our disposal, simply given through which truth, as if 'shot through a pistol', is a fixed and 'minted coin that can be given and pocketed ready-made' (Hegel 1977c: 16, 22). Even Debord, from the standpoint of spectatorship, concedes as much: 'So the already questionable satisfaction allegedly derived from *the consumption of the whole* is adulterated from the outset because the real consumer can only get his hands on a succession of *fragments* of this commodity heaven – fragments each of which naturally lacks any of the *quality* ascribed to the whole' (1995: §65). A whole is never that which is immediately given, least of all to the finite subject of consumption. Hegel's *Phenomenology of Spirit* demonstrates as much insofar as it is only absolute knowing, and not natural consciousness, that exceeds the diremption of subject and object. The whole can never be an object of consciousness nor grasped behind a curtain of appearance.

And yet, as the travails of sense-certainty reveal in the *Phenomenology of Spirit*, the particular, once enunciated, always exceeds itself and *says* more than it means. As Adorno affirms, 'there is no other possible way for us to reach the whole except by exposure to the partial' (2017: 33). Nevertheless, within Adorno we find Hegel's whole not simply as the endgame through which the particulars have carried the dialectic, but, at the level of social experience, an overwhelming impression irrespective of any individual moments of determination:

> What I am claiming is precisely that in a certain sense – and I am essentially speaking here, like Hegel, with an eye to our social and historical experience rather than to the specifically organized experience of the sciences – that in a basic sense we have more awareness of the system in which we live, that we possess a more direct experience in ourselves of the reality in which we are

caught up, than we do of specific individual situations on the basis of which we might gradually ascend to a view or to a concept of the totality within which we live.

2017: 93

Here, the generic whole impresses itself with greater weight and potency than any particular. Even if unable to be directly represented, total unfreedom can be recognized easily enough (Adorno 2005a: 144). As Adorno continues,

> . . . what is actually immediate here, what we first of all perceive, are the general relations much more than the particular relations in which we are involved – rather as a dog, for example, will generally react by specifically wagging its tail when well-dressed people enter the room, will act less excitedly when less well-dressed people come in, and will even start to bark if someone like a tramp appears at the door. I believe that human experience generally organizes itself in such a way.
>
> 2017: 94

There is a generality that acquires prominence through the immediacy of social apprehension and, as a result, 'we actually become aware of the whole before we become aware of what is more specific' (2017: 95). As illustrative, one finds within Debord's own archival notes on Karl Mannheim's *Ideology and Utopia* (1929) the following extract from Louis Wirth's preface: 'A society is possible in the last analysis because individuals in it carry around in their heads some sort of picture of that society' (Mannheim 2015: xxv). Debord adds the following fragment: 'So that at present it is only possible by a succession of external images, actually manufactured. What was internalized is exterior by the technique of the society, a reaper instantly recreating (for S of S).'[10] In this way, it may be said that the spectacle, as a totality of abstract social relations, does indeed impress itself directly within individual experience, that 'we can no more speak here of a priority of the individual parts than we can speak of a logical priority of the whole' (Adorno 2017: 106). Under the spectacle, apprehended partialities are substituted by the omnipotence of 'a new generality' (Debord 1995: §2), one for which the 'spectator feels at home nowhere, for the spectacle is everywhere' (1995: §30).

The manner in which the whole of the spectacle makes its appearance cannot be equated with the immediate intuitionism so repelled by Hegel. The spectacle remains a social form of mediation and therefore beyond the 'ferment of enthusiasm' (Hegel 1977c: 5) found within the works of Jacobi, Novalis and Schlegel. The spectacle bears *conceptual* and *experiential* weight irreducible to any lightning flashes of the absolute. It accords with Adorno's observation that 'we first effectively become aware of a certain pressure or oppressiveness, that we thereby become aware of the totality before we register more specific aspects, and that situations in this regard may be just as abstract as the whole' (2017: 95). Even if the whole cannot be directly given, there nevertheless remains a *speculative experience* of the unity of multiple and particular relations. On the whole it can thereby be said that while it remains the case that the society of the spectacle renders it 'increasingly hard for workers to recognize and name their own impoverishment' (Debord 1995: §122), the untruth of this world is not without the wherewithal to speak its own name.

Let us recap. For Adorno, Hegel's philosophy is viewed as a '*bad* positivity' (Adorno 2008: 28) that elicits the problem of a system of enclosure, in effect an endorsement of the world's course. This development refers to the speculative in Hegel as the whole for which the essence of all negations resign themselves to the positive. It is a circular procedure whose tautology devours and regurgitates all particulars as moments of its own becoming. This system, or what Marx referred to in his youth as the 'grotesque craggy melody' (1975e: 18) of Hegel's thought, gives internal coherence to all particular and differentiated moments and is, for Adorno, substantiated in a society dominated by exchange relations and in its universal imperative for commensurability. It can thereby be said that Adorno's critique of Hegel is at once also a critique of the society of the spectacle. 'The spectacle manifests itself as an enormous positivity' (Debord 1995: §12), one whose concept is identical to social reality. The spectacle *integrates itself* into reality to the same extent as it *describes* reality (Debord 1998: 9). As such, within a society that is objectively falsified through the autonomy of exchange-value, what appears as true can only ever be a moment of the false.

Fundamental to Hegel's system is the concept of the identity of identity and non-identity, an integral principle of speculation that, for Adorno, comprises a doctrine of adjustment to a social reality forged by exchange relations and which lays its abrogation upon its own results. It is a rationality that doesn't so much eradicate qualitative distinction as really subsume them. Although the point will be more closely examined within chapter 3, here the survival of differentiation within a system of commensurability solicits the issue of 'true' and 'false' needs within the society of the spectacle. Through Debord's concept of the true as a moment of the false, such a dichotomy for which true needs are in external fashion deformed by the false needs of the society of the spectacle cannot be sustained. As the SI write within the article 'Socialism or Planète' from issue 10 of *IS*, '[this] pseudo-reality itself shows, negatively, what it hides. That all the needs that solicit or *could* solicit the production of commodities are *equally* artificial or arbitrary is what belies the dazzling contradiction of *advertising* in the social spectacle, which *speaks of what it does not sell and does not sell that which it speaks of* (IS 1997: 409). Important here is the notion that the falsity of social need subsists at the level of *potentiality*: 'all the needs that solicit or *could* solicit the production of commodities are *equally* artificial'. As Debord expands within *The Society of the Spectacle*:

> Without doubt, the pseudo-need imposed by modern consumption cannot be opposed by any genuine need or desire which is not itself shaped by society and its history. But the abundant commodity [*la marchandise abondante*] is an absolute rupture of an organic development of social needs. Its mechanical accumulation liberates unlimited artificiality, in the face of which living desire is disarmed. The cumulative power of independent artificiality is followed everywhere by the *falsification of social life*.
>
> 1970: §68

Particular social needs within the society of the spectacle are constituted in and through a speculative system that renders all particularities as insidious instances of its own self-justification. Here, the totality remains false even if its purveyed means of social satisfaction are requited. The 'empty depth'[11] of the spectacle proliferates social satisfaction within the surface of society. As such, full integration into the concept accords with a mode of commensurable satisfaction.

If the lesson of exchange-value is the *Schein* of which everything is always *equally* possible, the spectacle indexes the *Schein* that proclaims everything is not only equally *possible*, but equally *necessary*. As will become clear in subsequent chapters, the logic of the spectacle is thereby closer to Hegel's *Erscheinungen* than it is to the illusory category of *Schein*. And yet, within the scholarship, interpretations seem content to rest at a reading of the concept of spectacle closer to a Hegelian category of *Schein*, one for which the spectacle conceals rather than 'irradiates' (*irradier*) reality (Debord 1998: 9).[12] Here one finds variations on a substance dualism for which it is alleged that there is a 'true life', one irreducible and residual, *behind* the illusion of the spectacle. One finds similar criticisms in Baudrillard, who accused the SI of staying too close to Marxian orthodoxy by purportedly positing labour-power as the irreducible essence of human nature (Baudrillard 1975: 119–29).[13] More recently, Nancy advances the misguided notion that the concept of spectacle pivots upon a fundamental separation between spectacular appearance and a non-phenomenal essence, the 'un-appropriable secret of an originary property hidden beneath appearances' for which the spectacle is a 'surface, secondary exteriority, inessential shadow' (Nancy 2000: 51–2). Additionally there is Rancière, for whom Debord, in order to make the critique of the spectacle, allegedly wields a Feuerbachian abstract essence and therewith merely replicates Plato's critique of mimesis (Rancière 2009: 6–7, 15, 44). All dualist readings of spectacle lose their traction, however, within an evaluation of the spectacle as the realization of Hegelian idealism. As will become clear throughout this book, 'there is no substratum beneath such "deformations", no ontic interior on which social mechanisms merely act externally' (Adorno 2005a: 229).

If the logic of the society of the spectacle speaks to an identity between its essence and particular appearances, a point that will receive greater attention in chapter 5, there is an allusion to that society's realization of positivist aspirations. Indeed, for Adorno, the measure of philosophy is in the collapse of *Schein* (Adorno 1982: 39), a critical movement striving to enunciate the distinction between appearance and essence. If, however, such a distinction is denied, or that a reign of bare facticity and givenness vanquishes any ontological priority to that which lies concealed behind appearances, there looms an 'arch sin' which 'stands in no simple terms as a definitive "fraud"' (Adorno 2008: 98). In no uncertain terms then does the spectacle, as 'the *real presence* of fraud [*la fausseté*] ensured by the organization of appearance' (Debord 1970: §219), realize the sobriety of positivism insofar as it is a reality *sans* an essential truth beyond its deception. In this sense, it can be said that the spectacle realizes positivism insofar as it rejects a 'two-world' ontology for the supremacy and self-equivalence of the factually given as a levelling of essence. As logical positivist Moritz Schlick has written, against the 'counterposing [of] two kinds of reality' (1974: 237), '[t]here is only *one* reality; it is always *essence*, and does not admit of being broken down into essence and appearance. There are, to be sure, different kinds of real objects, indeed infinitely many; but there is only one kind of reality, and it is to be ascribed to all objects equally' (1974: 240). The spectacle denies its essence as independent from appearances. Indeed, the essential truth of the spectacle is its insistence that there is no reality beyond the world of appearances. The spectacle is a world that crochets a pattern of particular lies through the unity of universal falsehood.

The determinate and necessary relation between truth and falsehood, between appearance and essence, is the reality of the spectacle, resulting in 'the fatal mischief of a world arranged so as to degrade men to means of their *sese conservare*, a world that curtails and threatens their life by reproducing it and making them believe that it has this character so as to satisfy their needs' (Adorno

2007: 167). Contrary to Adorno's suggestion here, the spectacle *does* in fact satisfy human needs, albeit by producing those needs and wants alongside the available means of their satiation. The 'mischief' disenchanted by Adorno within *Negative Dialectics* thereby succeeds within the spectacle in reversing the gap between the essential laws of society and the prevailing generality. The levelling of appearance and essence found within the logic of the spectacle is not simply a loss of individual subjectivity but the actualized fulfilment of social need. Essence still requires appearance, but it is not an appearance *qua* illusion. The spectacle allows for discrimination between appearances, but it is a mode of distinction internal to an essential commensurability for which truth is made identical with the untrue. An examination into how Debord conceives, under the spectacle, the notion of ideology – a term which tends to exude the association of falsehood – helps to drive the point home.

The materialization of ideology

With only ten theses, the concluding chapter of Debord's *The Society of the Spectacle* is its shortest. Entitled 'Ideology Materialized', Debord approaches the question of ideology through the preceding diagnosis of a society dominated by the spectacle, that is, by a mode of abstract domination which concretizes itself within the world through its forms of appearance. It is less a chapter on Debord's understanding of the concept of ideology per se than it is an analysis on how the spectacle has inherently ideological features, or more specifically, how the spectacle can be construed as *the materialization of ideology*.

Of course the use of the term 'ideology' here is strictly provisional in order to elucidate certain dimensions of Debord's theory of the society of the spectacle. A more thorough intellectual history of ideology, obviously beyond the scope of this book, would warrant an investigation into the prehistory of its concept and its distinct status within Enlightenment thought, whose early articulations, unlike the rendition found in Debord, were indeed situated in an abstract subjectivism for which the responsibility of innate blindness fell entirely upon a subject's cognitive fallibility, rather than in an objective social organization. In this way, it can be argued that the nature of the concept of ideology belongs exclusively to the bourgeois era, that is, for which the Copernican individual remains its perpetual precondition. Closer to Debord's understanding, however, ideology here can be generally construed as independent intellectual formations and the conditions by which they gain their autonomy jointly under a real historical development. This separation can be socially derived from the division of labour and develops in accordance with the transformations of social fragmentation characteristic of class societies beginning from the division between intellectual and manual labour. It is in this way that Debord generally adopts the concept of ideology as 'the *separate power* of ideas' (Knabb 2006: 286).

Alternative to the notion that ideology is an invention of the bourgeoisie, however, it can also be said that ideology is as old as myth itself, as a necessary component to the division of labour and in the distribution of surplus throughout pre-capitalist social formations. This would accord with Debord's idea that while the spectacle was always ideological, ideology was not always spectacular, a point make explicit in a 1969 letter to Gianfranco Sanguinetti (2004a: 455–6). Ideology is described there as not reducible to the capitalist mode of production and finds its expression within those first primitive efforts at rationalization. Here we find another correspondence between Debord and Adorno, this time in accordance with the ideas of *Dialectic of Enlightenment*. Myth as nascent rationalization finds not just the formation of classes and the dominance of a priestly class peddling cosmic awe but more crucially the constitution of nature as an objectivity which superstition, magic and the exchange relation of sacrifice seek to tame. As Adorno and Horkheimer recount, over time the practice of sacrifice refines into the accurate calculation of quantifiable proportions, anticipating the use of money. In a word, myth, in facilitating the development of exchange relations through the axiom of identification, points to both the prehistory of ideology and the prehistory of the spectacle independent from their existence within the capitalist mode of production. As Debord writes, in the spectacle, 'the most modern is also the most archaic' (1970: §23).

Yet Debord dispels the notion of ideology as a strict category of epistemology, not a phenomenon of thought itself but the '*foundation* of the thought of a class society' (Debord 1995: §212). Ideology is accordingly not reducible to a subjective error or cognitive blunder, nor confined to class partisanship, wherein one group imposes its interests and beliefs upon another. Nor does it refer to a terrain in the battle over ideas and as such reduced to a class prejudice. For Debord, ideology instead dominates at the level of the social whole, never this or that sphere, however capable of internal oppositions. In this way, the clash between ideologies more closely resembles the competition between individual capitals. Furthermore, ideology is never simply illusory, 'but rather a deformed consciousness of realities, and in this form they have been real factors which set in motion real deforming acts' (Debord 1970: §212). In a word, ideology is the consciousness adequate to the truth of a reality in its utter falseness.

For Debord, ideology bears the '*abstract* will to universality' which 'finds itself legitimated in modern society by universal abstraction' (Debord 1995: §213). Debord concedes that Mannheim recognized this 'internal logic' (1995: §214) of ideology when, in outlining the notion of 'total ideology' as the synecdochical manner by which the ruling class projects its own interests as the interests of the whole of society, the 'despotism of a *fragment* impos[es] itself . . . as a *totalitarian* worldview' (1995: §214). And yet, for Debord, this impulse of universality has in a sense realized itself within the spectacle. As his own notes on Mannheim attest, the total ideology executed by the bourgeoisie 'goes beyond realizing itself (spectacle and commodity)'.[14] While it might be said that for Marx, ideology refers pejoratively to the role of ideas within class struggle, an element in the balance of social forces for which a *social-historical* truth is concealed, for Debord there subsists mystification at the level of conceptual truth, that is, in the abstract universality of the concept striving for actualization. In this way, the commodity form and its abstraction inadvertently commands a particular epistemological structure adequate to the individuals of exchange relations. As Sohn-Rethel has written, '[n]othing could be wrapped in greater secrecy than the truth that the independence of the intellect is owed to its original social character' (1983: 77). Here it can be remarked that socially necessary modes of thought accord with historically specific forms of social synthesis. What Adorno referred to as 'socially necessary semblance' (*gesellschaftlich notwendiger Schein*) – as an objective and necessary illusion that legitimates the social structure of domination – is thereby maintained at the level of the social determination of form.

It is with this rendition of ideology as formal determination that Debord proceeds to trace the shift from an early bourgeois era of arousing and *particular* ideological rivals – best epitomized during the revolutions of the late eighteenth century, whereby ideals effectively rode in on horseback – to a really existing *universal* ideology under the society of the spectacle. Ideology thereby coheres with the commensurability of exchange relations, an indifference to qualitatively distinct belief systems under a relation of identity. Mimetic to the commodity, it is the *form* of ideology and not any of its particular *content* that ordains its substance. As Debord writes, '[t]he claims of ideology now take on a sort of flat, positivistic exactness: ideology is no longer a historical choice, but simply an assertion of the obvious. *Names* of particular ideologies have vanished . . . Which is another way of saying that the history of ideologies, plural, is over' (1995: §213). Consequently, ideology will always believe itself to be elsewhere: 'It can keep the original name for something secretly changed (beer, beef or philosophers). And it can just as easily change the name when the thing itself has been secretly maintained' (Debord 1998: 34). The internal coherency between competing belief systems rests at the level of form. Its logic accentuates and embellishes resemblances while disavowing and effacing differences. As a result, under the spectacle, the universality of ideology is fulfilled precisely at the point of 'its dissolution into society as a whole' (Debord 1995: §214).

Debord refers to the spectacle as the '*materialization* of ideology ... which is precipitated by the concrete success of an autonomous economic system of production' (Ibid: §212). While it can be conceded that ideology has *always* procured very real material consequences, to give greater distinction to what Debord has in mind, it is fruitful to observe what he has to say about the spectacle's relation to, for example, religious consciousness and 'the mist-enveloped regions of the religious world' (Marx 1996: 83). The essential difference here is that the spectacle is not confined to making *unrequited* promises for salvation. As Debord writes within the first chapter of *The Society of the Spectacle*:

> Religious contemplation in its earliest form was the outcome of the establishment of the social division of labor and the formation of classes. Power draped itself in the outward garb of a mythical order from the beginning. In former times the category of the sacred justified the cosmic and ontological ordering of things that best served the interests of the masters, expounding upon and embellishing what society *could not deliver* ... The modern spectacle, by contrast, depicts what society *can deliver*.
>
> 1995: §25

Debord here alludes to the work of Feuerbach – who is utilized as the epigram for the first chapter of *The Society of the Spectacle* – in which religious consciousness consists in the projection of human beings and their powers into a transcendental realm assuming the appearance of a god, rather than grasped as the result of their own activity. For Debord, correlative with the fetish-character of commodities is then the fetishism of religious practice, consisting in the contemplation by humanity of its own separated powers. The principle of separation found within religious alienation expresses itself within the historical origins of the spectacle as the heir of religious projection whose cunning intends to deceive the world to its ruin. The spectacle is thereby said by Debord to be the material constitution of the religious illusion, 'the technical *realization* of the exile of human powers into a beyond [for which] those cloud-enshrouded entities have now been brought down to earth' (1995: §20; emphasis added). Not merely a sermon of hot air, the spectacle is 'the general equivalent of whatever society as a whole *can be and do*' (1995: §49; emphasis added). The lie of religious consciousness attains its truth under the spectacle, one wherein the promises of the commodity do not remain unrequited, but are advertised precisely *because* they are attainable. As it is remarked in the infamous 1966 pamphlet, 'On the Poverty of Student Life', the 'spectacle is the terrestrial realization of *ideology*. Never has the world been so inverted' (Knabb 2006: 428).

The spectacle is only the dissolution of ideology insofar as ideology is simply regarded as an illusory mechanism for concealing class interests. Under the spectacle, social relations appear as what they in fact are: a fragmented social condition unified in its very fragmentation. If ideology functions as an alleged conceptual truth that both formalizes and naturalizes phenomena into a distorted shape, the spectacle is the exposition of those distortions as material facts of reality. The spectacle as the materialization of ideology evades the exposure of a concretely anchored reality by, as will be examined in the next chapter more closely, both generating and accommodating the most varied sensuous material out of its own spectacular logic. It respects a seemingly endless diversity of phenomena while furnishing an inner principle of organization. While politics may have been indispensible to Greek antiquity just as Catholicism was for the Middle Ages, the society of spectacle need not ascribe to any *particular* spiritual worldview. It is obliged to respect any illusions held by its adversaries. There can, of course, exist competing belief systems and *Weltanschauungen* inasmuch as there can exist individuated currencies. Nevertheless, it was always doubtful that a reversion to the drachma would flounder international trade.

If ideology consists in the distorted reflex of the real world, the spectacle amounts to the clarified reflex of a world *really* distorted. The duplicated social world under ideology, no longer hawking misshapen reflections, supersedes its duality under the spectacle. For this, there can be no chasm between the appearances of the spectacle and the essence of its social reality. Unlike the mere promise of a world proclaimed by ideology, the world that the spectacle offers is delivered *in full*. While religious illusion consists in a false projection, spectacular ideology *reveals* the truth of a false and inverted world. It is the appearance of reality *as false*, not simply false in its appearing. While ideology falsifies reality, the spectacle *unveils* a falsified reality, which in turn reproduces that reality as false. One cannot see the world *not* as it really is.

Conclusion

We have seen how Adorno's criticism of Hegel's philosophy of identity can be inadvertently construed as a critique of the society of the spectacle itself, which refers not to a duplicitous reality said to be split between the abstract forces of market relations and a concrete, originary and genuine human condition, but to a single social world sneering with a face that need not conceal its intent: to drag human beings along a road to ruin paved with social satisfaction. It is the *untruth* of a world whose monstrosity it has *truthfully* become. The concept of the spectacle is false precisely to the extent that it is a '*Weltanschauung* which has become actual' (Debord 1970: §5), a verdict of affirmative positivity in and through its claims about appearances which are nonetheless true in their tendency towards the speculative identity of subject and substance. It is the same critical verdict given by Adorno on Hegel's philosophy. The world in actual fact is exhausted by the reconciliatory concept of the spectacle and emerges as identical to the façade through which it appears. The false is the spectacular medium for the appearance of truth and the spectacle thereby consists in the interweaving of the truth and the false, in glaring contrast to the dichotomy of the untainted truth and the pure lie. It is rather *the autonomy of the lie*, an independence that ideology, in previous formulations, could never achieve so long as its proclamations could be revoked by the concreteness of social reality. Under the spectacle, '[s]ociety has become what ideology already was' (Debord 1970: §217). It is in this way that the spectacle can be identified as the materialization of ideology – *defining that which appears and embodying appearance as definitive*.

As immediacies are annexed by the reigning actuality, the false installs itself, as the identity of appearance and essence, as the predominant and cohesive mediation governing the whole of society. The spectacle is the concept for this development, what Adorno might align with what he describes as 'arch-ideology' and Debord incidentally calls 'the acme of ideology' (1995: §215): that tireless pursuit 'to deny the distinction between appearance and essence' which 'compels us to accept that the phenomena are just as they appear, since there is nothing behind them' (Adorno 2008: 102).[15]

This book is concerned essentially with the life at work in the concept of the society of the spectacle. It is a life for which 'the lie has long since lost its honest function of misrepresenting reality. Nobody believes anybody, everyone is in the know' (Adorno 2005a: 30). This chapter has discovered that the spectacle's 'deceitful publicity' (Bonefeld 2014: 38) cannot be convicted of untruth from the perspective of truth, nor can criticism of the spectacle proceed through a discontentment with façades. If the spectacle inverts reality, it does so by inverting the inversion, that is, by *falsely reproducing an already falsified concrete reality as false*. As such, that which appears as true can only ever be a moment of the false. Truth becomes the experience of the lie.

If 'this world is naught but deception' (Villon 1977: 48; translation amended), however, we must now turn to an analysis of how such a world, riddled with deceit and without any hidden honesty, might acquire conceptual purchase. The next chapter will thereby examine a specific section of the *Phenomenology of Spirit* that deals precisely with that, a physiognomic investigation on how appearances disclose an inverted world through a dialectic of the 'sensible supersensible'. It is through such a movement of appearances that we will discover exactly how it could possibly be said that the world is rendered identical to the façade through which it appears.

2

The Speculative of the Spectacle

If you invert the world only once more, you will turn it on its true side, and you will not then say that it is without reason.

Ludwig Tieck

In the previous chapter, we have seen how the identity of truth and falsehood constitutive of the society of the spectacle accords with Adorno's criticisms of Hegel's philosophy of identity. It is the same critique that admonishes a social reign of falsehood perpetuated by Hegel's speculative, the identity of identity and non-identity which has procured a social whole dominated by equivalence. Yet it remains to be seen how it is that a movement of appearances specifically constitutes such a false totality. In a word, how might we grasp the rationality of the spectacle's appearances? Can it even be said that the spectacle is rational?

The eighth issue of *Internationale situationniste* (*IS*) (1963) opens with an editorial entitled 'Ideologies, Classes, and the Domination of Nature'. Within the essay, the SI appropriate a title of one of Goya's etchings from the *Los Caprichos* series in order to characterize their era as one in which 'the sleep [*sommeil*] of dialectical reason [has] engendered monsters' (Knabb 2006: 138). Of course for Goya, it is a depiction not of reason's altogether eradication, but that within a certain fractious yet rhythmic state of fantasy – not simply sleep but dream (*sueño*) – reason yields irrational fruit. Such is a cursory figuration of the society of the spectacle, 'a world of *irrational rationalization*' (Knabb 2006: 201) which, despite formulations within *The Society of the Spectacle* on its undialectical posturing, nevertheless retains an element of dialectical reason. Indeed, a year prior to the publication of this editorial, at a meeting of the SI's Central Council in Paris, the discussion turned to the issue of 'the dialectic of the spectacle' (IS 1997: 289).

Despite the way in which it might be said that irrationality seems to typify the society of the spectacle (Debord 1998: 31), there remains a determinate rationality for which it acquires actuality in the world. As Debord writes in his notes on Hegel's *Philosophical Propaedeutic*, 'The mystification of [its] "autonomy" breaks out in the S of the S with its permanent education ... It is always necessary to learn more of the infinite unfolding of the reason of the machines, by the image of the commodity world of production.'[1] Under the spectacle, there is a generalized uncertainty, albeit it is '*organised* everywhere' (Debord 1998: 55); or as Debord writes in *The Society of the Spectacle*, 'What pushes for greater rationality is also what nourishes the irrationality' (1995: §72).[2]

The spectacle, 'which is so fundamentally unitary', wields for Debord a stringent logic that 'controls [an] abundant diversity' (1998: 6, 7). However, the inner connection and unifying force between its particular appearances have yet to be examined. Doing so would comprise investigating the spectacle as a speculative concept which is actualized in and through a relation of identity within difference and difference within identity. This chapter will thereby examine the unity and division of appearances characteristic of the spectacle. By first offering greater elucidation on Hegel's conception of speculative identity, we will then provide an interpretation of the 'Force and the Understanding: Appearance and the Supersensible World' section of the *Phenomenology of Spirit*. This section is in the distinctive position of offering a vignette on the spectacle as a society organized by way of appearances in and through a speculative identity of identity and non-identity. Crucial for the reconstruction here will be the way in which the structure of solicitation found therein stands as a relation of exchange and how a dialectic of *Erscheinungen* yields what Hegel calls a sensuous supersensible inverted world. We note at the outset that the concept of force employed by Hegel in that section of the *Phenomenology of Spirit* carries with it a structure of *unity-in-separation*: the unity of force is an *Erscheinung* that mediates over and against independent extremes or differences. As such, within the concept of force, diremption takes on the appearance of a unity that is perpetually divided into extremes: a unity of separations which does not abolish separations. This dynamic will subsequently be carried over into an analysis of chapter 3 of *The Society of the Spectacle*. Before concluding, this chapter will also integrate comments on the concept of speculation found in Feuerbach and the young Marx, with particular attention to those writings closely examined by Debord. It will thereby be argued that Debord's usage of the speculative for the concept of the society of the spectacle derives not simply from Hegel himself but also from some of his strongest critics.

Speculative identity

While bringing the first volume of his *Science of Logic* to publication, Hegel penned a letter to educational reformer Friedrich Immanuel Niethammer in October 1812. The letter is accompanied by a private report (*Gutachten Propaedeutik*) on teaching philosophy to gymnasium students and concludes with a threefold distinction between what he describes as abstract, dialectical and speculative thought. As Hegel writes:

> Philosophical content has in its method and soul three forms: it is, *1*, abstract, *2*, dialectical, and *3*, speculative. It is abstract insofar as it takes place generally in the element of thought. Yet as merely abstract it becomes – in contrast to the dialectical and speculative forms – the so-called understanding which holds determinations fast and comes to know them in their fixed distinction. The dialectical is the movement and confusion of such fixed determinateness; it is negative reason. The speculative is positive reason, the spiritual, and it alone is really philosophical.
>
> 1984: 280

Hegel conceived speculative thinking as the most difficult for gymnasium students, in contrast with both the thought of the understanding (*Verstand*) which grasps abstract determinations in their isolation or '[n]othing beyond tortuous antitheses' (1984: 281) and dialectical reason (*Vernunft*) for which every new concept proceeds out of a systematic whole. Less important is Hegel's classification of such differing modes of thought than is the way in which, through his philosophy, each proceeds immanently out of each other. Thus the speculative moment is born out of (*herborgehende*) the dialectic, or as Hegel writes in the *Encyclopaedia Logic*:

> When the dialectic has the negative as its result, then, precisely as a result, this negative is at the same time the positive, for it contains what it resulted from sublated within itself, and it cannot be without it. This, however, is the basic determination of the third form of the Logical, namely, the *speculative* or positively rational [moment] ... The *speculative* or *positively rational* apprehends the unity of the determinations in their opposition, the *affirmative* that is contained in their dissolution and in their transition.
>
> 1991b: 131

The speculative is the systematic unfolding of relations, a category of systematic unity in the structure of social experience. It is the development of *Vernunft* in its overcoming of the ordinary thought of the *Verstand* in its isolation of individual phenomena.

Verstand and *Vernunft* amount to different operations with respective propensities. Hegel describes their distinction thusly: 'The *understanding determines*, and holds the determination fixed. *Reason* is negative and *dialectical*, since it dissolves the determinations of the understanding into nothing; it is *positive*, since it generates the *universal*, and comprehends the particular therein' (2010: 10). *Verstand* preserves determinations as formal and static, differentiating one category from another and retaining that distinction. In contrast, *Vernunft* yields to the sublation of finite determinations and their passing into their opposites. *Vernunft* grasps the distinctions drawn by the *Verstand* although witnesses their dissolution into their opposite.

The speculative in Hegel is as such the procured and positive reconciliation of contradiction resulting from the movement between the *Verstand* and *Vernunft*, themselves not separate faculties of cognition but different aspects of the single activity of thought. Speculation finds as its basis *Vernunft* which has incorporated the antinomies of the *Verstand* into a higher unity. What is more, the speculative lays bare the totality of thinking in the identity of subject and object and is also at once a theory of social reality or spirit. That is, speculative identity for Hegel needs to hold true not simply as an exercise of the thinking subject but within objective reality itself.

Speculation is ingrained within the axiom of identity. The identity characteristic of speculative reason is the identity of identity and non-identity, the preservation of difference within identity; 'being opposed and being one are both together in it' (Hegel 1977a: 156). It is a concept of identity first formulated by Hegel in *The Difference Between Fichte's and Schelling's Systems of Philosophy* and one which he held throughout his life. There it is introduced alongside the distinction between the *Verstand* – a process of differentiating and holding to rigid oppositions – and speculative *Vernunft* – a process of giving differentiating unity through immanent mediation.

Within the speculative, identity coincides with positivity, incorporating within itself the negative moments of the non-identical into the differentiated, itself derivative of the identity principle and, we might say, its appetite. Speculative identification is reconciliatory at the level of the whole and removes concepts from their isolation, comprehending a given dichotomy as a unity with positive cohesiveness. 'The *speculative* or *positively rational* apprehends the unity of the determinations in their opposition, the *affirmative* that is contained in their dissolution and in their transition' (Hegel 1991b: 131). The speculative is the circumscription of the failure of any category to subsist on its own terms and, in so doing, turns it into its opposite.

It is the argument of this book that it is the *speculative* aspect of the dialectic which constitutes the spectacular logic of the society of the spectacle. We can build this idea from a thesis that appears early on in *The Society of the Spectacle*: 'Indeed the spectacle reposes on an incessant deployment of the very technical rationality to which that philosophical tradition gave rise. So far from realizing philosophy, the spectacle philosophizes reality, and turns the material life of everyone into a universe of speculation' (Debord 1995: §19). Our argument can be said to advance the notion that the implications of such a thesis, if they are fully developed in accordance with the spectacle as the *Hegelianization of reality*, as remarked in our introduction, unfurl a manner through which the spectacle can be given greater conceptual determinacy.

The rhythm of speculative identity is central to the spectacular logic of the society of the spectacle. However, a caveat is here needed to better distinguish speculation and dialectics more generally. Indeed, precisely because the spectacle yields positive reconciliation as a unity-in-separation does it not merely exhibit a generically dialectical logic. More specifically, speculation is, in the words of Hegel, 'the most important aspect of dialectic'[3] and the one which most fully accommodates an identity of opposites. Indeed, the spectacle itself is the speculative movement of turning categories into their opposites, always proving 'to be the other of itself' (Hegel 2010: 744). The spectacle is therefore not simply a dialectical concept but the trajectory of the dialectic as the revelation of its own reconciled positivity. As speculative, the spectacle produces the world as a socialized totality internally unified through the principle of separation, a speculative identity that sustains difference within itself.

The previous chapter demonstrated how, for Hegel, the false is generative of the true. However, with Hegel's speculative, we are no longer dealing with a simple identity between truth and falsehood. Rather, within the speculative, identity comes to coincide with positivity, incorporating within itself the negative moments of the non-identical mangled into the differentiated. Negation drives the disagreement between knowledge and its object, expressing differentiation into opposites but even further, as a moment of speculative thought, as an opposition to those opposites. As such, determinate negation contains within it the speculative aspiration of unifying disjointed moments into a higher concept. Opposed categories are given a positive relation; their opposition overcome and will yet begin again. The speculative is that aspect of the negative reason of the dialectic which overcomes its confusion of the determinations of the *Verstand*.

Gadamer makes the point that the German language is especially suited for speculative philosophy. Its 'speculative spirit' (Hegel 2010: 12) is endowed with the disposition for its lexicon to yield one word with opposite meanings. A speculative proposition breaks down any calcified relation between subject and predicate and undermines any conventional distinction between the two; 'their unity, rather, is meant to emerge as a harmony' (Hegel 1977c: 38). Such is the case that the speculative identity of the spectacle neither petrifies its predicates nor sets them above its subjectivity as a formal and abstract identity. Hardly reducible to a logic of classification, the spectacle organizes differentiated particulars to correlate with their opposites. It must, as Marx and Adorno observed of capitalist society, 'constantly expand, progress, advance its frontiers, not respect any limit, not remain the same' (Adorno 2007: 26). The speculative concedes the transition of categories turning into their opposite, overturning the ordinary understanding about opposites. The true turns into the false while difference rolls over into sameness without completely denying the difference between opposites, only their absolutization.

Both Adorno and Debord conceive society as a speculative concept, one which is irreducible to a single axiom or definition. Society is not a classificatory concept nor can it be empirically demonstrated. It subsists as a reified whole in and through every concrete social relation. That the spectacle constitutes itself as *society* already suggests itself to be both a process and an internally mediated and *speculative* totality. The society of the spectacle preserves the same resistance to reduction as a speculative proposition. Its concept is an abbreviation for complex social process of domination allergic to single precepts. The category of spectacle eludes a singular definition and should rather be grasped as a universal dynamic of society in general that contains within it a variety of social phenomena. In fact, it can been said that all 221 short theses that make up *The Society of the Spectacle* are themselves 221 different definitions of the spectacle from varying vantage points.

Force and the understanding

Hegel's speculative develops its self-identity within the manifold of phenomenal appearance forms. We thereby discover the necessity of having first elucidated, in the previous chapter, how the false is generative of the true. Such an account of falsehood remains incomplete without demonstrating that it is speculative thought which aims to give necessary justification and legitimacy to falsehood.

Indeed, its aspiration is a speculative identity between truth and falsehood, an identity that is carried through the movement of appearances themselves. Only as such can we understand the role of appearances in the speculative development of a false totality.

A cardinal speculative moment in the *Phenomenology of Spirit* occurs within 'Force and the Understanding', the first most profound moment of self-discovery for which consciousness concedes that to know its object is to also know itself, a preliminary anticipation of the speculative unity between subject and substance.[4] It is renowned as one of the most arduous and opaque sections of the *Phenomenology of Spirit*. Its difficulty primarily resides in its importance. It completes Hegel's criticism of varying epistemological perspectives in which consciousness is confronted with a seemingly alien and external object and has yet to grasp its own contributing *self* in the knowing of its object. The section also constitutes an intricate rendition of one of the central theses of the book: that the distinction between the object as it appears and as it is *in-itself* is a distinction made solely in and by consciousness. For this, the section witnesses a developing conversion of object into subject, or more specifically, it is here that the phenomenal consciousness pivotally transitions to a *self*-consciousness.

As a general overview, the chapter explores different candidates and versions of the non-empirical unity and discrimination of objects of experience, or how consciousness is to supply a supersensible ground for directly apprehending a *unity-in-difference* of manifold appearances. Simply put, how is consciousness to link empirical appearances with the thing itself? Hegel advances through various ideas found within Plato, Aristotle, Leibniz, Newton, Galileo and, most obviously, Kant, all for whom the problem of a duality between the sensual and non-sensual leads to what Hegel calls an inverted world (*die verkehrte Welt*). In providing alternative ways of characterizing the faculty of the *Verstand* in its experience of the object, Hegel first employs the category of force to grasp the non-empirical ground of the empirical. From there, he moves into a more in-depth discussion of appearances (*Erscheinungen*) and what he calls the supersensible beyond (*das übersinnliche Jenseits*). Hegel then proceeds to a nomological discussion of this supersensible beyond and, through the category of law (*Gesetz*), explores the manner in which non-empirical *necessary* relations among appearances are the truth of appearances themselves. He then examines the emergence of an inverted world (*verkehrte Welt*) which serves as a transition to 'Self-consciousness'.

It is important to first emphasize that the German 'verkehrt' does not simply mean 'false' (*falsch*). 'Reversed', 'turned-around', 'upside-down', 'backwards', 'topsy-turvy', 'deranged', 'perverse' and 'contorted' are all closer to the mark. The clarification serves as a useful instance in demonstrating that the experience of consciousness never falls within a simple duality between what is true and what is false. Further, Gadamer helpfully reaffirms the double sense of *verkehrt* as both an inversion and perversion and not simply 'the contrary, the mere abstract opposite of the existent world. Rather this reversal in which everything is the opposite of itself makes visible in a kind of fun house mirror the covert perversion of everything as we know it. If this is so, the topsy-turvy world would be the perversion of perversity' (1976: 48).[5]

We will now offer a rehearsal of the primary moves made within this section of the *Phenomenology of Spirit*. From there, its dialectic of appearance will be emphasized as an abridged portrait of the society of the spectacle, instantiated subsequently with an analysis of chapter 3 of *The Society of the Spectacle*. What proceeds will not be an exhaustive and detailed account of 'Force and the Understanding' but only a reading which highlights those moments in its development that assist in elucidating the logical structure of appearances in the society of the spectacle.

The interiority of things

Within the *Phenomenology of Spirit*, we find consciousness in the difficult position of trying to account, in the object that confronts it, for a unity of diverse sensory elements alongside the object's universality, without losing the ability to discriminate between any of those particulars or properties. Consciousness has failed to coherently relate the diversity and 'selfsameness' (*Sichselbstgleichheit*) of its object. The movement away from sensible reality without completely abandoning it now characterizes the emergent faculty of the *Verstand*. It begins with its object as an 'unconditioned universal' (*unbedingt Allgemeine*), an external object of *thought* neither seen nor heard, which, if it is not to regress, must part with the unstable conditions of sensibility. The object of consciousness now oscillates between a set of properties and a unity, and finds recourse in an inferred interiority to thinghood. The thing has emerged as the imperceptible binding of the one and the many. This is, for the *Verstand*, an objective and external essence that is now its non-sensual object.

As an object of the *Verstand*, the manifold properties of the thing appear as the empirical manifestations resulting from something *behind* the immediacy of the object. This transcendent sphere behind the realm of sense and perception is an experiential ground Hegel calls the supersensible world as that which subsists underneath the world of phenomena. The unconditioned universality becomes the mutually alternating appearing of passive multiplicity on one side and an invisible active unity on the other.

The back-and-forth movement of matters passing over into their unity and the unity dispersing into independent matters unfolding in their diversity is what Hegel calls force (*Kraft*). On the one hand, we have the dispersal of independent matters in their immediate sensuality as an *expression* of force. On the other hand, Hegel calls *force proper* or *genuine force* the movement of the disappearance of those independent matters, that is, their retraction into a unified whole, a force driven back into itself from its expression. Consciousness sustains the different moments *qua* different, as an unperceivable causal power which binds the properties of the thing together as an existent substance in the world with reference to the interiority of things while the perceived extended world is a plenum of independent matters.

The structure of solicitation

The *Verstand* posits force as an explanatory power as it observes empirical phenomena. It is the ground of perceptual diversity whose dynamic is one of expansion and contraction. Hegel describes this movement between each side of force through a structure of solicitation (*sollizitieren*). The plurality of matters solicits force into a unity. Yet force is also the universal medium of subsisting matters. Hegel concludes that *force is both what is solicited and what does the soliciting*, both the externalization of sensual properties and the withdrawal of those elements back into the medium of its unity. This unity of force is 'transformed into the same reciprocal exchange of determinatenesses' (Hegel 2018: 84). In appearance, there nevertheless remains a duality of forces, a self-diremption into two wholly independent forces whose only being is in truth their being posited by the other. Hegel describes the resulting scenario as a 'play of both forces' in which they are determined as mutually opposed in an alteration of immediacy. Each force has their determination and complete fulfilment only through the other as its reciprocal complementary. Force is doubled into both a self-manifesting force and the force to which it is manifest.

The composition of the play of forces consists in the mutual solicitation of two forces. What we have is an immediate alteration of back-and-forth solicitation, that is, 'the absolute exchange of *determinateness* which constitutes the sole content' (Hegel 2018: 89) of what is being exhibited, in other words, what is appearing. Decisive here for our analysis is that the true content of the appearance of the play of forces is *the unity of commensurability or of the absolute exchange of determinateness (das absolute Austauschen der Bestimmtheit)*. These two relations are one and the same. Their difference is only a difference of the *form* of appearing either as solicited or soliciting. What disappears in this dynamic is all distinction and separation between mutually contrasting forces. The appearance of separateness therefore dissolves into a unity. All distinction evaporates in this absolute flux, and what remains is 'a difference into which the many antitheses have been resolved' (Hegel 1977c: 90). The law of appearance is as such the simultaneous cancellation and affirmation of difference. It is a 'selfsameness of the non-selfsame, a constancy of inconstancy' (Hegel 2018: 94)

Through the *Verstand*, consciousness looks through the mediating play of forces into the true background of things. Hegel describes this 'developed *being* of force' as *appearance (Erscheinung)* insofar as '*being* that is directly and in its own self a *non-being* a surface show', or what Pinkard translates as a 'seeming-to-be [*Schein*]'. However, this being of force is not simply a semblance, seeming-to-be or surface show but is 'a *totality of show*' (Hegel 1977c: 87). Hegel here gives the category of *Erscheinung* a more thorough definition as 'ein Ganzes Scheins'. As such, *Erscheinung* can be said to consist in *a totality of semblances*. Said another way, the *Schein* of the *Verstand* transitions into a world of *Erscheinungen* when it is put together into a whole of dispersion and contraction. The development of *Schein* to *Erscheinung* is the *Verstand*'s explanatory movement of identifying the immediacies of sensual appearance to be governed by *a totality of appearance* that is the dynamic expression of force from a supersensible world. This totality is what constitutes the inner unity of things. *Erscheinung* is the whole of reality. The *Verstand* thereby sees itself as penetrating beneath the semblance or surface of things and arriving at what it understands to be the true background and objectivity of the world.

To recap, the sensuous world which Hegel calls the world of appearance (*der erscheinenden Welt*) has revealed behind itself a supersensible world (*eine übersinnliche Welt*). This is the true world above the vanishing and unstable world of appearances. This permanent beyond is for Hegel the first albeit imperfect or immature appearance of reason (*unvollkommene Erscheinung der Vernunft*). As Hegel writes:

> [W]hat is disclosed for the first time and henceforth is a *supersensible* world as the *true* world over and above the *sensuous* world as the *appearing* world. That is, over and above the vanishing *this-worldliness*, there is disclosed a persisting

other-worldly beyond, an in-itself which is the first and therefore incomplete appearance of reason, that is, which is the pure element in which the truth has its essence.

2018: 87

The *Verstand* is fastened into this position of *viewing* the inner world through the play of forces. This movement produces a new determination that derives from the experience of the *Verstand* beholding (*erblicken*) the *Hintergrund* via the appearance.

After consciousness has penetrated the supersensible world and passed through the movement of appearing, to its dismay, it finds nothing. This is not because its reason is mistaken or short-sighted, but simply because there is nothing there to be known. That which is beyond consciousness is unknowable *by definition*. The interiority of things is empty. The *thing-in-itself* is that which does *not* appear. There is difficulty in explaining what is in consciousness by an appeal to what is outside consciousness. As such, the *Verstand* can no longer maintain that the source of appearances is the supersensible world. Rather than characterizing force as a substance *that* externalizes itself within the phenomenal or empirical realm, *force becomes the externalizing appearance itself*. There is no substance to force that is more than its expression.[6] This occurs since the supersensible world derives from the world of appearance that has mediated it. Since appearances *produce* the supersensible world or that its beyond derives *from* appearance, *the essence of the inner world is its appearance*. Appearance is that which fills the inner world of things. The essential truth of the sensually perceived becomes the appearance itself. This is what is meant by Hegel's enigmatic and yet crucial formulation that '[t]he supersensible is therefore *appearance qua appearance*' (1977c: 89). Appearance is not the appearance of some other reality in opposition to that reality, but reality itself. In a word, *the supersensible world envelopes the sensual world*. Let it be emphasized, Hegel's point is that it is the supersensible world and not the sensible world that constitutes appearance. The inner world is the truth of appearance of which it negates its exteriority. The supersensible is thereby *the totality of appearance shown forth*.

Erscheinung as the totality of *Scheinen* gives real insight into the interiority of reality. The *Verstand* comes to appeal to what it takes to be the essence of reality, namely a substantive 'law of force' (*das Gesetz der Kraft*) which governs the reality of things. The *Verstand* now finds unity and stability for the ceaseless movement of phenomena in the law of force as the 'tranquil image' (1977c: 91) of continual change. This calming kingdom of law governing the erratic heteronomy of the phenomenal world – or the permanent supersensible *eidos* of the sensible world – is taken as an objective substance. Having understood its own mistake as grasping the empirical as an illusory appearance, the *Verstand* now posits the supersensible world as a sphere defined by the laws of mathematics and the natural sciences. This inner true reality is no longer unknowable beyond its compartmentalized categorizations. The *Verstand* thereby manoeuvres from the Kantian noumenal world to one of lawful scientific and mathematic precision and validity predominantly structured by quantitative properties. To borrow a formulation from Adorno and Horkheimer, '[t]he essence of the world coincides with the statistical law by which its surface is classified' (2002: 183).

The inverted world

Consciousness now wields two versions of the supersensible world. There is first the 'tranquil image' of the world of phenomenal appearance as the foundation of law. This world however turned out to be anything but a calm copy (*Abbild*). Its picture has only turned into a mirror of itself for which the world of sense and the supersensible world of its own thought has reversed into an 'inverted world'. The first supersensible world – 'the tranquil kingdom of laws' as the immediate copy of the perceived world – is changed into its opposite. Each of the two worlds becomes their own opposite. Selfsame becomes difference while difference becomes selfsame. Difference becomes now an *inner* difference. Like becomes unlike and unlike becomes like. Through this process, this inverted *second supersensible world* becomes appearance itself, or rather 'is completed as appearance' (Hegel 1977c: 96). The sensible world has becomes unintelligible without the supersensible world. The true world is therefore the inverted world. If the sensible world is to be known at all, it must be inverted. What is at issue here is not simply a distinction between what is the case and what seems to be, nor is it a presumption of two separate worlds of the sensible and supersensible, of appearance and reality. Instead, Hegel is calling into question the antithesis between inner and outer, of appearance and the supersensible as two different actualities.

The thesis of Hegel's inverted world is that the instability of the empirical world in which there is a constant disappearing into the supersensible world finds in this second world the truth of constant and perpetual change. The second supersensible world of abstracting from the empirical world becomes *the true world* for which its inversion is a requisite for the intelligibility of the *unity-in-separation* of the play of forces. The law of the inverted world says that like poles in the first world are the unlike of itself, and that the unlike poles in the first world becomes like itself: what is sweet in the first world is sour in the inverted world, or black *is* white, good *is* evil, oxygen *is* hydrogen, honour *is* contempt, punishment *is* revenge, and so on. The principle of the other world turning into its opposite is the intelligibility adequate to the abstractions of consciousness. Since both worlds elicit and require their own opposite, it is not the case that there are two worlds at all, but that there is simply *the self-inversion of one world*.

The sensible world is thereby contained within the supersensible world. This is the result of thinking through the unity of absolute exchange as an internal opposition of solicitation. The truth of the relation between an essence and its manifestation is that while there is an opposition between both sides, each is only the opposite of its opposite (*das Entgegengesetzte eines Entgegengesetzten*). As such, each side includes the whole opposition and its other within itself and that through the inverse of the sensible world, the supersensible world includes the sensible within itself.

The interiority, solicitation and inversion of the spectacle

While admittedly the above interpretation of 'Force and the Understanding' is not an easy development to follow, it has been necessary to establish the conceptual grounds and dynamics of the dialectic of appearance in order to best elucidate how it is that Debord's theory of the spectacle is a direct inheritor of the three central moments described above: an objective and sensuous reality enveloped by abstraction, a predominance of commensurable solicitation and an inverted world. It will be argued now that, together, these three developments of the 'Force and the Understanding' provide a vignette of the society of the spectacle's central peculiarities. Here Debord's personal notes on the section offer a synoptic rendition of the spectacle's speculative logic.

Debord's archival notes on 'Force and the Understanding' mark a series of important moments in the section. He explicitly traces how appearances, once penetrating mere *Schein* and thereby overcoming the separation of soliciting and solicited, become *Erscheinung*, the necessary manifestation of a totality of *Schein*. *Erscheinung* is the totality of *Schein* grasped as the universal interior to all things. Debord's notes conclude by emphasizing that the essential supersensible beyond comes from the world of *Erscheinungen* which mediates it. As Debord extracts in his notes, 'in other words, appearance is its essence and in fact, its filling' (Hegel 1977c: 89).

What Debord's notes on the section demonstrate is that if he acquired his concept of appearance from any part from the Hegel's *Phenomenology of Spirit*, the 'Force and the Understanding' section remains a pivotal and irrefutably important resource. Debord's notes on this section far exceed those compiled for 'The Revealed Religion' section of the book, a theme some commentators point to as demonstrable proof of Debord's usage of the *Phenomenology of Spirit* for his theory of the spectacle. However, because within 'The Revealed Religion' a diremption lingers between 'the colourful show of the sensuous here-and-now and the nightlike void of the supersensible beyond' (Hegel 1977c: 110–11), it remains an inadequate account of the manner in which the spectacle procures sensuous reality out of its supersensible essence. In a word, 'Revealed Religion' cannot be said to lay influence on the spectacle insofar as the problem of a *Jenseits* has returned as a mode of *Vorstellungen*.

Society is organized as appearance and exchange relations allow for the unity of appearances to become explicit while at once procuring an inverted world. This is the central idea derived from 'Force and the Understanding' that Debord imports as the logic of the society of the spectacle. As Debord's writes in his notes on Hegel's *Philosophical Propaedeutic*, 'We give to the interior the adequacy of the exterior.'[7] However, let us break down this logic more closely.

First, the *Verstand* discovers that the inner world of the supersensible has itself derived from the world of appearances which is the mediation between it and phenomenal reality. As such, appearance has itself become the essence. Appearance as *Erscheinung* is not therefore mere *Schein*; it is not illusory or false. It is the mediation of reality itself for which the phenomenal world is brought into existence. This empirical reality is as such *internal* to the supersensible world. As Debord writes in 'For a Revolutionary Judgment of Art', '[i]t is not in its surface meanings [*significations de surface*] that we should look for a spectacle's relation to the problems of the society, but at the deepest level' (Knabb 2006: 393–4). The postulate made by the *Verstand* that the essence of reality is *Erscheinung* is thereby constitutive of Debord's theory of the spectacle. For Debord, the spectacle as the totality of *Erscheinung* refers to the nature of capitalist society as a structural totality, the total and objective result of the unity of society and its phenomenal reality. While also a condition of fragmentation, the spectacle is always the claim of unity made at the level of appearances. Additionally, the movement from the *Verstand* to self-consciousness is a movement between division and unity, a speculative dynamic internal to the society of the spectacle. As the unification of separation, however, the spectacle preserves the separations and divisions of class society, with the difference that this mode of preservation, at the level of image, eclipses the isolated segments of a reified social existence. Through the mediation of the totality of appearances, the *Verstand*, in its speculative transition to self-consciousness, '*contemplates* itself in a world of its own making' (Debord 1970: §53) by observing the essential objectivity of the world as appearance.

Second, clarification is required for how 'Force and the Understanding' relates to the importance Debord places on the exchange relation for the development of the society of spectacle. While a more in-depth discussion on the spectacle's relationship to the determinations of value will be pursued in the next chapter, comments here on how already 'Force and the Understanding' provides some preliminaries, specifically by reading the structure of solicitation as a speculative model of exchange as that which unites while it divides. Hegel characterizes the structure of solicitation as an exchange process, using both German categories of *Wechsel* and *Tauschen*. While *Wechsel* is a term for the changing or switching of positions, terrain or objects, *Tauschen* is the word explicitly used by Marx for the exchange relationship of commodities through money. It is not uncommon, however, for each of the categories to overlap in common usage.[8] Again, Hegel himself employs both, often interchangeably. For example, 'Es ist hierin ebenso nur der unmittelbare Wechsel oder das absolute Austauschen der *Bestimmtheit* vorhanden, welche den einzigen *Inhalt* des Auftretenden ausmacht' (1970: 119). What is more, the *Verstand* wields the *Vorstellungen* of forces and laws for its investigation into the nature of reality. With its categories, it establishes the quantification and mechanistic contortion of phenomena for which *like* becomes *unlike* and *unlike* becomes *like*. The move from force to law consists in *the quantification of the empirical*. The abstractions of thought result in the commensurability of each side of the soliciting forces. Law appears as that which governs reality through the unity of the *exchange of forces*. The transition from force to law is therefore a transformation of *quality* into *quantity*. Additionally, because Hegel describes this process 'als *reiner Wechsel*' (1970: 126) whose predicate of 'pure' is always an indicator for the non-empirical and abstract, the thematic of quantitative abstraction as the content of the exchange process is all the more pronounced. The true content of the appearance of the play of forces is the unity of commensurability or of the absolute exchange of determinateness (*das absolute Austauschen der Bestimmtheit*) as a move from the qualitative to the quantitative. The exchange takes place within *Erscheinung* and refers to the alternation of two sides in the structure of solicitation. Distinctions come to be that are no distinctions at all and sublate themselves, while at the same time distinctions remain the selfsame.

The structure of solicitation as a dialectic of exchange is a decisive thematic insofar as the economic foundations of the spectacle can be grasped through the dynamic of both collapsing and preserving difference through exchange, or in the case of Hegel, a dialectic of identity and difference unfolding through the world of appearance as apprehended by the *Verstand*. As an inverted world, reality is the unity of opposite movements. As was demonstrated, however, these differences are only different in *form*, that is, in solicited and soliciting. Its unity exists only through its inversion, as in the case of the critique of political economy, in the equalization and commensurability of qualitatively different commodities. The maintenance of formal distinctions is nevertheless preserved insofar as the roles of soliciting and solicited express the respective positions of buyer and seller, which are distinctive positions that are always already the selfsame.

The structure of solicitation is an illustration of the dynamic of exchange. The resulting *Erscheinung* of unity is the law of the eternally selfsame. The *Erscheinung* of the spectacle is therefore the essence in which phenomenal difference is constant only through a law-like necessity of *equal becoming unequal and unequal becoming equal*. This is the fundamental structure of *Erscheinung*, which only acquires its status as a totality in and through a relation of exchange between the solicited soliciting play of forces. The selfsame commensurability between the play of forces is the ground by which appearance acquires its essential reality. Again, while the next chapter is devoted to the spectacle's relation to the development of exchange-value in Marx's critique of political economy, it is worth here emphasizing the centrality of equality for the logic of the spectacle.

From the beginning, the equalization of quality characteristic of commodity exchange was a fundament to the SI's diagnosis of modern society. As they write in the very first issue of *IS* (1958) in an article entitled 'The Situationists and Automation', '[t]he idea of standardization is an attempt to reduce and simplify the greatest number of human needs to the greatest degree of equality' (Knabb 2006: 57–8). In what would come to be an early draft of *The Revolution of Everyday Life*, Raoul Vaneigem, writing in 'Basic Banalities' within the eighth issue of *IS* in 1963, states that the spectacle is to a great extent 'a spectacle of confusion and equivalences' (Knabb 2006: 161). The collusion of disorientation and commensurability is a staple of the society of the spectacle. In fact, elsewhere Vaneigem provides one of the most aptly condensed definitions of spectacular logic: 'everything is equivalent to everything else in the perpetual spectacle of incoherence' (2012: 112).

Finally we consider the inverted world that has, through Hegel's analysis, enveloped both phenomenal reality and its intangible essence into one unity. Within the spectacle, it is not out of line to describe this development as a 'real inversion' (Marx 1989: 449). The inverted second supersensible world has phenomenality as its own internal plurality of distinctions. The trajectory of the movement of the faculty of the *Verstand* is ultimately to comprehend how the supersensible world embraces the sensible one. Empirical phenomenality becomes internal to the laws of abstraction and is enveloped and inverted as a moment of the *Verstand*, rather than an external object to be apprehended. The interiority behind the appearance of the world is only the rational construction of the *Verstand* itself. The entirety of the experience of the *Verstand* is therefore only the speculative movement from appearance to thought and back, the self-inversion by which the second supersensible world of abstraction envelops both the first and its phenomenal expression.

Debord's theory of the spectacle also contains the dynamic of the inverted world. As might be expected, however, it is first through Marx that one is best able to grasp the inversion of the spectacle as a particular development of the fetish-character of the forms of value. Both in *Capital* and *Contribution to a Critique of Political Economy*, Marx characterizes the commodity as a 'sensuous-supersensible thing'. It is an immediate and objective unity of use-value and value, of sensuous-concreteness and of abstractness that is the *in-itself* of money. That is, it is only when value is developed by Marx as *in process* through its forms of commodity, money and capital that the unity of the forms appears. Similar to the law of force, it is what remains in the disappearance of its individual instances. 'The sensuous object is here demoted to something that constantly vanishes. The objectivity of the general, the supersensible, is thus a vanishing objectivity' (Reichelt 2005: 46). In this way, it can be said that money is a selfsameness of the non-selfsame, an objectively existing constancy of inconstancy. Only within the development of value do commodities comprise the immediate unity of the specifically concrete and the abstractly supersensible.

Within this inverted world, active human practice creates its own opposite world which in turn concretely subsists only through that opposite. It is an inversion of the abstract and the concrete in which the sensible and concrete only appear as moments of forms of appearance of value. The world thereby exists in the inverted forms of the objective appearances of value. Inheriting Hegel's conception of appearance, an extrinsic duality of appearance and essence is called into question, distinguished however with the critique of political economy, wherein appearances actualize themselves in the inverted world of capitalist society. Marx thereby 'traces respective forms of appearance back to the general law of supersensible existence, an existence that contains within itself all its particularizations' (Reichelt 2005: 63), essentially revealing a contradictory dynamic whereby appearances are the expression of social reality, and yet social reality is the expression of appearances.

It is within this framework of inversion through appearance-forms, elaborated specifically by Helmut Reichelt but also elsewhere by Hans-Georg Backhaus (2005: 14), that Debord's theory of the spectacle can be situated. The essential truth of the sensually perceived becomes the appearance itself. This is what is meant by Hegel's enigmatic and yet crucial formulation that '[t]he supersensible is therefore *appearance qua appearance*' (1977c: 89). Appearance is not the appearance of *some other reality* in opposition to reality, but reality itself. The objectivity of the spectacle calls its own concrete phenomenality into existence as moments of its own abstraction. Herein lies the ontological essence of the spectacle which finds at its basis the inverted world of abstract labour, wherein 'the abstraction of all specific labor and the general abstraction of the entirety of production are perfectly rendered in the spectacle, whose mode of being concrete is precisely abstraction' (Debord 1970: §29). The representations of human activity, substantiated through abstraction, acquire the general authority of those abstractions. The spectacle is a form of social recognition mediated by the form of the commodity, wherein an individual and its activity are affirmed as alienated representations which are nevertheless themselves unconsciously constituted by the individual in its activity as the moments of instantiated concrete abstractions of the economy. As such, '[t]he spectacle constantly rediscovers its own assumptions more concretely' (Debord 1970: §28).

The spectacle speculatively conceives reality *as* appearance, as an inverted world for which the separation of the sensuous world of appearance and the first supersensible world of essence are sublated within a second supersensible world that both preserves and negates their differences. The second supersensible world is the actual reality of the world constituted through the movement of appearance. The content appears through its inverted forms. *The dreams of the spectacle become the material realities of men.* The spectacle thereby renders what Adorno calls a 'peephole metaphysics' (2007: 138–40) – a mere glance at the in-itself of objectivity – into a *gloryhole metaphysics*: full experiential satiation in what lies beyond the realm of appearances.

Unity and division of appearances

The conclusion of 'Force and the Understanding' as a speculative movement from the *Verstand* to an albeit nascent *Vernunft* yields a unity whose nature is that of identity-in-difference. The third chapter of *The Society of Spectacle* proceeds with a similar logical structure. Entitled 'Unity and Division within Appearances', Debord begins with an epigraph taken from a September 1964 article of the Chinese Maoist journal *Red Flag*, published between 1958 and 1988 after the Communist Party's Great Leap Forward towards intensive and rapid industrialization. It offers an instance of the internal ideological conflicts within the Chinese Communist Party,[9] replete with the vulgarized dialectics so characteristic of Mao's *Little Red Book*: '*A lively new polemic about the concepts "one divides into two" and "two fuse in one" is unfolding on the philosophical front in this country. This debate is a struggle between those who are for and those who are against the materialist dialectic*' (Debord 1995: §35). The extract pulled by Debord within the context of opening the third chapter is immediately lampooned by the theses that follow. There, Debord begins an analysis of the spectacle by isolating its double tendency to both divide and unify within its organization of appearances. He outlines a structure for which division takes on the appearance of unity and unity appears in the form of division: 'Like modern society itself, the spectacle is at once united and divided. In both, unity is grounded in a split' (1995: §54). The ground of the unity of the spectacle is its division. However, under the spectacle the grounding division is itself sublated by a reversal of the terms in and through the logic of appearing (*montrée*): 'As it emerges in the spectacle, however, this contradiction is itself contradicted by virtue of a reversal of its meaning: division is presented as unity, and unity as division' (1995: §54).

Importantly from our preceding analysis, this structure of unity-in-separation is described by Debord as a struggle 'between forces [*pouvoirs*]' (1995: §55), a disparity between unity and division overcome through the very logic of appearances. Recall that through the structure of solicitation, it is the dialectic of appearance that burgeons the unity of division and unity or, to put it in terms of Hegel's speculative, the identity of identity and non-identity. This essentially Hegelian insight into a structure of appearances for which differences subsist in and through identity is translated by Debord into geopolitical or factional conflict: 'Struggles between forces, all of which have been established for the purpose of running the same socioeconomic system, are thus officially passed off as real antagonisms. In actuality these struggles partake of a real unity, and this on the world stage as well as within each nation' (1970: §55).

Of course Debord maintains that these competing battles are not simply illusory and that they do in fact reflect the uneven and conflict-laden development of capitalism globally. Nevertheless, despite the high degree of political and economic differentiation between, for example, liberal democracies, colonialist, totalitarian or bureaucratic regimes, the specificity of each functions within a single overarching tendency of global capital accumulation; they are 'merely different aspects of a *worldwide division of spectacular tasks*' (1970: §57). The chapter as such aims to elaborate the specializations of the spectacle while grounding them within a unified structure of conceptual coherence, a mode of differentiation necessitating integrative mediation.

It could be said that the resurgence of protectionism, economic nationalism on both the right and left, alongside the consolidation of national identities and borders, are only the most recent phenomena with which to register the spectacular structure of reconciling differences within a unified identity. The *universal* turbulence of international growth rates over the last forty years transitions into an issue of national sovereignty exemplified through increasing deficit spending, leveraged investment, monetary financing by central banks and above all, the policing of surplus labour globally. Nevertheless, the spectacle dominates regardless of 'whatever ideological or police-state barriers of a protectionist kind may be set up by local spectacles with dreams of autarky' (Debord 1995: §58). As such, and again we find the spectacle's speculative logic, a real unity of identity does not abolish distinction: 'Just as the development of the most advanced economies involves clashes between different agendas, so totalitarian economic management by a state bureaucracy and the condition of those countries living under colonialism or semi-colonialism are likewise highly differentiated with respect to modes of production and power' (1995: §56).[10] Despite their differences, 'the specificity of each is subsumed under a universal system as functions of a single tendency that has taken the planet for its field of operations. That tendency is capitalism' (1995: §56).

Debord extends this logic further with a discussion of celebrity: 'Media stars are spectacular representations of living human beings, distilling the essence of the spectacle's banality into images of possible roles. Stardom is a diversification in the semblance of life ... intended to compensate for the crumbling of directly experienced diversifications of productive activity' (1995: §60; see also Knabb 2006: 334). All the paltry differences between media personalities – which, to borrow a formulation from Karl Kraus, effectively consist of clichés standing on two legs (1986: 16) – cannot dissolve their general unity as models of *Identitätszwang*.[11] The advertised personality appears in its immediate promise of freedom in the creation of a world that offers all possibilities. Although Debord writes that such individuals are 'incarnations of the inaccessible results of social labor' (1995: §60), it is worth remarking that in the present moment such personifications no longer have the status of the unattainable. Within the dominant platforms of online communication today, both the specialization of information control and the auratic exclusivity formerly monopolized by a select few of celebrity acclaim has been supplanted by the transformation of such communication technologies into durable consumer non-luxury goods and therewith through a democratization by which anyone with internet access and a voracious appetite for recognition can be catapulted to fame through a customized stylization of individual personas. However, despite these changes, Debord's analysis holds insofar as regardless of how high they ascend, a moment's notice will witness them dissolve into oblivion: 'When the only fame is that bestowed by the grace and favour of a spectacular Court, disgrace may swiftly follow. ... When the spectacle stops talking about something for three days, it is as if it did not exist. For it has then gone on to talk about something else, and it is that which henceforth, in short, exists. The practical consequences, as we see, are enormous' (1998: 18–20).

Within the spectacle, both political factions and competing models of individuality are contests 'meant to elicit devotion to quantitative triviality' (Debord 1970: §62). As Debord writes of individuality constituted within the spectacle, 'all official differences between them are thus cancelled out by the official *similarity* which is an inescapable implication of their supposed excellence in every sphere' (1970: §61). Any social difference appears within the spectacle in a manner for which 'spectacular antagonisms conceal ... the unity of poverty' (1970: §63), whether forged through deprivation or affluence. Here we find 'agreements which decide everything' (1998: 32). It is from this discussion that Debord broaches the two forms of the spectacle that dominated in the postwar period: *concentrated* and *diffuse*, terminology which again invokes the solicitation of force. While a close examination of the relation of these distinct forms of the society of the spectacle will be reserved for chapter 6, it is worth here noting again the spectacular logic of a unity-in-separation by which they are related.

For Debord, the categories of concentrated and diffuse spectacle refer to a certain global differentiation, or '*worldwide division of spectacular tasks*' (Debord 1970: §57), between different forms of the spectacle dominant in the 1960s. The *concentrated* form (see Figure 2.1) characterized the bureaucratic or planned economy in which property relations are mediated by a community of bureaucrats who appropriate the commodity of total social labour for the global market. It is a regime attended by permanent violence and 'an image of the good which is a resumé of everything that exists officially, and this is usually concentrated in a single individual, the guarantor of the system's totalitarian cohesiveness.

LE SPECTACULAIRE CONCENTRÉ

Figure 2.1 The Concentrated Spectacle, *Internationale situationniste* 10 (1966).

Everyone must identify magically with this absolute celebrity – or disappear' (Debord 1970: §64). The *diffuse* form of the spectacle (see Figure 2.2), on the other hand, is associated with the abundance of commodities in the postwar conditions of accumulation and prosperity. There, 'each commodity considered in isolation is justified by an appeal to the grandeur of commodity production in general' (1970: §65).

At the time, the *concentrated* and *diffuse* spectacle was held together as a speculative unity the world over. However, in 1988, with the gradual implosion of the Eastern bloc, Debord sees these two forms as having sublated into the unitary form of what he calls the *integrated* spectacle as the '*rational* combination' (1998: 8; emphasis added) of the two. This is specifically Debord's manner of conceiving the newly configured relation between state and economy since the 1970s and in the rise of new technological modes of communication. It might be said that neoliberal market forces adjoined with informal racket economies, neither of which subsists without the state's monopoly on violence, finds its unity in what Debord calls the *integrated* spectacle.

On the whole, the spectacle provides the 'image of the blissful unification of society' (Debord 1970: §69) against its contradictory divisions. As such, a laconic

LE SPECTACULAIRE DIFFUS

Figure 2.2 The Diffuse Spectacle, *Internationale situationniste* 10 (1966).

end to the division of labour is made manifest by the spectacle within its speculative logic of unity and division within appearance. In a passage worth quoting at length from *Comments on the Society of the Spectacle*, Debord writes:

> It is in these conditions that a parodic end of the division of labour suddenly appears, with carnivalesque gaiety ... A financier can be a singer, a lawyer a police spy, a baker can parade his literary tastes, an actor can be president, a chef can philosophise on cookery techniques as if they were landmarks in universal history. Anyone can join the spectacle, in order publicly to adopt, or sometimes secretly practise, an entirely different activity from whatever specialism first made their name. Where 'media status' has acquired infinitely more importance than the value of anything one might actually be capable of doing, it is normal for this status to be readily transferable; for anyone, anywhere, to have the same right to the same kind of stardom. Most often these accelerated media particles pursue their own careers in the glow of statutorily guaranteed admiration ... With the result that occasionally the social division of labour, along with its readily foreseeable singleness of purpose, reappears in quite new forms: for example, one can now publish a novel in order to arrange an assassination. Such picturesque examples also go to show that one should never trust someone

because of their job. Yet the highest ambition of the integrated spectacle is still to turn secret agents into revolutionaries, and revolutionaries into secret agents.

Debord 1998: 10–11; translation amended

This last sentence demonstrates that the *integrated* spectacle, as will be seen in chapter 6, carries over the speculative logic of turning something into its opposite. Further, the *Verdoppelung* of the spectacle's unitary logic sustains a speculative interchangeability by which, for example,

> Khrushchev had to become a general in order to have been responsible for the outcome of the battle of Kursk – not on the battlefield but twenty years later, as master of the State. And Kennedy the orator survived himself, so to speak, and even delivered his own funeral oration, in the sense that Theodore Sorenson still wrote speeches for Kennedy's successor in the very style that had done so much to create the dead man's persona.

Debord 1995: §61

The logical commensurability of state functionaries subsisting at the level of form, irrespective of differentiated content, thereby guarantees, through the realm of spectacular politics, which becomes effectively indistinguishable from entertainment, that Trump's Twitter account will live on and wield as much influence long after he is buried in the ground. Yet at the same time, as Debord remarks in his preparatory notes for *Comments on the Society of the Spectacle*, under the spectacle, we witness, 'the first time that one can be in power without knowing how to talk (since those who hold the mechanism of the spectacle no longer need to convince the like of Pericles, nor to impress Louis the XIVth)' (Le Bras and Guy 2016: 183). It is an insight given concrete illustration during the 2013 memorial for Nelson Mandela in Johannesburg when a sign language interpreter 'faked' his way through the eulogy service, spontaneously inventing new signals without any meaning. Attributed to a sudden attack of schizophrenia, the performance nevertheless assured all those not conversant in sign language that this society, its state dignitaries and the general penchant for recognition, will uphold, from a foundation of incoherence, the dignity of the less fortunate in the most spurious and meaningless way possible.

The third chapter of *The Society of the Spectacle* offers an explicitly speculative logic of unity-in-separation as a dynamic of appearances derived from Hegel's 'Force and the Understanding' given concrete illustration. Here, a play of forces separate entities which in truth are the expression of a fundamental unity constituted in and through the inverted reality of appearances. The unity of the world of the spectacle is at once not simply the ever-recurrent possibility of division but contains the persistence of difference within itself. In a word, as a unity, the society of the spectacle *requires* internal differentiation. 'Thus false conflicts of ancient vintage tend to be resuscitated – regionalisms or racisms whose job it now is to invest vulgar rankings in the hierarchies of consumption with a magical ontological superiority. Hence too the never-ending succession of paltry contests – from competitive sports to elections' (Debord 1995: §62). It is for this reason that the spectacle cannot simply be read as a problem of petrification, but a dynamically developing organization of appearance-forms of bacchanalian revel, one for which rigidity dissolves into the fluid possibility that things can always be worse: 'Whatever lays claim to permanence in the spectacle is founded on change, and must change as that foundation changes. The spectacle, though quintessentially dogmatic, can yet produce no solid dogma. Nothing is stable for it: this is its natural state, albeit the state most at odds with its natural inclination' (Debord 1995: §71).

The spectacle differentiates as it unifies and unifies as it differentiates. The manifold coheres within a unity that *verdoppelt* again into the many. Each is a condition for the other. Separation is a condition of unity while unity the condition of separation. The resultant symmetry is the burgeoning of the speculative, the rationality of a unity which must internally differentiate itself without collapsing into a heterogeneous manifold of selfsame division. Society appears *fragmented* only within the *unity* that is the concept of the spectacle. And yet the reverse is also true: society appears *unified* precisely to the degree that the spectacle is also *fragmentary*. The whole of the spectacle thereby carries its differences within itself. Marx, writing in his 1847 essay 'Moralising Criticism and Critical Morality', inadvertently captures the speculative logic of the spectacle with refinement: 'That where it succeeds in seeing *differences*, it does not see *unity*, and that where it sees *unity*, it does not see *differences*. If it propounds *differentiated determinants*, they at once become fossilised in its hands, and it can see only the most reprehensible sophistry when these wooden concepts are knocked together so that they take fire' (1976c: 320). Identifying Marx here is apt since we will now, before concluding, turn to Feuerbach and Marx on the question of the speculative, writings with which Debord was closely familiar and which help to further substantiate the spectacle as a speculative concept.

The speculative in Feuerbach and Marx

Within Debord's archival notes, there is seldom commentary upon Hegel's direct words about the speculative.[12] However, his notes on Feuerbach and the early writings of Marx offer an alterative indirect concentration towards speculative philosophy. In fact, many if not the majority of Debord's notes on Feuerbach comprise the theme of Hegelian speculation. It could be cursorily remarked that Feuerbach has bearing on Debord for the way in which the former outlined religion and philosophy as the projection of human powers, as the transposition of essential being outwards into an independent realm hidden as originating within human beings. However, something more specific can here be unearthed: specifically how it is that Feuerbach's interpretation of the speculative in Hegel came to give greater determinacy to the concept of the society of the spectacle.

Feuerbach opposed what he took to be an idealist metaphysics characteristic of modern epistemology in which reality is allegedly subordinate to a rationalized transcendent realm expunged of sensuousness. Over and against the sensible world, the intelligible world is castigated by Feuerbach for failing to adequately allow empirical reality to break in on the mind that attempts to master it. The consummation of such endeavours are for Feuerbach exemplified in the speculative philosophy of Hegel, for which thought is said to have cut itself off from the objective world, tarrying, as in the case of the opening of the *Science of Logic*, with merely the concept of being rather than being itself.

For Feuerbach, religion subordinated and degraded man by its transcendental supremacy. In his introduction to the *Essence of Christianity*, which grounds comments made by both the young Marx and Debord, Feuerbach writes:

> In order to enrich God, man must become poor; that God may be all, man must be nothing. But he also does not need to be anything for himself, because everything for himself, everything he takes from himself, is not lost, but preserved in God ... What man withdraws from himself, what he lacks in himself, he only enjoys in an incomparably higher and richer measure in God.
>
> Feuerbach 2012: 124

Inverted ratios between human beings and their metaphysical creations index a scenario by which what is denied on earth is affirmed into the heavens. Humanity exteriorizes its subjectivity into a deity that assumes anthropomorphic predicates no longer wielded by their originators. As such, the fundamental secret of both theology and speculative philosophy was, for Feuerbach, that it concealed an anthropology. As Feuerbach writes in a passage extracted into Debord's notes, '[w]e need only turn the *predicate* into the *subject* and thus as *subject* into *object* and *principle* – that is, only *reverse* speculative philosophy. In this way, we have the unconcealed, pure, and untarnished truth' (Feuerbach 2012 : 154)

On the surface, Feuerbach makes his first explicit appearance in *The Society of the Spectacle* as an epigram to the first chapter:

> But, naturally, for the present age, which prefers the picture [*Bild*] to the thing pictured, the copy to the original, representation [*Vorstellung*] to actuality [*Wirklichkeit*], or the appearance [*Schein*] to the essence … *illusion* alone is *sacred* to this age, but *truth profane*. Indeed, sacredness [*Heiligkeit*] grows in the eyes of this age in the same measure as truth declines and illusion increases, so that the *highest degree of illusion* is to it the highest degree of sacredness.
>
> Feuerbach 2012: 258; translation amended

Taken from the preface to the second edition of *The Essence of Christianity*, Feuerbach, in outlining the objectification of religious thought as the projection of alienated human powers, here distinguishes religious estrangement from 'the *appearance* of religion' in the form of the Church whose proliferation of external *signs* (*Zeichen*) of faith registers appearance as 'the essence of the age' (Feuerbach 2012: 258). The authority of appearances derives from the set of inversions between subject and predicate characteristic of speculative philosophy, in which a transcendent and absolute deity is accorded the status of a subject.

Religion is for Feuerbach the immediate objectification of human powers into a heavenly beyond. It is of note, however, especially with regards to Debord's terminology, that objectivity in general has for Feuerbach the ontological status of a mirror and he often describes the epistemology of his own philosophy with the categories of vision, optics and image: 'my only endeavour has been to *see* correctly' (Feuerbach 2012: 254; see also 103, 105, 225, 230, 231, 233, 284, 288). For Feuerbach, human beings acquire consciousness of themselves through a *reflective* structure instigated by their own objectifications. While a more in-depth discussion of the German Idealist tradition of *Reflexionskategorien* and its influence on Debord will be reserved for chapter 4, it is apt here to note that Debord's idiomatic references to imagery can in part be derived from Feuerbach's usage, not in the sense of a complete adoption of the latter's vernacular with regards to objectivity generally, but in accord with the way in which mirror reflections as a relation to objectivity subsist through the subject–predicate inversions. Here 'man celebrates the theoretical feasts of vision' in which 'the image is *no longer* an image but the thing itself' (Feuerbach 2012: 101, 218).

For Feuerbach's *Preliminary Theses on the Reform of Philosophy* and *Principles of the Philosophy of the Future*, Debord took detailed notes on passages which equate Hegel's spirit as a '*spectre*' (Feuerbach 2012: 157) and, more importantly, which repudiate the inversion of speculative philosophy. Here the finite that appears in and through the infinite of speculative philosophy is but a mystification which 'has made the determinations of reality or finiteness into the determinations and predicates of the infinite' (2012: 160). Reality appears as an inversion of unreality and in a passage extracted in Debord's own reading notes, the following fragment appears: 'The course taken so far by all speculative philosophy from the abstract to the concrete, from the ideal to the real, is an inverted one. This way never leads one to the *true* and *objective reality*, but only to the *realization of one's own abstractions* and, precisely because of this, never to the true *freedom* of the Spirit' (2012: 161). For Feuerbach, 'Hegel turns unreason into reason' (2012: 167), a verdict adopted by Debord in the concept of the spectacle but without the antidote provided by Feuerbach's simple reversal of the abstraction. While Feuerbach sought to shift the relation between thought and being and allot to the latter the status of subject and to the former that of predicate, the spectacle, as we'll see throughout this book, risks no abrogation in the abstract affirmation of sensual finitude. Instead, within the spectacle, we find all of Feuerbach's slander against the rationality of the speculative, which has 'fixed the separation of the essential qualities of man from man, thus deifying purely abstract qualities as independent beings' (2012: 171), without recourse to the category of being. As speculative, the spectacle is the rationalized actuality of abstraction, elevated above and yet constituted through the appearances of sensuous reality. It is precisely within the speculative nature of the spectacle, as an ontology of social reality, that the abstract negates the concrete only to positively reconcile that negation by affirming the concrete out of itself. As Vaneigem writes, 'We *survive* in a metaphysical landscape. The abstract, alienating mediation that estranges me from myself is terribly concrete' (2012: 78).

For Feuerbach the new anthropological philosophy whose principle remained sensualism aimed at an 'undeceptive [*truglose*] identification' (Feuerbach 2012: 157) of man's essence with himself, one no longer robbed by forces of abstraction. And yet, as we've seen from the previous chapter, for Debord, spectacular identification relinquishes any deceptive manoeuvrings conjured by abstractions. The abstractions of the spectacle instantiate the concrete as objects of undiluted identification. Therefore, under the spectacle, no longer does Feuerbach's thesis hold that matter remains in contradiction with thought. In a word, the speculative doesn't simply *measure* reality – *it is reality*. Feuerbach's words can thereby be replicated if the category of thought is instead supplanted by the speculative not as a mystical and illusory epistemic blunder, 'the dream of the human mind' (2012: 258), but as the fundamental structure of social reality. Without lacking flesh and blood, human beings remain abstractions reproduced through exchange. Consistent with Feuerbach's analysis, the sensuous under the spectacle remains a predicate of the subject of the speculative.

Feuerbach excoriated Hegelian speculation for its methodical abstraction of reality and in its rendering of the concrete as a predicate to the subject of thought whose autonomous and self-subsisting ideal movement proclaimed itself the order of reality. Debord was intimately familiar with these criticisms and it can be argued that the very concept of the society of the spectacle inherits these features of Feuerbach's interpretation of the speculative. This argument can be advanced by proceeding to those aspects of Marx's writings for which Debord was most familiar and which contains commentary on the speculative in Hegel's philosophy.

In his younger years, Marx dealt with the issue of speculation as a form of alienation, as the most 'dangerous enemy' of '[r]*eal humanism*' (Marx 1975d: 7). This appears most starkly within his *1844 Manuscripts* and *The Holy Family*. There, speculation is reproached much as Hegel's philosophy would suffer under the criticisms of Feuerbach. The goal of *The Holy Family*, co-authored with Engels as their first writing partnership, was a critique of the Young Hegelians, specifically the Bauer brothers and the articles which appeared in their monthly *Allgemeine Literatur-Zeitung*. In chapter 5, Marx and Engels confront a review of Eugène Sue's popular sentimental urban adventure novel *Les mystères de Paris*. Within this section entitled 'The Mystery of Speculative Construction', Szeliga is reproached for his speculative presentation of the novel; however, before doing so, Marx offers a brief synopsis on how he understands 'speculative construction *in general*' (Marx 1975d: 57). He does so by introducing the famous example of *the* fruit, a general substance whose particular forms of expression comprise the pear, the apple and the almond. Fruit is here the essence and the latter examples are its forms of existence, *modi* of being fruit. Important to bear in mind for our own analysis is the way in which the essence of *the* fruit renders the particular and sensuous expressions of apples, pears and almonds *commensurate* with one another. As Marx writes, 'my speculative reason declares these sensuous differences inessential and irrelevant. It sees in the apple *the same* as in the pear, and in the pear the same as in the almond, namely "*Fruit*". Particular real fruits are no more than *semblances* whose true essence is "*the* substance" – "*Fruit*"' (1975d: 57). Through the essential fruit, all of its particular forms of appearance are pregnant with commensurability; they become equal as only sensuous expressions of their essence.

Marx demonstrates how speculation derives the *diversity* of many individual fruits from the *unitary* substance of *the* fruit. Why *the* fruit as essence manifests itself as a *'semblance of diversity'* is interrogated in order to evaluate the seeming contradiction involved within this 'speculative conception of *Unity*'. Marx, however, continues by parody and gives voice to the speculative philosopher: 'This, answers the speculative philosopher, is because "*the* Fruit" is not dead, undifferentiated, motionless, but a living, self-differentiating, moving essence. The diversity of the ordinary fruits is significant not only for *my* sensuous understanding, but also for "*the* Fruit" itself and for speculative reason' (1975d: 58–9)

The qualitatively different expressions of *the* fruit are only the latter's modes of self-differentiation. As expressions of *the* fruit, they are commensurate. However, the speculative unity examined here is not an undifferentiated unity: the unity-in-difference of speculative reason does not liquidate all individual fruits to *the* fruit. Instead, *the* fruit as essence encompasses differentiation within itself; its oneness is thereby the *totality* of fruits, 'the living *unity* which contains all those fruits dissolved in itself just as it produces them from within itself'. Within this speculative world, particulars become *semblances* (*Scheine*) and have, for Marx, acquired a 'supernatural significance'. As Marx elaborates, 'when the philosopher expresses their existence in the speculative way he says something *extraordinary*. He performs a *miracle* by producing the real *natural objects*, the apple, the pear, etc., out of the unreal *creation of the mind* [*Verstandeswesen*] "the Fruit"' (1975d: 59).

Marx views speculation as dissolving real relations into moments of abstraction from the essence of the thinking subject, one which '*incarnat*[*es*] itself in real situations and persons so that the manifestations of its life are countesses, marquises, grisettes, porters, notaries, charlatans and love intrigues, balls, wooden doors, etc.' (1975d: 60). Although such imagery refers to Sue's *Les mystères de Paris*, the speculative structure reproached by Marx finds affinity in what will come to be in later years developed as the critique of political economy. Here, the real abstractions of value as capital-in-process give to themselves concrete expressions, semblances of its own autonomous process which develop out of themselves not Parisian tropes, but real personifications under the objective imperative of producing exchange-value – industrial capitalists, commercial capitalists, financial capitalists, petty-bourgeois, wage-workers, lumpen-proletarians and so on. As Marx wrote a year prior in his 'Contribution to the Critique of Hegel's Philosophy of Law', 'It therefore necessarily seems that the most profound, most speculative level has been reached when the most abstract attributes ... appear as the highest ideas directly personified' (1975d: 40). For this, it can be said that Marx's critique of speculation is at once his critique of political economy insofar as both speculation and capital produce a reality *a priori* out of themselves. This connection can be aptly illustrated through the shared structure of the fruit analogy above and its correlate within the first German edition of *Capital*, volume 1:

> It is as if alongside and external to lions, tigers, rabbits, and all other actual animals, which form when grouped together the various kinds, species, subspecies, families etc. of the animal kingdom, there existed also in addition *the animal*, the individual incarnation of the entire animal kingdom. Such a particular which contains within itself all really present species of the same entity is a *universal* (like *animal, god*, etc.).
>
> 1976a: 69

For both capital and speculation, 'its real mode of existence is *abstraction*' (Marx 1975c: 331). Both comprise experiences of alienation that give form to sensuous reality, restoring the empirical world in its own image.[13]

Marx's critique of the speculative is at the same time his critique of the abstractions of the capitalist mode of production. This critical symmetry – observed most notably from the *Neue Marx-Lektüre* work of Hans-Georg Backhaus and Helmut Reichelt and developed more recently within the authors of the International Symposium on Marxian Theory (ISMT) debate, particularly the work of Tony Smith, Riccardo Bellofiore, Patrick Murray and Christopher J. Arthur – helps demonstrate the speculative logic of the spectacle. As Backhaus writes in *Dialektik der Wertform*:

> Generally, in Hegel 'the spiritual world ... is recognized as self-alienation', as an 'alienated form' of man, as a 'product of self-denial.' If then Marx formulates the program of his criticism in such a way that, following the critique of religion, it is now also necessary 'to uncover self-alienation in all of its unholy forms', then of course he also had in mind the economy, although it is not expressly mentioned.
>
> 2011: 405–6

Not simply intent to illustrate the continuity of the critique of alienation in Marx's *oeuvre*, for Reichelt, 'Hegelian idealism ... is bourgeois society as ontology. The dilution of the non-identical to the pure category has its real substratum in this factual perversion [*Verkehrung*], in which the living individuality is absorbed by its own character-mask. From this aspect, Hegel's concept of presentation [*Darstellung*] appears in a new light' (Reichelt 2001: 90).

Within the ISMT readings, despite their differences,[14] the point remains the same: Hegelian logic 'was essential for the mature Marx *exactly* because its idealism accurately *reflects* the "idealist" and "totalitarian" nature of capitalist "circularity" of capital as money begetting money' (Bellofiore 2015: 172). The speculative world Marx took to be upside-down shares its inversion with the *modus operandi* of value's abstraction from and instantiation of the concrete. Marx was thereby more accurate than he knew when he wrote that 'Hegel's standpoint is that of modern political economy'; or that 'Hegel's *Phänomenologie*, in spite of its speculative original sin, gives in many instances the elements of a true description of human relations' (1975c: 333, 193). It is precisely *because* of its 'original sin' that we find within the development of capitalist society a mode of domination by abstractions, logically cohering through its speculative dimension. Although Marx always held speculative development to be independent from the development of reality – and in fact it is the conflation of the two that warranted so much attention towards the Young Hegelians – if the similarities between speculation and value are maintained, both entailing a domination by abstraction, then how it is that Hegelian speculation might come to inscribe social reality from within appears as an open question. It is the contention of our analysis that the concept of the spectacle is precisely an attempt to answer such a question.

In sum, from Feuerbach, Debord garners a critique of the speculative as a form of domination by abstractions, that is, by a supersensible beyond that inverts the relation of subject and predicate procured by an alienated objectivity constituted through *Reflexionskategorien*. From the early writings of Marx, Debord inherits a concept of the speculative whose unity propounds a logic of commensurability between concrete appearance-forms as moments of its own primordial substance. 'Speculative philosophy expresses this fact, this *actual relation* as *appearance* [*Erscheinung*], as *phenomenon* [*Phänomen*]' (Marx 1975b: 7–8). It is a world of inversion, one in which the actuality of empirical reality becomes a moment of appearance through which an essential unity differentiates itself.

Speculative alienation is not ontologically distinct from 'the *real* estrangement of the human being' (Marx 1975c: 334). Any yet for Marx, speculation remained illusory, a mode of thought which nullifies its objective character and blossoms as a '*false* positivism' (1975c: 339). Its illusions are brought together within the speculative unity of subject and substance, and as such, there are limits to Marx's critique of the speculative that Debord's concept of the spectacle helps to advance, whereby the world of speculation stands as the mirror image of the world of actuality. Namely, that the speculative ought not to be criticized as an epistemological neglect of material reality, but that it is the embodiment of a form of domination by the abstract. Indeed, to answer Marx's query on the significance of the result of Hegel's speculative logic, it is the spectacle which 'satisf[ies] itself with being a totality of abstractions or the self-comprehending abstraction' that, in the end, even '*resolves* nature into these abstractions' (1975c: 343, 345), an externality posited from within its own process. The speculative abstractions of the spectacle are made into their own substance, hypostatized into an objective reality.[15]

Conclusion

Within the present chapter, the speculative trajectory of the *Verstand* and the structure of solicitation led ultimately to an inverted world by which the supersensible embraces the sensible. For this, the spectacle emerges as 'the simplified summary of the sensible world' (Debord 1998: 28). We have seen how Debord offers an explicitly speculative logic of unity-in-separation as a dynamic of appearances derived from Hegel's 'Force and the Understanding' given concrete illustration through the third chapter of *The Society of the Spectacle*. Through the dialectic of appearances, empirical phenomenality becomes internal to the law of abstraction and it is through this process that the speculative logic of the spectacle becomes explicit. The appearances of the spectacle are thus not obstacles that conceal an inaccessible beyond but give positive albeit inverted order to the objective world itself. Furthermore, the society of the spectacle hardly appears as a seamless homogeneity that extinguishes all difference and heterogeneity derived from a *primis principiis*. Quite the contrary. Quality abounds everywhere we look as the spectacle demonstrably generates its own internal differentiations and divisions which can never be fully liquidated if it is to preserve itself as a totality. The spectacle exceeds the schematism of the *Verstand*; it does not simply blossom within a heteronomy of separations but emerges as the unifying principle of separation. For this, the spectacle can hardly be construed as a fixed 'monochromatic formalism' (Hegel 1977a: 9) but shines forth in colourful and immense diversity through a fundamental speculative logic of organization.

For Hegel, the speculative is the movement of thought capable of surmounting the dichotomies of the *Verstand* through the unifying power of *Vernunft* which, as Adorno observed, is 'a good deal more cunning even than Hegel believed' (2003a: 106). Speculative unity is the imposition of a harmonious state of affairs that nevertheless remains at odds with itself. Here, as speculative, we unearth the spectacle as offering '*scope both for the repression of qualities and for reconciliation*' (Adorno 2008: 161). It is 'to delight in the present' as 'the *reconciliation* with actuality' (Hegel 1991a: 22), a phrase found within the preface to Hegel's *Elements of the Philosophy of Right* which Debord extracted into his notes. As such and reversing Feuerbach's dictum, we can say that through the spectacle the *laws of speculative* have become *laws of reality*. However, let us for the moment leave this speculative logic aside and proceed to examine how it is that Hegel's dialectic of appearance examined above finds its way into Marx's critique of political economy and why it is that Debord's concept of the society of the spectacle remains incomplete without an analysis of the forms of capitalist wealth.

3

The Value of the Spectacle

The evils produced by extreme equality become apparent only gradually; little by little they creep into the heart of society; they are noticed every now and again so that, when they are at their most disturbing, habit has already nullified their effect.

Alexis de Tocqueville

Published a century after Marx's *Capital*, Guy Debord's *The Society of the Spectacle* was described upon its release as 'the *Capital* of the new generation'. However, the book's content has almost never been seriously examined alongside the dialectical logic of the social forms of value systematically ordered within Marx's *Capital*. Despite Debord's description of the modern spectacle as a development of the commodity-capitalist economy, discussions on Debord's debt to Marx customarily emphasize those early writings in which Marx enunciates the critique of alienation without having yet traversed the works of classical political economy.

And for good reason, as his archival notes can verify. A preliminary glance at *The Society of the Spectacle* elicits the impression that the 'ruthless criticism of all that exists' first enunciated by Marx in his early twenties successfully reverberated a century later. The book resounds with both implicit and explicit reference to the phenomenon of social alienation or estrangement described by Marx in the *1844 Manuscripts*. And yet, we find, early on in *The Society of the Spectacle* the following register of social alienation through which Debord situates the advent of the spectacle:

> The first phase of the domination of the economy over social life brought into the definition of all human realization the obvious degradation of *being* into *having*. The present phase of total occupation of social life by the accumulated results of the economy leads to a generalized sliding of *having* into *appearing*, from which all actual 'having' must draw its immediate prestige and its ultimate function.
>
> Debord 1970: §17

Here, the primacy of appearance over possession draws attention not simply to the way in which Debord's theory of the spectacle acquires theoretical determinations from Marx's early writings on social alienation, but, more specifically, how these developments of the commodity economy come to occupy, in Marx's later writings, a certain centrality to a dialectical structure of appearances in the critique of political economy.

The spectacle is a critical category of social organization specifying the multivalent aspects of the unity of capitalist society in relation to an underlying determinate structure of appearance that, as we've seen from the previous chapter, originates in Hegelian thought. However, it remains the case that the extent to which Debord is justified in his claim that the spectacle constitutes a qualitative development of capitalism has yet to be evaluated in accordance with the categorial determinations of the capitalist mode of production. As has sometimes been claimed, is it true that Debord's spectacle is simply a replacement for Marx's commodity albeit under conditions of postwar prosperity? Is the difference between Marx's critique of political economy and Debord's analysis of spectacle simply one of emphasis? Further, how does the spectacle relate to the other prominent forms of appearance of value, such as money and, perhaps more importantly, capital (Dauvé 2000 and 1996; Perspectives 1975)? Finally, in what sense ought, as Debord writes in a 1966 letter, '[t]*he revolutionary theory of Marx* ... be corrected and completed' (2003b: 188)?

This chapter will attempt to answer these questions by first highlighting the central role of appearance-forms in Marx's critique of political economy. Here, it will become clear that value – the social form of wealth within capitalist society – is ontologically structured as a totality through a set of appearance form-determinations (*Erscheinung Formbestimmungen*). As we know from Hegel, a totality cannot be given directly or immediately and so what becomes primary is the *form* of value or, again, what Marx refers to in a number of places as *Formbestimmung*. Here, value as formal determination or as the self-movement of form – not itself something directly perceptible and yet obtaining concrete appearances – derives from the self-reproducing logic of the totality of social relations necessary for the production and reproduction of capital.

The systematic exposition of *Capital*, volume 1, proceeds through a structured succession of categories that unfold immediate appearances to reveal their internal dynamics and, most crucially, the necessity through which essential social relations obtain the appearance-forms they do. It is the mode of presentation (*Darstellung*) that examines social reality as a totality of inner connections and determinations. Marx's *Darstellung* gives concrete conceptual unity to aggregated historical detail. It is a reconstruction that starts from the immediacies of how wealth appears within capitalist society and proceeds to unfold the mediating essence that is the retrospective ground for those forms of appearance.

It is through the logic of the *Erscheinungsformen* of value that Marx attempts to provide an answer to the problem of why value must assume its particular forms. This is a question never posed by classical political economy and yet, as we learn from Marx, remains fundamental for explaining the mediations between, for example, profit and labour. This problem cannot be adequately answered without Hegel, specifically his *Wesenslogik* in which essence must appear as something other than itself. For Marx, this logic – through which the mutually constitutive identity of appearance and essence calls into question the limits of formal dualisms – is a conceptual resource for conceiving not only the necessity for surplus-value to appear as profit, but also the necessity of value to assume its particular concrete shapes, such as commodity, money and capital.

Not only does the concept of spectacle derive from this essentially Hegelian movement of the self-development of appearance-forms inherited by Marx, but in the first instance, Marx's usage contains insight already disposed towards, let us say, the spectacular. One can identify attributes of the Latin *spectaculum*, and its connection to a 'mirror image' or 'arranged display', and from *spectare* – 'to view', 'watch' or 'behold' – within the development of the forms of appearance of value. However, this would at best only demonstrate that Debord is composing a theory of the spectacle by emphasizing certain methodological aspects of Marx's critique of political economy. This is certainly true and the gravity with which Debord aims to formulate a critique of society within the contours set by a Hegelian dialectic emerges as Debord scrutinizes different possible titles for *The Society of the Spectacle*:

- The real society of the spectacle.
- The dialectic of the society of the spectacle.
- The dialectic of society as spectacle.
- The dialectic in the society of the spectacle.
- The dialectic in society as spectacle.
- The spectacular moment of commodity society (or subtitle?).
- The society as spectacle.[1]

Besides the connotations involved in these working titles and their affinity with the method of Marx's critique of political economy, there are some considerable advances made by Debord with his concept of spectacle. We will first recall those general elements from Marx's critique of political economy from which Debord understands his own diagnosis. From there, how the spectacle relates to the appearance-structure of the forms of value will be examined, with specific attention thereafter to the select determinations of money. It will be seen that money, specifically as a monopoly on use-value, bears distinctive connection to the concept of the spectacle, yet is only fully substantiated by Debord's engagement with postwar economist John Kenneth Galbraith. This chapter will then assess the way in which Debord's society of the spectacle remains a critical category that both exceeds the specific determinations of the critique of political economy while yet having its conceptual basis within them.

The spectacle as a category of the critique of political economy

At the most elemental level, we recall Marx's description of the dual-character of the commodity. It is a 'sensuous supersensible [*sinnlich übersinnlich*]' (1962: 85, 86) thing whereby, in Marx's exposition in *Capital*, volume 1, the unity of sensuous use-value and abstract exchange-value of the commodity unfold corresponding concrete and abstract forms of human labour crystallized within. Marx refers to this unity as value, which is the form of wealth within the capitalist mode of production. For Marx, this unity becomes posited *for itself* when the products of labour are equalized in the exchange process; they are abstracted from their heterogeneous and concrete particularities by reducing the substance of their use-value to a quantity of socially-necessary abstract labour time, the measure of their value.

The incommensurability of the use-values of two commodities becomes momentarily displaced during the equalization of the exchange process. Value thereby comes to be realized in the exchange process through the negation of use-value in which the sensuous or qualitative aspects of the commodities are momentarily expelled by the quantitative equivalence of exchange. And yet, for Marx, this negation of use-value acquires a positive presence in the form of money and capital, each of which take possession of the materiality of production and consumption for the purpose of exchange. Within capitalist society, production is production *for exchange*, and in this way, the concreteness of the world is brought into existence by the abstract objective force of value.

The abstraction of exchange renders the concrete aspect of commodities, and the human labour embedded within, as the forms of determinations of value itself. Here, the natural form of the commodity becomes its value-form as its represented form of appearance. As Marx writes, '[w]ithin the value-relation and the value expression included in it, the abstractly general counts not as a property of the concrete, sensibly real; but on the contrary the sensibly-concrete counts as the mere form of appearance or definite form of realization of the abstractly general' (1978: 139–40). This inversion of the abstract and the concrete constitutes within Marx's *Capital* the development of the different forms of value beginning with its elemental form as the commodity. It is through this process that the sensuous world becomes subsumed by the supersensible. The constant expulsion and affirmation of concrete reality constitutes the essential movement of value, a process whereby the negation of use-value during exchange in turn objectifies itself, or negates its negation, by instantiating concrete reality through its development of forms (*Gestaltungsprozess*). It is *an abstract emptiness acquiring concrete constitutive power* (Arthur 2004). Such is the manner in which value gives itself its own reality, an autonomy of *real abstractions* constituting the world in its own image.[2] Through the form determinations of value, Marx outlines the extent to which social reality comes to be constituted through or mediated by the forms of appearance of value. The social world of commodity exchange thereby produces what Marx calls an objective domination (*sachliche Herrschaft*): human activity becomes subordinated to the objective social forms of the commodity, money and capital.

These are the conditions under which the notorious fetish-character of the commodity can be properly understood. Through the exchange process, commodities attain the forcefully abstract objectivity of value, whereby as sensuous things, they are at the same time, supersensible. The fetish-character of the forms of value refers thereby to the appearance of objectivity possessed by the social characteristics of labour as embodiments of abstraction, whereby 'the labour time socially necessary for their production forcibly asserts itself like an over-riding law of Nature' (Marx 1996: 86). As Marx famously continues, 'It is nothing but the definite social relation between men themselves which assumes here, for them, the fantastic form [*phantasmagorische Form*] of a relation between things' (1996: 83). Since a commodity enables its possessors to situate themselves in a determinate place of production and exchange, commodities become the necessary condition for the possibility of both sociality and concrete reality. In its exchangeability, the commodity possesses the ability, or the virtue, to establish relations among people. While people enter into these relations as owners of commodities, the commodity acquires a social agency for facilitating the exchange process. As a result, human beings become reified and subordinated to the social synthesis of commodity exchange. The commodities become the true social actors in the exchange process.

It is within such a framework that Debord unfolds the opening chapter of *The Society of the Spectacle*. Insofar as within capitalism, '[r]eality *is* inversion, *is* appearance, in which reason, in its inverted forms of existence, subsists contradictorily through – estranged – forms of social unity' (Reichelt 2007: 34), the spectacle is the culmination of this fetish. Debord aims to elucidate an autonomized social reality constituted through appearances, wherein social unity only exists in its inverted form, an appearance of a falsified social existence constituted through the commodity social form. As such, the spectacle is not a falsified representation *of* reality, but the phenomenal exposition of an *already* falsified reality given methodological register through the categories of 'image', 'representation' and 'appearance'. The spectacle is not a manipulation or distorted representation of the world, that is, a conspiratorial effort to mystify, nor does its genesis reside merely in the technological capacity to proliferate images (Debord 1970: §5). Instead, like the concrete instantiations of value, the spectacle is a social relation rendered into a materially objective force: 'a *Weltanschauung* which has become actual, materially translated. It is a world vision which has become objectified' (Debord 1970: §5).

By now it should be abundantly clear what the spectacle *isn't*. It is not the case that the spectacle chiefly concerns visual imagery or is reducible to the advertisements and entertainment that saturate modern society (Debord 1970: §24). Rather, it is a category that critically elucidates the abstract form of domination constituted by the exchange relations of the capitalist mode of production. In a word, the spectacle is the *total commodity* of society – the total result of social objectification rendered into an appearance of social unity in which separate spheres of social life, although dependent on capitalist production, have reached an accord organized into a totality.[3] A justification for one of its moments is a justification for its entirety. It is the reigning identity of production and consumption, of work and leisure, of culture and commodity, of state and economy, of ideology and the material environment. Such a mode of social organization must furthermore entail the organization of human perception, defining *what* is to be seen with *how* it is apprehended. This determination of consciousness is identically a definition of activity, of what is permitted and possible within prevailing society. As Horkheimer writes in 'Traditional and Critical Theory', 'Even the way they see and hear is inseparable from the social life-process as it has evolved over the millennia. The facts which our senses present to us are socially preformed in two ways: through the historical character of the object perceived and through the historical character of the perceiving organ' (2002: 200).

Value and its spectacular forms of appearance

We begin with §10 of the first chapter of *The Society of the Spectacle* and consider some of the issues embedded therein: 'Considered in its own terms, the spectacle is affirmation of appearance and affirmation of all human life, namely social life, as mere appearance. But the critique which reaches the truth of the spectacle exposes it as the visible negation of life, as a negation of life which has become visible' (1970: §10). What does it mean for a negation to gain positive form or obtain this appearance-form? For Debord, this is the result of the autonomous movement of the commodity economy in its abstract and quantitative structuring of social relations. But to fully grasp what this means, we have to tour Marx's theory of the form of value. It is there that we will see how it is that the economy acquires this independent force of objectivity through its forms of appearance.

Debord's opening chapter, 'Separation Perfected', continues within a framework derived from the opening sections of *Capital*. There, the 'sensuous supersensible' (*sinnlich übersinnlich*) feature of the commodity elicits the unity of sensuous use-value and abstract exchange-value which is named by Marx as value. It is a unity that becomes posited *for itself* when the products of labour are equalized in the exchange process and are abstracted from their heterogeneous and concrete particularities by the reduction of the substance of their use-value to a quantum or aliquot of socially-necessary abstract labour time. The use-values of two commodities become momentarily displaced during the exchange process. Value is thereby realized in the exchange process through the negation of use-value in which the qualitative aspects of the commodities are momentarily expelled by the quantitative equivalence of exchange. Here, the natural form of the commodity becomes its value-form as its form of appearance.

Insofar as within capitalism, social reality appears as an inverted world and subsists through estranged forms of abstract social unity, the spectacle is the culmination of a fetish in which the 'unity it imposes is merely the official language of generalized separation' (Debord 1995: §3). Debord aims to elucidate an autonomized social reality constituted through appearances, wherein social unity only exists in its inverted form. As such, the spectacle is not a falsified *representation* of reality, but the visual or phenomenal exposition of an already falsified reality; it is the development of value *becoming visible to itself*. Recall that the spectacle is not a distorted representation of social reality but the appearance and justification of the *actual* distortion or perversion of social reality *itself*. As Debord writes in the second chapter, 'The spectacle is the moment when the commodity has attained the total occupation of social life. Not only is the relation to the commodity visible, but it is all one sees: the world one sees is its world' (1970: §42).

However, if we are to regard the spectacle as *a visualization of the world of commodities*, then the category of the commodity itself doesn't yet obtain the features Debord is describing. We need instead to traverse the varied capacities and functions of money. Indeed, while the commodity features as a more prominent protagonist in *The Society of the Spectacle* on the surface of things, it will be argued that it is actually different aspects of the logic of money which better elucidates the spectacle as a development of the capitalist mode of production.

The spectacular nature of money

For Marx, the forms of appearance of value proceed through 'visual inspection' or *Augenschein*. This is Marx's formulation which comes to the fore most explicitly in the first chapter of the first German edition of *Capital* and the 'Value-Form Appendix' to that edition. There, it is appearances themselves that commence the dialectic on the forms of value: 'Der Augenschein lehrt ferner'. In a sense, Marx is simply observing (*betrachtet*) their development. Among the initial passages of *Capital*, volume 1, the *Erscheinungsformen* proceed through four basic moments – a dramaturgy between coat and linen – progressively gaining greater visual impact through a totalization of commodity values and culminating in the money-form whose fetish-riddle, as Marx writes, is 'the riddle of the commodity fetish, [but] now become visible and dazzling to our eyes' (1996: 103; translation amended). In other words, the money-fetish is only the commodity-fetish rendered *spectacular*.

Prior to this, Marx's exposition has traversed the simple form of relative value for which the being of value only 'comes to light' (*kommt dagegen zum Vorschein*) as a relation between two commodities, whereby their equal relation posits, on one side, 'the body of another commodity, sensibly different from it [and] becomes the mirror [*Spiegel*] of its own existence as value [*Wertsein*]'. Here, value 'reveals itself' (*offenbart sich*), or receives sensual expression (*erhält sinnlichen Ausdruck*), in the relation between commodities; that is, one commodity's use-value becomes the form of appearance (*Erscheinungsform*) or the objective reflection of the value of another commodity.

Second, Marx proceeds to the equivalent form of value, which unlike future editions, already broaches the discussion of the fetish-character of commodities whose mystical form elicits the famous optic metaphor in which subjective impressions are explicable 'not as a subjective stimulation of the optic nerve itself, but as the *objective form* of a thing outside the eye' (Marx 1978: 142). The equivalent form is, as Marx states, a 'reflection determination' of the use-value of other commodities. In his example, linen 'sees itself' as equivalent to the coat. There is a reciprocal and mirroring relation of opposites in the relative and equivalent forms of value.

Third, Marx proceeds to the developed form of relative value in which the form of value becomes an *environment* of commodities. Here we find the proliferation of many simple relative value expressions. The accidental character of the equation of two commodities immediately falls away to reveal an 'indefinite, constantly extendable series of its relative value-expressions [and] the linen relates itself to all possible commodity-bodies as mere form of appearance of the labour which is contained in itself' (Marx 1976a). Within this emergent *world* of commodities, the body of each becomes a mirror (*Spiegel*) for a universal equivalent.

Finally, Marx follows this series of development into a situation in which the totality of values can now obtain the appearance as exchange-values or what he calls the universal relative form of value. In this process, one commodity as a *specific equivalent* within the world or environment of relative forms of value remains. Marx is now tracing the developing money form of value out of the equivalent form's position within the universal relative form of value. Here emerges the universal (*allgemeine*) equivalent, the universal and yet individuated materialization of abstract human labour whose use-value is precisely its universal form of value as a universal equivalent. All commodities thereby 'mirror' or 'reflect' themselves in one and the same commodity as quantities of value.

Within this development, what appears as Marx's frequent use of visual similes cannot simply be regarded as a stylistic peculiarity. For instance, there is a determinate *reflective* structure between two commodities in the relative form of value; in turn, the equivalent form *reflects* within itself the relative use-value of all other commodities; the universal equivalent is the *visible incarnation* or 'reflection determination' (*Reflexionbestimmung*) of the totality of commodities in which the body and use-value of each become mirrors for the universal equivalent. Within the first German edition of *Capital*, volume 1, Marx makes clear that his usage of categories of reflection derive from what Hegel terms *Reflexionbestimmung* in his *Wesenslogik*. Marx offers the following analogy: 'There is something special about such reflection-determinations. This man is, for example, only King, because other men behave towards him like subjects. They believe, however, that they are subjects because he is King' (1976a: f5; translation amended).

It is, however, within the form of money that the *spectacular* nature of the value-form finds its most potent expression. Indeed, money emerges as a great visual embodiment and display of all that has preceded it. It can be argued that money within the capitalist mode of production is *spectacular* in nature. There are three aspects to Marx's theory of money that coalesce under the concept of spectacle, or rather, three important elements inherited from the money-form of value that come to constitute the spectacle: 1) money as the objective visualization of value; 2) money as an omnipotent purchasing power and therewith in its monopoly on use-value; 3) money as *Gemeinwesen*, which, as we'll see, is always already capital. But let us now briskly traverse these three aspects before discussing the relation between spectacle and capital.

Money as the visualization of value

The money-form necessarily follows from the exchange relation insofar as the exchange-value of commodities needs to acquire an objective existence. In fact, money emerges as the externalized community of commodities, the appearance of their unity given an independent existence. As a necessary and observable form of appearance of the total social labour within capitalism, money is the mirror in which the value of all commodities finds determinate reflection. Because every commodity receives its status in relation to *all others*, money appears, in Marx's exposition, as the actualization of commodity homogeneity and commensurability, the visual embodiment of the relation between all commodities. As Marx writes, through the money-form, value remains 'everywhere visible' (1987: 337); it is 'the social resumé of the world of commodities' (1996: 79).

It is within money that value obtains its most visible *incarnation*. It is important to emphasize here is that money is not, strictly speaking, the *representation* of the value of commodities, but an *exposition* of their relation as values. It is the *presented actuality* of the unity of value. As Marx writes:

> It is as if alongside and external to lions, tigers, rabbits, and all other actual animals, which form when grouped together the various kinds, species, subspecies, families etc. of the animal kingdom, there existed also in addition *the animal*, the individual incarnation of the entire animal kingdom. Such a

particular which contains within itself all really present species of the same entity is a *universal* (like *animal*, *god*, etc.).

1976a: §69

Money is the necessary *presentation* of value for itself, not as a representation of value but its *visual presence*. This further entails the way in which Marx is not conceiving a nominalist theory of money, or money as a mere symbol of value. Money is not a stand-in or reference for commodity values, but the totality of their relations given an independent form. If anything, money liberates itself as a form of representation and in turn transforms everything around it into *its representative*. As Marx writes, in money, 'everything is turned around, and all actual products ... become the representation of money' (1986: 126).

Through this aspect of money – which doesn't conceal the real material content of economic relations but instead makes them phenomenologically actual – it becomes clear in what sense the spectacle cannot be conceived as a manipulation or distorted representation of the world, in other words, a conspiratorial or orchestrated effort to mystify the world, or merely the technological capacity to disseminate images. Nor does the category refer to any semiological aspect of the commodity economy. Instead, like the monetary instantiation of value, the spectacle is a social relation rendered into a materially objective force: 'a *Weltanschauung* which has become actual, materially translated. It is a world vision which has become objectified' (Debord 1970: §5). It is a category that elucidates the abstract form of domination constituted by the *Erscheinungsformen* of value and its development into an objective phenomenal form.

Money as the monopoly on use-value

Let us move on now to a second aspect of money which is inherited by the spectacle. The value of money in the first instance is money's purchasing power: what money can command. As a universal equivalent, it can potentially purchase *anything*, even that which doesn't appear on the market. Further, while all commodities might not be products of labour, all are capable of acquiring a price-form (Marx 1996: 112). As such, money is a universality that renders in principle everything in the universe exchangeable with everything else. Its use-value is precisely its capacity to exchange the totality of use-values. Money is 'an appropriate expression of equivalence in the infinite variety of use-values' (Marx 1987: 281); it is 'the essence of all the use values' (Marx 1986: 200). It is for this that Marx describes money as the 'absolute commodity' (1987: 374) or 'the ubiquitous [*allgegenwärtige*] commodity' (1986: 164). As is already anticipated in 'The Power of Money' section of the *1844 Manuscripts*, money is *the* means of purchase, that which gives access to *all* objects and the only *true* need. Here, money as a means of purchase grants it its mystifying and omnipotent power; it is the medium under which *all* needs are potentially met. In fact, money emerges as the only true objective need governing the rest.

Within the second chapter of *The Society of the Spectacle*, Debord begins to address the relationship between the spectacle and use-value or social need. Between §§46–7, Debord brings his diagnosis closer to the *Formbestimmungen* of value. Here, the relation of exchange-value and use-value are constituted through a relation of subsumption, wherein use appears as *internal* to exchange, a development most clearly illustrated in Marx's identified 'four peculiarities' or 'inversions' of the equivalent form of value. As Debord writes, 'mobilizing all human use and establishing a monopoly over its satisfaction, exchange value has ended up *directing use*' (1970: §46). Subordinated to exchange, use becomes inseparably appended to the production of exchange-value, that is, to an utterly abstract and quantitative criterion. The spectacle here instantiates concrete human needs to its own standard, as a form of appearance wherein the abstract assumes the shape of the concrete. In this way, money is not simply a concrete universal binding together the heterogeneity of the world, but the form of appearance which conjures and arouses the very concreteness of the world into determinate existence.

So here the spectacle follows again an aspect of money insofar as it is by no means an idealist optical illusion, but the determinate reflection of the relations among all other commodities, the ontological objective actuality of relationality that gives structure and meaning to all empirical existence. It is in this way that Debord can characterize, in a 1969 letter, the spectacle as 'a *moment* in the development of the world of the commodity' (2004a: 79). This moment is the *Gestalt* of money which renders a *world* of commodities possible. The visible material world is in fact the determinate reflection, or spectacular image, of general equivalence which structures that world's concrete and differentiated heterogeneity. This framework elicits a situation in which reflection becomes reality itself and the matter and use-values reflected as ephemeral appearance. As Marx writes, money is 'the external, common medium and faculty for turning an image into reality and reality into a mere image' (1975c: 325). Within this framework, Debord identifies a '*tendency of use value to fall*' (1970: §47), appropriating Marx's own formulation of the rate of profit and referring to a loss of the autonomy of use from exchange. As Debord writes, 'use in its most impoverished form (food and lodging) today exists only to the extent that it is imprisoned in the illusory wealth of increased survival. The real consumer becomes a consumer of illusions. The commodity is this *factually real* illusion, and the spectacle is its general manifestation' (1970: §47; emphasis added).

Debord's second chapter builds from the exchange relation not just the spectacle as the prevailing model of social life, but that through the analysis of use-value as *internal* to exchange-value, the spectacle serves also as the total *justification* or *legitimation* of the existing system and ensures the permanent presence of that justification. In this way, the spectacle is both the embodiment of existing social meaning and its verification: 'In the inverted reality of the spectacle, use value (which was implicitly contained in exchange value) must now be explicitly proclaimed precisely because its factual reality is eroded by the overdeveloped commodity economy and because counterfeit life requires a pseudo-justification' (1970: §48). In this chapter we find that the spectacle refers to a pseudo-autonomy of use as it is emphatically lauded in order to justify the reigning domination of the commodity. As Debord will later write in the third chapter, 'The satisfaction which no longer comes from the use of abundant commodities is now sought in the recognition of their value as commodities: the use of commodities becomes sufficient unto itself' (1970: §67). Here again we find as a model the money-form whose use-value is its power of exchangeability. The spectacle asserts itself where the shadow of use has reappeared in its inverted form: the economy appears as an objective reality which mediates between need and satisfaction. Additionally, within this 'fraud of satisfaction' (1970: §70), the constitution of human needs within the movement of value cannot be contrasted with any opposing 'natural' or 'authentic' needs and desires. It is rather the case that social existence, in its real subsumption within the self-producing development of the commodity-form, becomes recalibrated as mediated moments within the autonomous economy:

> The pseudo-need imposed by modern consumption clearly cannot be opposed by any genuine need or desire which is not itself shaped by society and its history. The abundant commodity stands for the total breach in the organic development of social needs. Its mechanical accumulation liberates unlimited artificiality, in the face of which living desire is helpless. The cumulative power of independent artificiality sows everywhere the falsification of social life.
> 1970: §68

However, this is, to borrow a phrase from Adorno, the socially necessary semblance of an epoch wherein need and its satisfaction are merely the determinate and subordinated moments which mediate an economy developing *for itself* outside of anyone's control. Through this framework it becomes clear that the spectacle entails the commensurable identification with the predominant images of social need constituted in and through the money structure. In this way, while reiterating the trifling distinction between '*superficial needs* and *deep needs*' (Adorno 2003b: 392), the spectacle erects a model of social satisfaction integral to its domination. It is from this perspective that '[s]pectators do not find what they desire; they desire what they find' (Debord 2003a: 114).

This analysis comprises an advance beyond Marx, specifically with regards to the way in which the category of the spectacle elicits a sustained critique of use-value and need satisfaction, thereby sidelining what Hafner has called the tendency of 'use-value fetishism' (*Gebrauchswertfetischismus*) (Hafner 1993). From that perspective, one finds descriptions for the decay or degradation of use-value by exchange extrinsically eroded by market forces, a theme frequently found within critical theory but one which emerges as prominent in the work of Helmut Reinicke (Reinicke 1975: 205), Wolfgang Pohrt (Pohrt 1976), Stefan Breuer (Breuer 1977) and even Hans-Jürgen Krahl (Krahl 1971). The utility of the concrete is virtuously elevated as a barometer to vilify the abstraction of exchange, as if the dialectic of the 'sensuous supersensible' social world of value need only dispense with what erroneously might be conceived as the independence of its material reality. The concreteness of human practice subsists in and through the supersensible world, itself generative of material personifications and character-masks. To diremt this spectacular reality, in which the concrete is affirmed and naturalized as a bulwark against the abstractions of the economy, is itself to reaffirm the logic of the spectacle as the positivity of the concrete and *Gebrauchswertfetischismus*. As Bonefeld draws out the political implications, '[h]ere the distinction between use-value and concrete labour, on the one hand, and exchange value and abstract labour, including the manifestation of value in the form of money, on the other, appears in the form of distinct personalities – pitting the creative industrialist against the parasitic banker-cum-speculator' (2014: 196). It is in this capacity that, for example, struggles for national liberation, that is, in defence of national community in opposition to alleged forces of international financial globalization, are *spectacular* in nature, specifically bewitched by the charm of identification for which the nation stands as the generality through which self-determination can become actual. Here a further line can be drawn between the concreteness affirmed by the spectacle and anti-Semitism in which the *Volksgenossen* are draped in talk of ancestral and mythic bonds of blood and soil against the abstract parasitism of money and finance (Bonefeld 2014: 207).

The spectacle naturalizes the concrete as a moment of its own process, itself upholding the lie that the concrete ought to be celebrated as the undefiled source of credible industry, productivity and creativity against the abstract wealth of financial speculation. In a word, where pleas for the concrete to be extricated from the abstract proliferate, so does the spectacle's logic of *Gebrauchswertfetischismus*, itself derivative of the money-form. Here Debord can help make sense of the ways in which the contemporary resurgence of right-wing nativism holds to this dimension of spectacular logic, specifically for its characteristic elevation of local cultures and particular identities over what is perceived to be universalist globalism:

> The spectacle cannot be set in abstract opposition to concrete social activity, for the dichotomy between reality and image will survive on either side of any such distinction. Thus the spectacle, though it turns reality on its head, is itself a product of real activity. Likewise, lived reality suffers the material assaults of the spectacle's mechanisms of contemplation, incorporating the spectacular order and lending that order positive support. Each side therefore has its share of objective reality. And every concept, as it takes its place on one side or the other, has no foundation apart from its transformation into its opposite: reality erupts within the spectacle, and the spectacle is real. This reciprocal alienation is the essence and under-pinning of society as it exists.
>
> Debord 1995: §8

As the complement to money, the spectacle detaches the use-value of money as the medium of circulation, itself the necessary universal equivalent of all commodities, and establishes a pseudo-autonomy of *use in general* as a category for society as a whole. If money is the realization of exchange value's negation of use, then the spectacle is the return of use, now draped in a counterfeit independence. The spectacle is the appearance of value as use in its sovereignty while unrelentingly still draining the world of its detail. It is thereby as both the objective visualization of value and its monopoly on use that Debord can describe the spectacle as 'the money which one *only looks at*, because in the spectacle the totality of use is already exchanged for the totality of abstract representation' (1970: §49). To discover further insight into how it is that use-value comprises a central dimension of the society of the spectacle, however, Debord's notes on postwar economist John Kenneth Galbraith are of assistance.

Hunger is never simply hunger

In preparing *The Society of the Spectacle* for publication, Debord reviewed Galbraith's *The Affluent Society* (1958). Debord's notes traverse chapters 9 through 12 and it is from his critical comments on Galbraith's work that the theory of the spectacle as a monopoly on use-value is in part derived.[4] Writing during the economic boom of the 1950s, Galbraith upheld the importance of consumer stimulus and public spending, which, he argued, were internal to levels of productivity. Against notions of consumer sovereignty, for Galbraith, the means by which wants and needs are created and satisfied derived directly from productive capacity accompanied by the advertising industries and advanced salesmanship techniques. Together these elements synthesize and comprise consumer demand so that which is eminently useful is ultimately to be gleaned from what Galbraith called the 'prestige of production'. This perspective can of course be drawn from Marx himself, particularly when he describes, in the introduction to the *Grundrisse*, the identity of production and consumption, for which 'nothing is simpler for a Hegelian' to understand:

> Just as consumption gave the product its FINISH as a product, so production gives the FINISH to consumption. *For one thing*, the object is not an object in general, but a definite object which must be consumed in a definite way, a way mediated by production itself. Hunger is hunger; but hunger that is satisfied by cooked meat eaten with knife and fork differs from hunger that devours raw meat with the help of hands, nails and teeth. Production thus produces not only the object of consumption but also the mode of consumption, not only objectively but also subjectively. Production therefore creates the consumer.
>
> (3) Production not only provides the material to satisfy a need, but it also provides a need for the material. When consumption emerges from its original natural crudeness and immediacy – and its remaining in that state would be due to the fact that production was still caught in natural crudeness – then it is itself, as an urge, mediated by the object. The need felt for the object is created by the perception of the object. An *objet d'art* – just like any other product – creates a public that has artistic taste and is capable of enjoying beauty. Production therefore produces not only an object for the subject, but also a subject for the object.
>
> Marx 1986: 29–30

From a version of this identity, Galbraith criticizes the neoclassical perspective on diminishing marginal utility – which argues that the diminishment of individual product demand is derived from an increase in its consumption – insofar as it ignores a concept of satiation not reducible to the subjectivism of consumer disposition. In a fragment Debord pulled into his notes, with emphasizing scribbles in the margins not found alongside other sentences, Galbraith concludes his ninth chapter with the following: 'We do not manufacture wants for goods we do not produce' (1999: 113).[5] For Galbraith, the creation of wants is required to absorb output so that '[o]ne cannot defend production [in the name of] satisfying wants if that production creates the wants' (1999: 124). There is no such thing as independently produced or spontaneous needs and desires. It is an observation incorporated into Debord's concept of use-value as an internal moment of exchange-value. Within a capitalist economy, need always depends on and is in fact created by productive output. Here we find a source for how Debord can make the claim that the spectacle entails a development in the economy for which 'the use of commodities becomes sufficient unto itself' (Debord 1970: §67). The justification of exchange-value under the spectacle proceeds through its appearance as use-value. In a word, exchange-value is productive of its own presupposition so that 'the process by which wants are satisfied is also the process by which wants are created. The more wants that are satisfied, the more new ones are born' (Galbraith 1999: 126).

Yet there are important criticisms of Galbraith's work found within Debord's notes. However, it is within the tenth chapter of *The Affluent Society* that Debord's critical notes bear directly on the issue of the spectacle's relation to use-value. Debord continues with some remarks on Galbraith's general perspective that the profession of economics acts defensively when confronted by the increasing volume of allegedly frivolous products. As Debord writes, 'G. [Galbraith] seems not to see the weakness of his reformism. Is it not because it is necessary for any movement of production/consumption to "have" the misfortunes caused by inequality to always be compensated by the alienation of its positive and negative poles?' Here Debord rejects Galbraith's engagement with inadequate theories of consumer demand insofar as it fails to account for the speculative identity between immiseration and compensation. For Debord, each side of this relation is structured by the importance the society of the spectacle places on use-value, itself a dimension of exchange-value that, in different terms, is already garnered from Galbraith's position that consumer demand derives from levels of productivity and not from without. While inverted needs 'spiritualize our unconscious suffering under the material denial' (Adorno 2007: 93), under the spectacle material plenitude is but the continuation of privation by other means. As Vaneigem writes:

> The satisfaction of basic needs remains the best safeguard of alienation; it is best dissimulated by being justified on the grounds of undeniable necessities. Alienation multiplies needs because it can satisfy none of them; nowadays lack of satisfaction is measured in the number of cars, refrigerators, TVs: the

alienating objects have lost the ruse and mystery of transcendence, they are there in their concrete poverty. To be rich today is to possess the greatest *quantity* of poor objects.

Knabb 2006: 121

In his notes on Galbraith, Debord describes need as 'a mechanism that is now fatal and absurd' whose comforted satiation elicits a 'false pair: artificial needs – moderate needs'. To oppose this pair is described by Debord as 'the Marxian project', perhaps yet another way the SI intended to settle its accounts with Marx and to extend its revolutionary perspective not merely to a full stomach but to a full life. At one point, Debord's marginalia makes the point explicit: 'The society of the spectacle is the manufacturing, beyond our appearances, of the appearance of a satisfaction.' Here the spectacle, as the excess of particular appearances of want and need, is the generative mechanism of those appearances, a unity of *Erscheinungen* which, as we've seen in the previous chapter, gives to the concrete its falsehood.[6]

Within this framework, satisfaction must ultimately contain its opposite insofar as use-value becomes, under the spectacle, the pre-eminent apologia for society as a whole. Additionally, as is written in the 1962 article 'Ideologies, Classes, and the Domination of Nature' in the seventh issue of *IS*:

> Use value – indispensable still, but which had already tended to become merely implicit since the predominance of a market economy – is now explicitly manipulated (or artificially created) by the planners of the modern market. It is the merit of Jacques Ellul, in his book *Propaganda* (1962), which describes the unity of the various forms of conditioning, to have shown that this advertising-propaganda is not merely an unhealthy excrescence that could be prohibited, but is at the same time a remedy in a generally sick society, a remedy that makes the sickness tolerable while aggravating it.

Knabb 2006: 136

These observations are upheld in Debord's notes on Galbraith. There it is written – as of 'vital importance pour S du S' and which reaffirms the above remarks on the identity of production and consumption found with the introduction to Marx's *Grundrisse* – that 'all production is transformed when we must also produce the consumer. And that is a society of the spectacle.' For Debord, the 'manufacturing [of] the production of consumers' is an important index for the development of the modern spectacle as he locates within the first decades of the twentieth century:

> As the production of the assembly line became more efficient, there was need to develop a more responsive consumer market. In the twenties, advertising agencies worked on that by means of publicity image. Publicity for industrial design, brand names, slogans and jingles, testimonials, macho sexuality, and feminine seduction began to bombard us via the press and magazines, but also via the newly discovered radio broadcasting.
>
> Lowe 1983: 137

Of course, these comments by Donald M. Lowe in his 1983 underappreciated *History of Bourgeois Perception* are not meant to suggest that the spectacle is reducible to the proliferation of advertising agencies, or that if only the representations depicted there might yield more 'accurate' or 'just' portraits of society, then the spectacle would be overcome. The point is only to emphasize that crucial for the way in which the spectacle incorporates a monopoly on use-value is through the concreteness of satiation as an internal moment of capitalist production. In sum, any interpretations of the concept of the society of the spectacle as synonymous with consumerism or unregulated advertising ought to heed these commentaries: that in the development of capitalist accumulation, the production of consumption and therewith in the production of needs, is first and foremost only a moment in the developing autonomy of exchange-value.[7]

Money as *Gemeinwesen*

We return now to yet another aspect of money that helps prepare us for understanding the relation between spectacle and capital. For Marx, since the money-form of value is the concrete actualization of general equivalence, society appears as unified and as a whole within money. In money, one sees both, in the words of Anitra Nelson, 'the universality of the estrangement of individuals from themselves and from others' and 'the universality and generality of all their relations and abilities' (1999: 70). However, for Debord and within the spectacle, society is capable of appearing unified *everywhere*, not just in the money-form, but 'where the totality of the commodity world appears as a whole, as a general equivalence for what the entire society can be and can do' (Debord 1970: §49). How this relates to capital requires a look at money's function as a unified *Gemeinwesen*.

In the *Grundrisse*, Marx discusses, among the functions of money, its *third* determination from which it is distinct as both a measure of value and a means of circulation. Here money appears as an *end-in-itself*, 'money as money' or as 'the *universal material representative of wealth*' (Marx 1986: 151). Marx describes this third determination as the unity of the previous functions of money and which, as an *end-in-itself*, cannot be confined to the sphere of circulation. This third determination is already latent capital albeit only by preserving its fluid becoming and by withdrawing and re-entering the sphere of circulation. In a word, for exchange-value to become truly autonomous as money, it needs to develop into capital; it must exit and re-enter circulation and aspire towards imperishability. Money that is made autonomous and results from circulation as exchange-value but which re-enters circulation and perpetuates and valorizes itself is capital. In a word, only in capital has money lost its rigidity and become a process. And of course, the specific exchange through which money becomes capital and not simply a commodity is in the purchasing of labour-power, the use-value that money purchases in order to become capital through the immediate unity of the labour process and the valorization process.

Here, within the transition to capital, money is no longer simply independent exchange-value but the autonomy of exchange-value as 'self-positing' (*selbstsetzende*): 'money must be spent for productive consumption, that is it must be engaged in reproducing exchange-value' (Marx 1986: 113). Within the M–C–M circuit, money is 'exchange-value-for-itself' (*Der Tauschwert als sich selbstsetzende Bewegung*). Money as capital is independent of circulation and activates production with the purchase of labour-power. Capital must exist in both production and circulation, as both commodity and as money.

In its becoming-capital, money becomes the community or *the* social bond. 'It is itself the *community*, and cannot tolerate any other standing above it. But this implies the full development of exchange value, hence of a social organization corresponding to it' (Marx 1986: 155). As Marx continues, money is 'the *real community*, in so far as it is the general material of existence for all, and also the communal product of all' (1986: 158). It is in this way that capital *becomes* society, a development which includes the real subsumption of the labour process by the valorization process. The *Formbestimmung* of value strives to make itself a unified totality. We can trace this aspiration first through *Capital*, volume 1, in which Marx defines capital as value-in-process, then through circulating capital as the identity of variable and constant capital within *Capital*, column 2, and finally, within both *Capital*, volume 3, and the *Grundrisse*, capital is defined as the unity of the production and circulation processes. In a word, capital becomes the form of value that constitutes itself *as society*. We are now able to directly engage the relation between capital and the *society* of the spectacle.

Capital as spectacle

The spectacle cannot be reduced to the *commodity* because the commodity does not by itself yield the objective autonomy of exchange-value. This only occurs through the advent of the money-form. And yet, the spectacle cannot be reduced to *money* by itself since it is not a phenomenon confined to the sphere of circulation. Money only exits circulation as *capital*. So, is the spectacle synonymous with capital, or more specifically, with *value-in-process*? It will be argued below that it isn't, and not simply for the way in which Debord identifies some pre-capitalist tendencies of the spectacle.[8]

It has been indicated that the spectacle incorporates, from the commodity, exchangeability as the dominant mode of social synthesis. More importantly, however, are the tripartite aspects of money outlined above: 1) as the visual objectification and actuality of inverted social relations; 2) as the essence of all use-values; and 3) as the unified social whole or the unity of appearance-forms – that is, as capital. However, the purview of *The Society of the Spectacle* traverses an array of social phenomena not directly reducible to the category of capital. These broadly include the appearance of seemingly opposed political factions, the image of individuality as advertised celebrity personalities, the representation of the proletariat in various organizational forms, the appearance time structured by commodity production and circulation, the composition of the urban environment, the presentation of cultural products and discourses and the rendering of ideology. These are only a few of the aspects of social life that the multivalent category of spectacle is meant to critically examine, none of which can be easily reduced to the category of capital.

One of Debord's most explicit connections between capital and the spectacle comes at the end of the first chapter: 'The spectacle is *capital* to such a degree of accumulation that it becomes image' (*Le spectacle est le capital à un tel degré d'accumulation qu'il devient image*) (1970: §34). How are we to understand such a formulation? After all, from the perspective of value as the unity of the forms of appearance, capital is already 'image', understood here as *Erscheinung*. A solution to this cryptic thesis can be found by recalling the aforementioned discussion of the money-form of value. Just as money was the *becoming visible of commodity relations* in their totality, the spectacle is for Debord *the becoming visible of capital* as a totality, but not simply as the monetization of capital since this would be a redundant formulation. Capital is already the movement of money. Instead, the spectacle as the becoming visible of capital is *the becoming visible of the unity of appearances*, that is, *the mode of appearance of society unified under capital*. However, do not let the term 'visibility' suggest that the spectacle is a concept, again, primarily concerned with literal visual imagery or is reducible to an environment oversaturated with advertisements or consumerism. Visibility here refers back to the riddle of the money-fetish – to the inverted world become, in Marx's words, 'dazzling to our eyes'. In this way, the spectacle remains a category that critically elucidates the abstract form of domination constituted by the exchange relations of the capitalist mode of production and yet carries this structure well beyond 'economic' relations. As Debord writes, 'Capital is no longer the invisible center determining the mode of production.' Under the spectacle, '[s]ociety in its length and breadth becomes capital's faithful portrait' (1995: §50). Important to note here is that Debord conceived the category of spectacle as of a higher order than the category of society: 'It is not modern society that own the spectacle, but the inverse.'[9]

The notion that human beings are deprived of any substance not imported by the *Formbestimmung* of value, and therewith structured by *Erscheinungen*, derives from Marx's critique of political economy. However, from the perspective of the concept of spectacle, the totalizing implications of this general movement of appearance were not theoretically carried through. Central here is the manner in which the full autonomy of appearance-forms only arises with the emergence of fictitious or interest-bearing capital in which capital returns to the form in which it first arose as money and begets more money seemingly as a result only of itself or the increase in value directly from circulation. Here, the production process effectively disappears and for Marx, it is the culmination of the *Erscheinungsformen* in which everything is reduced to circulation, 'a complete *objectification, inversion* and *derangement*' (Marx 1989: 453). However, it remains the case for Marx that this 'completion of fetish capital' (Marx 1998: 390) nevertheless remains intrinsically related and dependent upon relations of production. It can thereby be said that Marx, in his analysis of capital, renders explicit the necessity between appearance forms and essential social relations.

However, the manner in which *Erscheinungsformen* detach themselves and come to reconstitute real concrete social relations indexes their triumph as social reality and therewith solicits the demand to examine how the autonomy and movement of appearances might come to pervade all aspects of social life. It is here that the category of the spectacle is of service. The major distinction to be made between the development of value in its particular forms of appearance and the spectacle is that, unlike the fetish-character of value, there is no masquerade operative in its mystification. The fetish of the commodity need not anymore contain a 'secret' and abandon its previously coveted opacity. The spectacle has a sole demand: that social reality appear in all of its *transparency*.

Recall that the spectacle adopts the mandate of exchange-value: everything is possible because everything is equivalent. As the negation of life and of concrete reality that has become visible *qua* appearance, the spectacle follows the objective form determinations of value by asserting a positive presence as the determinate negation of use-value. For this, the spectacle makes visible a world that is *at once both present and absent*. 'Indeed, it is only inasmuch as individual reality *is not* that it is allowed to *appear*' (Debord 1995: §17). While it has been the category of *Erscheinung* that has given us the optimal resource for connecting Debord's theory of the spectacle to Marx's critique of political economy, it is within this context, by which the negation of use-value acquires a positive presence in the form of capital, that the classical concept of *image* derived from antiquity can be of service for the analysis of the spectacle as 'le capital à un tel degré d'accumulation qu'il devient image'.

Capital takes possession of the materiality of production and consumption for the purpose of exchange. It is the reconstitution of use-value in and through its negation within circulation. Here Debord's equation of capital with image can justly take the latter category with seriousness and not simply as a rhetorical device. For Aristotle, image (*eikōn*) is the presence of that which is absent, or the eidetic impression of the copy of an object in its absence. It is the imitation of 'the kind of thing that was or is the case; or the kind of thing that is said or thought to be the case; or the kind of thing that ought to be the case' (Aristotle 1996: 42). Here, image is the presence of that which, in its absence, can no longer be recalled. The image is the return of the concrete whose likeness is not in dispute. It is the imitation not of what capitalist society has abolished, but of what capital momentarily displaces in the exchange process. For this, '[t]he world the spectacle holds up to view is at once *here* and *elsewhere*' (Debord 1995: §37). The category of image is an abridgement of the process by which capital both butchers and resurrects use-value and in so doing, accords to individual appearances a unifying structure. The spectacle described as capital become image is the abbreviation for which the increasing autonomy of exchange-value, through the visualization of the money-form, has given rise to a visible unity of appearances. As Sohn-Rethel has remarked, 'In a photograph, so to speak, capital always looks just like money' (Sohn-Rethel 2020: §34). The spectacle, as that which is *beheld*, refers to the identity of the non-identical of exchange value not merely as operative, but *disclosed*. It is the commodity social form 'shown for *what it is*' (Debord 1970: §37), a display of alienation *in its utmost clarity*: '[n]ot only is the relation to the commodity visible but it is all one sees: the world one sees is its world' (1970: §42).

As a structure of disclosure constitutive of its object, the spectacle is a luminosity unfolding upon the terrain of the false, the publicity of the commodity world having given exchange-value its full autonomy within the money-form. Within the spectacle, social activity is made to appear, and in doing so, is embedded with a meaning that contains both the image and the goal of social development under commodity society. Through the spectacle, the portrait of capital becomes all of society, for which '[a]t the moment of *economic* abundance, the concentrated result of social labor becomes visible and subjugates all reality to appearance, which is now its product' (1970: §50). In the words of Jacques Camatte, 'The spectacle has to show humans what they are, or what they must be' (1995: 170), in which the human being becomes 'no more than a ritual of capital' (1995: 108–9).[10] Here, capital becomes 'the mirror of all representations' (Camatte 2011: 251), divorced from any dependency on its transubstantiations, and reproducing itself, in part, through the form determinations of its *Erscheinungsformen*. Capital becomes spectacle to the extent that, as a social reality, only the *Erscheinungsformen* persist. It is for this reason that Debord can write, 'Revolution is not "showing" [*montrer*] life to people but making them live' (2006g: 561). For both Camatte and Debord, this movement of capital – as self-valorizing value or as a self-developing form of appearance without substance – proceeds to an anthropomorphization, which both capitalizes human beings and humanizes capital.

Reichelt reminds us that Marx's various phantasmic formulations cannot amount to mere rhetoric, but as features of reality, wherein '[r]eality *is* inversion, *is* appearance, in which reason, in its inverted forms of existence, subsists contradictorily through – estranged – forms of social unity' (2005: 34). Correspondingly, Debord's spectacle follows such an analysis and amounts to the most developed form of this unification within twentieth-century Marxism. The spectacle is the appearance of social unity in which separate spheres of social life, although dependent on capitalist production, have reached an accord that synthetically organizes each of its moments into a totality. Important to recall here is the way in which the spectacle is less a critical theory of appearances than it is a theory of the *unity* or organization of appearance-forms. A justification for one of its moments is a justification for its entirety. It renders commensurate not only the distinctions between production and consumption, monopoly and competition, use-value and exchange-value, but also class distinctions, leaving in their wake personifications, representations, appearances or images of its own movement. Such a mode of social organization, which, as Debord writes in a

1966 letter, 'monopolizes all human communication' (2003b: 157), entails also the organization of human perception, defining *what* is to be seen with *how* it is apprehended. The spectacle is the phenomenological terrain of value, a 'monopoly of appearance' (Debord 1970: §12) which, as Debord writes, 'naturally finds vision to be the privileged human sense which the sense of touch was for other epochs' (1970: §18). The spectacle thereby 'says nothing more than "that which appears is good, that which is good appears"' (1970: §12).

Conclusion

The key to grasping the respective relation between Marx's critique of political economy and Debord's theory of the spectacle is in the study of the structure of the *Erscheinungsformen* of value. As such, already in the first three chapters of *Capital*, volume 1, we find the *Elementarform* of the spectacle. However, for Marx, the form of appearance 'makes the actual relation invisible, and, indeed, shows the direct opposite of that relation' (1996: 540). This is in stark contrast to the way in which the spectacle operates by exposure, 'a *son et lumière* show that lights up the entire surface of society with the same factitious poverty' (IS 1997: 470). This is why the fetish-character of money is so important: the mystification acquires an objective and autonomous form unlike the commodity-fetish for which social relations remain concealed behind the social relations of things. Even if having its basis within them, it remains the case, however, that the category of spectacle *exceeds* the specific determinations of value, a broader model of social organization for which the structure of appearing outpaces that which appears, or more specifically, it gives particular appearances inner coherence as moments of a totality. Exceeding the logical ordering of Marx's categories, the spectacle nevertheless derives from the cadences of the concept of value and its form determinations.

The spectacle is a category that elevates Marx's *Erscheinungsformen* as a polyscopic and omnipresent element of social reality. As Lefebvre has written, 'there is more to *Capital* than political economy' (1991a: 80). In this way, the category of the spectacle attempts to provide a theoretical reconstruction of social reality as an organic whole which is constituted in and through the autonomy of the *Erscheinungsformen*. The spectacle ought then not to be measured by an attained quantitative degree of capitalist accumulation, but by the degree to which the total result of a society based on capital accumulation obtains objectivity at the level of ruling appearance-forms as the dominant social structure.

As a critical concept, the spectacle – 'whose role is to *inform* the commodity world' (Knabb 2006: 201) – elucidates and gives unifying structure to diverse phenomena within contemporary capitalism under a logic, derived from the structure of exchange, for which 'appearances of a socially organized appearance' have acquired 'enormous positivity' (Debord 1970: §10, §12). It is in the spectacular realm of appearance that the inner content of objectivity is manifest. In a word, the spectacle is the *total commodity* of society, that is, the total result of social objectification and its visible vindication. In this way, the spectacle is more suitably construed as the phenomenological terrain of value as a totality, or perhaps simply, as the phenomenality of value: the self-movement of appearance-forms which, to echo the dynamic of Hegel's *Phenomenology of Spirit*, draws into itself both subject and substance. Having here demonstrated how Debord's concept of the spectacle relates to the appearances-forms of value in Marx's critique of political economy, we will now take a closer look at what gives the spectacle its own distinct unitary structure.

4

The Reflection of the Spectacle

As he lay stretched out in the grassy shade,
he could never gaze his fill on that fraudulent image of beauty;
and gazing proved his demise.

Ovid

Within his epic poem, *Metamorphoses*, Ovid recounts the myth of Narcissus who infamously 'fell in love with an empty hope, a shadow mistaken for substance' (2004: 112). It was the comely hunter's reflection that deceived him, withering away there by the side of the pool into gold and white petals. Narcissus falls victim to his own reflection, helpless to tear himself away from the grip of identification or *Identitätzszwang*. His own wealth leaves him a pauper and yearning for a separation that might free him from his curse. It is a myth that, while excessively trodden, suitably illustrates the manner in which the category of reflection yields important insight for understanding what makes Guy Debord's concept of the spectacle, specifically with its unitary character, different from Georg Lukács' concept of reification.

Lukács' theory of reification has been regarded as having made a profound impact on Debord's theory of the society of the spectacle, standing as one of its principal predecessors for critically diagnosing a society dominated by the commodity social form and its fetish-character. When the sole criterion of thought is its agreement with an impervious reality, it fails to think its own historical present and falls under the phenomenon famously theorized by Lukács as reification (*Verdinglichung*). At the centre of *History and Class Consciousness* resides its most distinguished essay, 'Reification and the Consciousness of the Proletariat', wherein Lukács uncovers forms of thought adequate to the historically specific social form of the commodity and the abstraction of exchange relations. Not simply reducible, however, to the epistemological structure mimetic to the commodity, reification refers to prevailing index of objectivity which casts its shadow over both proletariat and bourgeoisie, the social form that objectification assumes under the abstract domination of the capitalist mode of production. As an antinomic relation between subject and object, the reification of the commodity structure consists of the objective forces of society and the subjective orientation necessary to them (Russell 2018).

Commentators have called attention to the way in which Debord's theory of the spectacle is the direct inheritor of Lukács' theory of reification. However, despite any affinity that might be said to characterize their respective frameworks, little effort has been made to establish the qualitative distinctions between what can be called these two theories of reification. At best, Debord is simply seen as having 'advanced' Lukács' concept of reification adequate to the conditions of postwar prosperity or simply as its derivative extension. Rarely is there an examination into how it is that the *logic* of each of their respective concepts differ.

This chapter will pursue this task through an analysis of the philosophical concept of reflection as it is developed within the philosophy of Hegel. Hegel remains a fundamental source for the work of both Lukács and Debord, and, as will be seen, the derogatory meaning Hegel assigns to 'philosophies of reflection' within his early *Faith and Knowledge* and the redemption that the concept of reflection receives within his later *Science of Logic* – specifically as a *speculative* concept – each offer registers for which to mark the logical difference between reification and the spectacle. In a word, for Lukács, reification remains riddled with reflective antinomies, while for Debord, the society of the spectacle adheres to a unified and inner coherence of separations. We will proceed by first offering an account of reflection as it appears within Hegel's *Faith and Knowledge* and how the criticisms offered there can be said to amount to an expanded version of Lukács' 'The Antinomies of Bourgeois Thought'. Thereafter, Lukács' later veneration of reflection as it appears in Hegel's *Wesenslogik* will be examined in order to call attention to the way in which Debord's theory of spectacle instantiates this superior speculative concept of reflection. While Lukács upholds Hegel's determinations of reflection as a decisive conceptual resource for Marxism to grasp social relations per se, our argument contends – as will become more explicit in chapter 5 – that Hegel's *Wesenslogik* expounds aspects of the reified structure of the spectacle. We find then, through Hegel's engagement with the category of reflection, an opportunity to demonstrate the manner in which Debord sublates Lukács' overestimation of the determinations of reflection. In this way, Lukács and Debord aren't simply in the same critical tradition, but wield substantively different concepts of reification. That which Lukács held as the mediated truth of relationality against the immediacy of reified life becomes the model for a form of reification that is the spectacle. This chapter will argue that the *historical* transition between Lukács' reification and Debord's spectacle is a *conceptual* transition between Hegel's critique of philosophies of reflection and the *Wesenslogik*.

Philosophies of reflection

Prior to the break with Schelling's philosophy of identity, Hegel's 1802 *Faith and Knowledge* (*Glauben und Wissen*) critically aligns the work of Kant, Jacobi and Fichte under the disparaging description of 'philosophies of reflection', which are characterized by the reduction of philosophy to the terrain of subjectivity and formal identity. Here, philosophies of reflection fail to become *speculative*, that is, they flounder in the task of bringing systematic unity to the conceptual dichotomies and antinomies that culminated with Kant's Critical Idealism and Fichte's *Wissenschaftslehre*.

It is Kant's *Verstand*, however, that amounts for Hegel to the most robust and developed faculty of reflection.[1] As we've seen in chapter 2, the *Verstand* is an analytic faculty of making distinctions or determinations grounded and fixed wholly on the side of a knowing subject which separates itself from its object. The reflective philosophy of the *Verstand* is for Hegel false because of its insistence on ready-made dichotomies of abstract universals such as the infinite and the finite, subject and object, universal and particular, freedom and necessity, inner and outer, causality and teleology, and so on. Further, the certitude of the *Verstand* is largely the certitude of the natural sciences, often pledging its allegiance to a concept of experience merely as the registration of sense perception governed by a line of causality and to an extensive atomism for which the world is reducible to the sum of its parts. While of course not all reflective philosophy need adopt these characteristics, they are only meant, for Hegel, to generally portray the unmediated and external relation of philosophical concepts found to constitute reflective philosophy.

The candidates of Hegel's choosing are 'the best minds that the age had produced' (Harris 1977: 3). Hegel is not, however, simply repudiating the work of Kant, Jacobi and Fichte, but rather critically demonstrating the limits of their reflective approaches and how speculative philosophy stands upon their accomplishments. In this way, *Faith and Knowledge* is a balance sheet of the debt that speculative philosophy owes to its forebearers. Further, Hegel's essay demonstrates not just the conceptual but also the historical significance of speculative philosophy. According to Hegel, the philosophies of Kant, Jacobi and Fichte are the culmination of a history of metaphysics that, in transitioning to the question of epistemology, allots to the faculty of reason a regulative function without access to the whole infinity of its substance.

While the reflective antinomies shared between Kant, Jacobi and Fichte are all dealt with differently, Hegel nevertheless sees them all as essentially absolutizing opposition as a fundament of subjective cognition. Together, 'these philosophies have to be recognized as nothing but the culture of reflection raised to a system' (Hegel 1977b: 64). The principle of subjectivity constitutive of reflective philosophy holds to the axiom that all knowledge is finite and that the infinite is only a thought *reflected in opposition* to the finite consciousness. When consciousness is only capable of *reflecting* upon a reality independent or indifferent to it without actually entering the objectivity of the world, knowledge finds recourse in the articulation of *faith* (*Glauben*) in a non-cognitive supersensible beyond (*übersinnliche Jenseits*). Since their concept of the subject is essentially finite, there remains in reflective philosophy the faith in a supersensible beyond to which conceptual structures cannot gain access. While only alluded to in the work of Kant, this faith in a projected beyond becomes in Jacobi an immediate sense-certainty and is explicitly systematized in Fichte. In sum, the central reflective structure is one of external opposition *formally* identified without any internal relation.

Reflective philosophy nullifies that which is objective into a programmatic principle of finite subjectivity. The absolutizing of the finite and the infinite – or what amounts to Hegel as the 'idealism of the finite' (Hegel 1977b: 64) – results in a version of the absolute that is empty of all reason. It is a fixed and by definition incomprehensible realm of faith that is nevertheless described as rational simply because reason recognizes itself in its own exclusion. Reason is abased to a subjective regulative principle that cannot gain access to the supersensuous. This exclusion is its saturation by finitude, prohibited from entering the nature of objects. Reflective philosophy attempts to derive a world from an empirically instantiated faculty of reason while the eternal remains in a realm beyond rational knowledge, a *übersinnliche Jenseits* inaccessible to rational cognition. The standpoint of reflection remains ignorant to a true and speculative identity between subject and object. The absolute distance reflective philosophy sets between itself and its pure object symptomatically accords a corresponding set of fixatedly opposed principles of the finite and infinite which proclaims: *never the twain shall meet.*

An antinomic theory of reification

Already we may grasp elements of this 'epoch of reflection' (Cerf 1977: xvii) to have endured within Lukács' theory of reification. Illustrative here is the way in which Hegel demonstrates not only the deficiency of a philosophy extrinsically separated into unreconciled dualisms, but that the task of overcoming the divisions of reflective philosophy is a cultural task to be gleaned from the travails of civilization itself. It is not a stretch to characterize this civilization, from the perspective of Lukács, as capitalist modernity. The category of reification allows Lukács to take the fetish-character of the commodity social form to be the most essential component of the sociality constitutive of capitalism. Through the historical transformation of the production process with its increasing fragmentation of the division of labour, Lukács distils a process of abstract and formal rationalization, effectively synthesizing the work of Max Weber and Georg Simmel within the framework of Marx's analysis of the commodity form as the universal structuring principle of society as a whole. The structure of the commodity relation provides a model of all the objective and subjective aspects of society, pervading social life in its entirety. Lukács' fundamental question is stated thus: 'how far is commodity exchange together with its structural consequences able to influence the *total* outer and inner life of society? Thus the extent to which such exchange is the dominant form of metabolic change in a society' (1971a: 84). As 'a multivalent term of social analysis' (Bernstein 1984: 7), the category of reification thereby allows Lukács to disclose the universal form of the commodity within the social spheres of, for example, bureaucracy, juridical relations, journalism and marriage. Reification is not therefore simply a problem of the economy, but 'the central structural problem of capitalist society in all its aspects' (Lukács 1971a: 83). In his generalization of Marx's critique of political economy, Lukács made explicit what could already be found in Marx himself – the *critique of society* for which the commodity yields, as is made clear in the *Grundrisse*, determinate forms of being (*Daseinformen*) and determinations of existence (*Existenzbestimmungen*) (Postone 2009). For Lukács, reification was the theoretical core of Marx's critique of political economy, a critical theory of objective social relations obtaining an autonomous movement which structures the forms of thought adequate to it. Marx's categories serve for Lukács as both forms of being and forms of consciousness. He appropriated Marx's categories of the critique of political economy as 'determinations of both the subjective and objective dimensions of modern social life' (Lukács 1971a: 64)

As a social critique, Lukács' theory of reification fundamentally concerns an inverted relation between subject and object left in perpetual antinomy, leaving the individual with little recourse other than to either hold fast to objective forces regarded as immutable and timeless or defensively project the centrality of subjectivity onto all that surrounds it. On one side sits the irrevocable and immediate facticity of reality as if operating by absolute necessity, while the subject of this fatalism finds only inward impotence as the world appears as only a moment within and created by its rational faculties (Russell 2018). Lukács outlines a series of particular antinomies that give both sociological and epistemological expression to this fundamental condition for which the antinomic relation between subject and object is given only a reflective or, at best, a mechanically mimetic relation (Lukács 1978: 28). Indeed, it is with different *Reflexionskategorien* that Lukács articulates reification as a failure of mediation for which a knowing subject sees, represents, reflects, imagines or pictures the world as its external object. The failure of mediation as reflection emerges as a mirroring of reality in thought which sets subject and object interminably apart. Lukács' critique of *Reflexionskategorien* generally refers to empiricist, rationalist and vulgar materialist philosophies that affirm an unmediated reflection of existence in thought. In place of an internal mediation, reflection appears as a mirroring of reality that is nevertheless set at a distance from the knowing subject.

Remarkably, the English translation of *History and Class Consciousness* is in the unfortunate position of having rendered the role of reflective philosophy within Lukács entirely absent as compared to the original German. For example, on many occasions, the German *Reflexionswissenschaft* is simply translated as 'fetishistic science' (1971a: 10); *Reflexionszusammenhang* as 'unmediated connections' (1971a: 9), 'unmediated concepts' (1971a: 13, 14) or 'unmediated relations' (1971a: 23); *Reflexionsbestimmungen* becomes 'unmediated formulae' (1971a: 15), 'unmediated abstractions' (1971a: 163), 'categories of thought' (1971a: 170) or simply 'mental categories' (1971a: 186); *Reflexionskategorien* is translated as 'abstract mental categories' (1971a: 165, 180), 'abstract categories' (1971a: 185), or simply 'categories' (1971a: 190). However, maintaining a philosophical connection between philosophies of reflection and reification is crucial not simply for registering the Hegelian influence on Lukács, but for grasping reification as a structure of reflection and its categories as a sociological extension of Hegel's *Faith and Knowledge*. In a word, what Hegel calls the '[p]latitude of reflection' (1977b: 127) becomes, in Lukács, a social theory.

Within his theory of reification, the antinomic relation between subject and object is frequently characterized through a philosophy of reflection. Here we find the reified subject seeing, representing, reflecting, imaging or picturing the world as its external object. Reflection becomes for Lukács a subject–object relation for which the 'contemplative stance' is most aptly given philosophical expression. A 'correspondence' between subject and object, between thought and existence, remains insufficiently mediated and within the antinomic structure of reification, one correlated with the fetish-character of the commodity. A petrified reflection of empirical reality within thought is itself the contemplative adherence to an unalterable mode of cognition confronted by an impenetrable existence.

In his 1967 preface to *History and Class Consciousness*, Lukács mentions that his 'rejection of the view that knowledge is reflection' has its source within his repudiation of the vulgar materialism of Second International Marxism. This hatred of mechanistic fatalism 'was the concomitant of reflection theory in mechanistic materialism' (1971a: xxv). With these themes, Lukács substantially departs from Marxian orthodoxy and rejects any 'materialist' theory of cognition as a mirror-image of the external world. Lukács describes this bourgeois materialism, following Heinrich Rickert, as an 'inverted Platonism', an implicitly dualistic approach that wields a contemplative and 'photographic' copy theory of epistemology, a tendency started within Marxism by Engels' *Dialectics of Nature* and extended with Lenin's *Materialism and Empirio-Criticism* (1971a: 202, 199).[2]

This contradiction between subject and object, universal and particular, and finite and infinite cannot adequately be dealt with by empiricist or rationalist frameworks and should be qualified as a relation within the thing itself and not merely as a deficiency of subjective approach. As Lukács concludes:

> Thus thought and existence are not identical in the sense that they 'correspond' [*entsprechen*] to each other, or 'reflect' [*abbilden*] each other, that they 'run parallel' [*parallellaufen*] to each other or 'coincide' [*zusammenfallen*] with each other (all expressions that conceal a rigid duality). Their identity is that they are aspects of one and the same real historical and dialectical process.
>
> 1971a: 204

As a coerced solution to the antinomies of bourgeois thought – which is of course no solution at all – all previous reflective philosophy is the epistemic correlate to the reification constituted through the commodity social form. For this reason, it would not be an exaggeration to state that the form of the commodity is an accurate *reflection* of consciousness.

An untarnished reflection

Against an antinomic and reflective theory of reification, Lukács suggests that the *Wesenslogik* of Hegel's *Science of Logic* philosophically indicates 'the emergence of the truly objective form of existence and the destruction of those confusing categories of reflection which had deformed true objectivity into a posture of merely immediate, passive, contemplation' (1971a: 166). Indeed, in his subsequent *The Ontology of Social Being*, Vol. 1: *Hegel's False and his Genuine Ontology*, written decades later, Hegel's determinations of reflection are revered for the way in which they assist in the philosophical overcoming of the bourgeois and reified nature of previous theories of reflection.

Within the *Wesenslogik*, Hegel's determinations of reflection emerge as the categorial thematization of relationality, redeeming thought of its dichotomous poles found within reflective philosophy. The *Wesenslogik*, to be examined in greater depth in the next chapter, provides an account of the inner nature of immediacies as mediations, determinations which mediate appearances, giving them essential unity as necessary manifestations of an essence. The reflection determinations between appearance and essence allow thought to comprehend relations, yielding an identity between that which appears and the appearance itself. Each side is the determinateness of the other and we thereby find within Hegel's *Science of Logic*, the conceptual framework for thinking immanently necessary categorial relations. It is a logic through which the identity of appearance and essence calls into question the limits of formal dualisms and expounds an internal relation between identity and distinction, content and form, inner and outer, and so on. While an appearance is the manifestation of an essence, equally, essence *must* take on an appearance. Hegel's *Wesenslogik* thereby overturns any 'standard essence–appearance model' (Murray 2015) in which essence is mistaken for a real but unobservable thing hidden behind a curtain of appearances.

Lukács views the triumph of Hegel's *Wesenslogik* over previous reflective philosophy as an integral step in the development of a social ontology freed from reification. Many pages of *The Ontology of Social Being* are devoted to Hegel's reflection determinations and how it is that they expresses the social and ontological truth that the essence of immediate appearances derives from its *determinate relatedness*. In contrast to the trend that reaches its zenith in bourgeois thought, in which human thought was regarded as unable to grasp the underlying essence of illusory and phenomenal appearance, Lukács sees Hegel as having advanced the discovery of giving to the categories of reflection an *internal and necessary correlation*, dissolving immediacy into a unified division, bridging the absolute separation between appearance and essence. Lukács makes clear how reality only makes sense as a set of internal relations, rather than isolated and petrified objects. In Lukács, reflection, once *the patron of antinomy*, has now become *the enemy of antinomy* and stands at the very centre of the Hegelian dialectic.

For Lukács, the determinations of reflection are characteristics of the structure and dynamic of reality, burrowing directly into the identity between subject and object and lead straight into 'the heart of the dialectic'. Here, the determinations of reflection salvage the complete and absolute identification of subject and object (1978: 84). The unitary character of the reflection determinations is Hegel's theory of identity. For Lukács, this demonstrates that identity is a category of existing objectivity which doesn't only belong to formal logic. The persistence and loss of identity, as the mediation of difference through reflection, is a real process and a concrete problem. Lukács holds that it is clear that 'the level of separation of these reflection determinations by the understanding is not only a stage prior to their dialectical unification by reason, but also a progress in civilization in relation to the original directly unitary perception' (1978: 105). All of these categories ontologically characterize definite structures and structural changes in society. For this, Hegel's reflection determinations unknowingly define an increasingly concrete dimension within an objective complex of social being. In this way, Lukács holds that Hegel's transition from *Verstand* to *Vernunft* bears an 'epochal significance' (1978: 78), one for which the power of unification has disappeared from society and opposites have lost their living relation to, and reciprocal influence upon, one another and become rigidly self-contained (Hegel 1977b: 91). While it has already been noted that Hegel describes reflective philosophy within a 'culture of reflection', it is within such a scenario that Hegel's criticism of reflective philosophy as the reunification of anguishing opposition – and in the measured shift from the *Verstand* to *Vernunft* – acquires its true meaning, one whose speculative unity has developed into *a spectacular epoch*.

A unitary theory of reification

The task before us is to demonstrate in what capacity the speculative logic of reflection determinations as the unifying and necessary relation between the opposites of appearance and essence, identity and distinction, inner and outer, form and content, immediacy and mediation inheres as a fundamental structural dynamic of Debord's theory of a society of the spectacle. Again, while a more sustained investigation into the *Wesenslogik* will proceed within the next chapter, it will suffice for the moment – in order to demonstrate the qualitative distinctiveness between Lukács and Debord on the question of reification – to outline a set of defining features of the spectacle altogether divergent from an antinomic theory of reification.

It is perhaps first apt to briefly illustrate how important Lukács was for Debord. Debord firstly follows Lukács in grasping the form of the commodity and its fetish-character to be of central importance as a structuring principle for society in general. Prior to the 1967 publication of *The Society of the Spectacle*, an article appearing the year prior in issue 10 of *IS* helpfully illustrates both the debt and differences between reification and spectacle. Entitled 'The Fundamental Structures of Reification' and authored by Strasbourg student Jean Garnault, the work stands as a suitable bridge in demonstrating how the notion of spectacle both integrates elements of Lukács' theory of reification and makes certain conceptual strides beyond its contours. Its opening passages largely remain within Lukács' framework, emphasizing 'the commodity *form*' and 'the *logic* of its real development'. Here, Marx is lauded for having given 'to the theory of the fetishism of the commodity an objective truth and a real-life ordinariness'. What becomes paramount for the SI is how the *form* of the commodity remains pivotal despite the historical transformations of capitalism, one which has acquired an autonomous existence that has created a social world in its own image, both an anthropomorphisis and mode of representing the world which has 'reduced the totality of social reality to the quantifiable and installed the totalitarian domination of the quantitative' (IS 1997: 448). Further, and here the SI largely adopts the concept of reification found within Lukács, the fetish-character of the commodity form anchors the concreteness of the world as a moment of formal rationalization.

Within *The Society of the Spectacle* itself, the indebtedness to Lukács is overwhelming,[3] markedly through Debord's frequent employment of the category of 'contemplation', itself a characterization regularly utilized by Lukács as the necessary relation of the reified antinomy between an alienated subject and its inaccessible world (Lukács 1971a: 126). As Lukács elaborates in one of the more focused passages on the concept:

> As labour is progressively rationalised and mechanised his lack of will is reinforced by the way in which his activity becomes less and less active and more and more *contemplative*. The contemplative stance adopted towards a process mechanically conforming to fixed laws and enacted independently of man's consciousness and impervious to human intervention, i.e. a perfectly closed system, must likewise transform the basic categories of man's immediate attitude to the world: it reduces space and time to a common denominator and degrades time to the dimension of space.
>
> 1971a: 89

For Lukács, the 'standpoint of contemplation' is largely associated with the faculty of reflection (1971a: 122), a stance unable to practically penetrate into the living and historical reality of the objective world. The above passage appears within *The Society of the Spectacle* as the epigraph for its second chapter, that section of the book which deals explicitly with the economic foundations of the spectacle and its modern origins with the fetish-character of the commodity social form. However, as an important distinction to Lukács, the agent of such contemplation is never simply the fragmented subject of reification but the objectivity of the society spectacle itself, wherein 'the commodity contemplates itself in a world it has created' (Debord 1970: §53). While contemplation as a register of reification is for Debord still signified as an absence of totality – much as it is for Lukács – within the theory of the spectacle it becomes not a passive disposition of an alienated subjectivity[4] but a reigning and, as it will be argued, speculative dominion over the concrete totality of social life.

Returning to the aforementioned 1966 article in *IS*, however, more stark conceptual differences between Lukács' theory of reification and Debord's spectacle begin to reveal themselves. The article begins largely with an adoption of the concept of reification found within Lukács, in which the fetish-character of the commodity form has anchored the concreteness of the world as a moment of 'formal rationalization'.[5] However, these remarks, echoing the reified structure found within Lukács, begin to take a qualitative turn once the category of spectacle is introduced a few sentences later. Unlike previous forms of capitalism, which 'was satisfied with crushing social man with a host of partial alienations', all of the 'old separated spheres' – which are described as 'a cohort of reified *abstractions*: *the* individual, *the* state, *the* consumer, *the* market' – are now reduced 'to one and the same reification'. This singular form of reification obtains insofar as the spectacle 'is a projection of *the entirety of life* [and a] prescriptive model of life itself' (IS 1997: 448–50).

It is within *The Society of the Spectacle* itself, however, that this unitary character becomes explicit. The preliminary clue demonstrating that Debord's theory of the spectacle is less a theory of appearances, than it is a theory on the inner coherence and cohesive organization of appearance-forms, is in the very title of the book. That is, it is a *society* of the spectacle, rather than a set of individuated *spectacles*. It is a peculiar form of society that Debord is diagnosing and therefore the task remains to expound the unifying logic which holds society together under the spectacle, rather than simply place focus upon a heterogeneous manifold of contingent and fragmented occurrences of alienation. The social cohesion achieved within the society of the spectacle adheres through the principle of separation. It is a social separation of human beings from their own activity falsified into an *appearance* operating outside of their control.

Debord's opening chapter, 'Separation Perfected' (*la separation achevée*), continues with this framework. Insofar as within capitalism, social reality appears as an inverted world and subsists through estranged forms of abstract social unity, the spectacle is the culmination of this fetish of the whole in which the 'unity it imposes is merely the official language of generalized separation' (Debord 1995: §3). Nevertheless, Debord opens the book with the first two theses making this point explicit: it is *the whole of life* that is presented under the spectacle, not simply an aspect or fragment of life. Social life fragmented, a condition already theorized under Lukács' concept of reification, develops under the spectacle by cohering into a 'common stream' in which 'reality unfolds in a new generality' (Debord 1995: §2). Under the spectacle, the universality of the commodity form no longer merely fragments social life, but has now developed the capacity to *unify* social existence to a degree previously unattainable. Notably for Lukács' theory of reification, the 'specialisation of skills leads to the destruction of every image of the whole'. If, 'despite this, the need to grasp the whole – at least cognitively – cannot die out' (Lukács 1971a: 103), then the spectacle, at the level of its concept, provides an answer, one for which all of the antagonisms of a fragmented social existence are given relief through spectacular modes of social integration. It is for this reason that Debord titles the first chapter 'Separation Perfected'.[6]

Precursors to such a model of false universality can be found in the early writings of Marx, of which Debord was intimately familiar. Accompanying the scattered remarks on the abstract universality of religion and speculative philosophy within these early writings, there figures also prominently an estranged and abstract unity of the state and civil society, specifically within 'Contribution to the Critique of Hegel's Philosophy of Law' (Marx 1975b: 58–9) and 'On the Jewish Question'. Such a unity reveals the individual as an 'imaginary member of an illusory sovereignty ... deprived of his real individual life and endowed with an unreal universality' (Marx 1975f: 153). For Marx, such unity remains empty and essentially mystical, 'the *postulated illusion* of the *unity of the political state with itself*' (1975f: 93). Similarly, within these early ruminations on the categories of bourgeois society, money assumes 'the universal self-established *value* of all things' (1975f: 172), which effectively elicits 'the omnipotence of its being [as] the bond of all *bonds*' (1975c: 323–4). Additionally, within 'Comments on James Mill', money as a '*sensuous* superstition' (1975a: 213) emerges as an abstract universality fastening together social relationships under its mediating logic.

Within Marx's early writings, religion, the state and money are all couched in terms of an abstract universality unifying heterogeneous particularity, individuality and difference in a mystified and inverted manner. It is no secret that Marx's early writings perhaps held more attention for Debord than the critique of political economy. Within the Guy Debord archive at the Bibliothèque Nationale de France in Paris there sits a small black moleskin notebook in which Debord assembled a copious amount of commentary and quotations on Marx's early writings. Here Debord predominantly finds accord with a youthful Marx incisively disseminating the critique of abstraction. Nevertheless, for Debord, *The Society of the Spectacle* and those issues of *IS* published during the 1960s burrow deeply into the critique of political economy, unravelling a form of reification through the *Erscheinungsformen* of value, which yield not simply a social situation in which fragmentation abounds without any reconciliation between subject and object, but rather a reconstructed 'lost paradise of unitary societies ... a reality entirely reduced to the quantitative, thoroughly dominated by the principle of identity' (IS 1997: 451). As Debord writes towards the conclusion of his book, 'The spectacle erases the dividing line between self and world, in that the self, under siege by the presence/absence of the world, is eventually overwhelmed; it likewise erases the dividing line between true and false, repressing all directly lived truth beneath the *real presence* of the falsehood maintained by the organization of appearances' (1995: §219). Indeed, the 1966 article makes explicit that the logical principle of *identity* has found its 'appropriate realization in the commodity-spectacle'. The 'flat and disincarnated positivity' (IS 1997: 450, 452) installed by the commodity-spectacle realizes the general identity not simply as an illusory fantasy but rendered actual through the formalization of social relations by exchange.[7] There is a principle of identity or an *Identitätszwang* between spectacle and spectators whereby the former furnishes the latter with an entire purview of social possibility and satisfaction.[8]

Although it will receive greater attention in the next chapter, it is instructive to note how the concept of identity in Hegel's *Wesenslogik* emerges and immanently demands and maintains the category of distinction within itself. For Hegel, identity is not simply the cancellation out of differing sides (Hegel 2010: 362). Here, the concept of identity ought 'not to be interpreted merely as abstract identity, i.e. as identity that excludes distinction' (Hegel 1991b: 181) in the ordinary non-speculative sense of the term. Identity and difference, each shining into another, only acquire respective meaning in their relation; 'where there is distinction, we require identity and, where there is identity, distinction' (Hegel 1991b: 184). The possibility of adequation between subject and object without either an abstract identification imposed by the law of the excluded middle or refuge within an absolute separation is precisely the logical and speculative structure of spectacular unification.

The spectacle adopts aspects of the *Wesenslogik*, specifically the determinations of reflection for which appearance and essence are identical without the liquidation of distinction. For Hegel, the reflective shining between identity and difference reaches its completion in appearance and its essential ground, the truth of which is in its very relationality; 'what appears shows the essential, and the essential is in its appearance' (Hegel 2010: 419). The true unity between reflection and its other is consummate, however, only within their complete interpenetration as actuality. The essential truth of appearance is thereby acquired only as a concrete existence, namely as thinghood. Hegel's logical development has thereby witnessed the sublation of being into the having of properties as thinghood, which is in turn the shining forth of appearance – not, however, as a structural layering over of some *übersinnliche Jenseits* or that which is merely inner, but as the necessary form under which that which is essential is made manifest and actual (Hegel 1991b: 195–201).

The spectacle is 'at once a faithful mirror held up to the production of things and a distorting objectification of the producers'. Making 'no secret of what it *is*' (Debord 1995: §16, §25), the spectacle assumes a mirror structure in which, rather than misrepresenting reality, accurately reflects a reality already mangled and perverted by the fetish-forms of the autonomous economy developing for itself. Again, as a structure of disclosure constitutive of its object, the spectacle is a luminosity unfolding upon the terrain of the false. There is no masquerade operative in its mystification. Within the spectacle, social activity is made to appear, and in doing so, is embedded with a meaning that contains both the image and the goal of social development under commodity society, *defining that which appears and defining appearance as essential*. A small feuilleton, entitled 'The Independence of the Commodity' and embedded within the same aforementioned article in *IS* issue 10 (see Figure 4.1), describes the spectacle aptly: 'The autonomy of the commodity is at the root of the dictatorship of appearance; of the fundamental tautology of the **spectacle**, where importance is always presupposed and defined by the staging of importance. The prefabricated pseudo-event which dominates and orients the real is an event that is no longer visible for what it contains, but which has no other content than to be **visible**' (IS 1997: 449).

Figure 4.1 The Independence of the Commodity, *Internationale situationniste* 10 (1966).

The spectacle thereby 'says nothing more than "that which appears is good, that which is good appears"' (Debord 1995: §12). The monopolization of social reality by the commodity form proceeds by way of a spectacular 'organization of appearance', one whose rational form 'reflects [*renvoie*] back to men the characteristics of their own lives by presenting them as objective characteristics' (IS 1997: 451).

Under the spectacle, the myth of Narcissus, from where this chapter began, is thereby given a modernized social ontology through a form of domination in and through reflective identification. Debord was well aware of how the category of spectacle elicited the reflective structure of a mirror. As he wrote in 1980 to a

Greek translator of *The Society of the Spectacle*, 'In French, "spectacle" has the merit of being linked to the Latin *speculum* and thus to mirror, to the inverted image, to the concept of speculation, etc' (Debord 2006c: 64). However, it is important to recall here that a mirror structure is not the image itself, but the means by which appearances take shape. The mirror shows only what is present; it is not a *camera obscura* whose optical projection appears through an illusory inversion. Following suit, the spectacle as a universal medium for which the totality of social relations within commodity-capitalist society appears is not to be conflated with the individual imagery that is only its result. The reflective structure of the spectacle is a structure for the movement of appearance-forms as the essence of reality. The appearances of the spectacle are not fundamentally distinct from any underlying 'authentic' reality but are the essence of reality itself. Debord aimed to elucidate an autonomized social reality constituted through appearances, wherein social unity only exists in its inverted form, an appearance of a falsified social existence constituted through the commodity social form. As such, the spectacle is not a falsified *representation* of reality, but the visual or phenomenal exposition of an *already* falsified reality given methodological register by Debord through the categories of 'image', 'representation' and 'appearance'. Like the concrete instantiations of value, the spectacle is a social relation rendered into a materially objective force: 'a *Weltanschauung* which has become actual, materially translated' (Debord 1970: §5). It is a concept that elucidates the abstract form of domination constituted by the *Erscheinungsformen* of value and that structure's inherited Hegelian *Wesenslogik*, a logic to be examined more closely in the next chapter.

The central claim of this book is that it is fundamentally Hegel's *speculative* logic that is instantiated by the spectacle and allows Debord to compose a theory of reification grounded within social unity, a far cry from the antinomic theory of reification found within Lukács. Lukács already critically theorized the 'generalized separation of worker and product [which] spelled the end of any comprehensive view of the job done, as well as the end of direct personal communication between producers' (Debord 1995: §26). For both Lukács and Debord, this 'triumph of an economic system founded on separation leads to the *proletarianization of the world*' (Debord 1995: §26). However, while inheriting a social world divided, the spectacle sublates that division and affirms a 'common language that bridges this division' as that world's sovereign 'self-representation'. As Debord summarizes, 'The spectacle thus unites what is separate, but it unites it only *in its separateness*' (1995: §29). While separation remains 'the alpha and omega of the spectacle' (1995: §25) and is its basis insofar as it is the development of the commodity-capitalist economy and its requisite class division and alienation, the spectacle nevertheless obtains a unity-in-separation insofar as the 'phenomena of separation is part and parcel of the unity of the world' (1995: §7). The spectacle therefore 'manifests itself as an enormous positivity', and a speculative one at that for which the negativity of one side always yields a positive result. On the whole, the spectacle is as such the 'monopolization of the realm of appearances' (1995: §12) and not reducible to any single and fragmentary appearance.

Conclusion

At the beginning of this chapter, we have seen how reflective philosophy, in Hegel's account, proceeds by way of an assumed independence to the givenness of objective reality, and then attempts, through its acquired capacity to think the representation of all that is possible, to overcome the immediacy of a sensory relation to world.[9] The structure of reflection becomes a subjectivity at odds and unreconciled with the world around it. For Lukács, this form of subjectivity is emblematic of the reified subject within capitalist society. Yet it is further in the work of Hegel that Lukács gestures beyond this antinomic mode of relating to the world, specifically as an alternative philosophy of reflection exemplified in relations of mediated otherness we find in Hegel's determinations of reflection in the *Wesenslogik*. Reflection there becomes an objective form of mediation of subjective knowledge, a movement between subject and object that both unifies and divides, thereby offering a model for the overcoming of the separated condition of reification.

In sum, reflective philosophy provides a model of reification for Lukács as a mode of antinomic *separation*. Yet as we have seen in the second half of this chapter, Debord's theory of reification as spectacle stands in contrast as a mode of reflective *identification* between subject and object, that is, a mode of *unification* – a form of social mediation not reducible to an unmediated division between subject and object, self and world, appearance and essence, abstract and concrete, spectator and spectacle, and so on. As this book has contended throughout, it is a social prognosis more suitably correlated with the logical dynamic of Hegel's speculative philosophy. The transition between *external* reflection criticized by Hegel in *Faith and Knowledge* and the determinations of reflection within the *Wesenslogik* thereby offers a philosophical reconstruction of the differences between Lukács' reification and Debord's spectacle. In a word, there is nothing antinomic about spectacular domination. Reification is no longer a problem of antinomies within Debord as it is within Lukács.[10] Finally, grounding the spectacle within the *Wesenslogik*, an investigation which will follow in the next chapter, has the added merit of putting to rest all those interpretations of Debord as excessively subjectivistic, derivative of French existentialism, or as subject to a dualistic framework in which 'inauthentic' images are extrinsically correlated with an ontologically 'authentic' and 'true' concrete social reality. In contrast, the interpretation set out in this chapter argues that the spectacle is the unity-in-separation of both subject and object devoid of the necessity of positing a *übersinnliche Jenseits* that is simply concealed by an illusory mystification. It is the 'the mirror-image of a world gone out of joint' (Lukács 1971b: 17), rather than an out of joint mirror-image of the world. However, as we will see in the next chapter, to fully grasp the spectacle as a speculative form of reflective identification between subject and object is also to inquire about its *essence*, that is, how a multiplicity of appearances might cohere within a common unity of speculative identification. It is by asking as much that we now turn to the spectacle's *Wesenslogik*.

5

The Essence of the Spectacle

No exile is possible in a unified world.

Guy Debord

Between 1 February and 10 April 1967 at the Collège de France, Jean Hyppolite conducted a seminar on Hegel's logic at which Guy Debord was in attendance. At the time, *The Society of the Spectacle* had yet to go to print and Debord's seminar notes are sprinkled with 'pour SdS'. His notes begin with a division of the *Science of Logic*, not according to its doctrines, but according to three different modes of cognition: 'understanding – negative dialectic – positive speculation'.[1] While the first, as we've seen in the previous chapter, is best accorded to the antinomic fragmentation characteristic of Lukács' theory of reification, the third, as this book has maintained, is most suitably a logical form achieved by the society of the spectacle.

The central argument of this book has been that it is the speculative element of Hegel's dialectics – a unitary structure that doesn't obliterate difference – that gives to the spectacle its spectacular logic. Indeed, over twenty years after it was written, Debord described his 1967 book as having sought to evaluate the spectacle in terms of its 'depth and unity' (Debord 1998: 3), a characterization invoking both a structure of essence and appearance, as well as a unity capable of self-differentiation. Here the spectacle wields a logic that controls a diverse abundance of particular phenomena. It will be argued in the present and final chapters that 'the depth and unity' of the spectacle requires Hegel's *Wesenslogik* and *Begriffslogik* for its determinate coherence to be understood as a social totality.

In this chapter, the *Wesenslogik* of the spectacle will be examined specifically for the way in which its *essence* consists in a unitary structure amidst a changing multiplicity of appearances-forms. Our final chapter, on the *concept* of the spectacle, will proceed to an investigation of its *Begriffslogik*. There, it will be the spectacle as a *self*-differentiating unity – that is, a conceptual structure whose internal differences are but the self-movement of its own universality that subsists in and through its individuated particulars – that will be elucidated. This final chapter will acquire a certain concretion hitherto absent from this book; it will be shown that the self-differentiated moments of the spectacle exhibit an inner speculative identity between its moments and argue that these moments are marked most notably in Debord's diagnosis through the relations between work and leisure, state and economy, town and country and the diffuse and concentrated forms of the spectacle, all of which, as determinations of the spectacle's *Begriffslogik*, give to it conceptual coherence as a social totality.[2]

Yet here, in the present chapter, a concept of essence is first necessary to examine if the spectacle is to retain its unitary character amid a changing multiplicity of appearances. Otherwise it would to regress into a circumstantial aggregation of appearances with no inner relation, a bad infinity overcome with empty chatter and collated arbitrarily. Indeed, the question of essence, starting with Plato, was always a question of unity, a query into how it is that the like and unlike might bear in their plurality some kind of structural coherence said to truly exist in and through exteriority. Heteronomous contingency cannot be sustained in a world of overwhelming administration and '[a] theory that wants to eradicate from science the concept of essence succumbs to helpless relativism' (Marcuse 2009: 32). The *essence* of the spectacle is thereby a problem of its unity and the truth of its being amongst its infinite manifold variation of appearance-forms. To preserve unity and difference without abandoning their reciprocal integrity or commensurability is then the task before us for elucidating the spectacle's coherence as a totality, as well as what Hegel's *Wesenslogik* seeks to demonstrate. For this, the spectacle inherits the philosophical problem of the one and the many. Ultimately, for Hegel, essence becomes the appearance of appearances, or the totality of appearances. And yet, as Debord writes in a 1973 letter, '"the appearances of this appearance" already constitutes a peculiarly unorthodox and baroque turn of phrase on which I settled somewhat reluctantly' (2005: 61). If Debord hesitated to utilize such a formulation, we must examine how the concept of the society of the spectacle nevertheless inheres with such a logical structure, giving to it its unitary character.

Through three distinct moments of the *Wesenslogik*, we will see how the spectacle's structure of appearances acquires actuality in and through the speculative identity of identity and difference: appearance, commensurability and actuality will therefore emerge as the three central determinations of spectacular logic. Held together through speculative identity, these three determinations will offer up the society of the spectacle as a reconciled unity or world of differentiated appearance-forms that has become an actuality through a determination of commensurability brought to totality. To examine the spectacle as a *Wesenslogik* is thereby to give full coherence to the following early thesis of *The Society of the Spectacle*: 'The spectacle cannot be understood either as a deliberate distortion of the visual world or as a product of the technology of the mass dissemination of images. It is far better viewed as a weltanschauung that has been actualized, translated into the material realm – a world view transformed into an objective force' (1995: §5). We will return to this thesis periodically throughout the present chapter. It will be argued that the spectacle, as a 'weltanschauung that has been actualized, translated into the material realm – a world view transformed into an objective force', cannot sustain its logical coherence without a *Wesenslogik*. Let us, however, begin with the problem of the spectacle's multiplicity of appearances.

The problem of indifference

Towards the end of 1973, at the conclusion of the production of the film version of *The Society of the Spectacle*, Debord prepared a legal document which, although never used, was to serve as a potential '[b]asis for a defense in a possible lawsuit' deriving from the film's usage of pre-existing commercial footage. There he writes, 'It is not the author's intention to criticize this or that particular aspect of the here and now, a trade unionist or a starlet, but rather the *generality* of this epoch – before which the particularities are *indifferent*. These have been selected by the author for their accessibility, thus for the actual extent to which they enjoy spectacular dissemination' (2005: 101; emphasis added). Note the *indifference* as a way of characterizing the relation between the spectacle's differentia and its overall generality. It is an apt beginning insofar as it is also the precise manner in which Hegel's *Wesenslogik* is propelled forward as the culmination of the *Seinslogik*.[3] The *Wesenslogik* explores different candidates for a two-tiered reality of varied perspectives, a duplicitous reality inaugurated by the category of indifference, a substrate underlying qualitative and quantitative alteration. The determinations of being have become *posited* determinations of being by their indifferent unity. The *self-relation* of being as an explicit category of the *Science of Logic* is the transition to the *Wesenslogik*.[4]

For Hegel, determinacy beyond directly apprehended qualities must be sought to give being coherent explication as qualitative and quantitative differentiation. It is precisely the same dilemma which Debord aims to resolve in the category of the spectacle. In a 1985 preface prepared by Debord for a collected volume of all twenty-nine issues of *Potlatch*, a great difficulty is described, 'due to the fact that these spectacular forms have apparently changed, every three months, almost every day' (2006i: 327). Indeed, as Debord describes such inconstancy in a 1978 letter, 'the current state of the world [is] surrounded by lies that *change from one day to the next*' (2005: 474). The variety and diversity of the spectacle requires therewith unitary coherence, one which must satisfy the following three central determinations:

1. The unity of the spectacle must emerge through an immanent logic of *Erscheinung* for which an originary or transcendent *Jenseits*, and with it the framework of a duplicitous reality, proves inadequate to the spectacle's inversion of the sensible and supersensible.
2. The unity of the spectacle must optimally express a totality of identity-in-difference, self-equality and commensurability, therewith upholding the centrality of exchange-value as constitutive of spectacular logic for which *all otherness is but its own internal moment*.
3. This unity of the spectacle must be an actuality both of its particular manifestations and in its general structure and, in so doing, render *fully visible and transparent* its inner necessity, an optics that allows the spectacle *to see* as much as *it is seen*.

As will become clear, it is only through the logical development of the *Wesenslogik* that the concept of the spectacle can comprise all such determinations and be given the abridged description as a 'weltanschauung that has been actualized, translated into the material realm – a world view transformed into an objective force' (Debord 1995: §5).

The relational world of the spectacle

With regard to the first central determination, as a complete identity between appearance and essence, we begin by recalling a passage from the seventeenth thesis from *The Society of the Spectacle*:

> An earlier stage in the economy's domination of social life entailed an obvious downgrading of *being* into *having* that left its stamp on all human endeavor. The present stage, in which social life is completely taken over by the accumulated products of the economy, entails a generalized shift from *having* to appearing: all

effective 'having' must now derive both its immediate prestige and its ultimate raison d'etre from appearances.

Debord 1995: §17

Here, where Debord registers the development of social alienation through the advent of the spectacle, specifically as *having* transitions to *appearing*, we find an uncannily similar logical development of Hegel's concept of *Erscheinung*. Indeed a near identical movement is found in the *Encyclopaedia Logic*, in which Hegel's logical development exhibits the sublation of *being* into the *having* of properties as thinghood, which is in turn the shining forth of *Erscheinung* – not, however, as a structural layering over of some *übersinnliche Jenseits* or that which is merely inner, but as the necessary form under which that which is essential is made manifest and actual (Hegel 1991b: 195–201). However, let us in brief traverse these steps as they appear within the *Science of Logic* so that we might correlate the similar logic of Debord's seventeenth thesis.

For Hegel, essence is first a simple negativity, that is, *not* the immediacy of being. It is *non-being*. *Schein* is the immediacy of non-being, itself the negativity of essence. In proving itself to be non-immediacy, being as immediate is therefore only what it initially *seemed* to be. Being is the immediate seeming or *Schein* of essence. An absolute distinction between essence and its own seeming collapses as the former is grasped *as* the generation of seeming. Essence does not thereby underlie *Scheinen* as a foundation but is the process of seeming itself. This immediacy of *Schein* in and through the negativity of essence demonstrates essence to be determinate as 'an infinite self-contained movement which determines its immediacy as negativity and its negativity as immediacy, and is thus the shining of itself within itself' (Hegel 1991b: 345). Hegel calls this self-movement *reflection*.

From *Schein*, Hegel arrives at the section on appearance through the *Reflexionsbestimmungen*. Reflection is the attempt to find an identity that can account for differentiated *Scheinen*. The nature of the *Reflexionsbestimmungen* is to demonstrate that 'the determinateness of the reflection is *the reference in it to its otherness*' (1991b: 353). For this, the *Reflexionsbestimmungen* derive a logic of relations, one in which otherness is determinate in and through identity. Within the *Seinslogik*, determination referred to the way in which *something* was determined as distinct from an *other* as a contrastive limit of being. Now, however, a *Reflexionbestimmung* is not a transitory category but self-identical within the unified and manifold relations. In fact, *Reflexionsbestimmungen* give to relations their coherence as moments of differentia.

The *Reflexionsbestimmungen* are the attempt to stabilize the relational unity of a manifold through a series of additional categories. The last of which, ground, finally allows for the maintained integrity of a unity in differentiation. Hitherto the relation between essence and *Schein* remained ungrounded. Only in its completion does ground exhibit the insight that there is nothing *behind* external reality and that it is the essential nature of interiority to fully manifest itself in an exteriority. This formation process is the manner in which identity shines forth. If it were merely a shining of differences, we would have regressed to the category of *Schein*. Instead, it is the identity within difference that has come to the fore in the ground connection. For this, the appearing differentiated within identity introduces the concept of *Erscheinung*, that appearance of essence as an identity within difference. Essence has developed *Schein* into *Erscheinung*, for which it emerges as 'not *behind* of *beyond* appearance, but since the essence is what exists, existence is appearance' (Hegel 1991b: 199). In sum and through ground, essence has come into existence and this existence Hegel calls *Erscheinung*.

Ground is no longer conceived as a substratum beneath a synthesized manifold but as the immanent interconnection of the manifold itself. It is a reciprocal grounding for which the ground is equally the grounded. Hegel calls this *existence*, 'the immediate unity of inward reflection and reflection-into-another' (1991b: 192). Concrete existence is a negative unity and is as such called by Hegel a *thing*. The determinations of the thing are its *properties* which it *possesses*. Here then Hegel makes explicit that the development from the *Seinslogik* up until now proceeds from *being* to *having*. The thing is a determination of concrete existence, whose properties are thing's distinguished existents. With the thing comes the relation of *having* or the *possession* of properties.

The appearance of essence as concrete existence, which, while able to convert *Schein* to *Erscheinung*, is not yet sufficient to fasten together the totality of the process. Concrete existence still fails to unify with that from which it is produced; 'as Musil quipped, a man without properties is properties without a man' (Cirulli 2006: 107). Since attempting to grasp the unity of the thing dissolves any such unity into an excitation of identity and difference, the thing has dispersed (*sich auflöst*) into *Erscheinung*. *Erscheinung* emerges as the immanence of essence within being and the thing will become the '[*shining forth* or] *appearance*' (Hegel 1991b: 198). We now have the conceptual resources to return to transition from *having* to *appearing* found within Debord's seventeenth thesis.[5]

What we discover in the chapter on *Erscheinung*, crucial for the spectacle, is that the essential truth of appearance is nothing independent from its appearing. This is a development from concrete existence or thinghood. Hegel's logical development has thereby witnessed the sublation of being into the having of properties as thinghood, which is in turn the shining forth of appearance – not, however, as a structural layering over of some *übersinnliche Jenseits* or that which is merely inner, but as the necessary form under which that which is essential is made manifest and actual. To disavow that there is an essence to the spectacle is to inadvertently affirm its appearances *as essential*. Here and consistent with Hegel's *Wesenslogik*, essence of the spectacle is only the visibility of its *Erscheinungen*, or 'the night of "spectacular society," whose spectacles presented nothing but an eternal positive façade' (Knabb 2006: 290). *Erscheinung* is not the screen through which reality lays concealed, but demonstrates the essential nature of reality to manifest itself.

However, it is not enough to affirm *Erscheinung* as the essential unity of the spectacle. As the fifth thesis of *The Society of the Spectacle* reminds us, it is also a *Weltanschauung* that has stabilized the movement of *Erscheinungen*. Further, perhaps most crucially and as Debord's fourth thesis states, 'The spectacle is not a collection of images, but a social *relation* among people, mediated by images' (1970: §4; emphasis added). For this, we must extract from Hegel's concept of *Erscheinung* three cadences: 1) the *law* of *Erscheinung*; 2) the *world* of *Erscheinung*; and 3) the *relations* of *Erscheinung*. Within Hegel's treatment of the *Wesenslogik*, all three such moments are not only found but made explicit moments of the concept of *Erscheinung*.

With the *law* of *Erscheinung*, Hegel is after a permanent element against the perpetual flux of externalities. The law of *Erscheinung* is the unity that holds together such an indifferent diversity of *Erscheinungen* in permanent subsistence. The content of law and *Erscheinung* is therefore identical as the substrate of appearance. Appearance here becomes a rule of quantitative consistency against a perennially unstable fluctuation of *Erscheinungen*. Further, 'the kingdom of laws is the *restful* copy [*Abbild*] of the concretely existing or appearing world' (Hegel 2010: 441). Here, to be restful is to remain selfsame despite changes. Importantly, together the kingdom of laws and the concrete existence of the appearing world constitute a single totality so that in law essence becomes appearance in its totality.

As his notes make clear, Debord garnered much of his knowledge of Hegel's *Wesenslogik* from Lefebvre's *Logique Formelle, Logique Dialectique*. With regard to the law of *Erscheinungen* specifically, Debord extracts the following passage:

> And that is why we can reach essence from appearances. Essence is nothing but *a stream deeper* in the flow of appearances and phenomena. All facts are not on

the same plane, and essence, the law below the surface is in the calm and deep part of the river. It is necessary to pass through the surface and plunge towards these deep waters.

1982a: 200

The law of appearance procures externalization in existence, producing finitude as what Hegel calls the copy or image (*Abbild*) of its own process. It is here that Debord's employment of the category of image (*image*) throughout *The Society of the Spectacle* is afforded greater meaning. For Hegel, the kingdom of lawful *Erscheinungen*, as we will recall from chapter 2, is the image of tranquil stability within a world of instability. *Erscheinung* as law does not simply stabilize the tumultuous heteronomy of the phenomenal world, but produces concrete existence out of itself. This consequence is but the finite image of *Erscheinung*. In *The Society of the Spectacle*, the category of image echoes this very dynamic. Only as the law of *Erscheinung* does the spectacle generate 'images [which] fuse in a common stream' (Debord 1970: §2). Thus the spectacle cannot simply be accorded with the mere diverse dissemination of images themselves. Such a collection would, in Hegel's terms, be an externally connected and aggregated ensemble (*das Zusammen*) of differences without unity. As Hegel writes in the third part of his *Encyclopaedia of the Philosophical Sciences*, 'A higher activity than mere reproducing is the *relating* of images *to one another*' (2007: 190). Under the spectacle, the 'ruling economy' (Debord 1970: §14) as the law of *Erscheinung* wields the image of concrete existence and gives to that existence structural coherence. As Debord comments, '[w]here the real world changes into simple images, the simple images become real beings' (1970: §18). As such, capital become image is the affirmation of a harmonious reality despite the heteronomy of diverse *Erscheinungen*.

These remarks, however, insofar as Debord here again refers to 'images of the world', remain partial without comment on the *Erscheinung* as *world*. In the *Encyclopaedia Logic*, the category of *Erscheinung* is for Hegel almost immediately the invocation of a *world* of appearance: 'The essence does not remain behind or beyond appearance, but manifests itself as essence precisely by reducing the world to mere appearance' (1991b: 200). *Erscheinung* becomes a *world* of *Erscheinungen* through a unity of both inward reflection and reflection into another. In the latter, the ground of what appears is as much its own appearance so that the existence of *Erscheinung* 'is developed into a *totality* and a *world* of appearance, or of reflected finitude' (1991b: 201).

The *world* of concrete existence, as a negative diversity of an indifferent manifold, is transposed into the stable copy or duplicated image (*Abbild*) that is the kingdom of laws. There the world acquires tranquillity against its heteronomous and unconnected diversity. However, as a world, 'the appearing things have their grounds and conditions in other appearing things' (Hegel 2010: 443). Such is the case that law, as the identical content of *Erscheinungen*, also carries over this reflective othering of appearance as a further appearance. The world of *Erscheinung* discloses itself (*auftut*) as now dirempted into an appearing world and a world as it is in and for itself. This duplicity of the world of *Erscheinung*, divided into a diversified manifold of alterable appearing and a supersensible world, is as a totality what Hegel calls 'the total reflection of this world' (2010: 444). The world as it is in and for itself is thereby internally split into an opposition between the sensible and supersensible. The identity of these two worlds is 'specifically this, that the world that exists in and for itself is the *inversion* [*verkehrte*] of the world of appearance' (2010: 446).

As might be recalled, the path which we currently traverse has in large part already been examined within chapter 2 and its analysis of the inverted world. There, the sensuous supersensible inverted world of the *Phenomenology of Spirit* was imported into the logic of the society of the spectacle insofar as society is organized as appearance and it was through an exchange relation of force solicitation that allowed for the unity of appearances to become explicit while at once also procuring an inverted world of the supersensible.[6] The inversion proceeds as such: the lawful world of *Erscheinungen* separates itself from the heterogeneous world of the *Erscheinungen*, and in so doing, assimilates this manifold as its own supersensible *Abbild* of the sensible world. The supersensible thus inverts the sensible as a moment of itself. The duplicitous world of *Erscheinung* develops into a reigning commensurability between essential law and heterogeneous appearing.

For Hegel the *world* of appearance is a reflected finitude of existence whose totality encompasses as an identity both its externalization and self-relation. *Erscheinung* becomes a *world* of *Erscheinungen* insofar as it derives from a manifold of concrete and self-subsisting existents a unified selfsame relation. We now reach a more determinate meaning of Debord's fifth thesis: the category of *Welt* 'signifies in general the formless totality of a manifoldness; this world has foundered both as essential world and as world of appearance; it is still a totality or a universe but as *essential relation*' (2010: 448).[7] Prior to its essential relation, however, the world *as sheer manifold* lends itself to the claim that the spectacle 'originates in the loss of the unity of the world, and the gigantic expansion of the modern spectacle expresses the totality of this loss' (Debord 1970: §29). As Debord writes in his seminar notes on Hyppolite's spring lecture, 'the world is immediate, melting before us, but the other is the world of essence'.[8] Such is the case that the spectacle as a world of *Erscheinung* accords with the concept of a world found in the *Wesenslogik*: a negative diversity of an indifferent manifold yet to exhibit its unifying principle. This principle will emerge 'as a tendency to make one see the world' (Debord 1970: §18), rather than the world itself which is, through this development, only the manifold finitude produced out of the logic of *Erscheinung*. Therein, the world as manifold is not confronted by the spectacle, as if it were its 'supplement [or] additional decoration' (1970: §6), but is, as a *relation*, its offspring. As Debord writes further in his notes to Hyppolite's lecture, '[i]f the relation to the other is a relation to itself, one escapes the bad infinity' of perpetual and mere accumulating finitude. On the final day of the seminar, Debord writes that 'Hegel only wants to understand a world that makes itself', that is, through the inner unity of its exterior *Erscheinungen*.

The truth of *Erscheinung* is the essential relation between its two worlds, a unity by which each immanently references the other. For Hegel, the essential relation will assume three distinct forms: a relation between whole and parts, force and its expression and inner and outer. It is only through the final relation of inner and outer that the inequality (*Ungleichheit*) characteristic of the duplicitous world will collapse a complete commensurability between *Erscheinung* and essence. This full commensurability will assist then in the transition into an analysis of the spectacle as a unity of identity-in-difference whose self-equality gives further logical determinacy to the centrality of exchange-value as essential to the *Erscheinung* of the spectacle.

One of Debord's most cited theses from *The Society of the Spectacle* is the fourth: 'The spectacle is not a collection of images; rather, it is a social *relationship* between people that is mediated by images' (1995: §4; emphasis added). It is through the dynamic of essential *relation* at the conclusion of Hegel's section on *Erscheinung* that this identification of the spectacle as relation can receive its full meaning, particularly as the central feature of the spectacle is that its truth does not resides within a concealed interiority but strictly through the movement of exteriority that is internal to an inverted supersensible world. We move then directly to the essential relation between inner and outer in the *Wesenslogik*. The inner ground of appearance is here coupled with its outer existence. However, again, it is the unity of each side that is crucial. 'What is internal is also present externally, and vice versa; appearance does not show anything that is not within essence, and there is nothing in essence that is not manifested' (Hegel 1991b: 209).

This section, in an anticipatory fashion, provides the conceptual resources of the spectacle's *revelatory* character. The inner and outer of the spectacle have identical content, a fundamental equivalence between essential reality and its manifest and diverse *Erscheinungen*. The nature of the spectacle's interiority is to bare all, to *sich offenbaren*, and to exhibit reality as speciously self-evident. In a word, externality is as much this totality as is its inward reflection into itself. At last we find in *Erscheinung* 'the revealing [*Offenbaren*] of its essence, and this essence, accordingly, consists simply in being self-revealing [*sich Offenbaren*]' (Hegel 2010: 464). However, as will be seen, the visibility of reality as *Erscheinung* is the visibility of a manifest inner necessity, a revelation progressively disclosed by the category of actuality. In a word, *to actualize is to make visible* insofar as identity is *seen* as an inner unity of difference. Only there will the spectacle as the interiority of *Erscheinung* made manifest shine as an identity of identity and difference with the exterior of *Erscheinung*.

Essence is the immanent organization of appearances. 'The whole logic of essence is the logic of appearance; being has entirely become *appearance* and we can just as well say "this is only appearance," and "everything is in appearance"' (Hyppolite 1997: 173). For this, Hegel's *Wesenslogik* is indispensible for the logic of the society of the spectacle: 'Diversities and contrasts among such phenomena are the appearances of the spectacle – the appearances of a social organization of appearances that needs to be grasped in its general truth' (Debord 1995: §10). The essence of the spectacle is not to be grasped as an underlying or common thread, denominator or abstract universality that somehow accords with a manifold of differentiated immediacies and sensible appearances. Instead, as a *Wesenslogik*, the concept of the spectacle is the very unifying structure of particular appearance-forms in their very exteriority and is thereby afforded explanatory power as the essential of manifold appearances against their sheer multiplicity, a position derived from a tripartite analysis of *Erscheinung* as law, world and relation. The totality of the sensuous manifold turns into its own opposite as a result of its own relationality. Within the spectacle, exteriority is but the inverted world of essential unity that has given to sensuous reality its coherence. Having thereby distinguished how the spectacle refers to no more than that what it appears to be, we can now proceed to the second determination of its spectacular logic.

The spectacle as a reign of commensurability

In order to satisfy the second central determination of the spectacle as a *Wesenslogik*, we need to examine how it is that the doctrine on the whole is increasingly constitutive of what we might call a second-order determination of exchangeability for which its couplets are progressively commensurate with one another. This development is also at once an accelerating interiorization of otherness untenable with categories of Hegel's *Seinslogik*. However, before proceeding to analyse such moments of selfsameness as a dynamic of the spectacle, it is necessary to return to the category of indifference as a guiding thread through which the unitary structure of the spectacle is composed, specifically in accordance with Marx's critique of political economy, from which, as we have seen in chapter 3, the concept of the spectacle in part derives.

Indeed, the problem of indifference riddles the *Wesenslogik* on the whole and is not simply its embarkation. Everywhere it appears, indifference – as the German term *Gleichgültigkeit* indicates – also invokes a reign of identity, a commensurability that comes close to swallowing differentiation *in toto*. Now, if identity, as the rudimentary logic of exchange-value, is also the *movement of indifference*, we must recognize how exchange-value assumes the form of indifference. This takes place most starkly within *Contribution to a Critique of Political Economy* and *Grundrisse* where Marx gives to the autonomous movement of exchange-value the predication of indifference at almost every level of the particular forms of value: commodities are indifferent 'to all religious, political, national and linguistic barriers' (1987: 384); money as universal equivalent is indifferent to everything under its 'GENERAL POWER OF PURCHASING' (1987: 215); capital is indifferent to any use-values 'and can with equal indifference adopt or shed any of them as its incarnation' (1987: 84). Fundamentally, the propensity of indifference extracted from the critique of political economy is the result of the identity of exchange (1987: 472; see also Marx 1986: 94).

As we have seen throughout this book through various registers, the spectacle inheres within itself a speculative logic of identity of identity and non-identity. Its *Identitätszwang* was most closely rooted in the critique of political economy within chapter 3, wherein certain determinations of money, specifically as, in following Marx's descriptions, the *visible incarnation* or *Reflexionbestimmung* of the totality of commodities were argued to comprise the spectacle. How then to locate this structural fundament of identification – whether it is between competing ideologies, exchangeable commodities or the true and the false – requires a closer look at the *Reflexionsbestimmungen* of the *Wesenslogik*, specifically with an eye towards how this logic renders all otherness as an internal differentiation of itself.

Debord considered identity to be the deadening core of Hegel's philosophy. In a statement on Vaneigem's resignation from the SI, Debord quotes a passage from the *Wesenslogik* describing the benumbing of identity in distinction to the category of contradiction:

> ...what Hegel, in *The Science of Logic*, called 'the most profound and most essential quality,' which is *contradiction*. 'In relating to it, actually, identity is only the determination of what is simple and immediate, of what is dead, insofar as contradiction is the source of all movement, of all life. This is only to the extent that a thing includes within itself a contradiction that shows itself to be active and alive.'
>
> 2004a: 317⁹

If, as we maintain, the spectacle also inheres a logic of identity, one which exudes otherness and difference out of itself as a world of *Erscheinungen*, then closer examination into that Hegelian concept of identity, which contains differences within itself, is warranted.

As a *Reflexionbestimmung*, Hegel names identity as a self-relation, an 'equality with itself' established by the self-negating negative of reflection. In the development of essence heretofore, otherness has 'disappeared into pure self-equality' and through the inner repelling activity of reflection, essence has become 'simply self-*identity*' (Hegel 2010: 356). As a result, identity contains otherness within its own self-equality or is the process of 'the disappearing of otherness' (2010: 361). In and through its negative, identity is therefore also *difference*. Wholly self-relational, difference within identity is the self-negating negation and is as such not a difference from something *else* – or akin to the otherness (*Anderssein*) found in the *Seinslogik* – but a difference not mediated through externality or through the otherness of existence but the difference of reflection itself. As a differing from itself, difference is thereby still identity: an identity *of* difference.

Identity has turned into its opposite, whereby everything is both identical to itself only through differentiation. Reciprocally, there is no identity without difference and no difference without identity. However, a relation of self-related identities, which Hegel calls *diversity*, returns us to the problem of indifference. It is in fact diversity's central defect. Reflection as the essence of things must assume the form of diversity insofar as it constitutes both identity and difference 'as two self-relating, self-identical moments that differ because they are *separately* self-relating' (Houlgate 2011: 150). Diversity is a *breaking apart* of identity into *indifferent* differentiations. An external reflection constitutive of diversity dirempts itself into the categories of *equality* (*Gleichheit*) and *inequality* (*Ungleichheit*). External identity is accorded the category of equality while external difference that of inequality. As a relation of external reflection, differences can only find affinity, and not any immanent identity, through the activity of *comparison (vergleicht)*. Comparison is a process which 'moves back and forth from likeness to unlikeness and from unlikeness to likeness' (Hegel 2010: 364).

Equality and inequality thereby comprise a '*negative unity*' for which likeness and unlikeness disappear into each other. Equality and inequality, initially the determinations of *external reflection*, have therefore deepened as the self-equality of reflection developed through the unity of identity and difference assuming the form of diversity. They comprise 'a difference which is no difference' (Hegel 2010: 365). We find then here in the *Reflexionbestimmung* a logic of identity that, despite the heteronomous threat of diverse differentiation, contains difference within itself. In a word, it is the *commensurability* of all sides that prevents external reflection from fracturing everything into a heteronomous manifold.

The movement of reflection within the spectacle is given illustration within issue 10 of *IS* (1966). In the short article entitled '"Le Monde" as Reflection', the French newspaper is first satirically lauded for its 'impartiality [and] respect for the facts' and by offering an 'intellectual valorization for the majority of its readers'. The respect commanded by *Le Monde* is, however, given critical determinacy precisely for its 'absolute respect for facticity', for what merely exists and for its 'benevolent comprehension' of the already accomplished. Its 'politeness beyond ideological conflict' recognizes all perspectives as 'fundamentally equal'. *Le Monde* is for the SI a transparent reflection of the world and this is precisely its spectacular function:

> The eager recognition of all powers at once is the best expression of this cynicism and naivety that are inseparable from impartial information. The realism of *Le Monde* is to admit that all powers are equal; futility is to believe that its lucidity for detail is better than that of any power ... *Le Monde* is precisely of the position of this educated and respectful spectator that it helps to train among its readers.
>
> IS 1997: 478

There is an overwhelming *apologia* to the commensurability of the spectacle in its movement of reflection as the identity of identity and non-identity. In the words of Asger Jorn, '[e]quivalence is the complete elimination of any notion of situation, of event' (IS 1997: 229)

Within reflection, equality and inequality are each a 'shining into the other' (Hegel 1991b: 184). Ultimately, however, it is *Gleichheit* that reigns supreme and whose logic of commensurability tightens even further within the progressive development of the *Wesenslogik*. For example, within the subsequent concept of opposition and its correlate categories of the positive and negative, each side can only refer to itself by referring to its other. For Hegel, the determination of this mediation is a certain *commensurability*: 'to each side, therefore, there belongs indeed one of the two determinacies, the positive or the negative; but the two can be interchanged [*verwechselt werden*], and each side is such as can be taken equally as positive or negative' (2010: 369). As Debord remarks in his notes on the *Phenomenology of Spirit*, 'the logic of opposition to reconciliation must be a problem that is capable of being contiguous'.[10] Indeed, Hegel continues to describe each side as not simply separate but wholly interchangeable.

The *Wesenslogik* progressively abandons the integrity of all external otherness in which the *Reflexionsbestimmungen* develop categorial couplets that are the reflective shining of one into the other as essential determinations. We have then satisfied the second central determination of the spectacle as a *Wesenslogik*: it is a unity modelled on the *Reflexionbestimmung* of exchange-value, which, as a totality of identity-in-difference, self-equality and commensurability, includes otherness within itself. Indeed, the spectacle admits of otherness, but always in relief. In his seminar notes for Hyppolite's lectures, Debord indicates an understanding of difference with respect to the *Seinslogik* and the *Wesenslogik*. For the former, he writes that, 'the qualities [of *Dasein*] are at the same time their limit ... not an external determination ... *Dasein* is identical to its limit'. As he continues with respect to difference in the *Wesenslogik*, 'in positive appearance ... a finite thing is not only what it seems to be. What happens to it does not happen only from the outside, but from within ... *Dasein* encountering alterity and alteration finds the problem of being for itself and this is already the immediate beginning of quantity [very difficult problem].'

The *Identitätszswang* of the spectacle is a determination of its essence which expounds internal and equiprimordial differentiation. We will reserve examining the specific inner differentiations of the spectacle until the next chapter, namely in accordance with the spectacle as a *Begriffslogik*. It only here needs to be emphasized how crucial the identity of equivalence is for the speculative logic of the spectacle, particularly with regard to the dialectic of *Erscheinung*. This came to the fore within our second chapter, in the structure of solicitation as an exchange-relation for which Hegel's analysis of force attempted to grasp the problem of internal relations as the interiority of sensible appearances. Within both the *Phenomenology of Spirit* and the *Wesenslogik*, the identity structure of solicitation emerges as the unity of variability as well as the exteriorization of that unity into a manifold, an inversion of the supersensible. However, unlike the 'Force and the Understanding' section of the *Phenomenology of Spirit* examined in our second chapter, the *Wesenslogik* provides the complete and purified sublation of the façade and its *Jenseits* within the movement of appearances devoid of any commonplace presuppositions or *Vorstellungen*. We are then, unlike within the *Phenomenology of Spirit*, in a better position to grasp the spectacle as a logic of appearances without a contingent prejudice of exteriority, as speculative of a higher order.

For the spectacle as a *Wesenslogik*, here emerges a totality wrought with a commensurability between its opposed sides, which, as we have seen from its dialectic of interiority and exteriority, 'is an inner that has equally become an outer but, in this outer, is not something-that-has-become or something-that-has-been-left-behind but is self-equal [*selbst gleich*]' (Hegel 2010: 460). The spectacle is as such immanent to its exterior appearance-forms, a logical structure demonstrable only through the centrality of identity-in-difference of commensurable equivalence.

A fair portion of Debord's understanding of identity and equivalence as a logic of exchange-value derives from Lefebvre's *The Sociology of Marx*. Throughout his marginalia on the book, 'pour SduS' constantly appears. On one of his index cards, the word 'equivalence' underlined and heading the subsequent comments comes to inform his notes on the twofold nature of the commodity as both a use-value and exchange-value. Here Lefebvre is examining the equation for which x quantity of commodity A is equal to quantity y of commodity B: $xA = yB$. Lefebvre follows this development and states that '[t]hings internally split in this way become related and equivalent to other things' (1982b: 95). Debord's notes draw attention to the way in which the internal differentiation of the form of the commodity makes explicit its universal commensurability with all other commodities. Debord's notes continue with Lefebvre's description on how this inner relation assumes the form of a sensuous *Erscheinung*.

If the relation between equivalence and appearance as constitutive of the society of the spectacle requires theoretical derivation out of Hegel's *Wesenslogik*, the argument currently underway, its explicit affirmation becomes clear in the writings of fellow SI member Raoul Vaneigem. Written and published the same year as Debord's *The Society of the Spectacle*, Vaneigem's *The Revolution of Everyday Life* (*Traité de savoir-vivre à l'usage des jeunes générations*) has admittedly not aged nearly as well as the former. The book, whose early drafts were published in *IS* issues 7 and 8 under the title 'Basic Banalities', adopts many of the themes of Debord's concept of the spectacle, however here they are predominantly accompanied by a belated *Lebensphilosophie* whose romantic lyricism affirms the primacy of subjective experience, spontaneity and poetry as the bulwark against spectacular domination. Less diagnostic than Debord's book, Vaneigem's work can at once be regarded as both sharing affinity with *The Society of the Spectacle* but also exhibiting important distinctions, even antitheses, in its critical theory.[11]

The concept of *Identitätzszwang* features prominently within Vaneigem's work. Whether through nation, religion or any other communal abstractions, identity is for Vaneigem 'a blood-soaked delusion' (2012: xii). Adaptation to the world through identification adheres to the speculative affirmation of positivity over the negative (2012: 26). It is an 'integration of people into the well-policed universe of things. Which is why the hidden cameras of celebrity are always ready to catapult the most pedestrian of lives into the spotlight of instant fame' (2012: 117). It is to the world of *Erscheinungen* that people affix themselves without remainder, and in 'Basic Banalities', Vaneigem links the development of private appropriation to the domination and organization of appearances that will come to instantiate itself within the society of the spectacle. In its pre-capitalist forms, the servants regards themselves as the 'degraded reflections of the master' (Knabb 2006: 154), while the master identifies with mythical transcendent forces, the represented abstractions of the social totality in which the class society is reproduced. In an analysis remarkably close to Adorno and Horkheimer's *Dialectic of Enlightenment*, this rationalized mimesis is then for Vaneigem fastened through the exchange relation of sacrifice, a unity of alienation whose 'objective (and perverted) harmony is sustained by myth – this term being used to designate the organization of appearances in unitary societies, that is, in societies where slave, tribal or feudal power is officially consecrated by a divine authority and where the sacred allows power to seize the totality' (Knabb 2006: 154)

For Vaneigem's spectacle, such a harmony culminates, through the repetition of images, stereotypes, models and roles, in unprecedented dominance in its reconstituted social unity, 'a showroom of stick figures' whose modes of behaviour 'are simply debased forms of the old ethical categories: knight, saint, sinner, hero, felon, faithful servant, *honnête homme*, etc' (Vaneigem 2012: 111). Their repetitive and indeed industrially frequent iteration through photography, radio, cinema, celebrity, election pageants, magazines, newspapers, television, but also now, it can be said, digital platforms, slogans, lifestyles and catchphrases, constitute individuals, together with the collapse of the great ideologies of yesteryear, into prefabricated personifications of *Erscheinungen* 'so as to constitute a sort of automatic dispenser of ready-made explanations and emotions' (Vaneigem 2012: 111–12). As Vaneigem continues, 'It falls to roles to integrate individuals into the mechanisms of culture; this is a form of *initiation*. It is also the medium of exchange of individual sacrifice, and in this capacity performs a *compensatory* function. And lastly, as a precipitate of separation, roles strive to construct a behavioural unity; in this endeavour they rely on *identification*' (2012: 115). The reflective search for identity, under the society of the spectacle 'degenerates into identification' (2012: 121). Here the *Reflexionbestimmung* of identity and its selfsame commensurability prevails. Indeed, 'what makes capitalist exploitation so repulsive is the very fact that it occurs between "equals"' (2012: 103). Fragmented and socially separated through private labour, individuals become interchangeable, '[a]n epitome of the prosaic' (2012: 75) whose only inner unity becomes the spectacle of common *Identitätzszwang*. The equivalence therein set with the world of *Erscheinungen* dominates the reification of the spectacle:

> What are the traditional 'revolutionaries' doing? They are struggling to eliminate certain distinctions, making sure that no proletarians are any more proletarian than all the others. But what party is calling for the end of the proletariat? ... That's what reification is: everyone and everything falling at an equal speed, everyone and everything stigmatized with an equal value. The reign of equal values has realized the Christian project, but it has realized it outside Christianity (as Pascal surmised) and more importantly, it has realized it over God's dead body, contrary to Pascal's expectations. The spectacle and everyday life coexist in the reign of equal values.
>
> Knabb 2006: 170–1

Despite spectacular divergences, peaceful coexistence along a horizontal social unity is for Vaneigem 'infinitely finite. It creates an unlimited appetite for the absolute' (Knabb 2006: 104). In a word, '[t]here are no gradations in castration' (Knabb 2006: 94), and with Vaneigem's invocation of the absolute, we can move to the category of actuality, the final determination of the spectacle as a *Wesenslogik*.

The optical actuality of the spectacle

For Debord, the full commensurability of the spectacle is achieved only through the category of actuality. We move now to the final central determination of the spectacle as a *Wesenslogik* and are reminded again of the fifth thesis of *The Society of the Spectacle* in which the spectacle is described as a 'weltanschauung that has been actualized' (1995: §5). Let us now turn in brief to what, for Hegel, the category of actuality entails.

The categorial sequence of a thing with properties, a play of soliciting and solicited forces or a dynamic of inner and outer are all attempts to express a relational structure and yet risk regressing into a substratum logic. This all changes with the introduction of the category of actuality. The identity of *Erscheinungen* with interiority is what Hegel calls actuality, the *full illumination* of essential reality. We are now dealing entirely with reality as a totality of inner differentiation. Hegel has given to facticity necessity as a process of formation, both an inner becoming outer and an outer becoming inner.[12] The totality of the world of *Erscheinungen* unfolds only as manifestations of inner necessity and not simply as an aggregated ensemble.

We have surpassed mere existence (*Dasein*) and have introduced actuality (*Wirklichkeit*), a category 'higher than *concrete existence*' (Hegel 2010: 477), which concerns again the problem of identity through differentiation. Here, reflection has turned inward into the determination of identity, which, through itself, transitions into an opposition with difference. This *Reflexionbestimmung* must, however, fully exteriorize in all of its clarity. The flux of *Erscheinungen* has therewith emerged as a process of externalization through which a unity of interiority is fully displayed. Indeed, prior to actuality, it could be said that identity remains *unseen*. It must yet exteriorize itself as a manifestation of its own process to demonstrate the coherence of reality as an absolute self-manifestation. This is precisely what the category of actuality accomplishes and which, as will see, is a structural determination of the spectacle.

In this section of the *Wesenslogik*, Hegel develops the idea of actuality as a manifest necessity through a series of modal terms and substantive relations. However, actuality is also the culmination of the *full transparency* of essence as concrete existence. What began as the immediate albeit incomplete seeming opticality of *Schein*, akin to the mirror image of an essential locus, for which the independence of *Schein* was completely illusory, has, through reflection, become a mirror image less *derivative* of the originary thing itself than a wholly determinate essential manifestation. In this way, the movement of *Schein* remained at first only the existent non-being of essence, or, in the words of Debord, 'inasmuch as individual reality *is not* that it is allowed to *appear*' (1995: §17). *Schein* as the immediacy of non-immediacy was here the absence of an existent presence given existent presence through the seeming of essence. And yet, this progression failed to reconcile the thing in itself with its *visible* properties which were not the showing forth of the thing itself. *Erscheinung* resolved the diremption as the preservation of the unity of the thing in itself and its differentiated properties, acquiring a higher stability of *visibility* as the dispersal of essence as an identity within difference. It is only within actuality, however, that *Erscheinung* becomes the full revelation (*Offenbarung*) of essence, a visibility of a manifest inner necessity. In a word, to actualize is to make the *Wesenslogik* in its entirety visibly transparent. Only as actuality will essence, as the interiority of *Erscheinung*, manifestly shine as an identity of identity and difference with the exterior of *Erscheinung*.

It is through this conclusion of the *Wesenslogik* that the spectacle can be grasped as an essence that strives to bare all, *sich offenbaren*, and to exhibit reality as speciously self-evident. In the penultimate thesis of *The Society of the Spectacle*, Debord makes the point explicit: 'By eagerly embracing the machinations of reformism or making common cause with pseudo-revolutionary dregs, those driven by the abstract wish for immediate efficacity obey only the laws of the dominant forms of thought, and adopt the exclusive viewpoint of *actuality* [*actualité*]. In this way delusion is able to reemerge within the camp of its erstwhile opponents' (1995: §220). The spectacle is only the revealing (*Offenbaren*) of its essence, and this essence, accordingly, consists simply in being self-revealing (*sich Offenbarende*). However, we find within Lefebvre's *The Sociology of Marx* a description of appearances that, without invoking the category of spectacle, nevertheless speaks to Debord's importation of Hegel's concept of actuality as a central determination of the spectacle:

> The various types of social praxis within specific social structures and modes of production give rise to 'representations'. These representations increase or decrease the degree of a given society's 'opacity'. They illumine or obscure the society. Sometimes they illumine it with a false clarity and sometimes they plunge it into shadow or darkness in the name of a doctrine even obscurer than the reality generating it. Social reality, i.e. interacting human individuals and groups, produces *appearances* which are something more and else than mere illusions. Such appearances are the modes in which human activities manifest themselves within the whole they constitute at any given moment – call them modalities of consciousness. They have far greater consistency, let alone coherence, than mere illusions or ordinary lies. Appearances have reality, and reality involves appearances.
>
> 1982b: 62

This is an exceptional passage not simply for the fact that Debord extracted it into his notes. It accomplishes several tasks for elucidating the society of the spectacle as the actuality of the *Wesenslogik*. First, it helps situate the spectacle as a system of appearances along a spectrum of opacity. In this case, however, the spectacle amounts to the extreme pole of such a continuum, a glaring transparency and 'general equivalence for what the entire society can be and can do' (Debord 1970: §49). Second, the passage gestures towards the spectacle as more than mere illusory *Schein*, but as a structure of *manifestation*. Finally, Lefebvre's remarks additionally help locate the appearances of the spectacle as modalities of consistency, terminology that bears directly on the actuality of the spectacle as a *Wesenslogik*.

Within the first moment of actuality, we are no longer dealing with a duplicitous reality – as between the manifold of the phenomenal world and its essential interior. As positivity, it is the exposition of all previous determinations whose finitude are considered only expressions (*Ausdruck*) or copies (*Abbild*) of itself. Thus the 'transparency of the finite' (Hegel 2010: 468) positively asserted by the absolute dissolves into its own medium; 'it is absorbed by that through which it shines' (2010: 468). The absolute of the absolute relation is therefore a process of exposing finitude as copies or images of its own reflected medium. Furthermore, this exposition of the absolute – from absolute identity to attribute and then to mode – is in fact the reflective movement itself in which the absolute '*posits itself as self-equal*' (2010: 471). The *mode* emerges as the absolute's own reflective movement: *a transparent externality pointing only to itself*. Its exteriority is as much its interiority. Here we then find, in the middle of actuality and with regard to the analysis of the spectacle, a precise logical illustration of what the spectacle shows: its content is only the shining forth of itself. As Hegel describes in words which carry directly over the analysis of the spectacle:

> When therefore one asks for a *content* of the exposition, for *what* the absolute manifests, the reply is that the distinction of form and content in the absolute has been dissolved; or that just this is the content of the absolute, *that it manifests itself*... in this way alone is the absolute self-identity which equally is *indifferent towards its distinctions* or is absolute *content*. The content is therefore only this exposition itself.
>
> 2010: 471

Here we find captured the logical structure on how the spectacle is only the manifestation of itself, or how its content is identical to its form. The spectacle is as such only its own exposition, a 'self-bearing movement of exposition' (2010: 471) not propelled by interiority but through its own absolute self-manifestations. It is of course a 'self-illuminating light' but one which gives to itself '*emanation*' in and through differentiated *Erscheinungsformen* of 'unclouded clarity' (*ungetrübten Klarheit*) (2010: 474).

The spectacle as manifestation – whose 'most glaring[ly] superficial manifestation[s]', we can recall, are what Debord calls 'mass media' (1970: §24) – is its own inner necessity made manifest. It has no content save for the manifestation of itself. What is more, the category of manifestation can here be accorded to Debord's use of the category of 'representation', or that which is made to appear as an externalization of essentiality reality which has dispensed with any duplicity. Indeed, Debord utilizes the category of representation frequently within *The Society of the Spectacle* and interpreters are tempted to associate its invocation with a form of duplicitous delegation, political or otherwise. And yet, any such overemphasis on the category of representation would do well to consider a 1973 letter by Debord to his Dutch translator: 'The majority of the quotations from German texts that I employ in *Spectacle* were of course drawn solely from their French translations, either because they would have been reasonably familiar to the readership at that time (the éditions Costes translation in the case of Marx) or because I never found time to tackle the German originals (as in the case of Lukács). You are obviously right to use only the German originals as your guide' (2005: 79). The use Debord made of French categories ought not to overshadow their German origins. For example, regarding the category of representation, its frequent use in the French translation of Lukács' *History and Class Consciousness*, a book of great importance to Debord's concept of spectacle, is in fact the German *Vorstellung*. Now, for Hegel, *Vorstellung* collapses the subject into its predicate and only the latter is made to appear. More specifically, within the *Phenomenology of Spirit*, *Vorstellung* most cogently appears within the 'Religion' section and 'is a mode of knowing that renders the immaterial and the abstract as sensuous, material, and concrete. [It is] an inverted reality and through its sensuous, particular, imagining, produces an inverted consciousness' (Ebert 2014: 1). For Hegel, religion is a mode of thought at the level of the pictorial whose picture-thinking reality is inverted. Here resides the *illusory*, albeit necessary, character of *Vorstellungen*, which are always conveyed through imagery. Spirit becomes represented through a *Vorstellung* in the Christian incarnation of Christ, an embodied and immutable figuration. *Vorstellung* is as such an oversaturation of thought by finitude with an appeal to the purely sensuous and empirical. Yet in the movement of the speculative we find in *Vorstellung* the displayed 'depth of a suprasensuous world' (Hegel 1975: 8). For all this, we can say that Debord's employment of the category of representation is more closely an invocation of exteriority in its claim to self-subsistence. In fact, such *Vorstellungen* are only the manifestations of concrete existence brought to a higher level, that is, to the level of actuality. In this sense, Debord's use of the category of representation is not, as some commentators exclusively focus on (Mattick 2018), invoked in the commonplace usage as a political satellite for constituency. If it were, we would have regressed to the something and other relation of the *Seinslogik*. Instead, we find Debord's use of representation to be an abridged exposition of the necessity for the spectacle to appeal to its own sensuous reality.

Hegel gives to actuality a set of further determinations through the categories of *possibility, contingency* and *necessity*.[13] With this logical structure, we can regard the actuality of the spectacle as decreeing what is possible, a concept that reigns over and beyond mere facticity. The whole of the spectacle in its manifest appearances is its actuality, whose movement returns to itself as a self-determination of its possibility. We find here in the spectacle, Hegel's identity between actuality and possibility, the latter of which depends on the totality of the spectacle's moments of actuality and demonstrate its necessity. As Debord writes, 'Absolute conformism in existing social practices, with which *all human possibilities are identified for all time,* has no external limit ... Here, in order to remain human, men must remain the same' (1970: §130; emphasis added). Hence we find that the possibilities permitted by the spectacle, as internal to its actuality, are but the further expression of a domination by equivalence. While the spectacle then 'expresses what society can do', it is a range of possibility situated within its actualized necessity made manifest. For this, 'the permitted is absolutely opposed to the possible' (1970: §25), or as Debord writes in a 1991 letter, '[i]t is a necessity of the system, which must simply show [*montrer*] that there no longer exist traces of what had sought at one time to oppose it' (2008a: 280).

In Hegel's exposition, the determination of necessity shows itself to be contingency. However, this is a determination that necessity has given to itself. In becoming fully transparent (*durchsichtig*), the form of necessity dissolves the distinction between itself and its content. It is therefore *blind*. This *absolute necessity* is the form of the absolute relation whose differences are of a differentiated actuality. Absolute necessity is blind and '*averse to light*' (Hegel 2010: 488). Its actualities are therefore reflectionless (*scheinlos*). As such, Hegel proceeds to examine the further modal category of *substance* wherein '*blind transition of necessity is rather the absolute's own exposition,* its movement in itself which, in its externalization, reveals itself instead' (2010: 488). Within the category of absolute necessity, however, necessity becomes self-conditioned, a *causa sui* dependent only upon itself. It becomes, in a word, *sighted*.

Essence has exhausted itself in the actuality of appearance: 'what is inner and what is outer' (Hegel 1991b: 213). Difference therein is 'only the *reflective shine* of the movement of exposition'. The self-exposition of the absolute is illuminated as the result of its own positing: 'Just as the *light* of nature is not a something, nor is it a thing, but its being is rather only its shining, so manifestation is self-identical absolute actuality' (Hegel 2010: 489). Absolute necessity therein becomes the expositor (*Auslegerin*) of the absolute. No longer blind, necessity has become fully sighted and transparent. Actuality is progressively then becoming the stage of '*seeing* reality as totality expressive of essence' (Taylor 1975: 280; emphasis added). Crucial for our purposes is the way in which actuality amounts to the most concrete expression of *the visibility of necessity*, a publicity of itself into external reality, the climax of the objective logic. Actuality emerges as the emanation of reason as a pellucid totality of reality, one which, as detailed in the *Begriffslogik*, discloses its own self-differentiation without any shadow of dissimulation.

The spectacle similarly determines the logical structure of contingency and its relation to necessity. Necessity within the speculative is not as such predictive. It is not a determinism for which anything must always not be otherwise by some metaphysical iron law of history. Instead, necessity for Hegel, and as we extract it from the spectacle, is but a determination of actuality, a moment of the *Wesenslogik* which grounds necessity. Debord's twenty-first thesis of *The Society of the Spectacle* condenses this development: 'To the extent that necessity is socially dreamed, the dream becomes necessary. The spectacle is the nightmare of imprisoned modern society which ultimately expresses nothing more than its desire to sleep. The spectacle is the guardian of sleep' (1970: §21). Although a determination of actuality, such comments are not meant to minimize the necessity with which the spectacle offers up its differentiated *Erscheinungen*. Its actuality is inseparably linked to its objectively exerted necessity. As Debord quotes Rudolf Hilferding's *Finance Capital* (1910), 'it is one thing to recognize a necessity, and it is quite another thing to put oneself at the service of this necessity' (1970: §95). Necessity is a service *freely chosen* by the spectacle rather than 'the necessary product of technical development seen as a natural development. The society of the spectacle is on the contrary the form which chooses its own technical content' (1970: §24).

Comments such as these, for which the spectacle is accorded subjective agency, is already a broaching of its *Begriffslogik*. However, before proceeding to the next chapter, it is important to emphasize how the *Wesenslogik* itself arrives there. Hegel comes to define the absolute relation as a relation of *substance* and *accidents*, which will in turn develop into the relation of *causality* and finally into a relation of *reciprocal action*, which will open the door to the *Begriffslogik*.

Substance, differentiated into a totality of accidents, becomes power and mediates difference. It is a power of necessity which transitions into the relation of causality. Necessity has deployed reality as a substance with correlated accidents. We reach now the finale of the *Wesenslogik* for which substance as the totality of accidents offers a version of the unity between inner cohesion and outer multiplicity.

Substance as power dirempts itself into the posited, the *effect*, and its own inward reflection, the *cause*. Causality is as such an activity of presupposing its own conditions. It is no longer a simple substrate but is itself an act upon itself, a *passive substance* as upon an other. This passive substance is therewith doubled. For Hegel, importantly, the passive substance to which causality directs itself therein suffers a violence upon itself. Returning to the power of substance, Hegel offers the following:

> Violence is *the appearance of power*, or *power as external*. But power is something external only in so far as in its action, that is, in the positing of itself, the causal substance is at the same time a presupposing, that is, posits itself as sublated. Conversely, the act of violence is therefore equally an act of power. The violent cause acts only on an other which it presupposes; its effect on it is its negative *self*-reference, or the manifestation of *itself*.
>
> 2010: 501

Crucial for own analysis of the spectacle is how here violence as power is *internal* to the actuality of the *Wesenslogik* as absolute relation. It is an important point to emphasize for drawing a fundamental divergence between Debord's analysis and the aforementioned work of Raoul Vaneigem. First, on the whole, Vaneigem's diagnosis of appearances is saturated with a certain dualism not found within Debord's concept of spectacle. The very structure of *The Revolution of Everyday Life* expresses an external distinction between 'oppression and freedom', with the first outlining 'the perspective of power' and the second, 'the perspective of supersession' (2012: 4). For Vaneigem, '[t]he organization of appearances is a system for shielding the facts' (2012: 106) rather than immanent to manifest facticity. More important, however, is the way in which Vaneigem's diagnosis sets the category of hierarchical power above spectacle as of a higher order concept. As Vaneigem makes explicit, the supersessions are '[t]he spontaneous acts we see everywhere forming against power and *its* spectacle' (Knabb 2006: 162; emphasis added). Here, the spectacle is but one instance of hierarchical social organization. While on occasion offering remarks such as '[p]ower stands or falls with its organization of appearances' (Knabb 2006: 125), it remains the case that for

Vaneigem it is from a metaphysics of power that the spectacle draws its actuality. This is in glaring contrast to the present analysis, for which power, as a dynamic *internal to actuality* as absolute relation, is but a force wielded by the spectacle for its own reproduction. Vaneigem assumes the opposite whereby it is power that *illuminates* the spectacle rather than the spectacle as a *Wesenslogik* of *illumination*. On the contrary, the spectacle is for Debord frequently couched in terms of luminescence. For example, in a 1986 letter to Jaime Semprun, Debord chides what he calls 'a dominant trait of the epoch: there is *nothing new under the sun of the spectacle*'; or that a media personality may 'from the shadows come ... into the light of the spectacle' (2006c: 431).

The spectacle as *Wesenslogik* is nothing less than an actualized structure of *revelation*, 'the revealed mystery of the ultimate goal of production' (Debord 1970: §69). As completely transparent in its actuality, the spectacle harbours no itinerary for manipulation, sophism or persuasion. In this way, 'no one really believes the spectacle [only] *believing what is revealed*!' (Debord 1998: 60–1). To speak of the *actuality* of the spectacle is to pose, in abbreviated form, the identity of its differing appearances as its *essential* structure. The rendering visible of the essential structure does not lie in waiting behind *Erscheinungen* but derives from the very pulsation of those *Erscheinungen*. We may name this process of externalization as the *spectacularization* of the spectacle itself. This is why, for the SI, '[r]evolution [could never be] "showing" [*montrer*] life to people, but bringing them to life' (Knabb 2006: 396). The conceptual tools have now been introduced in order to speak of the spectacle as subject, that is, as entailing its own distinct *Begriffslogik*.

6

The Concept of the Spectacle

To convince is to conquer without conception.

Walter Benjamin

In the previous chapter, we have seen how the *Wesenslogik* offers a fundamental account of the society of the spectacle insofar as the unitary structure of essence provides a thoroughly determinate account of how it is that particular appearances immanently relate to that unifying structure and are not simply an externalized exteriority contingently related to the whole. And yet, the whole of the spectacle requires its own determinate logic as a self-differentiated totality whose parts are not substantively distinct from its overall structure. For this, the *Begriffslogik* becomes the macro social ontology of the society of the spectacle that exhibits internally differentiation as a self-operation. Here, the differences within the spectacle are but the necessary movement of its own archetypal self-developing unity, a perspective not yet broached within the *Wesenslogik* and its reflection relations. We have seen how the spectacle as a *Wesenslogik* concerns the relation between appearance and essence as a necessary and inner connection, or as an identity that contains differentiation within itself. Yet, if this speculative structure concludes as a substance which is in fact only *self*-differentiating, the nature of the spectacle as self-differentiation must be examined. It is here that we turn to Hegel's *Begriffslogik* and how the spectacle self-differentiates itself into a number of concrete and varied appearances that bear speculative unity.

Only as what Hegel calls concept, a self-developing whole, do subject and substance truly appear as a speculative unity. In his writings, Debord frequently accords conceptuality to the spectacle when referring, not to its individual elements but to its totality as a self-development. For example, in his 1979 preface to the fourth Italian edition of *The Society of the Spectacle*, Debord writes that since the book's 1967 publication, 'the spectacle has done nothing but meet more exactly its concept' (2006h: 1465). The spectacle as speculative concept must exhibit a unity which is at once a separation, an identity which preserves the non-identical within itself as a movement of its own internal differentiation. The concept of the spectacle must thereby at once provide a '*coherence of the separate*' (Debord 1995: §105) while demonstrating its transparency to be *self*-articulating. Fulfilling such requirements is to expound the spectacle as a *Begriffslogik*, a logic for which no absolute distinction remains for a reality divided between its appearance and its concept.

Unlike our analysis of the spectacle as a *Wesenslogik*, which proceeded through each of its major moments and determinations, the following procedure will take a different approach with regard to the *Begriffslogik* or the logical form by which, it will be argued, the spectacle comprehends itself conceptually and in doing so procures concrete self-differentiation and external opposition. We will first offer a note on how the spectacle is most suitably examined within Hegel's subjective doctrine insofar as Debord's analysis can be traced back to Marx's comments on capital as an automatic subject. From there, it will be argued that Hegel's *Begriffslogik* logically illustrates the spectacle's most concrete diremptions and how, through Hegel's structural distinctions between universality (*Allgemeinheit*), particularity (*Besonderheit*) and individuality or singularity (*Einzeinheit*), the concept of the spectacle, in the most precise meaning of *Begriff*, can be grasped as a syllogistic structure, a self-differentiating and self-externalizing totality. Here, examples of unities of opposites perfectly willing to tolerate partisan class power and other *membra disiecta* so long as the speculative system remains dynamically reconstituting its whole will be elucidated. These oppositions will be explored as the relation between work and leisure, state and economy, town and country, and diffuse and concentrated spectacle. Concluding remarks will be offered on how the spectacle's *Begriffslogik* gives it full rational and spiritual coherence as a critical theory of society.

The spectacle as automatic subject

In order to elucidate the spectacle as a *Begriffslogik*, we must first emphasize the *self-acting* nature of its concept as a universal substance whose content is objectively and immanently determined. We may cite here the affinity with which the spectacle appears as, in the words of Marx, something akin to an 'automatic subject'. For Marx, capital as value-in-process is described as follows within *Capital*, volume 1:

> [M]oney and the commodity represent only different modes of existence [*verschiedne Existenzweisen*] of value itself, the money its general mode, and the

commodity its particular, or, so to say, disguised [*verkleidete*] mode. It is constantly changing from one form to the other without thereby becoming lost, thus becoming an automatic subject [*automatisches Subjekt*]. If now we pin down the specific forms of appearance [*Erscheinungsformen*] which self-expanding value successively assumes in the course of its life, we arrive at the following explanation: capital is money, capital is commodities. In truth, however, value is here the subject of a process in which, while constantly assuming the form in turn of money and commodities, it changes its own magnitude, differentiates itself by throwing off surplus value from itself considered as original value, and thus valorizes itself independently. For the movement in the course of which it adds surplus-value is its own movement, its valorization is therefore self-valorization [*Selbstverwertung*]. Because it is value, it has acquired the occult quality of being able to add value to itself. It brings forth living offspring, or, at the least, lays golden eggs ... value now in the circulation M–C–M['], or the circulation of capital, suddenly presents itself as an independent substance, endowed with a motion of its own, passing through a life process of its own, in which money and commodities are mere forms which it assumes and casts off in turn.

1996: 164–5; translation amended

For Marx, the M–C–M' circuit of capital as self-valorization is a reflexive unity with itself and, as subject, is a movement through *Erscheinungsformen*, which presupposes its own results. Entering into relations with itself, capital is in this way self-presuppositioning, instantiating its own *Erscheinungsformen* as requisite moments of its own self-development as a totality. Here, for example, individual capitals, governed by the equalization of profits rates and competition, are but individualizations of capital in general as a universality that has particularized itself. While the identity between the categories of universality, particularity and individuality will receive more attention shortly, it is worth here only recalling that for Marx, the higher category of universality or of capital in general, as it appears within *Capital*, volume 3, and in the *Grundrisse*, speaks to, in the words of a contemporary French communist theory journal, a 'necessary relation of particular capitals among themselves which differentiate themselves from it and the differentiation of this relation is a necessary moment of the existence of the reproduction, at their own risk and peril, of particularities and individualities *as capital*' (Théorie Communiste 2010)

From here, we can draw out capital's fetish-character from its general law as an automatic subject that not only self-differentiates into individual capitals, but also into what Marx calls its personifications as capitalist and labourer. The former is but 'capital personified [*personifiziertes*]. His soul is the soul of capital';

the latter also a mere personification of abstract labour time (1996: 241, 251). As Marx elaborates with regard to the figure of the capitalist, it is but

> ...the conscious representative [*Träger*] of this movement, the possessor of money becomes a capitalist. His person, or rather his pocket, is the point from which the money starts and to which it returns. The expansion of value, which is the objective basis or mainspring of the circulation M–C–M, becomes his subjective aim, and it is only in so far as the appropriation of ever more and more wealth in the abstract becomes the sole motive of his operations, that he functions as a capitalist, that is, as capital personified and endowed with consciousness and a will.
>
> 1996: 163–4; see also 10, 95

As with Hegel's *Begriffslogik*, implicit in the concept of capital is the impulse to posit its own presuppositions, reproducing all the requisite concrete *Erscheinungsformen* of its own existence in its own movement of self-determination, a process through which the concrete labour process appears as but a moment in the development of self-valorization. It is only through these Hegelian conceptual dynamics that, for Marx, labour can logically be both the result and presupposition of capital (Russell 2015).

Capital is in sum its own absolute resource, giving to itself specification most crucially in the form of labour-power as the origin of surplus value. Its fetish-character subsists at all levels of its individuated relations, a confirmation witnessed in the movement of capital in general as a process of differentiation whose parts are but the concrete self-subsistence of its moving universality. These *Erscheinungsformen*, whether conflicting classes or competing capitals, are the social forms mediated in and through capital in general. Just as labour can only become productive once integrated into the valorization process, so does it only become social through the fetish-character of the exchange relationship. The fetishistic-character of the forms of value refers to the appearance of objectivity possessed by the social characteristics of labour as embodiments of abstraction. Fetishized social relations only exist as *Erscheinungsformen* of value-in-process and are not inversions of a pre-existing and untarnished substratum.

Following suit, for Debord the spectacle is also an autonomous subject that procures its own inverted reality, as having its own overarching subjective agency. Indeed, its *Begriff* is the grasping of reality in its movement of actuality whose conceptual externalization is a development of its own process. The spectacle is an extension of the automatic subject of capital and its fetish-character. Within chapter 3, we found the spectacle as inheriting the autonomy of exchange-value insofar as the money-form of value propounds a unity of all differences, or an identity of identity and non-identity between all commodities with its own independent and objective existence. The spectacle thereby derives from money a principle of unity which incorporates and reproduces differences without fully extinguishing them. Here the developing autonomy of exchange becomes not merely paradigmatic but constitutive of the society of the spectacle. And yet still further, as a society, the money-form as *Gemeinwesen* brought us to the relation between the spectacle and capital. Here money as a unity-in-difference is brought to a higher level as capital emerges as a structure in which the commodity and money are themselves unified in their differences. Through the previous analysis of the spectacle as it derives from the logical movement and increasing autonomy of exchange-value, its relation to capital emerged as the *becoming visible* – derived from the money-form of value – of the unity of appearances, that is, the mode of appearance of society unified under capital. It is here that '[s]ociety in its length and breadth becomes capital's faithful portrait' (Debord 1995: §50). The spectacle as 'socially organized appearance' (Debord 1970: §10) can thereby be contrasted with capital as a principle of organization that no longer requires any concealment as constitutive of its own actuality as a *Wesenslogik*.

Harbouring no secrets about what it is in the very generation of actuality, the spectacle nevertheless inherits the fetish-character of the forms of value as procures an inverted world. The fetish-character of the economy entails a 'principle [that] is absolutely fulfilled in the spectacle, where the perceptible world is replaced by a set of images that are superior to that world yet at the same time impose themselves as eminently perceptible' (Debord 1995: §36). In its very transparency it gives justification and legitimation to existing society. It is Marx's fetish-character *sans* its 'secret'. It is the economy become so autonomous so as to inaugurate a form of domination that only needs to give translucent emphasis to the reigning actuality, itself structured by commensurable appearance-forms that, as a totality, engages in 'an uninterrupted monologue of self-praise' (Debord 1995: §24). Further, as a concept which is entirely self-presuppositioning, the spectacle 'is essentially tautological, for the simple reason that its means and its ends are identical ... cover[ing] the entire globe, basking in the perpetual warmth of its own glory' (1995: §13). As a totality, value can also be grasped tautologically, that is, with no purpose outside of itself and its process of self-valorization. The spectacle inherits this dimension with its entirely self-referential prerogative. It therefore becomes the transparent model of everyday life within capitalist society. Insofar as the movement of value, in its concrete instantiation of its own abstract directives, establishes material content as the appearance of itself, '[t]he spectacle's form and content are [correspondingly] identically the total justification of the existing system's conditions and goals' (Debord 1970: §6). However, to give full conceptual determinacy to the society of the spectacle as subject, one which yields its own immanent concrete differentiations, it is necessary to examine its *Begriffslogik* more closely and assess how is it that the concreteness of the spectacle logically derives from its concept.

The concreteness of the concept

The spectacle as concept gives truth and verification to its finite appearance-forms as moments of its own self-development. With its substantive self-identity and immanent determinacy, its totality, according to Hegel's logic, is now *free*. Further, for Hegel, as 'the principle of all life' in which it both encloses all content within itself while releasing it, the concept 'is what is utterly concrete' (Hegel 1991b: 236), an achievement procured through its own development throughout the *Science of Logic*. Indeed, for Hegel, it is only within the *Begriffslogik* that an unprecedented level of concretion makes its appearance, 'precisely because it contains Being and Essence, and hence all the riches of both these spheres, within itself in ideal unity' (1991b: 237). While common sense might customarily associate the notion of a concept with that which takes flight into abstraction, or that which couldn't be further away from the real, Hegel's concept of the concept develops concrete reality out of itself. It is not simply a content of subjective representation or *Gedankendingen* but that which gives to all finite determinateness and differentiation a structure of coherence and inner necessity and, in so doing, deploys the world. In a word, Hegel, in the final doctrine, demonstrates the necessarily conceptual structure of all actuality. The *Begriffslogik* procures reality out of itself, a universality that particularizes itself and an inner necessity generative of externality as its manifestation. In these developments, the *Begriffslogik* expounds its own opposite as an immanent othering and therewith exposes a self-articulating totality of both subjectivity and objectivity as the exteriorization of interiority.

Like the other doctrines, the *Begriffslogik* progressively discloses differentiations; not, however, through a *passing over into another* such that can be found in the *Seinslogik*, or in a *reflective shining* as in the *Wesenslogik*. Instead, Hegel names the procession of the *Begriffslogik* as a *development* in which the nature of the concept *shows itself*. This development proceeds into three distinct moments: the subjective concept, the objective concept and the idea, the final of which Hegel expounds as the complete unity of subject and object, or of concept and reality as '*self-unveiled truth*' (Hegel 2010: 527). The concept derives reality from itself and all such forms of the concept are thereby for Hegel '*the living spirit of what is actual*; and what is true of the actual is only *true in virtue of these forms, through them* and *in them*' (Hegel 1991b: 239). Yet, the precise manner in which the concept generates reality out of itself, or '[t]he *derivation* of the real from the concept' (Hegel 2010: 522) requires elucidation through the predominant moments of its development as subjectivity, objectivity and idea. Through this process, reality will emerge as the concept's own determination, and in so doing, the concept categorizes itself as categorizing its other.

Within his seminar notes for Hyppolite's spring 1967 lecture on Hegel's philosophy, Debord divides the *Wesenslogik* into the categories of mediation, reflection and relation. He then writes that the *Begriff*, while perhaps appearing immediately, is nevertheless the 'mediation of the immediate' or 'the truth of the world'. Debord remarks here that both the *Seinslogik* and the *Wesenslogik* 'are false in their disposal [*enlèvement*]'. Indeed, the concept is the internalization of both being and essence, a category of the self-developing whole that, through the *Begriffslogik*, exhibits greater determinate coherence than the reflection determinations: 'the whole as essential unity, is to be found only in the *concept*' (Hegel 2010: 388). The *Begriff* of the spectacle thinks the possibility of objects and relations, having integrated both the logic of being and essence. Only in the concept will the finite receive its due as a moment or appearance of the self-developing whole, itself a progressive unfolding which will give to life itself its rational coherence. As Debord synoptically provides a description of this development,

> The *concept* of the spectacle brings together and explains a wide range of apparently disparate phenomena. Diversities and contrasts among such phenomena are the appearances of the spectacle – the appearances of a social organization of appearances that needs to be grasped in its general truth. Understood on its own terms, the spectacle proclaims the predominance of appearances and asserts that all human life, which is to say all social life, is mere appearance.
>
> 1995: §10; emphasis added

The *Begriffslogik* is as such not an abstract realm of ideas with only a mere correspondence relation to reality whose universality only gestures towards the particularities that comprise the empirical world. Reality becomes a moment in the development of the concept since, as a determinacy of *Dasein*, it is what allowed for deeper determinations to rise to the surface. The reality of the spectacle's being has given way to the self-movement of the spectacle as concept.

We find within Hegel's subjective doctrine a conceptual structure of reality, one not empirically derived, yet which gives to empirical reality structural determinations. Through the *Begriffslogik* we then reach, after having traversed its physiology, the truly concrete of the spectacle, 'not as a chaotic conception of a whole, but a rich totality of many determinations and relations' (Marx 1986: 37). Indeed, as Marx continues in his introduction to the *Grundrisse*, '[t]he concrete is concrete because it is a synthesis of many determinations, thus a unity of the diverse' (1986: 38). As Hegel prefigures Marx's rendering of the concrete in his *Introduction to the Lectures on the Philosophy of History*, '[t]he truth of the differentiated is its being in unity. And only through this movement is the unity truly concrete' (1985: 83).[1] Such becomes the case that only through the *Begriffslogik*, the 'concrete is no longer merely phenomenal but is concrete through the unity in the concept of opposites that have determined themselves as moments of the latter' (Hegel 2010: 594). Only as concept does the spectacle as such receive its full concreteness. Conceptual differentiation is at once also a conceptual concretization. As Debord writes in the margins of Papaïoannou's introduction to Hegel's *La Raison dans l'histoire*, the spectacle is 'rooted in the development of "the science of the finite"'.[2] We will momentarily examine the most prominent concrete oppositions of spectacular differentiation, a set of experiential appearances or concretizations of the spectacle's self-differentiation. However, before doing so, we must call attention to how Hegel's conceptual architecture of universality, particularity and singularity, a tripartite series of categories which help carry the *Begriffslogik* through to objectivity, appear within Debord's spectacle as concept.

The syllogistic structure of the spectacle as concept

In our introduction, we emphasized that Debord divides the concept of the spectacle into a syllogistic structure: it is at once *all of society* and a *part of society*, each side of which is connected through the spectacle as a *means of unifying society* (1970: §3). With Hegel's *Begriffslogik*, we can now fully cash out this division. It is indeed the concept of Hegel's concept that provides a model for this tripartite division. In the opening of the subjective concept, Hegel provides three essential categories with which to carry the *Begriffslogik* to the culminating idea, each moments of the concept itself that structure its self-differentiation: *universality, particularity* and *singularity*. Their unity, dynamically interpenetrated through the various forms of judgement and syllogism, comprise the whole of the concept in its development into objectivity. The moments of the concept cannot be absolutely separated and it is in the self-developing identity of universality, particularity and singularity that the concept acquires full and transparent concretion. While the details of this development cannot be given their full elaboration here, we can in brief remark that the universal as substance culminating the *Wesenslogik* proceeds to particularity, which presupposes universality while including additional determinations in order to further differentiate itself. In this way, particulars are particulars *of* the universal. The universal is therewith both a substance and subject that particularizes itself. Finally within singularity, the universal acquires concrete existence and is the superior embodiment of particularity. In sum, the *Begriffslogik* is a logic of 'unclouded clarity', a subject particularizing itself and therein 'remaining at home with itself in its other' (Debord 1970: 240).

Expounded through the *Begriffslogik* is how universality intrinsically relates to individuality as a necessary development of the concept. Debord was fully cognizant of this logical structure. As he extracts again from Papaïoannou, '[t]his Universal is the infinitely concrete that contains everything and that is everywhere'. The unity of universality cannot be sustained without the plurality of its particulars. At the same time, a plurality dissolves into heterogeneity if universality does not preserve its constitutive character. In a word, the conceptual unity of the universal requires for its determinacy the differentiation into particulars sustained as individual moments or differentiated particulars. As Debord notes from Lefebvre's *Logique Formelle, Logique Dialectique*, '[b]etween the universal and the concrete, it is impossible to suppress the mediation of the *particular*' (1982a: 220). We can here return to the analytic distinction made by Debord in regard to the spectacle as concept at the outset of *The Society of the Spectacle*. There, as was remarked in our introduction, Debord divides the spectacle into a tripartite structure of sectors: it is at once *all of society* and a *part of society*, each side of which is connected through the spectacle as a *means of unifying society* (1970: §3). We find then a syllogistic structure of the spectacle as a *Begriffslogik* for which its universality (all of society) particularizes itself (part of society), whose unity acquires concrete and singular instantiation (means of unifying society). To identify the spectacle with only its individual or particular moments is to adopt a nominalism that fails to grasp what is universal in the real. Similarly, to simply posit the spectacle without references to its own concrete particularization is to accord it the status of a subjective illusion, that is, as thoroughly *begriffslose* or, as is often indulged, equated with mere theatrics. It is only as concept that the spectacle can sustain its totality which renders commensurable its universality, particularity and singularity.

The universality of the society of the spectacle determines itself as both part of society and as a means of its unification. Each moment is but the universality of the spectacle with varying emphasis. As *universal*, the spectacle is self-relating in a manner that proceeds not despite of but in and through its differences. Here, the *particularity* of the spectacle is its universality made explicit as a moment of differentiation. The spectacle as *individuation* is its differentiated particular standing self-subsistent within its universality. Together, the *Begriffslogik* of the spectacle is the process of its own self-differentiation as an objectivity of being characteristic of capitalist society. The entirety of the spectacle is immanent in each of its particular moments, which together, in a seeming relation of opposed and individuated externalities, cohere in and within their differentiation in a speculative unity of the universal. Every moment of the spectacle, while perhaps in their isolation experienced as 'an existential laceration, a conflict of the individual against society' (Cirulli 2006: 8), is nevertheless identical with every other in the harmonious unity of its concept, a copula elevated to a height of synthesis.

For Hegel the universal has to particularize itself and therein maintain the integrity of its content. However, still further, the universal particularized must in turn give to itself concrete instantiation as distinct from other particulars and therewith individualize. For this, taking the categories together as a rational unity of the concept, 'the *look* of any particular thing, no matter how trendy [*branché*] it is supposed to be, derives its swank from the society of the spectacle which controls the entire network' (Debord 1985: 100). It is not that the particular simply contains the universal, or that every part of society merely holds within it as a container some universal propensity. Rather, the universality of the society of the spectacle exhibits itself in and through its particular and determinate moments or individual appearance-forms, the latter of which are, as Debord's extracted notes from Lefebvre's *The Sociology of Marx* remark, 'part of reality' (1982b: 118). We can now examine the spectacle as a structure of self-differentiation into its particulars.

The spectacle as self-differentiation

In the previous chapter, we examined how the categorial relations of the spectacle's *Wesenslogik* developed in such a manner that what is grounded was effectively the result of itself and for which reciprocal causal relations exchange determinations. Yet the residual problem of differentiation remains and is carried over into the *Begriffslogik* as a conceptual development of *self*-differentiation. Unlike the *Wesenslogik*, whereby the moment of positing maintains a distinction from the posited or that *relations* remain explicit between differences, within the *Begriffslogik* we find a *complete identity* between that which is determined and that which does the determining. Differences within the concept derive from its own self-identity. In fact, the concept is for Hegel the very process of self-differentiation. More specifically, it is the *full identity of self-differentiation* and it is this aspect of Hegel's *Begriffslogik* that is structurally exhibited by the society of the spectacle.

The spectacle is a totality, a genetic whole of self-division and self-opposition that reintegrates its individual moments and appearance-forms into itself. As a *Begriffslogik*, it thereby distinguishes itself within itself from itself. Its conceptual self-determination is precisely its ability to ground the totality of actual appearances, both self-determining and self-individuating, thereby overcoming the problem of *differentia* found within the *Wesenslogik*. In the words of Hyppolite, '[b]y comprehending itself, it comprehends all alterity' (1997: 70). The concept of the spectacle has therewith no identity behind or outside of its differences. There is no *deus absconditus* operating in its mode of self-externalization; 'its *differences* are themselves the *whole concept*' (Hegel 2010: 526), one which is purely self-relating and self-identical while remaining internally differentiated.[3]

The concept of the spectacle is not a concept *about* the spectacle, but marks its self-development as actuality, one whose *Arbeit des Begriffs* is immanent to its own reality. However, to conceptualize is to also *identify* and '[t]o be real, identity must manifest itself in difference' (Wright 1983: 25). The concept of the spectacle as such gives itself its own determinacy through the differentiation of its particulars. As Debord makes explicit, 'every concept, as it takes its place on one side or the other, has no foundation apart from its transformation into its opposite ... The concept of the spectacle brings together and explains a wide range of apparently disparate phenomena' (1995: §8, §10). Discovered within speculative identity is *a totally socialized society*, a unity *ens realissimum* for which experience is affirmed in the identity of opposites within the social whole. The spectacle is true only to the extent that it integrates as a moment of itself all that opposes it. It is here then, approaching now the conclusion of our investigation, that we can give to the nomenclature *spectacular* the predication of *internal opposition*. It is a dynamic summariy albeit inadvertently captured by Marx in *The Poverty of Philosophy* for which in 'the yes becoming no, the no becoming yes, the yes becoming both yes and no, the no becoming both no and yes, the contraries balance, neutralise, paralyse each other' (1976d: 164).

This process of dialectical reversals as a constitutive element of the spectacle is given concrete illustration by Debord and the work of the SI. Internal opposition is the spectacle's most incisive and formidable cultivation, a propensity that exceeds in its critical purchase the simple dichotomy invoked by proclamations of 'recuperation'. Despite the frequency with which the SI employs the category of 'recuperation', it is a shorthand that doesn't do justice to the concept of the spectacle. Emergent in the postwar period and basically synonymous with 'corruption', 'recuperation' is a notion that always presupposes the absolutization of exteriority and idealization of opposition. It is a military simile that has impoverished the vernacular of critique to great lengths. Recuperation is the dualistic ideology of resignation and defeat, a terrain in which the manoeuvre of eluding capture is always possible, but never successful. Here, equal pay and exploitation, or a prosperous healthcare system and police brutality, are each purportedly couplets whose independent poles couldn't be further apart, rather than individuated moments within a single totality. Yet in this way, 'the theory of recuperation has always been recuperated' (Dupont 2009: 244). In the spectacle we find instead 'the "peaceful coexistence" of reigning lies' (Knabb 2006: 192). It is this spectacular mode of internal opposition that ought to be expounded in a critical theory of the spectacle, one through which 'official capitalism had the greatest interest in upholding the pretense of its adversary' (Dupont 2009: 240). Here, domination is situated not within an irreducible opposition of enmity between subject and object but within their seamless and comprehensive identity. It is in this way that the spectacle's 'highest ambition . . . is still to turn secret agents into revolutionaries, and revolutionaries into secret agents' (Debord 1998: 11).

Spectacular unity, which is at once a separation of internal opposition and self-externalization, subsists as an identity which preserves the non-identical within itself. Often forewarned by the SI was as such not to 'get caught up in the spectacle of *opposition*' (Knabb 2006: 457). The externalization of the spectacle's concept therewith registers what can be described as inclusionary exclusions, placations that on their surface appear as external to the society but are in fact wholly immanent yet generated as an exteriority. Such a tendency becomes an explicit concern for Debord in a 1985 posthumously published article on immigration in France, 'Notes on the "Question of Immigrants"', wherein the alleged exteriority of foreigners is as external to society as environmental pollution and detritus: both are but the immanent exteriorization lambasted as an external threat. As the article begins:

> As is the case with every matter raised *openly* in present-day society, everything is false in the 'immigrant question' ... Should we assimilate them or 'respect cultural diversity'? A false and absurd choice ... And the French themselves can hardly be said to be much better off. Wretched new surroundings and a wholly misguided grasp of everything having brought the entire planet down to the same level, the French, who have gone along with all this without much of a fight (1968 aside), are scarcely in any position to say that they no longer feel at home *because of immigrants*! They do indeed have grounds for no longer feeling at home since in this horrible new world of alienation there is nobody else *apart from immigrants*.
>
> 2006d: 1588–92

Assimilation becomes a superfluous political category within a society integrated and unified through a fragmentation not without the propensity to equalize everything. What assumes the appearance of exteriority is but an internal moment in the self-development of the whole.

In the mid-1980s, Debord contributed three unsigned articles to the journal *Encyclopedie des Nuisances*. For the eleventh issue, in 1987, Debord composed the entry 'Abolir'. One of his more literary writings, there we find a sketch of the various differentiations of social life rendered commensurate within the spectacle, a levelling in which, sounded in its infancy by bourgeois civil equality against the rights and the privileges of the nobility and clergy, distinction itself is undermined:

> The abolition of the town/country separation has been attained by the simultaneous collapse of both. The work/diversion separation is undone when work becomes so massively unproductive and inept (in the derisory 'tertiary sector') and when diversion becomes a boring and tiring economic activity. The inequalities in culture have been abolished almost everywhere and for almost everyone with the new illiteracy – the old project of the suppression of ignorance has been transformed by *suppression of the ignorance deprived of diplomas*.
>
> Debord 1987: 245–6

It is the fundamental speculative self-identity of the spectacle as a *Begriffslogik* that these comments bring to the fore, an identity-in-difference that externalizes itself as a moment of its own self-development.

The spectacle as *Wesenslogik* was necessary in order to grasp it as a *Begriffslogik* insofar as the opposition discovered within essence is integral to the self-differentiation of the concept, that is, for the way in which the concept of the spectacle expounds its various *Verdoppelungen*. These oppositions are not therefore dualities, a series of couplets external to one another.[4] If they were, the spectacle would not retain its inner unity and the opposing duplications would cease to attain determinacy as moments of the whole that is the society of the spectacle which divides itself and unifies itself in its division. Each side exists only in its relation to its other, so that the spectacle acquires the complete self-determinacy in its self-division.

It is important here to emphasize that the internal oppositions of the spectacle are not simply empirical oppositions, that is, each mere species of a single genus called spectacle so that the immanence of their opposition falls away. Just as the truth of the concept is not dependent on any prior sensual or more genuine reality, we are not dealing here with a simple movement of comparison characteristic of an aggregated diversity for which self-sustained positive existents externally relate. Similitude and dissemblance cannot do justice to how each side of the *Verdoppelung* essentially relate. Rather, the internal self-differentiation of the spectacle comprises a concrete unity that identifies itself in its differentiation while differentiating in and through identity. It is for this reason that we are here dealing with the speculative oppositions of the spectacle: surmounting external reflection, it is a self-opposition that procures distinctions of itself from itself. Difference emerges as internal difference for which each side reflectively shines through its opposite without a separated interiority. Let us now traverse the most pronounced and concrete internal oppositions found within Debord's critical theory of the spectacle: work and leisure, state and economy, town and country, and diffuse and concentrated spectacle.

Unity of work and leisure

Towards the end of the first chapter of *The Society of the Spectacle*, the relation between work and leisure is examined as part of a unity of everyday life under the spectacle. It is a critique appearing frequently throughout the writings of Debord and the SI, wherein leisure – an immense and burgeoning industrial sector of amusement and entertainment services compelling relaxation – structurally corresponds to the restoration of labour-power expended within the process of production. The unity of work and leisure, a specificity of the identity between production and consumption, is described by Debord thus, in which leisure

> ...is in no way liberated from productive activity: it depends on productive activity and is an uneasy and admiring submission to the necessities and results

of production; it is itself a product of its rationality ... Thus the present 'liberation from labor,' the increase of leisure, is in no way a liberation within labor, nor a liberation from the world shaped by this labor. None of the activity lost in labor can be regained in the submission to its result.

1970: §27

Consistent with both Lefebvre's concept of everyday life and elements of Adorno's writings on industrial culture, we find within the spectacle 'no alternative between work and recreation' (Adorno 2005a: 130). Having abolished the scarcity of 'free time' within conditions of postwar prosperity – which accelerated both the general need for leisure, as well as the differentiated needs within that framework – the realm of leisure activity becomes the necessary correlate to abstract labour spent in the production process, an internal self-diremption of the spectacle for which leisure both justifies the social whole and its individuated moment within the time of work.

It is, for the SI, 'the era of industrial culture' which 'integrates and formulates the unity of work and leisure' (IS 1997: 260). Debord's thoughts here accord largely with Adorno's analysis of the culture industry. For both, the products of leisure are pre-digested and standardized, whose various mediums elicit mass psychological behaviour for which base survival and integration assume the form of need satiation and satisfaction. Here we find again, as examined in chapter 2, a form of pathological projection and *Identitätszwang* in which people strive to adapt to a schematism that is accompanied by a set of ready-made reactions to the cultural products on display.

For Adorno, specifically in the case of photography and film, the resulting reification of the audience is a degradation of human perception. It does this, first and foremost, through a certain *domesticated naturalism* to which the photographic image is disposed, infusing empirical life with meaning: 'the duplicity of which viewers can scarcely see through because the nightclub looks exactly like the one they know' (Adorno 1998: 62). The continuous presentation of what exists is the sole possible horizon. Again, here the spectacle need only display the reigning actuality through its cultural products. 'Such a photological proof is of course not stringent, but it is overpowering' (Adorno and Horkheimer 2002: 118). Like the culture industry, the spectacle upholds the world in reverence as its own object. 'It exploits the cult of fact by describing bad existence with utmost exactitude in order to elevate it into the realm of facts' (Adorno and Horkheimer 2002: 119; see also Debord 1995: §213). Everything is reduced to recognition, to 'whatever the camera reproduces' (see Figure 6.1), therefore

Figure 6.1 The Domination of the Spectacle over Life, *Internationale situationniste* 11 (1967).

stunting the power of discernment in an absolute emaciation of perception through its *Identitätszwang*.

Accommodating various layers of behavioural response patterns, the cultural products of the spectacle, as derivative of the unity between work and leisure, refine their ability to directly identify reality with its representation. The more densely and completely its techniques duplicate empirical objects, the more easily it creates the verifiable conviction that the world outside is a seamless extension of the one which, for example, has been revealed in the cinema. In this way, like Adorno's concept of the culture industry, the spectacle is geared to mimetic regression, to the manipulation of repressed impulses to copy. Its orientation is to anticipate the spectator's imitative practice by making it appear as if an agreement already exists which it intends to create. 'Immediacy, the popular community concocted by films, amounts to mediation without residue, reducing men and everything human so perfectly to things, that their contrast to things, indeed the spell of reification itself, becomes imperceptible' (Adorno 2005a: 201, 206). We find then as the physiognomy of the spectacle in its development of leisure a mixture of streamlining photographic hardness and precision on the one hand, and an individual's pathological identification with standardized formulas and clichés on the other. Here, the revelation of brute existence and the objective legitimation of its meaning is given direct exposition. It is through this framework that for the SI, art adopts the meaning of entertainment itself: it is the society of the spectacle's apologia. To be entertained means to be in agreement, to reconcile oneself and find rapport with the world through *Identitätszwang*. Artistic form is therewith supplanted by representational and documentary function and in the uninterrupted packaging of standardized models. The entire system is justified on the basis of an infantile public which it itself has created.

At a time when Amazon is reorganizing warehouse work on the model of a video game, it is admittedly difficult to recall a period in which the clear distinction between work and leisure was so adamantly pronounced. It is in many ways a trenchant scenario of the advanced industrial nations of postwar prosperity with their high levels of GDP, wages, productivity and social safety nets culminating in an unprecedented purchasing power of the proletariat. It is a situation all the more exotic when contemporary conditions, specifically since the early 1970s with the proliferation of flexible labour markets, elicits a workforce of casualized employment contracts, twenty-four-hour availability or a general informality to labour relations typified by temporary, part-time, seasonal, internship and freelance work. Obscuring further any absolute line between work and leisure in the present moment is the insidious feint of entrepreneurialism under what is inanely described as the 'sharing economy', as well as the infantilization of workplace comradery, with its mini-golf, foosball tables and blue jeans exemplified in Silicon Valley. This is all not to mention, if a residual connection to what was once called leisure might be made, the compulsion of perpetually persevering with the nearly industrial-grade branding of oneself requisite to participating in digital social media communication and the socio-psychological narcissism and diminution of the self that tends to follow suit.

The point here is only to emphasize that during the period of Debord's diagnosis, the demarcation between work and leisure appeared absolute. Each serving as the justification of the other, their implicit unity provided an exemplary and socially palpable register for the unity between production and consumption, of use-value and exchange-value. For Debord and the SI, to abolish one was to abolish the other. It is therefore only at the level of immediacy that the compensatory character of leisure activity displaces work as the centre of social arrangements. The relation between the time of work and the time of recreation cohere as a harmony with which the system of capitalist production reproduces itself (Knabb 2006: 85–6). The reduction of working time finds positive affirmation in the free time of 'the industry of vacations, of leisure, of spectacles'. The organization of consumption as leisure is the 'counterbalance [of] the organization of work' (Knabb 2006: 182). In its unity with work, the realm of leisure, 'furnished with the emptiness of culture', is reduced to 'a satisfying positivity' that, in its speculative identity to its other, 'justifies its own existence tautologically by the mere fact that it exists, which is to say that it is granted recognition within the spectacle' (IS 1997: 374).

Unity of state and economy

This chapter seeks to make explicit a logic of the spectacle which self-differentiates itself while preserving an essential and speculative identity. Nowhere else perhaps does this self-diremption in its most capacious form occur than in the relation between the economy and the state under the spectacle. At the outset of his 1988 *Comments on the Society of the Spectacle*, Debord describes *The Society of the Spectacle* as having sought to expound the spectacle '*in essence*: the autocratic reign of the market economy which had acceded to an irresponsible sovereignty, and the totality of new techniques of government which accompanied this reign' (1998: 2; emphasis added). Here, the *essential structure* of the spectacle consists in the identity of the capitalist economy with the modern state. The internal relation between economy and state under the spectacle, or as the spectacle's differentiated exteriorization, can already be surmised in various guises throughout *The Society of the Spectacle*. The social separation constitutive of the spectacle, examined through the workings of the capitalist economy, is accordingly identified through the modern state structure. As Debord writes, '[t]he social cleavage that the spectacle expresses is inseparable from the modern State, which, as the product of the social division of labor and the organ of class rule, is the general form of all social division' (1995: §24). For Debord, it was the mercantile system of trade and commodity exchange that integrated a form of the state adequate to the demands of an ascending bourgeoisie class. As Debord remarks further on, 'Marx was already able, under the rubric of Bonapartism, accurately to depict a foreshadowing of modern State bureaucracy in that fusion of capital and State which established "capital's national power over labor and a public authority designed to maintain social servitude"...Already discernible in outline here are the sociopolitical bases of the modern spectacle' (1995: §87).

Despite these comments, and the ways in which the state appears sporadically throughout *The Society of the Spectacle* as an expenditure of the spectacle itself, it is within the aforementioned *Comments on the Society of the Spectacle* that the state under the spectacle is given greater attention. There, Debord gives new significance to the spheres of production and distribution under the development of the spectacle since the 1960s, specifically in accordance with the unity of state and economy. As already noted in chapter 2, *Comments on the Society of the Spectacle* proposes that the two forms of the spectacle reigning during the late 1960s, the *concentrated* and *diffuse*, have, since that time, coalesced into what Debord in 1988 calls the *integrated* spectacle as the 'rational combination' (1998: 8) of the two. Here, with the collapse of the Soviet bloc, the concentrated and diffuse forms of the spectacle cohere into the integrated spectacle. One principal feature identified by Debord characteristic of the integrated spectacle is indeed an unprecedented 'integration of state and economy', which is

> ...the most evident trend of the century; it is at the very least the motor of recent economic developments. The defensive and offensive pact concluded between these two powers, economy and state, has provided them with the greatest common advantages in every field: each may be said to own the other; at any rate, it is absurd to oppose them, or to distinguish between their reasons and follies. This union, too, has proved to be highly favourable to the development of spectacular domination – indeed, the two have been indistinguishable from the very start.
>
> 1998: 12

With further analyses of political assassinations, terrorism and surveillance, all phenomena teeming from contemporary events in, for example, Italy in the 1970s and Latin America in the 1980s, Debord offers comments on how such mechanisms of state control derive from the logic of the spectacle. It is, however, with his particular remarks on mafia organization that the unity constitutive of spectacular organization comes to the fore. As Debord writes, 'the first requirement of any Mafia, wherever it may be, is naturally to prove that it does not exist, or that it has been the victim of unscientific calumnies; and that is the first thing it has in common with capitalism' (1998: 63–4). Debord further elaborates on the mafia as a social form or informal racket that, while seemingly an anomaly or aberration of legitimized commercial practices, has in fact as its model the form of the state and economy:

> It is always a mistake to try to explain something by opposing Mafia and state: they are never rivals. Theory easily verifies what all the rumors in practical life have all too easily shown. The Mafia is not an outsider in this world; it is perfectly at home. Indeed, in the integrated spectacle it stands as the *model* of all advanced commercial enterprises.
>
> 1998: 67

For Debord, the modern state in general has as its prerogative the 'management of economic affairs' (1998: 69). The unity of state and economy is then for Debord,

> ... a natural product of the concentration of capital, production and distribution. Whatever does not grow must disappear; and no business can grow without adopting the values, techniques and methods of today's industry, spectacle and state. In the final analysis, it is the particular form of development chosen by the economy of our epoch which dictates *the widespread creation of new personal bonds of dependency and protection*.
>
> 1998: 69[5]

As such, under the spectacle we find a certain internal relation between state and economy, an affinity of self-differentiated identity. A similar relation can of course be found within Marx himself. Although never able to complete his planned volume on the state within the project of *Capital*, the introduction to the *Grundrisse* offers formulations that adhere to the notion that the state is the political form in which capitalist social relations appear. In Marx's planned outline, the state is described as 'the concentration [*Zusammenfassung*] of bourgeois society. Analysed in relation to itself' (1986: 45; translation amended). Further, at the outset of the second chapter of Marx's *Capital*, volume 1, we find a reflective relation between commodity relations and juridical relations, or what are symmetric abstract legal personalities of contractual relations necessary for exchange (1996: 95).

Drawing insight from these first few chapters of *Capital*, Soviet economist E. B. Pashukanis argued in the first decades of the twentieth century that the bourgeois form of law derives not from class interests but from the logic of commodity exchange itself and that it is not the case that the categories of bourgeois law are simply abused or manipulated by the ruling classes, but that the juridical concepts themselves are the necessary legal forms of the objective mediation of commodity exchange. For Pashukanis, there is an inner connection between the two social forms and his central thesis within *The General Theory of Law and Marxism* is to approximate the legal form as a necessary correlate to the commodity form. The formal equality of juridical relations develops parallel to the equality of exchange-value in which each commodity owner recognizes in the other a bearer of legal rights and interests of proprietorship.

Law becomes then not simply an ideological mystification or mere superstructure. It is the political form of commodity exchange whose purpose is to comprise a subjectivity with formal rights adequate to social relations. It is in and through the relation of private individuals with their fully developed abstract legal rights that we find the legal form as the necessary correlate to commodity exchange. As a result, the fetish-character of the commodity social form is therewith said to necessarily approximate a fetish-character of the legal social form, specifically by procuring an abstract legal subject necessary for the equivalence of exchange relations. As Pashukanis writes, '[t]he social relation which is rooted in production presents itself simultaneously in two absurd forms: as the value of commodities, and as man's capacity to be the subject of rights' (2002: 113). As distinguished from a pre-capitalist system of privileges and specific social claims – for which relations were mediated by personal dependence and authority – the abstract universality of equivalent rights only develops in accordance with the dominance of exchange relations. Here, '[l]egal fetishism complements commodity fetishism' (2002: 117). State coercion thereby detaches itself as the particular mechanism of one class over another and becomes 'the impersonal apparatus of public power, separate from society' (2002: 139).

Although there is no archival evidence indicating that Debord was familiar with the work of Pashukanis, it can nevertheless be argued that the latter's framework for grasping legal relations as internally necessary to and yet differentiated from the fetish-character of commodity exchange gives to Debord's characterization of the spectacle as the unity of state and economy a logical foundation deriving directly out of Marx's critique of political economy. Here the state could be said to constitute, through the necessity of facilitating a legal form of private property and its exchange, an internal moment of the development of the capitalist mode of production. It is an inherent relation explored more recently by Bonefeld when he writes that '[c]oncentrated and organized coercive force is thus the precondition of free economy. The laws of equivalent exchange are premised on order, and the establishment of order is a political matter' (2014: 176). For Bonefeld, the nation-state is the *political form* of capitalist society. Further, just as the economy is a requisite condition for the state and vice versa, so is, more specifically, the world market a condition for a system of inter-national relations (2014: 149). Here, the nation-state subsists in and through the world market so that regardless of the level of protectionism, such states subsist in and through the global flow of capital in general. 'In this context, the notion of the national economy is misleading' (2014: 159). Despite the level of state regulation, whether laissez faire or Keynesian, we find within the concept of the spectacle a state-form adequate for the development of the commodity economy: 'The spectacle has its roots in the fertile field of the economy, and it is the produce of that field which must in the end come to dominate the spectacular market, whatever ideological or police-state barriers of a protectionist kind may be set up by local spectacles with dreams of autarky' (Debord 1995: §58). The unity-in-separation of national states and the global economy, as well as, on a more elemental level, the determination of the state as a unifying force within a society of competition, affirming bourgeois rights of equality, justice, utility and liberty – in a word, the laws of privation – together comprise the spectacle in its self-differentiated exteriorization. Within this framework, regional nationalism, although palpably real, is nevertheless subordinated to a larger objective conceptuality. It is for this reason that Debord and the SI always refrained from supporting, and in fact actively criticized, the struggles for national liberation during the 1960s, conflicts whose essential banner announced 'economic development'. It is another instance of what was understood to be the unity of state and economy under spectacular domination. Whether with regard to Russia, China, Egypt or even Algeria (Dolto and Sidi Moussa 2019), Debord's diagnosis circled opposingly around the bureaucratic classes emergent within struggles of national liberation. If they are to assume the political destiny of the bourgeois, such movements must align their struggles to the mandates of economic industrialization (Debord 1995: §113), a resignation in harmony with the global division of the spectacle.

Despite these comments, it is perhaps within Debord's 1965 essay, 'The Decline and Fall of the Spectacle-Commodity Economy', that the identity between state and economy under the spectacle receives its most potent and concrete instantiation. This essay, originally distributed in the US in December 1965 and subsequently appearing in the tenth issue of *IS*, in 1966, examines the Watts riots of Los Angeles which took place in the summer of 1965. In response to police violence, a social eruption took place over the week, with the California National Guard called in to pacify the situation, resulting in over thirty deaths. For the SI, despite seemingly prompted by the state and its police force, this 'was a rebellion against the commodity, against the world of the commodity in which worker-consumers are *hierarchically* subordinated to commodity standards'. We find in Debord's analysis a direct connection between the commodity and the state, specifically by which black youth, cynically aware of the limits it faces for a social integration offered more readily to other segments of the population, have in their refusal taken the publicity of capitalist abundance '*literally*'. This wealth, so often dangled above their means, was taken at its word as a life worth living. In doing so, through mass collective looting and redistribution amongst themselves, 'they are challenging their exchange-value, the *commodity reality* which moulds them and marshals them to its own ends':

> Looting is a *natural* response to the unnatural and inhuman society of commodity abundance. It instantly undermines the commodity as such, and it also exposes what the commodity ultimately implies: the army, the police and the other specialized detachments of the state's monopoly of armed violence. What is a policeman? He is the active servant of the commodity, the man in complete submission to the commodity, whose job is to ensure that a given product of human labor remains a commodity, with the magical property of having to be paid for.
>
> Knabb 2006: 197–8[6]

Under the spectacle, the absolute distinction between state and economy becomes obscure, each side, in their fundamental internal commensurability, emerging as the justification and legitimation of the other. In this way, confronting the ebb and flow of the economy means confrontation with the state, as recent developments such as deficit spending, monetary stimulus, liquidity injection, austerity and repression demonstrate against the background of a global economic restructuring and its corresponding devaluation of total labour-power, regardless of any social democratic aspirations. The spectacle as an internal self-differentiation of state and economy is at once also the objectification or exteriorization of the mediations of state and economy. Further, it is here, as a moment in the social totality, that, if maintenance of social order should require, 'a policeman [can] appear as what he [is] in essence: an entertainer, a psychologist, a humanist' (IS 1997: 469). For this reason, demands for greater police transparency can only ever be spectacular: that the police should greater accord and find superior harmonization in a society false from the ground up.

Unity of town and country

Having examined the speculative identity and differentiation between work and leisure, and state and economy, we turn now to the spectacle's internal opposition between town and country. Chapter 7 of *The Society of the Spectacle*, 'The

Organisation of Territory', is the shortest and begins with the tendency of the capitalist mode of production to have unified space by breaking down regional boundaries between one society and the next. Although the current political climate suggests the commodity labour-power to be temporarily prohibited from freely traversing national boundaries, it remains the case that with, for example, instantaneous communication and transportation networks, capital, as Marx writes in the *Grundrisse*, 'by its nature drives beyond every spatial barrier. Thus the creation of the physical conditions of exchange – of the means of communication and transport … becomes an extraordinary necessity for it' (1986: 448).[7] Marx refers to this international tendency of capital as 'the annihilation of space by time' and is an observation integrated by Debord in his diagnosis on how the spectacle renders commensurable the relation between town and country.

For Debord, capital has 'shattered all regional and legal boundaries' (1995: §165). Here it is said that the spectacle renders commensurable the distinctiveness and independence of places into a spectacular unity of 'interchangeability' (1995: §168). It is a power of homogeneity, and yet, importantly, one which unifies, battering down, as Debord paraphrases Marx, with its heavy artillery all Chinese walls. We find then within the spectacle a dialectic of proximity, in which '[t]his society eliminates geographical distance only to reap distance internally in the form of spectacular separation' (1995: §167); or as Adorno writes, '[e]strangement shows itself precisely in the elimination of distance between people' (2005a: 41).

Indeed, drawing on the work of Lewis Mumford, Debord describes the social isolation brought out by capitalist urbanism as requiring also a 'controlled *reintegration* … based on the planned needs of production and consumption. Such an integration must recapture isolated individuals as individuals *isolated together*. Factories and cultural centers, holiday camps and housing developments – all are expressly oriented to the goals of a pseudo-community of this kind' (1995: §172). The togetherness garnered through the commensurability of different places, or what Debord calls an 'environment of abstraction' (1995: §173), close to what Lefebvre refers to as 'abstract space' (1991b), is given a number of exemplary instances throughout the chapter. These include a discussion of tourism, itself the derivative of commodity circulation, which emerges as 'the chance to go and see what has been made trite' (1995: §168). Also examined is the proliferation of social housing for which '[t]he same architecture appears everywhere' (1995: §173). One also finds mention of what Debord calls the 'dictatorship of the automobile', itself the 'pilot product of the first stage of commodity abundance' (1995: §174) under the arterial expansion of freeways, parking spaces and circulation networks. Urbanism thereby emerges as a modern mechanism of both safeguarding class power for which the population incurs geographical isolation to match their own internal isolation, as well as a mechanism of 'controlled reintegration' based on the planned needs of production and consumption.

The spectacle's near obliteration of spatial distinction abolishes the separation of town and country so crucial for the emergence and development of bourgeois society. Rural landscape, largely deindustrialized since the publication of *The Society of the Spectacle*, is replete with the detritus of capital investment. As a result, Debord writes, 'urbanism institutes a *pseudo-countryside* devoid not only of the natural relationships of the country of former times but also of the direct (and directly contested) relationships of the historical cities. The forms of habitation and the spectacular control of today's "planned environment" have created a new, artificial peasantry' (1995: §177). Alongside this erosion of the countryside due to the expansion of commercial urban imperatives, distant realities are brought ever closer together through various technologies. The rural naïf, once ignorant to anything outside of the inner circle of their vocation and family life, disappears within the interconnected world, the tragedy of Gretchen in Goethe's *Faust*. In this transition from *Gemeinschaft* to *Gesellschaft*, cosmopolitanism replaces traditional illiteracy through a culture industry traversing class and geographical boundaries, with greater technological capabilities than film, radio and magazines were for the previous century (Hesse 2018). The *natural* isolation of rural life and its attendant provincial ignorance has been replaced, for Debord, by the *manufactured* isolation and falsity of unitary social interconnection. The fully accessible world has not simply exorcized the notorious idiocy of rural life inasmuch as it has established a *unitary* idiocy between rural and city life, whose now universal parochial outlook traverses both the city centres and its concrete suburban landscape, and emerges in the spectacle through the techniques of urbanism by 'refashioning the totality of space into *its own peculiar decor*' (Debord 1995: §169).[8]

Long since having lost its etymological origin in 'travail' as a laborious effort, to travel within the spectacle between different places and to make the exotic our own has become a commonplace exercise. 'A publicity poster of a well-known airline, utterly confusing provincialism and globalism, appeals to its customers with these words: "When you use our services, you are everywhere at home"' (Anders 1956: 21). The dangers of travel have become for the most part obsolete as differences of place are brought within a commodity purview supplemented by technologies allowing us to at once both supplant and render omnipotent inexorable laws of familiarity; here, 'adventure' is reserved for culinary pleasure or the 2018 Dodge Journey. For the traveller, the most pressing concern appears as what is the proper regional etiquette for tipping your bartender. As Günther Anders has written, 'when all the various and variously distant regions of the world are brought equally close to us, the world as such vanishes' (1956: 24). Travelling is increasingly robbed of landscape. The tourist 'is not invited to become acquainted with an unfamiliar world; instead, people, countries, situations, events, particularly the least familiar of them, are presented to him as though he had always known them; they are thoroughly philistinized in advance' (1956: 22).[9]

Nevertheless, for the figure of the tourist, a holiday in Marseille *appears* qualitatively different to, for example, a weekend in Oaxaca. Despite that both may offer their own set of experiential gratifications for those ready to spend, distinction is *not* wholly extinguished, but preserves itself within a unity of nevertheless commensurable commodity nuances and market relations. Fresh Mediterranean seafood and indigenous regional cheeses are not in themselves identical but find equivalent and objective expression in the money-form. The point isn't that spatial organization under the spectacle produces identical places, but that the speculative power of commensurability means that an English breakfast can be had in the heart of Africa; or alternatively, that place is rendered into caricature, such that an Airbnb flat in a seedy district of Rome is hygienically adorned with movie posters of *Roman Holiday*. The emphasis here is that for Debord's spectacle, we are not simply dealing with individually identical appearances of social life but, more centrally, the *organization of appearance-forms*. As Lefebvre has written, '[a]bstract space *is not* homogeneous; it simply *has* homogeneity as its goal' (1991b: 287), a homogeneity of form whose content allows for differentiation. Despite differentiation, alterity with a structure of appearance-forms must remain amendable to accommodated commensurability and reconciliation.

Unity of diffuse and concentrated spectacle

We turn now to a final self-differentiation found within the spectacle as *Begriffslogik*, a *Verdoppelung* already described in part within the previous analysis: the *diffuse* and *concentrated* as two forms of the spectacle, each harmoniously balanced within the spectacle as such but whose identity only becomes explicit with Debord's later category of the *integrated* spectacle. During the 1960s, the diffuse spectacle corresponded to the Western society of commodity abundance while the concentrated corresponded to that of the Eastern societies of bureaucratically controlled state planned economies. To bring what was observed as their fundamental unity to the fore, let us first turn to a fragment found in the tenth issue of *IS* (1966). In an analysis on the reifying structure of the commodity, one which in part derives from comments found in Lukács (Lukács 1971a: 95–103), it is argued that '[t]he commodity, like the bureaucracy, is a formalization and a rationalization of praxis … The bureaucratization of capitalism does not mean an inner qualitative transformation, but on the contrary is an extension of the commodity form. The commodity has always been bureaucratic' (IS 1997: 450).[10] Although here only an abbreviated and elementary connection, the rationalization of the commodity as a latent bureaucratic structure indexes the SI's larger geopolitical diagnosis on the symbiotic and equitable relation between the liberalism of the diffuse spectacle and the authoritarianism of the concentrated spectacle, or on the whole what Debord called 'the bourgeois-bureaucratic spectrum' (1995: §113).

Although on the surface seemingly without any social affinity to the open markets and unrestrained industries of Western societies of commodity profusion, the concentrated spectacle – often under alternative titles such as the 'degenerated workers' state', 'state socialism', 'bureaucratic collectivism', 'state capitalism' or the 'transitional society' – while differentiated from the diffuse spectacle, nevertheless adopts a form of domination wholly compatible within the global division of the society of the spectacle. Informed by the criticisms of *Socialisme ou Barbarie*, Debord's ideas concerning the concentrated spectacle are also influenced by the work of Bruno Rizzi. In 1976, Debord advocated to Gérard Lebovici that it was 'indispensible' (2005: 364) to publish Rizzi's *The Bureaucratization of the World* (1938) with Editions Champ Libre. This book, in Debord's words 'the most unknown book of the century' (2005: 365), examined the nature of the Soviet economy as a bureaucratic form of domination. Rizzi puts forth a version of bureaucratic domination which, in the Soviet Union, 'has swollen the state to unheard proportions' (1985: 58). Rizzi argues that this society inaugurated a new form of class domination by bureaucracy and, through state nationalization and state planning, developed a form of property whose owners were 'careful not to declare officially that it does possess this property' (1985: 50). As, in the words of Debord, a 'cheap remake of the capitalist ruling class' (1995: §104), this new class of state functionaries, political officialdom, party technocrats and trade union bosses together, with official journalists, intelligentsia and police, comprise a bureaucratic ruling class.

The social form emergent within the Soviet Union, although not constituted through an open capitalist economy or through the principle of private property, nevertheless, through its form of collective state property and its police state perpetuated exploitation and the extraction of surplus value. The state here becomes 'the sole employer of labour' (Rizzi 1985: 80), exploiting the proletariat en bloc and fixing 'its standard of living by means of wages and by the prices set for goods in the state shops ... [T]he bureaucracy has given itself a monopoly position, thus perfecting the system of exploitation' (1985: 50–1). Rizzi affirms a theory of state monopolization of labour-power in the interest of economic productivity with policies of industrialization, wage and retail price controls, land rent and nationalized property (Debord 1995: §101). For all this, just as within the diffuse form of the spectacle, we find a variation on the domination by the economy. Bureaucratic centralization becomes here the resultant requirement for the state's relation to the economy whose phenomenal appearance ratifies and concentrates itself in the personality cult of the leader (Debord 1995: §64). As Rizzi anticipates Debord's own observations,

> ...the state expresses itself in a grand, theatrical manner, as in the western totalitarian states, and the real or feigned veneration of the Leader, raised almost to divinity, is equal or, perhaps, even greater. The hierarchy is held in great esteem and servility is pushed to its ultimate limit. The population lives in an atmosphere of fear, as though walls could hear and speak.
>
> 1985: 45

The concentrated spectacle of bureaucratic regimes perpetuates the reigning domination of the economy. 'Planning is merely the other face of the free market. The only thing planned is *exchange* – along with the mutual sacrifices it entails' (Vaneigem 2012: 15). As Debord writes, 'The economy in its independence thus showed itself so thoroughly able to dominate society as to recreate for its own purposes that class domination which is essential to its operation. It proved, in other words, that the bourgeoisie had created a power so autonomous that, so long as it endured, it could even do without a bourgeoisie' (1995: §104). Within this framework, Debord describes what he calls an 'image of socialism' that was 'soon to emerge as the mortal enemy of the proletariat in Russia and elsewhere' (1970: §97). Essentially, this image had but one meaning, exemplified in the words of German SPD leader Friedrich Ebert: 'working hard'. Within *The Society of the Spectacle*, this point begins a criticism of the Leninist vanguard party and Bolshevism generally as propagating an ideological model in which 'the task of directing the proletariat from without, by means of a disciplined clandestine party under the control of intellectuals who had become "professional revolutionaries"' (1970: §98). As Debord continues, 'This same historical moment ... also marks the definitive inauguration of an order of things that lies at the core of the modern spectacle's rule: this was the moment when an *image of the working class* arose in radical opposition to the working class itself' (1970: §100). Debord thereby begins to establish that the spectacle as a social reign of appearances has pervaded the workers' movement itself in the varied institutions of the state, the party, unions and bureaucracy (1995: §114). Each exemplified a spectacular monopoly over the representation of the proletariat as a separate power over and against it. 'By this time the revolutionary image of the proletariat had become both the main element in, and the chief result of, the falsification of society' (Debord 1970: §101).[11]

For Debord, it nevertheless remained the case, and contrary to Rizzi's own analysis, that the bureaucracy of the concentrated spectacle was inferior to the diversified market relations of the diffuse spectacle (Debord 1995: §104). The localisms of each of its satellite bureaucracies, within a global market, could not fully coincide, either economically or politically, with mandates from Moscow; 'interbureaucratic relations have always contained underlying conflicts' which, for the SI, were seen in the upheavals of Poland, Hungary and contemporaneous Czechoslovakia. It nevertheless remains the case that in its concentrated form, '[t]his was a local primitivism of the spectacle that has nonetheless played an essential part in the spectacle's worldwide development' (Debord 1995: §105).[12]

Crucial to the present analysis, however, for which an underlying unity between the concentrated and diffuse spectacle stands as an exemplary instance of the spectacle's own self-differentiation, is to emphasize the commensurable concordance between each side:

> Never underestimate the importance of East–West exchanges! In the West, *homo consumator* buys a bottle of whiskey and receives the lie that comes with it; in the East, Communist man buys ideology and gets a bottle of vodka for free. Paradoxically, Soviet and capitalist regimes are on the same path, the one by virtue of a production-driven economy, the other by virtue of a consumption-driven one.
>
> Vaneigem 2012: 56

Regardless of the seeming differences of Cold War opposition, a single social totality inaugurated by the global capitalist economy under the spectacle held sway. In time, this fundamental unity would become explicit under the category of the *integrated* spectacle.

It is within *Comments on the Society of the Spectacle* that Debord introduces the *integrated* spectacle as the combination of the *concentrated* and *diffuse*. It is a book written around the impending fall of the Berlin Wall and is Debord's attempt at theorizing the global unification of the spectacle that was to soon emerge. As integrated, it unprecedentedly combines the triumph of commodity circulation with pervasive state management. In a draft foreword to the third French edition to *The Society of the Spectacle*, Debord describes the integrated spectacle in a passage he requested appear on the back cover of the book:

> It is this will for the modernization and unification of the spectacle, tied to all the other aspects of the simplification of society, that led the Russian bureaucracy to suddenly convert itself, like a single man, to the current *ideology* of democracy: that is to say, the dictatorial liberty of the Market, tempered by recognition of the Rights of the Spectator.
>
> 2008a: 351

The pseudo-rivalry of the diffuse and concentrated spectacle has, under the integrated spectacle, ceased its bickering and conceded, in triumphant procession, its ultimately shared prerogative of immense spectacular positivity: reconciliation, despite its differences, to the reigning actuality. Here, as the culmination of its *Wesenslogik*, the integrated spectacle is described as a thorough penetration and identity between appearance and essence:

> For the final sense of the integrated spectacle is this – that it has integrated itself into reality to the same extent as it was describing it, and that it was reconstructing it as it was describing it. As a result, this reality no longer confronts the integrated spectacle as something alien. When the spectacle was concentrated, the greater part of surrounding society escaped it; when diffuse, a small part; today, no part. The spectacle has spread itself to the point where it now permeates all reality... the globalization of the false was also the falsification of the globe.
>
> Debord 1998: 9–10

Almost overnight, the division of the Iron Curtain shattered, exposing the mechanisms of secret police with televised transparency. And yet, even before Debord's *Comments on the Society of the Spectacle*, the East and West held within the society of the spectacle a 'deep affinity' (Knabb 2006: 336). Indeed, despite the manner in which each side posited the other as its competitive nemesis, their quarrel helped stabilize the global economy (Goldner 1991). 'The peaceful coexistence of bourgeois and bureaucratic lies ended up prevailing over the lie of their confrontation' (Knabb 2006: 254). While the concentrated spectacle has its police, the diffuse has its sociologists; on one side is venerated the leader of statecraft, the other, gadgets and consumables. Juridical and ideological differences cohere within a broader structure of social reconciliation and *Identitätszwang*.

The coherence of the spectacle

The above series of self-differentiated concrete moments that acquire inner speculative identity as the developing actuality propounds the spectacle as a *Begriffslogik*. Together, the unity of work and leisure, state and economy, town and country, diffuse and concentrated, all comprise what can now be concluded as the spectacle's coherence as a social totality. The society of the spectacle as a distinctly critical theory of society thereby refers to how each of the aforementioned social phenomena necessarily presuppose their opposite as a determinate condition of themselves. It is through the speculative identity of spectacular logic that this unitary structure has come to the fore. It is a critique that cannot acquire full coherence without making explicit the interconnections of society as a whole. In fact, it demands that only with attention towards a comprehensive whole, one constituted by the falsehood of commensurability through a dialectic of appearances, can critical theory do justice to the individual phenomena of capitalist society.

Indeed, the whole to which speculative logic gestures proves itself in the development of its concept. It has been necessary to expound this development insofar as 'the spectacle does not always aim at being understood, no more than current society' (Debord 2006c: 389). Despite its propensity for irrationality, as remarked in chapter 2, the present analysis has thus sought to make explicit what the SI termed at one point, 'the bourgeoisie's oppressive coherence' (Knabb 2006: 281). For Debord specifically, the notion of coherence (*cohérence*) implies the distribution of equivalence, as can be drawn from his 1963 unpublished 'Notes on Coherence'. Although the short fragments in that text concern an internal debate within the SI on the organization's anti-hierarchical aspirations,[13] it is not out of line to extract this association between coherence and commensurable exchangeability which inheres as a rhythm of the spectacle's speculative logic, that is, as 'the identity of identity and non-identity' (Hegel 1969: 74; Hegel 2010: 33). The resultant positivity, in its fully luminescent revelation, is the spectacle's distinctive coherence as a speculative totality, one whose logic has come to the fore through the self-exteriorization of its *Begriffslogik*.

An object can only be presented as a totality if its differentiated elements emanate out of a unifying concept. This gives to the object *coherence* as a comprehensive reality, a unity-in-difference whose moments or constituents are exhibited as the result of its self-differentiation. It is for this reason that Hegel, the great 'partisan of unity' (Adorno 2007: 158), has been so paramount for making coherent the spectacle's conjunctive horrors. Such a unitary actuality without remainder is the coherent totality of the society of the spectacle:

> In a certain sense, the coherence of spectacular society proves revolutionaries right, since it is evident that one cannot reform the most trifling detail without taking the whole thing apart. But at the same time this coherence has eliminated every organized revolutionary tendency by eliminating those social terrains where it had more or less effectively been able to find expression: from trade unions to newspapers, towns to books. In a single movement, it has been possible to illuminate the incompetence and thoughtlessness of which this tendency was quite naturally the bearer. And on an individual level, the reigning coherence is quite capable of eliminating, or buying off[,] such exceptions as may arise.
>
> Debord 1998: 80

For Debord and the SI, '[t]he coherence of the critique and the critique of incoherence are one and the same movement' (Knabb 2006: 278; see also 190, 285–6). To therewith give to the spectacle optimal coherence as a speculative rationality[14] is then not simply to dilute it of arbitrary contingency, but also to make explicit its immanent necessity as a totality of positivity. However, to pursue and render coherent the spectacle in its full rational development is to follow the *Begriffslogik* in its final moment: the spectacle as *idea*.

The idea of the spectacle

Following the *Begriffslogik* of the spectacle, we discover that its *concept* and its *idea* each lay different emphases on its spectacular structure. For Hegel, the idea is the unity of the concept and objectivity whose content is what the concept gives to itself in the form of external otherness. The idea is as such not a subjective representation or *Gedankendingen* but 'the objectively *true*' (Hegel 2010: 670) or, as Hegel describes later on, the idea 'has the *entire essentiality* of the objective world in its concept' (2010: 696). The idea is the unity of the subjective concept and objectivity, or the externalization of the concept within the objective world; it is everything actual and through which the concept acquires realization. Like the concept, the idea is not therefore an idea *of something*, but that which 'is essentially *concrete*, because it is the free Concept that determines itself and in so doing makes itself real' (Hegel 1991b: 287). The reality of the world, despite its external heterogeneity, only has coherence through the concept, and in the latter's development, integrates, through the idea, objective reality within itself. It is only here, in the end, that the concrete becomes fully concrete, as the idea for which '*being* has attained the significance of *truth*; it now *is*, therefore, only what the idea is' (Hegel 2010: 672).

The idea can be grasped as a unity of subject and object. It is fundamentally reason, a development of the concept that has determined itself as both subjectivity and objectivity. It is the concept as it distinguishes itself from an objectivity it itself has externalized. Likewise, this objectivity becomes a moment of the subjective idea itself, one side of a negative unity for which 'the idea has its reality in a materiality' (2010: 674). While the moments of the idea in their development will give to the concept a soul that is *fully animated* (2010: 675), let us refrain from a detailed analysis of the remainder of the *Science of Logic* and instead call attention to the way in which such an idea appears within the logic of the spectacle.

In brief, it can be said that the unity of subjectivity and objectivity as idea within the *Begriffslogik*, that is, as the speculative identity of subject and substance, elaborates an essential identity between spectator and spectacle as internal to a more holistic concept of the spectacle. In a word, only as *idea* does the spectacle's *Identitätszwang* receive full elucidation whereby the opposition between subjectivity and objectivity is speculatively overcome. As Debord extracts from his reading of Lefebvre's *Logique Formelle, Logique Dialectique*, 'Subjectivity (or concept) and the object are therefore *the same and not the same* because: "it is perverse to regard the objective and the subjective as a solid and abstract opposition; both are dialectical." (HEGEL.)' (1982a: 283). For Hegel, the objectivity of the concept is first set in contrast to the concept. It is as such that the difference between spectacle and spectator, a formulation appearing frequently in Debord's writings, can be held as a remedial opposition. However, as an *Identitätszwang*, the otherness between spectacle and spectator folds in on itself through the congruity between substance and subject. As Lefebvre writes elsewhere, people recognize themselves 'in the fictive drama of the Idea' (1968: 58).

It is only if the self-determination of the concept and of objectivity procures a structure which contains their correspondence can it be said that there subsists a full identity between the subjective conceptual aspirations of the spectacle and its objective spectators. This is the spectacle as idea, whereby 'the separation of concept and objectivity eliminates itself, that their opposition resolves itself into a unity into which both are absorbed' (Winfield 1999: 44). The concept of the spectacle as idea is the unity of its particularized forms of subjectivity and objectivity. The spectator and its spectacular world are two sides internal to the development of the spectacle's *Begriffslogik* as idea. Each poses the reciprocal definition of the other since each requires the other for its own completion. We find then through the idea of the spectacle no external distinction between spectacle and spectator. The concept of the spectacle has thereby given itself determinacy in and through the totality of objectivity while its objectivity has acquired subjectivity through its immanent determinations.

The life of the spectacle

Having determined the extent to which both the *Wesenslogik* and the *Begriffslogik* structurally inhere within the society of the spectacle, we are now able to recast a concept Debord employs in the very first thesis of *The Society of the Spectacle*: 'The whole *life* of those societies in which modern conditions of production prevail presents itself [*s'annonce*] as an immense accumulation of *spectacles*' (1995: §1; emphasis added). This prompting category of 'life' has for interpreters given cause to read Debord's theory of the spectacle as essentially dualistic, that is, as a quasi-Feuerbachian approach to grasping the spectacle as a distortion of some pre-existent and natural condition of social life mangled by the spectacle – that is, everything this book has attempted to dispute. However, if we take the category of life as a culminating category of the *Begriffslogik*, that is, as a moment in the self-development of the concept of the spectacle which has exteriorized itself into actuality, then the self-presentation of life becomes constitutive of the spectacle's mode of appearing, and not in fact as that which has been replaced or dispossessed by the spectacle.

For Hegel, life breaks with the ideality of the concept and is the latter's developing actuality. Life is as such the process by which the concept 'gives itself reality through a process of objectification' (Hegel 2010: 677). Now, as we've seen above, the unity of spectacle and spectator is, strictly speaking, the *idea* of the spectacle in its self-determination. The purposiveness of its concept returns to actuality in the form of *life*, which is the truth of the idea, as the unity of concept and object. It is the manner in which the spectacle creates the concrete world for itself. As the SI write in the sixth issue of *IS*, in 1961, 'The spectacle system that is in the process of integrating the population manifests itself both as organization of cities and as permanent information network. It is a solid framework designed to reinforce the existing conditions of life' (Knabb 2006: 87–8). The spectacle as such has as its trajectory the reinforcement and promulgation of life in all of its positive concreteness. Whether through the affirmation of an authentic life propagated by self-help industries and New Age positivity, the reactionary cult of action and practicism amongst political partisans or an overwhelming pragmatism for which truth is reduced to validity and thought reduced to vital impulse, in all cases with the glorification of life and overstimulation – in which the metaphor of 'blood and soil' is never far off – we find the spectacle and its spleen of want gratification. We thereby reverse an adage of the SI: boredom *isn't* always counterrevolutionary.

Anything which assumes the appearance of externality is but a spectacle that the idea of the spectacle gives to itself. We can now, after traversing a long and logically strenuous road, give greater meaning not just to the opening thesis of *The Society of the Spectacle*, but also to the notion that '[u]nderstood on its own terms, the spectacle proclaims the predominance of appearances and asserts that all human life, which is to say all social life, is mere appearance' (Debord 1995: §10). Following a notion of the dialectic from Lefebvre's *Dialectical Materialism*, Debord's spectacle, rather than expressing or reflecting the movement of the content, actually produces this movement. Such a notion of the dialectic, which is less in the business of *application* than *exposition*, 'is the most authentically Hegelian' (Lefebvre 1968: 53). The content of the spectacle derives from its own *Begriffslogik*. The speculative is the revelation of the dialectic's positivity. It is precisely in this element of the dialectic, in the transition from *Verstand* to *Vernunft*, that we discover the logic of the society of the spectacle. The speculative logic of the spectacle thereby reunites the positive thought of empirical observation, a life from which the spectacle is said to reassemble. The spectacle posits its own presuppositions. Only on the basis of its speculative movement can we 'embrace the existence of an anthropology, while on the basis of an anthropology, we can never raise ourselves' (Hyppolite 1997: 96) to grasping the essential determinations of the society of the spectacle without recourse to aimless contingency. 'Thus this speculative life of the Logos is the light that clarifies itself ... it is the light that is simultaneously immediacy and reflection' (Hyppolite 1997: 104). Spectacular life is the manner in which the spectacle comprehends all alterity. It does so merely by comprehending itself. As a *Begriffslogik*, the spectacle has thereby demonstrated that its thought and the life which it procures are one and the same, a life of speculation or, in the words of Debord, 'the material life of everyone [turned] into a universe of speculation' (1995: §19).[15] In sum, the objective world of the spectacle becomes in and for itself the idea in its positing itself as the purposive life of the genus, and in so doing, as the full 'transparency of the finite' (Hegel 2010: 468), brings it to actuality. The life of the idea of the spectacle has become speculatively identical to its concept and, in this development of its *Begriffslogik*, we are now able, nearing the conclusion, to grasp the spectacle as a shape of spirit.

The spirit of the spectacle

In our analysis, the *coherence* of the spectacle has referred to the overall speculative unity of its commensurable social phenomena. The *idea* of the spectacle has undermined any attempt to render its category as a dualistic framework between spectacle and spectator without identification. The *life* of the spectacle has advanced the criticism that the spectacle is not in fact a dualism between image and life but that the latter is a moment precisely generated out of spectacular logic. On the whole then, the *Begriffslogik* of the spectacle offer these different cadences of the spectacle as a critical theory of society. But since spectacular logic does indeed refer to the rationality of society itself, we must here place final emphasis on how this rationality is itself a *spiritual* process, that is, how a process of socialization is contained in the very notion of spectacular logic. For this we examine the spirit of the spectacle.

For Hegel and beyond the finitude of individual life, spirit emerges in the *Begriffslogik* and is 'constituted by the absolute unity *in the concept* of opposites, and in its appearance ... it must be possible to adduce an experience in support of each of the opposite determinations of reflection' (Hegel 2010: 690). For all of this, as Hegel continues, 'it is from the *idea of life* that the idea of spirit has emerged', and for which one can 'compare the empirical reality or the appearance of spirit to see how far it accords with it' (2010: 694). Spirit emerges as a moment of the *Begriffslogik*. The logical forms hitherto examined thereby comprise a logical framework of spirit and therewith have their place in Hegel's *Realphilosophie* as categorial forms with real embodiment. Their logical stringency have not therewith abandoned the 'concerned with "the spiritual bond"' (Adorno 2000: 69). For this, we have taken the form-determinations of Hegel's *Science of Logic* not simply as forms of thought but also that which comprises the forms of the world. The *Science of Logic* as such exposes the necessary determinations implicitly at work in the *Phenomenology of Spirit*, the logical requirements for the development of spirit. A science of logic holds the connection between the structures of subjective concepts *about the world* with the actual affirmative structures *of the world*. It was an insight well familiar to Marx in which 'the categories express forms of being, determinations of existence ... of this particular society' (Marx 1986: 43).

This book has argued that the society of the spectacle is the actuality of the categories of Hegel's speculative positivity. Hegel's conception of positivity is the speculative spirit having traversed the determinations of the identity of identity and non-identity. Spirit here demonstrates a movement of the unity of opposites or of internal opposition which sustain immanent contradictions. Only as concept, however, does this physiognomy become explicit. The society of the spectacle as a critical theory of society thereby signifies a *Realphilosophie* with logically overwhelming speculative cohesion.[16]

The spirit of spectacle thinks its own essential nature through a series of speculative social forms – as unities of opposites, or, to put it in its most unadulterated anatomy, the movement of identity of identity and non-identity – the *rhythm of exchange-value* – builds the concept of the spectacle. It is this spectacular logic – as a social spirit whose determinate rationality sediments itself through a form of commensurable identification carried through a dialectic of appearances – that has been the central focus of this book. That is, how what appears as the heteronomy of the spectacle can be rationally translated into a unity of opposites whose differences are but the self-difference of the spectacle's *Begriffslogik*. The content of the spectacle in all of its diversity and richness is raised to the level of its concept, as exteriorized moments of its own rational logic. Here we find '[t]he official thought of the social organization of appearances' as speculative, 'the unchallengeable internal logic of the spectacle's language' (Debord 1995: §195). The speculative spirit of the spectacle remains in the reconciliatory and binding articulation of society, one whose command need only disclose an actuality it itself has created, and in so doing, trumpet without duplicity that everything is, in truth, as it seems.

Conclusion: A Nightmarish Baroque

Effective refutation must infiltrate the opponent's stronghold and meet him on his own ground; there is no point in attacking him outside his territory and claiming jurisdiction where he is not.

G. W. F. Hegel

This book has taken measure of, as a balance sheet, the spectacular logic of the society of the spectacle. Discovered is a critical theory of society reconstructed through a dialectic of appearances that results in unitary social cohesion through a speculative identity of differences. What is more, the spectacle's spectacular logic gives to itself actuality in the world as a development of its concept. The concept of the spectacle, provided here in its most undiluted form, is its developing actuality inasmuch as its actuality is the self-development of its concept.

The society of the spectacle as a critical theory of society refers to how appearances of differentiated social phenomena necessarily relate and together procure a false totality. It is a critique acquiring full coherence only in making explicit the interconnecting logic of society as a whole. At base, it is a critical theory whose primary demand is that only with attention to a comprehensively social totality, one constituted by the falsehood of commensurability through a dialectic of appearances, can the individual phenomena of capitalist society be adequately criticized. Furthermore, it is a critical theory of a society whose individual appearances emerge as moments which *ratify* that same society. The immediate publicity and distressing clarity with which the world broadcasts its turmoil is a distinct situation not shared by earlier periods of alarming uncertainty. With the spectacle, to *disclose* the calamities of society is no longer a condition for its *undoing*. Unlike our predecessors, we 'see every tear in the tissue and hear every cracking of the joints' (Huizinga 2019: 5). In this way, the programmatic exposition and appearance of social conditions becomes itself a mystification of those social conditions, not however as an illusory veil but merely in rendering the actuality of society illuminate.

Such a critical theory puts to bed those interpretations of the spectacle as either a mechanism of pacification or depoliticization in which industries of mass consumption or advertising are castigated as means of manipulation and distraction. Indeed, the spectacle is a structure that instills passivity no less than unbridled and vigorous activity, often intensely political and yet in and through a speculative organization of *Identitätszswang*, in which human beings 'recognize', as Debord writes, their 'own needs in the images of need proposed by the dominant system' (1995: §30). It is therefore not simply the case that what binds the work of Debord to the critical theory of the Frankfurt School is the common concern over generic issues of alienation and reification, or that both tendencies merely scrutinized more closely how human beings subordinate themselves to things. It is more specifically in the spectacular logic of identification, of rendering commensurable like with like as the rationalization of mimesis, so central to Horkheimer and Adorno's *Dialectic of Enlightenment*, that Debord's critical theory finds accord.

For Hegel as much as Debord, here we find a rationality whose purpose is to reconcile us with the positivity of its historical moment, in a 'manner of only conceiving of a positive adhesion to *all that exists*' (Debord 2006c: 339). While it is true that Debord provides an extrapolation of the critique of political economy, the concept of the society of the spectacle takes liberties within that distance as a further development of Marx's categories through the speculative of Hegelian thought as the unity of separations. This book has therewith provided an ideal reconstruction of the spectacle as a concept, itself a nevertheless historical totality in its particular self-determinations. Such an approach – reconstructing Debord's diagnosis and expounding its logical determinations which are themselves historical – assists in advancing a critical theory of the society of the spectacle to resonate beyond its own peculiar historical moment, and it is the hope of this author that such a procrustean bed in which we find ourselves provides a theoretical framework through which to comprehend further developing social relations.

The structure of the spectacle, as has here been elucidated as a spectacular logic, upholds and restores the conditions of its own actuality through the historical development of capitalism in the aftermath of the economic crisis of the early 1970s. During this period and after, the individualization of class struggle and its 'culturalization', the ongoing regime of austerity and in general the imposition of crisis management globally which dealt a severe blow to the offensive capacities of the global proletariat, can all be examined within the diagnosis of the society of the spectacle set forth in our analysis, having rendered explicit a spectacular logic not confined to a single period of capital accumulation. Indeed, from industrial productive capital investment to fictitious capital at the base of this restoration after the postwar period, we can easily enough discover a reconfiguration of spectacular dynamics. Poverty assumes *the appearance* of individual responsibility, the state assumes *the appearance* of an obstruction to open market circulation flows, the commodity assumes *the appearance* of base survival, a satiated proletariat assumes *the appearance* of a good credit score, an unsatiated proletariat assumes *the appearance* of the excluded other, culture assumes *the appearance* of a mechanism of empowerment, and so on. None of these appearances are strictly false insofar as they are the true manifestations of the necessarily false. Only through a dialectic of appearances, fundamental in the analysis of spectacular logic, can the conditions of the spectacle's actuality procure reinvention, a development which certainly took place after postwar prosperity and into the twenty-first century. None of the changes since that time could have been possible without a logically existent structure of appearances and forms of commensurable identification constitutive of our analysis of the spectacle, whereby the actuality of the world need only disclose itself in order to justify itself.

The spectacle becomes that ruthless unity of difference whose conjunctive whole of relations and particulars pivots upon unbridled circulation and reconciliation. A brief scroll through one's social media feed elicits its nightmarishly baroque quality: the celebration of a newborn, a Coney Island hotdog eating contest, an appeal to help pay next month's rent, hysterical ebullience over the latest social democratic baby-kisser, a suicidal cry for help, raging California forest fires that you can 'Watch with your friends', colonoscopy discounts, crippling depression, holocaust denial, student loan refinancing, investment opportunities, petitions, gossip, eulogies and base entertainment all rolled into one singular engagement with the world. Indeed what was for the postwar period of the society of the spectacle the automobile (Knabb 2006: 69–70) is in its twenty-first-century advancement the digital apparatus of telecommunications and social media data distribution, a rationalized world of instant communication situated within total and immediate global interconnection. Both ascend, one no more concrete than the other, as requisites for social participation and operate as baseline form-determinations for all possible movement, however versatile. Yet the panorama of mass media remains the spectacle's 'most stultifying superficial manifestation' (Debord 1995: §24). Nevertheless, it is a field of experiential potpourri not altogether dissimilar from the latest museum curatorial programme, the contours of the next presidential debate or just an afternoon stroll along the avenue.

Emblematic for its tendency to the *pastiche* remains the Las Vegas Strip: at once landmarks of New York City cajole with Venetian façades; Parisian lights illuminate the tomb of King Tut; Caesar engages the quest for Excalibur; erupting volcanoes keep warm the prime rib buffets – all in all, an incoherent coherence fortified with neon brilliance.

Every momentary verisimilitude is as valid as the next, a veritable equalization between the most trivial and the deadly serious. It is their commensurability, schizophrenic in nature, that gives inner coherence to the heterogeneity of the world in the present moment as a society of the spectacle. The spectacle in this sense is hardly an exercise in mere representation, least of all a vendor of the fictitiously fabricated, but instead the pinnacle of mimetic fidelity within the social fabric. Nor can the logic of the spectacle, despite more common interpretations, be grounded as a semiotic function. As the true inheritor of the general equivalent, it is rather the manner in which society allows us to switch from one indulgence to the next, a burlesque parade that converts anything into its opposite within a harmonious cornucopia of variation by which we might identify, find recognition and, if lucky, call home.

Throughout this book, we have intentionally relinquished any fidelity to other features of Debord's thought, but instead sought to assess a particular diagnostic concept and give to it greater logical elucidation. Allegations that the examination seemingly lacks any criticism of Debord can be therefore assuaged in the general liberty with which the analysis diverges from a faithful reading of Debord and the SI project generally. Its excessively systematic approach, justified in this conclusion, can with legitimacy be reproached for failing to account for Debord's aversion to conceptual systems (Debord 2004a: 95).[1] However, this is less a weakness of our work than it is its strength.

Unease that within the present analysis the spectacle appears in an overtly idealist register, or that the materialist critique of Hegel is nowhere to be found, can be given the response that the investigation has sought to provide a concept of the spectacle as a centre of gravity of its speculative logic, an account of its fluctuating tendencies for accommodating differentiation irrespective of any contingent historical circumstance and that regardless of the historical moment it finds itself, its essential logical structure as a dialectic of appearance, which develops an unified inverted actuality through self-differentiation, gains purchase. For this, the spectacle has admittedly possessed something of an exaggeration throughout this book. Nevertheless, if its seemingly idealist logic bears little trace of a materialist underpinning – not a wholly justified admonishment given the centrality with which its historical genesis derives from the developing specificity and autonomy of exchange-value – it remains the case that the society of the spectacle realizes an idealist programme and gives to Hegel's speculative a really existing rationality, one whose postulates form together a social totality to which nothing remains extraneous. Any cosmetic associations between the society of the spectacle and Hegelian terminology thereby fail to live up to the former's speculative logic as a reality of Hegelian idealism.

For all this, this book has in large dose adopted the perspective *of* the society of the spectacle itself, an account of the vanity of the world it aspires to create. The cruelty of this approach resides in presenting its object as a full and virtually inescapable envelopment. It is for this reason that this book has offered no political prescriptions for the overcoming of the society of the spectacle – nor is it obliged to do so despite the frequently heard clamouring of this society to participate, with the utmost expediency, in its own improvement. 'The optimism of the left repeats the insidious bourgeois superstition that one should not talk of the devil but look on the bright side' (Adorno 2005a: 114). Rather, a meticulous exposition of the spectacle's conceptual objectivity is necessary in order to exorcize any ambiguity and arbitrariness from Debord's critical diagnosis. Further, critique does well to resist the incessant demand to immediately yield concrete solutions and avoid the abundance of apologetics that pervade society. In a word, it is of the utmost importance to prefer the bad against *the appearance of the good*. A record of the bad is what this book has sought to provide, and in so doing, uphold the adage that 'the possibility of a valid practice presupposes the full and undiminished awareness of the *blockage* of practice' (Adorno 2008: 54). There is no danger in overemphasizing unfreedom, especially when that unfreedom prevents the formation of something not yet experienced.

The impossibility of intervention cannot be overstated as a potential ground and possibility for immanent negativity. For this, we remind our readers that in no way has the investigation precluded the immanent contradictions and social antagonisms derived from Marx's critique of political economy. Instead, what thorough insight into the impossibility of intervention elicits are the limitations of particular interventions. A fully elucidated totality makes swift work of half-measures. For example, scrutiny of particular images found within the society of the spectacle can at best yield an aggregate of empirical studies that cease their criticism the moment such images encroach upon the more 'realistic', 'representative' or 'empowering'. Similarly, in an era of abounding apologetics, promises of greater exposure, visibility and transparency, or simply in the prerogative to be noticed, are all aspirations brightly lit by the society of the spectacle. There are immense illusions involved in efforts to emancipate this society by perfecting it. For this, again, interpretations emphasizing the spectacle as 'disempowering', 'depoliticizing' or 'devitalizing' miss the mark on its spectacular logic of social organization. Human beings today are not ashamed by their reification but by an insufficiency of it, tinged with the fear of not becoming exploited, compensated or vindicated. Nor can demands for the equitable distribution of wealth accord with a critique not aimed at hierarchical power, but as an indictment of requited equivalence. Indeed, Debord always considered debate 'on the activities of the world's owners' to be 'empty debate on the spectacle [and as such] organized by the spectacle itself' (Debord 1998: 6). A critical theory of the society of the spectacle extends itself beyond problems of wealth differentials, and as such, any analysis of particular *Vorstellungen* of this society risks ignoring what makes the spectacle a totality of accommodated differentiation. A central lesson of both Debord and the SI's critical theory remains that the world at present has forgotten how *more* can feel interminably like *less*. Said another way, malnourishment is still nourishment.

For Debord, *The Society of the Spectacle* is 'simply record [of] what is' (1998: 5). Such a critical diagnostic assumes greater importance and urgency in periods of extreme ignorance. We witness a time when the transparency of communication serves as a universal medium of untruth, where 'sidewalk-vending thinkers are so esteemed for reinventing lukewarm water' (Debord 2001a: 26). Here, amidst an environment where emoji keyboards can be argued to advance discourse, imprecision and arbitrary concepts reign supreme and 'serve definite forces' (Knabb 2006: 238). Furthermore, imitation of the fluency and tone of modern advertising, of conveying an idea in the most economical and accessible manner possible, drives critical theory to the terrain of its enemy. It is for this reason that our analysis has found recourse in a theory of the society of the spectacle as a thoroughly rational structure. The society of the spectacle as an eminently logical system, as here expounded, is ultimately justified from the prerogative to exorcize from the critical theory of society any of the flippant, capricious or incoherent orientation so prevalent within desultory dissatisfaction today. It has been the argument of this book that to give the concept of the spectacle its greatest explanatory power is to isolate its logical structure as the rational actuality of Hegel's speculative. Indeed, it is only by proceeding through reason, despite its reprehensible brood, that we discover what it still has to offer, lying in wait. Until then, any animosity towards the present investigation by the milieus of spectacular organization is assuredly and without impudence a great bounty and honour.

Appendix: *The Society of the Spectacle* and Its Time

What follows below is an outline of the philosophical, political and economic atmosphere surrounding the 1967 publication of Guy Debord's *The Society of the Spectacle*. It is an historical contextualization that helps to give greater historical meaning to the book's postwar arrival. The first part offers an abridged survey of Hegel reception in France from the interwar to the postwar period and how it is that Debord's Hegelianism amounts to an anomaly to postwar Hegelian reception. The second places Debord's Marxism within the context of France's annexation by Stalinism and how it is that Debord ought to be situated within the dissident Marxism that proliferated after 1956 as a crisis in Marxian orthodoxy. The final part places *The Society of the Spectacle* within the context of the development of capital accumulation within the *Trente Glorieuses* years and how the concept of capitalism as a society of the spectacle acquires historical determinacy through the peculiarities of postwar prosperity. The background as a whole bears important pertinence for the preceding investigation, insofar as a more logically coherent investigation of the concept of the spectacle as a critical theory of society ought to be weighed against the contingencies under which Debord was writing.

The fear of integration

Debord's return to the Hegelian thought took place at a time of its illegitimacy – or what Judith Butler has referred to as 'Hegel's dissolution in France' (1999: 7). It was a scandal not just for the major trends within French philosophy but also for the standards and developments of French Marxism. The way in which *The Society of the Spectacle* integrated aspects of Hegelian thought long since rejected functioned as a kind of assault upon the language, style and currency of the prevailing discourse and its various public intellectuals. The dialectic's 'epigrammatic' and 'insurrectional style' (Debord 1970: §206) lambasted the literary sensibilities of French intellectual periodicals. As *Le Monde* wrote in February 1968, one finds in the writings of Debord '[a] snarling, extravagant rhetoric that is always detached from the complexity of the facts upon which we reason [which] not only makes the reading disagreeable but also staggers thought'. However, for Debord, such confusion amounted to a strategic leverage, a mantra, upheld by Sun Tzu, in which the whole secret of victory lies in the enemy's intellectual and moral disorientation. By amalgamating French literary intimation with heavy German conceptuality, the dynamic category of the spectacle served broadly, in the words of Clausewitz, to confuse 'the enemy and lowers his morale' (1984: 198).

In this way, first, Debord, and the SI generally, sought to *weaponize* the dialectic, which was grasped as one of 'the truest and most important concepts of the era', and yet was surrounded by 'the greatest confusions and the worst misinterpretations' (Knabb 2006: 239).[1] For Debord, the dialectic amounted to that method best suited to both comprehend and contest the totality of the era, and in this way, as he concludes the preface to the third French edition of *The Society of the Spectacle*, '[t]his book should be read bearing in mind that it was written with the deliberate intention of doing harm to spectacular society. There was never anything outrageous, however, about what it had to say' (1995: 10). An intellectual atmosphere taking political positions, in the case of Sartre, '*to the right of Khrushchev*' (Knabb 2006: 235), when it wasn't liquidating subjectivity altogether, could only therefore receive *The Society of the Spectacle* and its return to a Hegelian thought, outside the discursive parameters of select figurations from the *Phenomenology of Spirit*, with animosity.

Second, it can be remarked that the distinctly French concern over conceptual unity stands as an unacknowledged concern over the spectacle itself, rather than simply a development within the history of philosophical thinking. The dream of the 1960s to think non-conceptual difference and absolute heterogeneity was a flight from the unifying power of objective social conditions. It is, at base, *a fear of integration*. As Adorno has remarked, 'the dialectic is reproached for revealing the compulsive character of the world' (2017: 78). Commenting further in his spring 1968 lectures on sociology, integration, first diagnosed by Herbert Spencer, refers to networks of socialization tightly woven together, 'so that even those who were outside bourgeois society, or rather half-outside it, like the industrial proletariat in the 1830s and 1840s, have been increasingly incorporated' (Adorno 2000: 24)

The society of the spectacle pivots upon a unifying logic of integrating, although without extinguishing, difference within itself. In this way, it might be said that the concerns said to occupy existentialism, structuralism, deconstruction and poststructuralism could be construed as essentially *reactionary*. In various capacities, too many and complex to review here, postwar French philosophy is itself responding in different ways to the same social conditions of the society of the spectacle, a flight towards what Adorno describes in *Negative Dialectics* as a 'logic of disintegration' (*Logik des Zerfalls*) within a society dominated by a principle of identity structuring both the equalization of exchange relations and modes of conceptual thought. Recourse to intense heterogeneous diffusion and an immersion into fragmentation and perspectivism inimical to objective universality and totality does not sit well for a social ontology pivoting upon the objective *unity* of organized appearances constituted through the commodity form and given actuality through the structure of its concept.

The illegitimacy of Hegel's system in the interwar years originates in the way in which, largely propagated by French neo-Kantianism, its alleged pan-logicism violently falsifies reality and reconciles thought to an unacceptable and traumatic social situation. Even by the late 1940s, the decline in Hegelian historicism, with the shift in focus of Alexandre Kojéve and Jean Hyppolite, and in the general loss of faith in the meaning of history, can be read as emblematic of a harrowing scenario in which the unifying power *Vernunft* had procured immense horror. And yet, up until the 1920s, the French almost always understood Hegel in terms of the system elucidated in the *Encyclopaedia of the Philosophical Sciences*. In the postwar period, it was easy to forget that contemporary readings were in many ways a reaction *against* the prewar interpretation of Hegel. Indeed, despite postwar interpretations to the contrary, French interest in Hegel did not first appear in the 1930s as a product of phenomenology, existentialism and Marxism. The postwar humanistic and anthropological version of Hegel was, in many respects, an attempt to correct what was seen as the error of Hegel's alleged pan-logicism in which the heterogeneity and alterity of phenomena are forcibly caught and encased within a rational system, rejecting anything that might fall outside.

However, prior to the ascendance of this criticism, French philosophy found itself in a situation captivated by the science of the nineteenth century and actively sought a new epistemological approach adequate to the scientific developments of the time. Upheld then was the logical system of the *Encyclopaedia*. The Hegelian dialectic allowed for the cognition of totality as a system of becoming which neither collapsed the particular into an abstract universal nor sacrificed conceptual intelligibility to the immediacy of intuition. It was the *speculative* component of the dialectic that was venerated in this period, the capacity of conceptual thinking to integrate opposites into itself. It is the superiority of *Vernunft* over *Verstand* that stood as a crucial pole of attraction in the prewar period, precisely the point of vehement contention and criticism that would appear in the postwar period. However, prior to that moment, it was Hegel as the philosopher of reconciliation that was lauded in France, even among some neo-Kantians such as Émile Boutroux.

On the whole, then, it can be argued that Debord stands not simply as an anomaly to postwar Hegelian reception, but more importantly, as a *reconciliation* of prewar and postwar Hegelian thinking. On the one hand, within Debord's thought, there is the adoption of Hegel's speculative as a moment within the dialectical logic that integrates difference within the unity of *Vernunft* over the antinomies of the *Verstand*. However, at the same time, Debord gives social ontology to this system as that which 'satisfies Spirit' in the form of the spectacle. Indeed, a comment from the preface to Hegel's *Phenomenology of Spirit* repeatedly appears within Debord's writings: 'By the little which satisfies Spirit, we can measure the extent of its loss' (Hegel 1977c: 5).[2] It is from spirit reduced to what *satisfies* it that Debord will begin his prognosis. Debord's Hegelian thinking bears the residue and maintains the falsification identified in postwar Hegelian reception by extending it into a social philosophy of spirit. On this view, Debord can be read as a synthesis of the pan-logicist and *Geisteswissenschaftler* Hegel without, unlike most postwar French Hegelianism, an excessive infatuation with the unhappy consciousness, the lordship and bondage dialectic, the structure of desire, and so on.[3]

Beneath the 'French fiddlededeee', Parisian socialists are all liars and rascals

Towards the end of the 1950s, Henri Lefebvre observed that 'Marxism has become *boring*. It has been a disappointment; young people are disappointed with it because it bores them' (1991a: 84–5). To what does Lefebvre attribute such decomposition? While it was through its leadership in the Resistance in the mid-1940s and its role in the anti-fascist coalition a decade prior that the French Communist Party (PCF) commanded significant influence in France and transformed it into a mass movement, the period between the 1930s and 1950s witnessed the gradual encroachment and clout of Stalinism over French

Marxism, in which the supreme prerogative of intellectuals became the defence and justification of the Soviet Union. Following the war and Moscow's stabilized relations with de Gaulle, the PCF substituted Bolshevist militancy with a tactical conservative republicanism. As a result, the PCF restrained all pugnacity in support of Stalin's policy of European stability and propagated collaboration with the Fourth Republic for economic reconstruction.

Debord and the SI held the utmost contempt for party Marxism. What is more, Debord's inspiration wasn't Lenin, for example, but nineteenth-century poet Lautréamont, whom the Surrealists held as the supreme exemplar of an individual utterly at war with all bourgeois values. Indeed, Debord, sharing in part a position similar to Lefebvre, stands at a considerable distance from the purview of official Marxism, taking a cue from the avant-garde before him. In a passage not altogether dissimilar from Debord's own trajectory, Alfred Schmidt writes that '[w]hat made Lefèbvre (by no means without conflict) turn to Marxism had little to do with university philosophy. It was the political and social upheavals of the postwar period, and more particularly personal problems, psychoanalysis, and association with the literary and artistic avant-garde, the surrealist movement' (1972: 325).

Besides affinity with the ideas of Lefebvre, which are beyond the scope of this book, Debord would come to supersede orthodox Marxism also through his brief participation, between 1960 and 1961, in *Socialisme ou Barbarie*. Against the 'academic thinkers with paid vacations' (IS 1997: 334) of *Arguments*,[4] it was *Socialisme ou Barbarie* that remained one of the few political organizations which exerted some momentary influence on the SI (1997: 250–6). It was specifically the group's critique of the vanguardism of Marxist-Leninism and the bureaucratic state of the Eastern bloc, as a variation on its Western reciprocal, that Debord would take heed. However, despite these insights, Debord would come to critically articulate a spectacular image of the political militant and its activism based on his own observations within *Socialisme ou Barbarie*, wherein a division of labour split leading theoreticians from rank and file members (2001b: 82–8). Further tension would soon arise, specifically with Castoriadis' orthodox and normative conception of labour and in general *Socialisme ou Barbarie*'s emphasis on self-management. For the SI, which infamously rejected labour *tout court* rather than idealized its self-management,[5] Castoriadis' positive conception of labour (Postone 1993: 171) resulted in 'maintaining, more or less unconsciously, a sort of nostalgia for older forms of work' (Knabb 2006: 132). Self-managed industrial production, with a mere changing of the guard, remained a far cry from a notion of the self-management of everyday life in all its aspects propagated by Debord.[6]

Debord's Marxism did not as such develop through academia, 'like Daniel Cohn-Bendit, or teachers like Althusser'. Nor did '[it] hail from the literary world like Sartre or even from the variegated milieu of left-wing militantism' (Jappe 1999: 84), which Debord deplored as either bureaucratic and economistic orthodoxy or theoretically aimless anarchism. Against the dogmatism of the PCF and its derivatives, what held Debord's attention were the new forms of social rebellion, from wildcat strikes to youth vandalism, student strikes, race riots and looting. Whereas the classical workers' movement took aim at capitalist deprivation, the new struggles were seen to theoretically elucidate the attack on capitalist affluence, a point shared with Lefebvre's scepticism over the idea that revolutionary transformation need derive from 'absolute poverty, want and pauperization' (Lefebvre 2002: 32). Indeed, as is emblematic of the dissident Marxism of the postwar period, it would be through that reading of Marx, in which the critique of capitalism as a form of impersonal and abstract domination and alienation acquires theoretical precedence over empirical and morally-laden concern over the worsening economic conditions of the working class, that the concept of the society of the spectacle as a critical theory of society would appear.

The *Trente glorieuses* years

It has been said that only as a *symptom* was the SI important. Such a judgement derives from the fact that the critique of the society of the spectacle emerges under very specific historical circumstances which witnessed an 'amelioration of the conditions of social life under capitalism' (Perspectives 1975: 10). The Marxism and critical theory that appeared in this moment develops against the background of a period of capital accumulation under the *Trente glorieuses* years of postwar prosperity (Arrighi 1994: 296–300; Harvey 1990: 121–40). Here, rapid per capita economic growth within the high-income countries – along with quickening technological innovation, historically high profit rates and employment levels and low inflation – witnessed an exponential increase of the non-agricultural workforce entering into industrial markets concomitant with rising levels of productivity and productive capacity.

Postwar Europe underwent breakneck development not seen since the eighteenth century, with the economic stagnation of the 1920s and 1930s seeming to vanish overnight.[7] As for France, in the 1930s, it was still a relatively underdeveloped country economically in comparison with some of its neighbours. Within only a few years, France's industrialization and productivity grew at an incredible rate, increasing faster than anywhere else in the world at the time. Crucial to this rapid industrialization was the role of state planning during the aftermath of the war, most notably with mixed economies operating not so much as 'a partial transformation of private enterprise into state-enterprise, but as a full employment program realized through government initiative in order to increase production within the private-enterprise system' (Mattick 1969: 145). The state sought to regulate the business cycle through a combination of fiscal and monetary policy that would direct investment towards public infrastructural development such as suburbanization and urban renewal along with a geographical expansion of communications and transport systems necessary for the growth of mass production and consumption. The Fifth Republic of De Gaulle continued these policies, and by 1960, France appeared as an absolutely different country from the France of 1950. A new social situation had emerged, one that witnessed an increasingly non-competitive economy characterized by state subsidization, strong regulation of certain sectors of the economy and the organization of consumption.

Important here is the way in which Debord sketches the modern origins of the spectacle within various developments that culminate in postwar prosperity. Debord identifies the advent of the spectacle proper within the period of the 'second industrial revolution', commonly regarded as the period from the late nineteenth century until the First World War, the historical moment in which 'alienated consumption becomes for the masses a duty supplementary to alienated production' (Debord 1970: §42). At this point, roughly from the beginning of the 1920s and accelerating after the Second World War, the economy no longer disregards the manner in which its working class satisfies its needs. Focused efforts on cultivating the *consuming* aspect of the proletariat inaugurated a deeper integration of the proletariat into the accumulation process. 'It is *all the sold labor* of a society which globally becomes the *total commodity* for which the cycle must be continued' (Debord 1970: §42). For Debord, the historical specificity of the spectacle unfolding in accordance with the development of the autonomy of the commodity can thereby be witnessed through a greater absorption of labour into the circulation sphere, an effort devoted strictly to the realization of surplus value, rather than to its creation. '[A]s soon as the production of commodities reaches a level of abundance which requires a surplus of collaboration from the worker' (Debord 1970: §43), consumption in general becomes, as the proletariat gains greater access to the total commodity, a dialectical determination of capitalist production, or said another way, the real subsumption of use in and the abstractions of commodity exchange.

This historical moment produced – in exchange for the immense growth in productivity and the cheapening of commodities deriving from the massive devalorization of capital during the war – increased purchasing power and greater integration of the proletariat into the spheres of consumption. While this was reflected as a *relative* decrease in the value of labour-power to the total social value produced, it nonetheless occasioned an *absolute* increase in the real value of wages. This tendency was additionally accompanied by direct subsidies to the productive sphere as well as an increase in the indirect wage of the proletariat, which thereby obtained the luxuries of a slight increase in the price of its labour above the minimum necessary for the reproduction of that labour-power, as well as various supplements such as loans, credit, welfare and retirement benefits.[8]

Overall, the concept of capitalism as a society of the spectacle acquires historical determinacy through the peculiarities of postwar prosperity. Again, it is a critique of society that need not pivot along theses of immiseration nor empirical sociologies on the working class which conceive the proletariat along the lines of income distribution. The impoverishment elicited by the concept of the spectacle expands proletarian wretchedness more capaciously into a 'nouveau prolétariat' (IS 1997: 253),[9] one beyond classical relations of exploitation and deteriorating working conditions, instead grasping the poverty of affluence. Through the critique of the spectacle, no longer would revolutionary class struggle find orientation in an emancipation from want, but from the dissatisfaction implicit within the dominant images of satisfaction and social meaning. The 'nouvelle pauvreté' (IS 1997: 256) exceeds material poverty and instead proliferates within the amelioration granted by postwar prosperity. As Debord proclaims in his 1961 film, *Critique of Separation*, 'The point is not to recognize that some people live more or less poorly than others, but that we all live in ways that are out of our control' (2003a: 31).

Notes

Foreword

1   In the course of the book, the reader will discover that Debord had a close relationship to the interpretation of Hegel's Logic proposed by Jean Hyppolite (Hegel's greatest French translator and commentator in the postwar period), where the category of the 'speculative proposition' played a central role. This is paradoxical in a sense, because Hyppolite's lectures at the Collège de France, which Debord attended and transcribed in his personal notes, were taking place in the last months in which Debord prepared his book for publication. Even if he wrote rapidly and with great assurance, I find it unlikely that he had not reached his main ideas and formulations before those lectures, on the basis of his own familiarity with Hegel's work. But I agree that this encounter was decisive and may have confirmed and 'sealed' his entire 'speculative' construction. In other places in his book, Russell rightly insists on the importance of Debord's familiarity with the work of Henri Lefebvre, and in particular the commentary on Hegel's *Logic* included in his book from 1946 (with new editions in 1969 and 1982), *Logique formelle et logique dialectique*, whose 'Hegelianism' earned Lefebvre severe rebuttals from the official philosophers of the Communist Party. Lefebvre, however, was not insisting on the 'speculative' dimension of Hegel's thought, but rather on its move from 'abstract' to 'concrete' forms of knowledge.
2   *The Society of the Spectacle*, § 215. I may be permitted a more personal remark here: an 'Althusserian' Marxist reads this with excitement and some puzzlement, because the 'materiality of ideology' is considered a cornerstone of Althusser's revision of the concept of ideology in classical Marxism. It was enunciated only two years after the publication of Debord's book (with the 1968 insurrection in the middle). It is impossible for me to say if Althusser had read Debord (perhaps the archives can clarify this point), but in any case it is clear that the two philosophers belong to antithetic branches of twentieth-century Marxism, in France and elsewhere, with the relation to the institutional Communist Party and the appreciation of the Hegelian legacy in Marx as radical points of incompatibility. It would be interesting to reflect here on the intrinsic ambivalence of this philosophical language (materiality, materialism, materialization), but also on the 'objective' pressure of revolutionary consciousness on both sides in a critical conjuncture. A 'dematerialized' (purely 'epistemic') concept of ideology is an extremely weak instrument of critique, if at all critical.

3 Adorno is not mentioned in the most recent and comprehensive dissertation on Debord and philosophy written in France, also quite remarkable and systematically investigating the Debord archive, that of Bertrand Cochard at Université de Nice (2019), except for a quick allusion to the analogy between some aspects of the 'spectacle' according to Debord and the 'cultural industry' according to Adorno and Horkheimer. See http://crhi-unice.fr/membres-statutaires/362-bertrand-cochard.

Introduction

1 Debord began writing *The Society of the Spectacle* as early as autumn of 1963 (Debord 2001: 262). An infamously artful drinker, Debord vowed two years later not to pick up a glass until the book was complete. As to whether or not he stuck with such a pledge, one can never know, although it is rumoured that during the final months before publication, Debord replaced his daily intake of alcohol with tomato juice (Frayssé 2017: 71). As he writes in a 1965 letter to Raoul Vaneigem, 'Although I've been fortunate enough to have had other demands on my time over the last month, my focus has been away from many of the charms and meanders of everyday life in order to put the finishing touches to the critique of the spectacle. I have cut out drink until the last line is written: an example worthy of classical antiquity! Like the Spartans at Thermopylae . . . In a best-case scenario it should be a weight off my mind in a matter of six to eight weeks. The trap I have set myself is nevertheless a clever one' (Debord 2003b: 21).
2 The rest of the Anglophone literature fares no better with mere cursory remarks, such as that Debord was 'inspired' by Hegel (Hussey 2001: 52) or that *The Society of the Spectacle* could be considered 'a détournment of Hegel' (Wark 2013: 50). Elsewhere the 'Hegelian tradition' was simply 'on Debord's mind' and that *The Society of the Spectacle* is in a 'forced conversation' with Hegel (Clark and Nicolson-Smith 1997: 24, 25) or that Debord 'more seriously enters into dialogue' with Hegel (Gilman-Opalsky 2011: 60). In terms of the French scholarship, exceptional mention ought to be made of Jean-Louis Moinet's *Genèse et unification du spectacle*, published in 1977 by Editions Champ Libre. Moinet was a Kierkegaardian and his book is divided into three sections: 'Against Hegelian Dialecticism', 'Pale Imitations of the Hegelian System' and 'Recent Forms of the Spectacle'. Also worth mentioning as a more recent engagement with the relation between Debord and Hegel is Bernard Cochard's 2019 doctoral dissertation from the Centre de Recherche en Histoire des Idées, titled 'Guy Debord et la philosophie'.
3 Marx's *Capital*, Volume I, begins as such: 'The wealth of those societies in which the capitalist mode of production prevails, presents itself as "an immense accumulation of commodities"' (1996: 45).

4 As Hegel writes, 'Hence this acquired property still has the same character of uncomprehended immediacy, of passive indifference, as existence itself; existence has thus merely passed over into figurative representation [*Vorstellung*]' (1977c: 17–18). This is a passage copied out of Debord's copy of Jean Hyppolite's translation of the *Phenomenology of Spirit* with the word 'détournable?' written adjacently; Bibliothèque nationale de France, Département des Manuscrits, NAF 28603, Fonds Guy Debord, Fiches rassemblées sous l'intitulé: Hegel 80 f. Phénoménologie de l'esprit 8 f.125 x 75 et 135 x 105 mm. References and citations from Debord's archival materials will be made thusly throughout the present work.

5 Within the present work, selections from *The Society of the Spectacle* will be procured from both the 1970 Black & Red and 1995 Nicholson-Smith translations. Thesis number to indicate their exact location will follow the quotations. Although it should be noted that Debord couldn't read English well, he was at least under the impression that the Nicholson-Smith translation was superior to what he took to be the 'mediocre' Black & Red translation (Debord 2008a: 122, 214–15, and 2005: 259–60).

6 For Sohn-Rethel, particularly through his concept of *Realabstraktion* as the way in which material life is dominated by the impersonal and objective forms of value, commodity exchange becomes a decisive medium of social synthesis which historically develops into a universal form of social mediation. Within Sohn-Rethel's analysis, the abstraction of exchange first appears within Ionia in the seventh century BCE and corresponds to the development of epistemological abstraction culminating in the philosophy of Kant. Here, intellectual labour, in employing universal non-empirical concepts, moves within the formal elements of the social synthesis of exchange, going so far as to 'define the Kantian "transcendental subject" as a fetish concept of the capital function of money' (Sohn-Rethel 1983: 77). Sohn-Rethel adopts the term 'social synthesis' as an appropriation of Kant's 'synthetic a priori judgements', paying 'transcendental idealism back in its own coin' (Sohn-Rethel 1983: 37)

7 In a May 1969 letter to the Italian section of the Situationist International (SI), Debord offers his own synoptic chapter breakdown of *The Society of the Spectacle* (2004a: 79–80). It is worth noting that as late as 8 March 1965, Debord had yet to finalize the precise chapter organization. As he reveals at the time in a letter to Vaneigem, an early draft manuscript consisted of twelve chapters, rather than what would become nine (2003b: 21–2).

8 As Debord writes in his notes on Clausewitz, 'A dialectical thought without strategy is the fault of the Hegelian system' (2018: 430).

9 Those quick to interpret Debord as the great opponent of imagery would do well to consider not only his films, but also more specifically he remarks in his foreword to the second volume of *Panegyric*, an autobiography composed mainly of

photographs: 'The reigning deceptions of the time are on the point of causing us to forget that truth may also be displayed by means of images. An image that has not been deliberately separated from its meaning can add great precision and certainty to knowledge. Until very recently, no one has ever doubted it. I intend, however, to provide a reminder of it now. An authentic illustration sheds light on true discourse, like a subordinate clause which is neither incompatible nor pleonastic' (2004b: 73–4).

10 These tripartite sectors of the spectacle are also invoked by Debord in a 1973 letter: 'The matter you raise prompts me to make the following points: behind the spectacle (for example, television, print advertising, government pronouncements, etc.), i.e. specific forms of deception, lies the overall *reality* of the spectacle itself (as a point in time determined by a specific mode of production). The dialectical relationship between the stark reality of socio-economic development unfolding historically and the spectacle's overall configuration which is both illusory and real is examined in the immediately preceding theses (7–9). Thus, by eliminating the idea of the social *organization* underpinning the spectacle, the German translation makes nonsense out of my original formulation, given that "the appearances of this appearance" already constitutes a peculiarly unorthodox and baroque turn of phrase on which I settled somewhat reluctantly. The only way its use can be justified is in reference to the following three stages: mere technological and ideological appearances / the reality of the social organization of appearances / historical reality' (2005: 61).

11 Derivative of this nominalism is what Hayes calls 'the common doxa of splitting the SI into two distinct phases (at least up until 1968): the so-called artistic SI of 1957–1961, and the political SI of 1962–1968' (2017: 14). The Anglophone literature almost exclusively proliferates within the elevation of this first period, spellbound by early practices of the SI such as *dérive* and psychogeography, although occasionally engaging the SI as political militants who precipitated the upheaval of May 1968 in France. In both cases, what is absent is a sustained evaluation on the concept of the spectacle as a critical theory of society utilizing the categorial sources of Hegelian thought and the dissident Marxism of the postwar period.

12 Clark and Nicholson-Smith offer an amusing anecdote, although there is no archival evidence that Debord attended a separate seminar the year prior: 'One of us remembers him at the Collège de France in 1966, sitting in on Hyppolite's course on Hegel's *Logic*, and having to endure a final session at which the master invited two young Turks to give papers. [Debord announces that there are] [t]hree stages in French middle-class culture's degeneration: first, standard scholarship, even if based on a certain general knowledge; next the Stalinist idiot with his passwords, "labor," "force," and "terror"; and finally – the lowest of the low – the semiotician' (1997: 24).

13 This is a formulation noted by Lenin in his 'Conspectus to the *Science of Logic*'. The remark is made near where Hegel writes of negativity as 'the *turning point* of the movement of the concept' (Hegel 2010: 745). Originally written in Russian as

'соль' and accurately appearing in German as 'Salz', the English translation inexplicably renders the description as 'the kernel of dialectics' (Lenin 1981: 228), even mistaking the singular conjugation of 'dialectic'.

14. As Debord writes in a 1971 letter, 'Although the concept of the spectacle is the center of the book, the title is merely provisional [*occasionnel*] and intends an agitation-effect: one could just as well have called it "The Society of the Proletariat." But it would be necessary to guard against the historical recuperation of the words. This is why this book, which is *communist* if it is anything, almost never uses this term' (2004a: 457).

15. Debord's attention to war theory, strategy and chance undoubtedly informed his delicate relationship to language. An overwhelming amount of his archival notes are devoted to war strategy and a scrupulous attention to the history of both modern and ancient warfare. Standing above the rest, however, is the inspiration drawn from the writings of Prussian military general Carl von Clausewitz. Clausewitz wants to strategically think the simultaneously contradictory factors of war, and for Debord, '[t]o think dialectically and to think strategically is the same thing' (2018: 430).

16. Along with Adorno, there is in Debord an appreciation of the parataxical approach to writing, illustrated in volume two of *Panegyric* with a quote from seventeenth-century Savoyard courtier Claude Favre de Vaugelas: 'But because my sole intention here has been to make remarks that are entirely distinct from one another, with the comprehension of a particular one in no way depending upon an understanding of the ones placed either before or after it, connecting them would only have caused difficulties, and I might very well have found myself going out of my way to make my work less agreeable and less useful to the reader. For there is no doubt that this continual diversity of subject matter creates the spirit anew and renders it more capable of carrying out what is proposed to it, especially when, as is the case here, brevity has been added to the general aspect, and one has been assured that every remark will make its effect felt' (Debord 2004: 163).

17. The reader of this book can, at any time, jump to the Appendix for a historical contextualization of *The Society of the Spectacle*. The Appendix consists of a tripartite division that outlines the philosophical, political and economic atmosphere surrounding the 1967 publication *The Society of the Spectacle*.

18. Beginning with 'Introduction to a Critique of Urban Geography', which originally appeared in the sixth issue of Belgian surrealist journal *Les Lèvres Nues* in 1955, the category is utilized by Debord generically to refer to publicity theatrics and the impressions and ambiances garnered from urban excursions. As might be expected, the term 'spectator' is also employed in a more commonplace capacity to refer to the subjectivity of passive reception. However, within the 1957 article 'Report on the Construction of Situations and on the International Situationist Tendency's Conditions of Organization and Action', the category gets the specific definition as

'non-intervention' and for which '[t]he construction of situations begins beyond the ruins of the modern spectacle'. It thereby begins to acquire a more technical meaning as a mode of 'psychological identification' (IS 1997: 699). It is within this early article – which was one of the preparatory texts for the July 1957 conference at Cosio d'Arroscia, Italy, at which the Situationist International was founded – that the spectacle emerges as 'the spectacle of the capitalist way of life' (IS 1997: 701).

19 All of the aforementioned passages from Hegel's *Elements of the Philosophy of Right* appear within Debord's own archival notes. Bibliothèque nationale de France, Département des Manuscrits, NAF 28603, Fonds Guy Debord, Fiches rassemblées sous l'intitulé: "Hegel" 80 f. "Principes de la philosophie du droit" 10 f.125 × 75 mm.

Chapter 1

1 While Debord owned a copy of *One-Dimensional Man*, it is only on *Eros and Civilization* that he compiled notes. Debord designates these notes as relevant for chapter '6/12 of SduS'. In an early draft chapter outline, this chapter six out of twelve would be referred to as 'The relations of the spectacle and of time'. Further, there are scattered indications throughout the writings of the SI which suggest a familiarity with Marcuse's *Soviet Marxism* (1958), such as Mustapha Khayati's 1966 article in *IS* 10 entitled 'Captive Words: Preface to a Situationist Dictionary'.

2 In a 1966 article in issue 10 of *IS*, entitled 'Some Theoretical Topics that Need to be Dealt With without Academic Debate or Idle Speculation', Raoul Vaneigem makes clear that problems of political economy, the social sciences and psychoanalysis are each elements of a unitary critical project (IS 1997: 454), a discursive itinerary not altogether dissimilar from the critical theory of the Institut für Sozialforschung.

3 Although predominantly dealing with their contrasting perspectives on the prospects of modern art in the twentieth century, Jappe 1999b is remarkably the only sustained comparative approach to elements of Adorno and Debord. There, Jappe convincingly argues that both thinkers take the domination of human beings by exchange-value to be pivotal for their respective critiques of modern society and that a common project in part emerges by correlating aspects of the culture industry and the spectacle. For a more recent account of this topic, see Jappe 2018.

4 *Vorstellung* is most appropriately translated as 'representation'. It also means what is laid out or stands before us. Its verb, depending on the context, is also sometimes rendered 'to imagine', 'to have in mind' or 'to have/frame/form an idea'. *Sich vorstellen* is 'to picture something to oneself'. It means a general or vague thought without determinacy, ill defined or even pictorial. *Sich vorstellen* is also used when portraying or painting a picture of oneself through introduction. It is the thinking at the level of everyday or ordinary life. The category is thereby used to denote an initial, unrefined

apprehension or presupposition, one without reflection. *Vorstellungen* thereby register a naivety that takes something for granted or at face value.

5 It is worth noting that within the 1960 issue of *Arguments* 19 featuring a translation of Adorno's 'Music and Technique', Debord made note of a footnote citing Adorno's 'The Experiential Content of Hegel's Philosophy' which appeared in an earlier issue of *Arguments*. It cannot be confirmed whether or not Debord actually read this essay. At the least, the highlighted footnote demonstrates Debord's orientation, however perhaps brief and wanting, towards Adorno's reading of Hegel. As will be illustrated throughout this book, similarities between Adorno and Debord on Hegelian philosophy are not biographical but reside in their respective concepts of a critical theory of society.

6 Whether or not Adorno is offering an accurate portrayal of Hegel's philosophy is beside the point for the present argument on the latter's relevance for Debord's concept of spectacle. Indeed, in many ways, it will be Hegel's philosophy rendered somewhat into a *trope* that matters for our analysis. Taking Adorno's interpretation of Hegel is important inasmuch as it is a portrayal that brings us closer to the logic of the spectacle, regardless of whether or not Adorno's interpretation is accurate. We find a similar departure within the systematic dialectics (ISMT) tradition of examining the categorial homologies between Hegel and Marx: 'it is exactly Hegel's idealism which made the Stuttgart philosopher crucial for the understanding of the capital relation' (Bellofiore 2015: 164).

7 This formulation appears in a preface Debord composed to a 1983 reprint edition of Polish Young Hegelian August von Cieszkowski's *Prolegomena for a Historiosophy* (1838), published by Editions Champ Libre. Although Debord did not discover Cieszkowski's work until 'after 1972' (Debord 2008a: 84), we find there comments on Hegel and his system as having 'ultimately accepted glorifying his present' (Debord 2006i: 1536), a verdict in accordance with remarks in *The Society of the Spectacle* (1995: §76). Notably, Debord venerates Cieszkowski who presented the 'first sketch of a philosophy of praxis' (Debord 2006i: 1536) prior to the work of Feuerbach. For further analysis on the relation between Debord and Cieszkowski in terms of a philosophy of praxis, see Bunyard 2018: 34–5, 73–4.

8 Bibliothèque nationale de France, Département des Manuscrits, NAF 28603, Fonds Guy Debord, Fiches rassemblées sous l'intitulé: 'Philosophie, sociologie' 156 f. Gabel, Joseph 5 f.210 x 135, 155 × 70 et 20 × 90 mm and Gabel, Joseph 8 f.125 × 75 et 75 × 125 mm.

9 It is within his 1988 *Comments on the Society of the Spectacle* that Debord returns to the ninth thesis of *The Society of the Spectacle*: 'Reversing Hegel's famous maxim, I noted as long ago as 1967 that "in a world that has really been turned upside down, truth is a moment of falsehood." In the intervening years, this principle has encroached upon each specific domain, without exception' (1998: 50–1).

10 Bibliothèque nationale de France, Département des Manuscrits, NAF 28603, Fonds Guy Debord, Fiches rassemblées sous l'intitulé: 'Philosophie, sociologie' 156 f. Mannheim, Karl, Idéologie et utopie; et Wirth, Louis, préface à l'édition de Idéologie et utopie 5 f.125 × 75 et 75 × 125 mm.

11 The formulation 'empty depth' (*leere Tiefe*) is employed by Hegel within the *Phenomenology of Spirit* to characterize spirit apprehended in various diminished capacities overwhelmed by finitude (1977c: 6, 436).

12 Incidentally, in the preface to *Elements of the Philosophy of Right*, Hegel describes 'spectacle' (*Schauspiel*) as the reduction of 'all thoughts and all topics *to the same level*' (1991a: 19).

13 Through this misreading, Baudrillard would then bestow the honour upon himself of advancing the indistinguishability between spectacle and reality, a critique already put forth by Debord a decade earlier. Jappe outlines the extent of Baudrillard's buoyant plagiarism in Jappe 2010.

14 Bibliothèque nationale de France, Département des Manuscrits, NAF 28603, Fonds Guy Debord, Fiches rassemblées sous l'intitulé: 'Philosophie, sociologie' 156 f. Mannheim, Karl, Idéologie et utopie; et Wirth, Louis, préface à l'édition de Idéologie et utopie 5 f.125 × 75 et 75 × 125 mm.

15 Within his 1962 seminar, 'Marx and the Basic Concepts of Sociological Theory', Adorno characterizes the commodity as 'the archetype [*Urform*] of ideology' (2018: 7). However, as chapter 3 will demonstrate, it is actually the value form of money that more closely resembles the pinnacle of ideology under the spectacle.

Chapter 2

1 Bibliothèque nationale de France, Département des Manuscrits, NAF 28603, Fonds Guy Debord, Fiches rassemblées sous l'intitulé: Hegel 80 f. Propédeutique philosophique 6 f.125 × 75 et 135 × 105 mm.

2 In *Comments on the Society of the Spectacle* theses ten and eleven examine what is described as 'the dissolution of logic … pursued by different, but mutually supportive means', including popularized technology and techniques linked to mass psychology (1998: 27). However, such a dissolution does not preclude a logical structure to the spectacle itself, only to those without the 'room for any reply' (1998: 29), that is, a logical structure which proffers illogical results. As Debord writes further in his notes on the political situation of 1963, 'CAPITALISM IS AND WANTS THE RATIONAL' (Le Bras and Guy 2016: 24). Additionally found in his preparatory notes for *Comments on the Society of the Spectacle* is that 'the spectacular actuality is *sufficiently* rational' (Le Bras and Guy 2016: 181)

3 The full passage proceeds as such: 'It is in this dialectic as understood here, and hence in grasping opposites in their unity, or the positive in the negative, that *the speculative* consists. It is the most important aspect of dialectic, but for the still unpracticed, unfree faculty of thought, the most difficult' (Hegel 2010: 35). Notably, the passage – which alludes to a conflict between speculation and the unfreedom of 'the concrete representations of the senses' (2010: 35) – was extracted by Debord and appears in his archive notes. Bibliothèque nationale de France, Département des Manuscrits, NAF 28603, Fonds Guy Debord, Fiches rassemblées sous l'intitulé: Hegel 80 f. Science de la logique 1 f.70 × 95 mm.

4 While at first it may seem anachronistic to describe the transition from consciousness to self-consciousness in the *Phenomenology of Spirit* as a speculative transition – insofar as it is only within the culmination of the book in absolute knowing that the speculative proper emerges – attributions of prematurity can be assuaged with consideration of how it is that Hegel describes the speculative within the *Phenomenology of Spirit*. While not yet a speculative *system*, the speculative is nevertheless described by Hegel in the preface as 'the rhythm of the organic whole' (1977c: 34), a process through which the *Phenomenology of Spirit* will acquire its ultimate truth. Its attention in the preface, there received more than anywhere else in the book, is situated to repudiate its conflation with any argumentative structure of the *Verstand* and the way in which the latter holds fast to fixed distinctions. The speculative is not strictly absent early on in the *Phenomenology of Spirit*, but is rather only implicit but yet to acquire an explicit orientation for the naïve consciousness. It is in this way that the speculative as absolute knowing is the surmounted purification of the momentary oppositions traversed throughout the *Phenomenology of Spirit* and derives from the experience of consciousness as a whole. Absolute knowing is indeed present throughout the *Phenomenology of Spirit*, albeit not explicitly so as an object of the naive consciousness. It is through the movement of appearances that absolute knowing comes to know itself. For this reason, the speculative is not independent of the particular developments of the *Phenomenology of Spirit*, but forged through the various moments of the phenomenal world. Furthermore, as it is described in Hegel's preface, the speculative is precisely what is alluded to in the first major transition from consciousness to self-consciousness. As Hyppolite writes, the speculative 'suspends the hypothesis of a source alien to knowledge, of an object distinct from thought, beyond it' (1997: 136). The 'Force and the Understanding' section is indeed the first section of the *Phenomenology of Spirit* that begins such a suspension, one for which the purported object of consciousness is integrated as a moment of the knowing subject's own activity.

5 It should be mentioned that Hegel's use of the category of an inverted world is in all likelihood in reference to the Romanticist poet Johann Ludwig Tieck and his play *Die Verkehrte Welt* (1798). Most Hegel commentators have not taken notice of Tieck's

work although as Verene notes, '[a] look into Tieck's play readily reveals that it concerns the kind of reversal of the order of things that concerns Hegel in the last pages of "Force and Understanding"'. Although there is no direct evidence that Hegel read Tieck's play, some of its admirers include the Schlegel brothers, William Grimm, Eichendorff and Schleiermacher. In fact, 'Tieck was part of the circle of the Schlegels at Jena just prior to Hegel's arrival there' in 1801. Further, '[i]n the general introduction to the *Lectures on Aesthetics*, Hegel comments on Tieck's irony and refers to the Jena period as the focal point for this aspect of Tieck' (Verene 1985: 50, 51)

6 Hegel's criticism here concerns a metaphysical idea of force rather than a direct engagement with categories of the natural sciences. For this, his concept of force is distinctively his own. Pinkard remarks that Hegel's critique is more applicable to Herder who 'posited a very generalized metaphysical conception of force as the explanation of the determinateness of appearance' (1996: 356), rather than an engagement with Newtonian laws of motion. The point for Hegel is that the separation between knowable perceptual expression and unknowable metaphysical force is thoroughly untenable.

7 Bibliothèque nationale de France, Département des Manuscrits, NAF 28603, Fonds Guy Debord, Fiches rassemblées sous l'intitulé: Hegel 80 f. Propédeutique philosophique 6 f.125 × 75 et 135 × 105 mm.

8 Within contemporary German, both *Wechsel* and *Tauschen* can connote economic phenomena, the former referring, for example, to a bill of sale while the latter a transaction. *Tauschen* thereby normally refers to the exchange of commodities while *Wechsel* more commonly means a 'switching' or 'alternating' of positions. However, there remains overlap between the categories as *austauschen* might be used for 'replacing' a battery.

9 For the SI's own analysis on these geopolitical developments, see their article in the eleventh issue of *IS* (1967), 'The Explosion Point of Ideology in China' (Knabb 2006: 240–51).

10 The concept of the spectacle thereby overturns traditional discourse on anti-imperialism: 'The society that brings the spectacle into being does not dominate underdeveloped regions solely through the exercise of economic hegemony. It also dominates them in its capacity as *the society of the spectacle*. Modern society has thus already invested the social surface [*la surface sociale*] of every continent – even where the material basis of economic exploitation is still lacking – by spectacular means' (Debord 1995: §57). In this way, 'a fundamental law in these spectacular times ... ensure[s] there is no such thing as a backward country' (Debord 1998: 5). For the SI's general criticism of leftist anti-imperialism, see 'Two Local Wars', which appeared in the eleventh issue of *IS* in 1967. There, both the Six-Day War and Vietnam are analysed in terms of the way in which they evoked, amongst the European left, absurd political positions.

11 The concept of *Identitätszwang* derives from Joseph Gabel's *False Consciousness: An Essay on Reification* (1962), a work which greatly informed Debord's thinking on reification in a number of ways. Gabel draws a parallel between reification and schizophrenia, an association that, for Debord, relates to the process of abstraction concretely realized by the exchange process which elevates the axiom of identification. Here, reification is said to be analogous to the pathologies of schizophrenia and, as a result, the aporetic gap between subject and object is filled with pathological identification or *Identitätszwang* – the compulsion or obsession for identification (Gabel 1975: 154). Most explicitly, within his concluding chapter, Debord employs Gabel's concept of *Identitätszwang* as a 'virtual identification' (Debord 1995: §212), an injunction set in motion by the spectacle: 'The spectacle erases the dividing line between self and world, in that the self, under siege by the presence/absence of the world, is eventually overwhelmed; it likewise erases the dividing line between true and false, repressing all directly lived truth beneath the *real presence* of the falsehood maintained by the organization of appearances' (1995: §219). All of Debord's notes on Gabel's book are marked with either 'SduS très important' or 'import. pour SduS'. Bibliothèque nationale de France, Département des Manuscrits, NAF 28603, Fonds Guy Debord, Fiches rassemblées sous l'intitulé: 'Philosophie, sociologie' 156 f. Gabel, Joseph 5 f.210 × 135, 155 × 70 et 20 × 90 mm and Gabel, Joseph 8 f.125 × 75 et 75 × 125 mm.

12 The exception remains, as was remarked in footnote 3 of chapter 2, an important extract from the *Science of Logic* (Hegel 2010: 35). Also worth remembering is that Debord, while attending his lectures, also took scrupulous notes on Hyppolite's work on Hegel. There one also finds an attention to Hegel's speculative. As Hyppolite writes in a comment of which Debord took note, '[Both Marx and Feuerbach] show that speculative philosophy, Hegel's absolute knowledge, is itself also a form of alienation, a substitute for religion. Man believes in another world in order to escape from the hostility of the one in which he lives; he projects into the "beyond" his own essence because his own essence is not realised in this world' (1997: 178).

13 As Backhaus writes, '[t]he isomorphism between the various "forms of self-alienation" is obvious; the economic and onto-theological basic concepts can be interchanged in the context of the alienation problematic' (Backhaus 2011: 414).

14 Smith, the most restrained when it comes to affixing Hegel's dialectical logic to the method of exposition within Marx's critique of political economy, nevertheless observes that Marx never 'waver[ed] in his condemnation of the metaphysics of absolute idealism . . . In his view *the structure of capital is precisely isomorphic with the structure of Hegel's Absolute*' (2015: 23). Murray continues in a similar vein in which the autonomous and self-realizing logic of Hegel's *Begriff* 'resembles' (1988: 217) the movement of capital. In an earlier article appearing in the 1983 volume of the *Hegel-Jahrbuch*, Murray brings such an isomorphism closer to the point at hand,

to the shared criticisms between Marx's interpretation of Hegelian speculation and the critique of political economy. There it is argued that Marx's *1844 Manuscripts* 'deciphers the logic of Hegel's philosophy in an amazing anticipation of his later critique of political economy. From the logic of Hegel's absolute idealism Marx sketches the logic of capital' (1983: 187). More generally, however, Murray has argued that '[a] thorough understanding of *Capital* requires the study of Hegel's philosophy, the philosophy of the Young Hegelians, *and* Marx's critique of the entire cycle of speculative thought' (1983: 57). For Arthur, capital emerges as the actuality of Hegelian idealism, 'a very peculiar object, grounded in a process of real abstraction in exchange in much the same way as Hegel's dissolution and reconstruction of reality is predicated on the abstractive power of thought' (Arthur 2004: 8). Both sides are said to share in 'an objective reality [which] has the shape of an ideality' (2004: 9), one which inheres within material practices and structures.

15 It is worth noting that the relation between alienation and the speculative was an idea that Debord also likely discovered within Hyppolite (Hyppolite 1969: 126, 134).

Chapter 3

1 Within Debord's archival materials, a rummage through his notations on Lefebvre's *Sociology of Marx* reveals these few additional working titles for what would eventually become *The Society of the Spectacle*. It can be deduced from textual evidence that Debord finalized the title of the book no later than September 1964 (Bernstein 1964). The final title is also confirmed by Debord in letters of 17 October and 25 November 1964 (Debord 2001: 302, 307).

2 The category of *Realabstraktion* derives not from Marx but from Alfred Sohn-Rethel, even if its conceptual content can be traced to the former's analysis of exchange abstraction and equalization. Within *Intellectual and Manual Labour: A Critique of Epistemology* (1977), Sohn-Rethel examines the correlation between the social synthesis of the exchange abstraction, along with its anthropological genesis within antiquity, and the epistemological abstractions culminating in the philosophy of Kant. While there is no available evidence indicating that Debord was familiar with the work of Sohn-Rethel, the way in which the concept of the society of the spectacle bears an unmistakable affinity to the concept of a real abstraction will become clear throughout this book.

3 Debord derives the concept of total commodity in part from Marx's notion that the 'total labour power of society, which is embodied in the sum total of the values of all commodities produced by that society, counts here as one homogeneous mass of

human labour power, composed though it be of innumerable individual units' (Marx 1996: 49). As Debord makes the connection explicit, 'The *entirety of labour sold* is transformed overall into the *total commodity*. A cycle is then set in train that must be maintained at all costs: the total commodity must be returned in fragmentary form to a fragmented individual completely cut off from the concerted action of the forces of production' (Debord 1995: §42).

4 This latter aspect of the spectacle is also one of the strongest distinctions between Debord and fellow SI member Asger Jorn on the critique of political economy. Jorn's *Value and Economy: Critique of Political Economy and the Exploitation of the Unique* (1962) presents many of the categories of Marx's critique of political economy albeit often abstracted from their determinate meaning within the capitalist mode of production and instead provided as elements of a certain rationality of cultural life. At once both deforming Marx and diverging from Debord, Jorn reads the concept of value 'as a purely *metaphysical* and thus immaterial phenomenon, as an *agreement by convention*, and thus as nothing other than a concept' (2002: 124). Also odd is the way Jorn upholds an arbitrary distinction between use-value and utility, a difference he develops into an ahistorical engagement with the categories of political economy.

5 Bibliothèque nationale de France, Département des Manuscrits, NAF 28603, Fonds Guy Debord, Fiches rassemblées sous l'intitulé: 'Philosophie, sociologie', 156 f. Galbraith, John Kenneth, 8 f. 210 × 135 mm. All hitherto references to Debord's notes on Galbraith derive from this archival source.

6 It could be said, regarding the way in which the spectacle produces the concrete out of itself, that the entirety of Debord's 1971 essay – entitled 'Sick Planet' and slated for the never published thirteenth issue of *IS* – can be interpreted as the spectacle's reconstitution of nature itself: 'A society that is ever more sick, but ever more powerful, has recreated the world – everywhere and in concrete form – as the environment and backdrop of its sickness: it has created a *sick planet*.' Here, political economy, as 'the complete denial of man', has now achieved 'its perfect *material conclusion*' (Debord 2008b: 81, 84).

7 The return of use as consumption within the spectacle also emerges in Debord's concept of pseudo-cyclical time: 'This time manifests nothing in its effective reality aside from its *exchangeability* . . . The general time of human non-development also has a complementary aspect, that of a *consumable time* which, on the basis of a determinate form of production, presents itself in the everyday life of society as a *pseudo-cyclical time*. Pseudo-cyclical time is in fact merely the *consumable disguise* of the time-as-commodity of the production system, and it exhibits the essential traits of that time: homogeneous and exchangeable units, and the suppression of any qualitative dimension' (1995: §§147–9; see also §153).

8 Debord sketches the historical and pre-capitalist origins of the spectacle within both religious projection and the phenomenon of specialization, both of which

have at their foundation a social division of labour requisite for the production and exchange of commodities. While it is the *spectacular essence of capitalism* within the twentieth century that concerns the present monograph, its pre-capitalist origins are noted by Debord in a 1971 letter: 'I arrived at this concept through lived, albeit eminently avant-gardist, experience of revolutionary activity during the 1950s and 1960s – but the phenomenon is considerably older. With its basis in ancient Greek thought, the spectacle underwent further development at the time of the Renaissance (with capitalist thought) and developed further still in the eighteenth century when private collections were opened to the public as *museums*. It emerged fully formed in the years 1914–1920 (with the ballyhoo of the war and the collapses of the workers' movement). Certainly "the concept is operational," as our enemies say. I would even say that it is increasingly so. The following question nevertheless remains: is this the *central* concept that defines the present *stage* of capitalism (just conceivably and hopefully for a few good reasons its "final stage")? I'm rather inclined to think that it is; but let us – or others – wait and see' (2004a: 455–6).

9 Bibliothèque nationale de France, Département des Manuscrits, NAF 28603, Fonds Guy Debord, Fiches rassemblées sous l'intitulé : 'Marxisme' 231 f. Frölich, Paul. Rosa Luxemburg, sa vie, son oeuvre. 2 f.

10 Camatte is an important resource for illustrating the way in which objective forms of appearance come to dominate social relations within capitalist society. While there was no direct correspondence between Debord and Camatte, their respective analyses comprise a similar picture. Camatte came out of the political tradition of the Italian left communism, strongly influenced by early Italian Communist Party member Amadeo Bordiga and argued that capital had anthropomorphized itself as a material community. Camatte, who has barely received any attention from the Anglophone world, never claimed any affinity with *Socialisme ou Barbarie* or the SI because they were formal organizations and, in his eyes, held to outdated council communist programmes. Debord, for his part, left no evidence of any contact with Camatte. In a passage that could have appeared within *The Society of the Spectacle*, Camatte writes, 'Capital has become absolute representation: everything men do is reflected in it; it can be the spectacle of the world in that it reflects, returns to all beings their various movements integrated into its life process' (2011: 339–40). The affinity with Debord is unmistakable. In another passage which, in all likelihood, is a direct appropriation of §17 of *The Society of the Spectacle*, Camatte writes, 'They are stripped of their activity, which is restored to them in the form of representations; the movement of alienation no longer bears on the being or the having, but on appearing: their life is organized for them, and thus they increasingly tend to perceive of themselves as being thrown into non-life' (2011: 252)

Chapter 4

1. The introduction to the *Science of Logic* offers a succinct characterization on the reflective disposition of the *Verstand*: '*reflective* understanding took possession of philosophy. We must know exactly what is meant by this expression which moreover is often used as a slogan; in general it stands for the understanding as abstracting, and hence as separating and remaining fixed in its separations. Directed against reason, it behaves as ordinary common sense and imposes its view that truth rests on sensuous reality, that thoughts are only thoughts, meaning that it is sense perception which first gives them filling and reality and that reason left to its own resources engenders only figments of the brain. In this self-renunciation on the part of reason, the Notion of truth is lost; it is limited to knowing only subjective truth, only phenomena, appearances, only something to which the nature of the object itself does not correspond: knowing has lapsed into opinion' (1969: 45).
2. Lukács' criticisms of Engels on the theory of dialectics, its relation to nature, and the latter's interpretation of the Kantian *Ding-an-sich* are located throughout *History and Class Consciousness* and make up most of *Tailism and the Dialectic* (Lukács 1971a: 3, 132–3; 2000: 94–137). However, the reader will find no explicit criticism of Lenin's *Materialism and Empirio-Criticism* in Lukács' writings. His critique of reflective epistemology nevertheless bears direct implication on Lenin's work and the latter's concept of reflection (*otrozhenie*), which became a dogmatic precept within Soviet *Diamat*.
3. Jappe remains the authoritative investigation on the relation between Lukács and Debord (Jappe 1999a). One of the more important associations between Lukács and Debord examined by Jappe is the way in which both conceive reification as entailing the degradation of time's fluidity to an abstract spatial dimension for which its 'qualitative, variable, flowing nature ... freezes into an exactly delimited, quantifiable continuum filled with quantifiable "things" ... in short, it becomes space' (Lukács 1971a: 90). The reduction of space and time to an abstract common denominator is explicitly articulated by Debord when he writes of a '*spatial alienation*, whereby a society which radically severs the subject from the activity that it steals from him separates him in the first place from his own time' (Debord 1995: §161, §170). As Jappe writes, '[f]or Debord, as for Lukács before him, one of the fundamental modes of reification is the *spatialization of time*' (1999a: 27).
4. As Debord writes in his notes comparing the work of *Socialisme ou Barbarie* to the theory of the spectacle, '[i]t is too simple to say that capitalism both requires and prevents participation ... Capitalism organizes "participation" as spectacle – in the spectacle ... It is wrong to say that [capitalism] prevents participation where in fact it is at the same time dependent on participation' (Le Bras and Guy 2016: 29). It has become a common endeavour for interpreters to justify the introduction of their

own categorial variations on Debord's diagnosis, such as the 'interactive spectacle' (Best and Kellner 1999) or 'spectacle 2.0' (Briziarelli and Armano 2017). What is here understood to be an advance on or renewal of Debord's critical theory is only the maturing tumour of preponderant interpretations that myopically elevate the predication of passivity over the very active and participatory requisite of spectacular identification.

5   In name, Debord engages with Lukács directly in *The Society of the Spectacle* within §112. There, Lukács is situated within the book's critique of Marxist-Leninism in all of its variants from Lenin himself, through Lukács, Trotsky and Stalin and in its institutionalization with the Second and Third Internationals and social democracy. For Debord, Lukács' description of the Bolshevik Party corresponded to everything the party *wasn't* (1995: §112).

6   Debord procured the title of the first chapter of *The Society of the Spectacle* from Hegel's *The German Constitution*: 'for madness is the complete isolation of the individual from his kind' (Hegel 2004: 101). Here, the original German, 'die vollendete Absonderung', is translated into French as 'la séparation achevée' in the Jacob and Quillet edition of Hegel's *La constitution de l'Allemagne*.

7   As the article describes in an earlier passage, 'In the structure of the commodity form – before its explosive growth – the general identity of commodities was only obtainable by diverting their fictitious identification into a general abstract equivalent. This illusory identity, assumed daily, ended up inducing the identity of all needs – and thus of all consumers – and in this way attains a certain degree of reality. The complete realization of the old abstract equivalence would be the climax of this process. Due to this expansion, the area of cultural production, or advertising, has more and more trouble differentiating between products and so prophesizes the great tautology to come' (IS 1997: 450).

8   Debord's adoption of Joseph Gabel's concept of *Identitätszwang* is yet another instance by which the critique of the spectacle bears affinity to ideas found within Adorno and Horkheimer's *Dialectic of Enlightenment*, specifically the rationalization of mimesis. As Debord writes, [t]he need to imitate . . . is indeed a truly infantile need, one determined by every aspect of his fundamental dispossession' (1995: §219). For further comment on Debord's engagement with Gabel, see footnote 11 of chapter 2.

9   When the knowing subject wasn't simply fixating itself to the empirical world through sense impressions, Kant's transcendental philosophy raised its newfound confidence of the self-referential thinking I to a new level and released subjectivity from the given. For Schelling and Fichte, the pure transcendental I becomes absolute and exercises its reflection as its own *causa sui* by which it fashions the entirety of the world around it.

10 Although again beyond the scope of the present chapter, it is worth suggesting an alternative conceptual prehistory to Debord's theory of the society of the spectacle,

one which does not overemphasize the impact of Lukács' theory of reification but instead introduces the spectacle's affinity to the concept of reification found within Isaak Illich Rubin's *Essays on Marx's Theory of Value* (1928), a book which Debord could not have read prior to the publication of *The Society of the Spectacle* and yet which contains some important and yet inadvertent correlations. Although hardly a robust Hegelian, Rubin's attention to *Formbestimmung*, the primacy of exchange and his emphasis on the relation between appearance and essence together share important similarities to Debord and could be argued as an approximation to Debord's theory of the society of the spectacle, a point that assumes greater importance once the differences between spectacle and reification are elucidated. In a word, we can suggest that it is with Rubin's concept of reification that Debord's theory of spectacle finds greater accord, rather than with the reification of Lukács (Rubin 1973: 21–43).

Chapter 5

1 Bibliothèque nationale de France, Département des Manuscrits, NAF 28603, Fonds Guy Debord, Fiches rassemblées sous l'intitulé: Hegel 80 f. Hyppolite, Jean. Notes de cours sur Hegel 5 f.125 × 75 mm. All subsequent citations from Debord's seminar notes derive from this archival source.
2 It is worth clarifying that an engagement with Hegel for a critical theory of society ought not to proceed as a mere formal application or transfer of Hegelian categories. As Marx wrote to Engels in 1858 criticizing Lassalle, 'it is one thing for a critique to take a science to the point at which it admits of a dialectical presentation, and quite another to apply an abstract, ready-made system of logic to vague presentiments of just such a system' (1983: 261). It is in this way that to observe either the *Wesenslogik* or the *Begriffslogik* within the dynamism of the society of the spectacle is not to adopt the perspective of merely upholding a happenstance isomorphism so commonplace today amongst Marxist commentators on Hegel's *Science of Logic*. It is instead a substantive and meaningful connection that will be established through the reconstruction of the peculiarly speculative object that is the society of the spectacle.
3 It is from real measure that Hegel transitions to the *Wesenslogik*. Differences in ratio produced a plurality of measure-relations that are each self-subsistent. Their self-subsistent unity has it that being has become *indifference*, or a that a problem emerges of failing to stabilize determinate ratios. Every hitherto determination of being (quality, quantity and their immediate unity within measure) remains distinct from an indifferent (*gleichgültig*) *substrate* of being which has resulted from a series of differentiated measure-relations. The indifference of being to its determinations, as a substrate, relates to itself in its negation of all such determinacies. This

mediation contains both *negation* and *relation*. Measure-relations thereby introduce the explicit problem of *relating* and, as such, the determinations to be unfolded within the *Wesenslogik* will be wholly *relational*. For Hegel, the dilemma here is that the resulting determinacy of being is indifferent and yet is the result of a set of determinations now regarded as external to the substrate of being. How we are to reconcile the substrate as *determined* while itself *determining* as an emergent logic of being is a central aporia of the *Wesenslogik*.

4   In contrast, the categories of Hegel's *Seinslogik*, the first division of the *Science of Logic*, do not incorporate relational structures of internal difference. Only the inner relatedness *Wesenslogik* can provide the desideratum necessary for determinate relations of unity and division. The patterns of reflection found therein acknowledge the necessity of relations within a unitary structure.

5   Textual evidence that Debord was familiar with the section on thinghood in the *Encyclopaedia Logic* can be derived from a passage found in a November 1975 letter to contacts in Portugal, which concludes with a quote from Hegel (1991b: 203): 'To sum up: the fact that you have gone from occupying what was undoubtedly the most advanced position of the entire movement in the summer of 1974 to coming up with these ludicrous theoretical justifications for your practical shortcomings in no way permits me to approve of your "thoroughly bad" – in the Hegelian sense – political stance: "because a work that is not a work ought to be called bad"' (2005: 312).

6   Hegel's analysis of *Erscheinung* within the *Wesenslogik* and its development into essential relation invokes a similar although not identical dynamic. Indeed, these passages in large part rehearse the dynamic of the 'Force and the Understanding' section of the *Phenomenology of Spirit*. The fundamental difference, however, between the logic of appearances there and its appearance now is that, no longer situated as a problem of the naive consciousness confronted by the instability of the objective world, the dialectic from thinghood to the world of appearances 'shows itself here in its genesis' (Hegel 1991b: 194), that is, as an explicitly speculative logic no longer tethered to the *Vorstellungen* of consciousness. We find here a logic of appearances in its purified form without the prejudices of the naive consciousness, proceeding first from existence and the problem of the one and the many to its resolution in the category of *Erscheinung*.

7   The philological connection between French translations of Hegel and Debord's employment of the German category of *Weltanschauung* is not altogether impertinent here: 'Another consequence of the dynamic of Hegelian language is the necessity the French translator encounters of sometimes varying, more or less lightly, the translation of terms identical in the German text ... *Anschauung* ranges from "contemplation" to "intuition," by way of "vision" pure and simple, or even "spectacle"' (Lefebvre 2014: 391).

8   There is an irony contained in the original French lost in the English. The French 'essence' (*l'essence*) can also be translated as 'gasoline' or 'petrol'. As such, we might say

that the other of this spectacular *Welt* is the fuel through which it can be burned to cinders; what Debord calls later in his notes 'le germe de mort'.

9   Debord extracted this corresponding quotation from the *Science of Logic* (Hegel 2010: 381–2) and kept it in his notes on Hegel. Bibliothèque nationale de France, Département des Manuscrits, NAF 28603, Fonds Guy Debord, Fiches rassemblées sous l'intitulé: Hegel 80 f. Science de la logique 1 f.70 × 95 mm. Additionally noteworthy is the way in which Debord also associates the dead with money, specifically through Hegel's early Jena writings: 'The spectacle extends to all social life the principle which Hegel (in the Realphilosophie of Jena) conceives as the principle of money: it is "the life of what is dead, moving within itself"' (1970: §215).

10 Bibliothèque nationale de France, Département des Manuscrits, NAF 28603, Fonds Guy Debord, Fiches rassemblées sous l'intitulé: Hegel 80 f. Phénoménologie de l'esprit et autre à identifier 3 f.125 × 75 mm.

11 Debord had high regard for *The Revolution of Everyday Life* and held it to be continuous with his own critique of the spectacle: 'with their clear focus on the same problem and their convergence of views, our respective contributions are going to forge a way through as distinct, albeit complicit and frequently criss-crossing entities: akin to buttresses, as it were, in Gothic architecture? For two works whose finer points had scarcely ever been aired between us, the convergence is serendipitous yet counter-proof too of coherence' (2003b: 20; see also Debord 2004a: 313–14 and SI 2003).

12 It is worth remarking here that the German *Wirklichkeit* is appropriately associated with a 'working out' or 'becoming true' – as a variation on Aristotle's *energeia* – rather than the simple *Realität* or Latin *res*.

13 On the whole, the modal concept of possibility has its necessary correlate in the category of actuality, insofar as the possible or impossible can only be set against the actual. Further, contingency arises in this relation between possibility and actuality as that which is actual but weighed against an environment of possibilities. It would be necessary and not contingent if it were otherwise. Any yet, measured against the actual, certain possibilities are possible while others impossible. Given then certain conditions, some possibilities are necessary even if contingent. In contrast, those *real possibilities* which cannot be otherwise are what Hegel calls *real necessity*. What Hegel subsequently calls *real actuality* is always determinate and contains real possibility that in turn becomes actual. What *could be* is always already immanently derivative of *what is*.

Chapter 6

1   As Hegel markedly writes in the introduction to *Elements of the Philosophy of Right*, 'it is the *concept* alone ... which has *actuality* in such a way as to give it itself' (1991a: 25).

2   Bibliothèque nationale de France, Département des Manuscrits, NAF 28603, Fonds Guy Debord, Fiches rassemblées sous l'intitulé: Hegel 80 f. La Raison dans l'histoire 8 f.125 × 75 mm. All subsequent citations from Debord's notes from Papaïoannou's work derive from this archival source.
3   The *Begriffslogik* consists in maintaining the identity and determinateness of the concept in and through the other. Otherness here – unlike within the *Seinslogik* as completely excluded from something or in the *Wesenslogik* as only partially included by preserving its independence – is fully integrated as an immanent determination of the concept.
4   Albeit with differences in their concepts already elucidated, Vaneigem described this fundamental unity of opposites under the category of 'decompression' (*décompression*), the common ground or agreement between opposition that, in their equilibrium, stabilizes the reigning society (2012: 42–5).
5   As the SI write in the eleventh issue of *IS* (1967), 'Since the great crisis of 1929, state intervention has been more and more conspicuous in market mechanisms; the economy can no longer function steadily without massive expenditures by the state, the main "consumer" of all noncommercial production (especially that of the armament industries). This does not save it from remaining in a state of permanent crisis and in constant need of expanding its public sector at the expense of its private sector. A relentless logic pushes the system toward increasingly state-controlled capitalism, generating severe social conflicts' (Knabb 2006: 254).
6   When discussing potential titles for what would become *The Decline and Fall of the Spectacle-Commodity Economy*, Debord wrote the following in a December 1965 letter to Mustapha Khayati: '"The Reasons of Wrath"? It would appear that the pun does not carry over into English and our title needs to work for an anglophone readership ... Alice immediately came up with "The Reasons of Colour" ... I thought of "The Empire of the Visible and its Decadence" but the reference to the Ku Klux Klan's "invisible empire" is a bit flimsy. Might an overtly political, less literary title be more appropriate? After all, the subject of the article is not so much the rebellion of the Blacks but rather the early stages of the prevailing social spectacle's collapse *in its American field of operations*, just as the ludicrous Beijing–Moscow squabble is the ideological and bureaucratic equivalent of this impending collapse' (2003b: 97).
7   Marx also describes the way in which bourgeois society abolishes national distinctions in the *Manifesto of the Communist Party* (1976b: 488, 503).
8   In *Comments on the Society of the Spectacle*, Debord offers a passage elaborating on the unity of town and country found in *The Society of the Spectacle*: 'Villages, unlike towns, have always been ruled by conformism, isolation, petty surveillance, boredom and repetitive malicious gossip about the same families. Which is a precise enough description of the global spectacle's present vulgarity, in which it has become

impossible to distinguish the Grimaldi–Monaco or Bourbon–Franco dynasties from those who succeeded the Stuarts' (1998: 33–4).
9 Here is movement socially and objectively indexed not by concretely differentiated space but by time in the abstract. It is within Debord's concept of 'irreversible time', as the time of the commodity measured as abstract and homogeneous, outlined in chapters 5 and 6 of *The Society of the Spectacle*, that such a notion of space is expanded. In this way, capital's 'annihilation of space by time' is the tendency which gives determinacy to Debord's account of the spectacular organization of spatial territory. Debord's debt to Lukács can here be traced directly. This concerns the way in which both thinkers conceive reification as entailing the degradation of time's fluidity to abstract spatial dimension for which, in the words of Lukács, its 'qualitative, variable, flowing nature ... freezes into an exactly delimited, quantifiable continuum filled with quantifiable "things" ... in short, it becomes space' (1971a: 90). The reduction of space and time to an abstract common denominator is explicitly articulated by Debord when he writes of a '*spatial alienation*, whereby a society which radically severs the subject from the activity that it steals from him separates him in the first place from his own time' (1995: §161; see also §170). As Jappe follows, '[f]or Debord, as for Lukács before him, one of the fundamental modes of reification is the *spatialization of time*' (1999a: 27).
10 As the 1966 essay 'On the Poverty of Student Life' further emphasizes, 'Despite their superficial disparities, all existing societies are governed by the *logic of the commodity*; it is the basis of their totalitarian self-regulation' (Knabb 2006: 427).
11 If during the early and mid-twentieth century, the spectacular representation of the proletariat assumed the appearance forms of union leadership and party constituent, it can be argued that within the present moment, the spectacular appearance of the proletariat obtains an overtly sociological guise and image of the morally clad 'excluded', thereby insinuating that a more allegedly just integration into forms of direct exploitation is the only trajectory the proletariat can aspire to (Surplus Club 2015; Zamora 2013).
12 Debord ascribes to the formation of the modern spectacle not simply the development of bureaucratic regimes but also twentieth-century fascism: 'Fascism was an attempt of the bourgeois economy to defend itself, *in extremis*, from the dual threat of crisis and proletarian subversion ... Fascism presented itself for what it was – a violent resurrection of *myth* calling for participation in a community defined by archaic pseudo-values: race, blood, leader. Fascism is a cult of the archaic completely fitted out by modern technology. Its degenerate ersatz of myth has been revived in the spectacular context of the most modern means of conditioning and illusion. It is thus one factor in the formation of the modern spectacle' (1995: §109).
13 'Coherence implies that, as [both] precondition and consequence, none of the situationists can be regarded so inferior (or superior) with respect to the others that

dialogue with him [or her] on a single subject would be impossible. *A fortiori*, none of us can ever *feign* such a "regard"' (Debord 2006e: 635).

14 As Debord extracts from Papaïoannou's introduction to Hegel's *La Raison dans l'histoire*, 'Philosophy is more than consolation. It reconciles; it transfigures the real which seems unjust and raises it to the rational, showing that it is based on the Idea itself and capable of satisfying reason.'

15 Debord's occasional use of the term 'non-life' within *The Society of the Spectacle* (e.g. 1995: §2, §123, §185) does not compromise the present interpretation, which rejects any fundamental dualism to the logic of the society of the spectacle. It ought not to be forgotten that Debord's use of various terminology does not unfold by itself with systematic consistency. For this, the contrast between 'non-life' and 'life' in *The Society of the Spectacle* is not a technical distinction. In fact, it is the 'life' of the spectacle that preponderates throughout the book (e.g. 1995: §6, §153).

16 As Debord extracts again from Papaïoannou, spirit 'finds its own center in itself; it also tends towards this center – but it is itself this center. Its unity is not outside of it, but in itself. It is in itself and remains in its own element (bei sich).' Importantly, Debord adds next to this quotation in the margins 'très important pour SdS [society of the spectacle]'.

Conclusion

1 Yet as Debord writes in issue 16 of *Potlatch* (1955), 'But opinions do not interest us, only systems. Certain comprehensive systems always seem to incur the anathema of individualists armed with their fragmentary theories, whether psychoanalytic or merely literary. These same Olympians, however, are happy to align their entire lives with other systems whose reign, and whose perishable nature, become more difficult to ignore by the day' (2004: 23).

Appendix

1 For the SI, neither the consciousness of the left or the ratiocination of party bureaucracy were capable of conceptualizing the society of the spectacle. For both sides, '[d]ialectics is their common enemy' (Knabb 2006: 253). It is important to note, however, that Debord and the SI never claimed 'to have a monopoly on the dialectics that everyone talks about; we only claim to have a temporary monopoly on its *use*' (Knabb 2006: 176). The dialectic for Debord would therewith operate as only a moment within strategic thinking generally. As he wrote for his 1978 film, *In girum imus nocte et consumimur igni*, 'theories are only made to die in the war of time. Like

military units, they must be sent into battle at the right moment; and whatever their merits or insufficiencies, they can only be used if they are on hand when they're needed. They have to be replaced because they are constantly being rendered obsolete – by their decisive victories even more than by their partial defeats. Moreover, no vital eras were ever engendered by a theory; they began with a game, or a conflict, or a journey' (2003a: 150–1).

2 This quotation appears frequently not just in Debord's notes on Hegel, but also cited by him in a 1960 letter to Patrick Straram (1999: 376). It is likely that Debord first came across the quotation within Lefebvre's *Logique Formelle, Logique Dialectique*, which he extracted into his notes along with the following remark: 'An admirable thought, to which however we object that only a "spirit" is satisfied, and that a man worthy of the name knows neither the satisfaction nor the vain anxiety and anguish of the "spirits"' (1982a: 225).

3 For a bibliographic guide to Hegel's reception in France, including a list of some of the earliest and major translations of Hegel, from the mid-nineteenth century to the mid-1970s, see V. Y. Mudimbe and A. Bohm 1994. Other valuable surveys include Roth 1988, Sinnerbrink 2007 and Baugh 1993, 2003, all of which have been utilized in this appendix.

4 In February 1963, the SI published a document entitled 'Into the Trashcan of History', which celebrated the dissolution of the journal *Arguments*, which, due to its 'exhaustion of ideas', 'now presents us with the spectacle of the disappearance of absence' (Debord 2006a: 624–5).

5 Despite these criticisms, both Roland Simon and Gilles Dauvé have argued that the SI never exceeded the limits of workerist productivism in their adherence to councilist self-management (Dauvé 1996; Dauvé 2000; Dauvé 2015; Simon 2001). For Debord's own comments on the organization of workers' councils, see Debord 1970: §§116–18, §179.

6 For further literature on the relation between the SI and *Socialisme ou Barbarie*, see Thomas 2016, Hastings-King 1999, and NOT BORED! 1996, 1998 and 1999. Also, for a thorough account of the mutual influence between the SI and *Socialisme ou Barbarie*, as well as an analysis of the dubious accusation that Debord plagiarized the concept of spectacle from Castoriadis, see Hayes 2017: 253–96, 309–16.

7 Between 1948 and 1952, 'the Western European economy expanded at a rate of more than 10 percent per annum. By 1951 production was fully 55 percent above levels reached four years before. Western Europe then embarked on two decades of rapid growth unmatched in its prior or subsequent history' (Eichengreen 1995: 3).

8 Debord briefly outlines the contradiction of the organic composition of capital by describing the phenomena of automation as that which 'objectively eliminates labor [and yet] must at the same time preserve *labor as a commodity* and as the only source of the commodity' (1970: §45). Since the total social labour time must not

diminish alongside increasing technical forces, which expel labour from the production process, Debord identifies what has been referred to as the 'post-Fordist service economy' as necessary for absorbing the disregarded labour. As he writes, '[s]ervices, the tertiary sector, swell the ranks of the army of distribution and are a eulogy to the current commodities; the additional forces which are mobilized just happen to be suitable for the organization of redundant labor required by the artificial needs for such commodities' (1970: §45).

9   The concepts of 'new proletariat' and 'new poverty' are located in the 1962 article, 'The Bad Days Will End', which appeared in *IS* 7. The article outlines the way in which 'irreducible dissatisfaction spreads subterraneanly, undermining the edifice of the affluent society' (IS 1997: 250).

Bibliography

Adorno, T. W. (1976), 'Sociology and Empirical Research', in Adorno et al., *The Positivist Dispute in German Sociology*, trans. G. Adey and D. Frisby, London: Heinmann.
Adorno, T. W. (1977), 'Music and Technique', *Telos* 32: 79–94.
Adorno, T. W. (1982), *Against Epistemology: A Metacritique. Studies in Husserl and the Phenomenological Antinomies*, trans. W. Domingo, Cambridge and Malden, MA: Polity.
Adorno, T. W. (1993), *Hegel: Three Studies*, trans. S. W. Nicholsen, Cambridge, MA: MIT Press.
Adorno, T. W. (1998), 'Television as Ideology', in *Critical Models: Interventions and Catchwords*, trans. H. W. Pickford, New York: Columbia University Press.
Adorno, T. W. (2000), *Introduction to Sociology*, trans. E. Jephcott, Stanford, CA: Stanford University Press.
Adorno, T. W. (2003a), 'Reflections on Class Theory', in *Can One Live after Auschwitz?: A Philosophical Reader*, trans. R. Livingstone, Stanford, CA: Stanford University Press.
Adorno, T. W. (2003b), 'Thesen über Bedürfnis', in R. Tiedemann (ed.), *Gesammelte Schriften Band 8: Soziologische Schriften I*, 392–6, Frankfurt: Suhrkamp.
Adorno, T. W. (2005), *Minima Moralia: Reflections from a Damaged Life*, trans. E. P. N. Jephcott, London: Verso.
Adorno, T. W. (2007), *Negative Dialectics*, trans. E. B. Ashton, London: Bloomsbury.
Adorno, T. W. (2008), *Lectures on Negative Dialectics*, trans. R. Livingstone, Cambridge: Polity.
Adorno, T. W. (2017), *An Introduction to Dialectics*, trans. N. Walker, Malden, MA: Polity.
Adorno, T. W. (2018), 'Theodor W. Adorno on Marx and the Basic Concepts of Sociological Theory', trans. V. Erlenbusch-Anderson and C. O'Kane, *Historical Materialism* 26, no. 1: 154–64.
Adorno, T. W. and M. Horkheimer (2002), *Dialectic of Enlightenment: Philosophical Fragments*, trans. E. W. Jephcott, Stanford, CA: Stanford University Press.
Anders, G. (1956), 'The World as Phantom and as Matrix', *Dissent* 3, no. 1 (Winter): 14–24.
Aristotle (1996), *Poetics*, trans. M. Heath. London: Penguin Books.
Arrighi, G. (1994), *The Long Twentieth Century: Money, Power, and the Origins of Our Times*, London: Verso.
Arthur, C. J. (2004), *The New Dialectic and Marx's Capital*, Leiden: Brill.
Backhaus, H. (2005), 'Some Aspects of Marx's Concept of Critique in the Context of his Economic-Philosophical Theory', in W. Bonefeld and K. Psychopedis (eds),

Dignity: Social Autonomy and the Critique of Capitalism, 13–29, Aldershot: Ashgate.

Backhaus, H. (2011), *Dialektik der Wertform: Untersuchungen zur Marxschen Ökonomiekritik*, Freiburg: Caira.

Baudrillard, J. (1975), *The Mirror of Production*, trans. M. Poster, New York: Telos Press.

Baugh, B. (1993), 'Limiting Reason's Empire: The Early Reception of Hegel in France', *Journal of the History of Philosophy* 31, no. 2: 259–75.

Baugh, B. (2003), *French Hegel: From Surrealism to Postmodernism*, New York: Routledge.

Bellofiore, R. (2015), 'Lost in Translation? Once Again on the Marx-Hegel Connection', in F. Moseley and T. Smith (eds), *Marx's* Capital *and* Hegel's Logic*: A Reexamination*, 164–88, Chicago: Haymarket.

Bernstein, J. M. (1984), *The Philosophy of the Novel: Lukács, Marxism and the Dialectics of Form*, Minneapolis: University of Minnesota Press.

Bernstein, M. (1964), 'The Situationist International', *Times Literary Supplement*, 2 September.

Best, S. and D. Kellner (1999), 'Debord, Cybersituations, and the Interactive Spectacle', *SubStance* 28, no. 9: 129–56.

Bonefeld, W. (2014), *Critical Theory and the Critique of Political Economy: On Subversion and Negative Reason*, London: Bloomsbury.

Bonefeld, W. (2016), 'Bringing Critical Theory Back in at a Time of Misery: Three Beginnings within Conclusion', *Capital & Class* 40, no. 2: 233–44.

Breuer, S. (1977), *Die Krise der Revolutionstheorie: Negative Vergesellschaftung und Arbeitsmetaphysik bei Herbert Marcuse*, Frankfurt am Main: Syndikat.

Briziarelli, M. and E. Armano (eds) (2017), *The Spectacle 2.0: Reading Debord in the Context of Digital Capitalism*, London: University of Westminster Press.

Bunyard, T. (2018), *Debord, Time and Spectacle: Hegelian Marxism and Situationist Theory*, Leiden: Brill.

Butler, J. (1999), *Subjects of Desire: Hegelian Reflections in Twentieth-Century France*, New York: Columbia University Press.

Camatte, J. (1995), *This World We Must Leave and Other Essays*, New York: Autonomedia.

Camatte, J. (2011), *Capital and Community*, trans. D. Brown, New York: First Prism Key Press.

Cerf, W. (1977), 'Speculative Philosophy and Intellectual Intuition: An Introduction to Hegel's Essays', in *Faith & Knowledge*, trans. W. Cerf and H. S. Harris, Albany, NY: State University of New York Press.

Cirulli, F. (2006), *Hegel's Critique of Essence: A Reading of the* Wesenlogik, New York: Routledge.

Clark, T. J. and D. Nicholson-Smith (1997), 'Why Art Can't Kill the Situationist International', *October* 79 (Winter): 15–31.

Clausewitz, C. (1984), *On War*, trans. M. Howard and P. Paret, Princeton, NJ: Princeton University Press.

Dauvé, G., aka Barrot, J. (1996), 'Critique of the Situationist International', in S. Home (ed.), *What is Situationism? A Reader*, trans. L. Michaelson, Edinburgh: AK Press.

Dauvé, G., aka Barrot, J. (2000), 'Back to the Situationist International', in *Aufheben*, No. 9.

Dauvé, G., aka Barrot, J. and F. Martin (2015), *Eclipse and Re-emergence of the Communist Movement*, Oakland, CA: PM Press.

Debord, G. (1970), *The Society of the Spectacle*, trans. F. Perlman and J. Supak, Detroit: Black & Red.

Debord, G. (1985), 'Abat-faim', *Encyclopédie des Nuisances* 5 (November): 96–102.

Debord, G. (1987), 'Abolir', *Encyclopédie des Nuisances* 11 (June): 245–50.

Debord, G. (1995), *The Society of the Spectacle*, trans. D. Nicholson-Smith, New York: Zone Books.

Debord, G. (1998), *Comments on the Society of the Spectacle*, trans. M. Imrie. London: Verso.

Debord, G. (1999), *Correspondance, Volume 1: Juin 1957–Août 1960*, Paris: Librairie Arthème Fayard.

Debord, G. (2001), *Correspondance, Volume 2: Septembre 1960–Décembre 1964*, Paris: Librairie Arthème Fayard.

Debord, G. (2003a), *Complete Cinematic Works: Scripts, Still and Document*, trans. and ed. K. Knabb, Edinburgh: AK Press.

Debord, G. (2003b), *Correspondance, Volume 3: Janvier 1965–Décembre 1968*, Paris: Librairie Arthème Fayard.

Debord, G. (2004a), *Correspondance, Volume 4: Janvier 1969–Décembre 1972*, Paris: Librairie Arthème Fayard.

Debord, G. (2004b), *Panegyric, Vols 1 and 2*, trans. J. Brook and J. McHale. London: Verso.

Debord, G. (2005), *Correspondance, Volume 5: Janvier 1973–Décembre 1978*, Paris: Librairie Arthème Fayard.

Debord, G. (2006a), 'Aux Poubelles de l'Histoire!', in *Œuvres*, Paris: Collection Quarto, Gallimard, 623–34.

Debord, G. (2006b), 'Cette Mauvaise Réputation', in *Œuvres*, Paris: Collection Quarto, Gallimard, 1796–840.

Debord, G. (2006c), *Correspondance, Volume 6: Janvier 1979–Décembre 1987*, Paris: Librairie Arthème Fayard.

Debord, G. (2006d), 'Notes sur le "question des immigrés", Notes pour Mezioud', in *Œuvres*, Paris: Collection Quarto, Gallimard, 1588–92.

Debord, G. (2006e), 'Note sur la coherence', in *Œuvres*, Paris: Collection Quarto, Gallimard, 635–7.

Debord, G. (2006f), 'Notice pour la Fédération française des ciné-clubs', in *Œuvres*, Paris: Collection Quarto, Gallimard, 70.

Debord, G. (2006g), 'Pour un jugement révolutionnaire de l'art', in *Œuvres*, Paris: Collection Quarto, Gallimard, 558–63.
Debord, G. (2006h), 'Préface à la 4ᵉ edition italienne de *La Société du spectacle*', in *Œuvres*, Paris: Éditions Gallimard, 1460–73.
Debord, G. (2006i), 'Présentation inedited des *Prolégomènes à l'Historiosophie* d'August von Cieszkowski', in *Œuvres*, Paris: Éditions Gallimard, 1536–7.
Debord, G. (2008a), *Correspondance, Volume 7: Janvier 1988–Novembre 1994*, Paris: Librairie Arthème Fayard.
Debord, G. (2008b), *A Sick Planet*, trans. D. Nicholson-Smith, London: Seagull Books.
Debord, G. (2010), *Correspondance, Volume 0: Septembre 1951–Juillet 1957*, Paris: Librairie Arthème Fayard.
Debord, G. (2018), *Stratégie: La Librairie de Guy Debord*, Paris: Éditions L'échappée.
Dolto, S. and N. Sidi Moussa (2019), 'The Situationists' Anticolonialism: An Internationalist Perspective', in A. Hemmens and G. Zacarias (eds), *Rethinking the Situationist International*, London: Pluto Press.
Dupont, M. (2009), *Nihilist Communism: A Critique of Optimism in the Far Left*, San Francisco: Ardent Press.
Ebert, T. L. (2012), 'Hegel's "picture-thinking" as the interpretive logic of the popular', *Textual Practice* 28, no. 1: 9–33.
Eichengreen, B. (1995), 'Mainsprings of Economic Recovery in Post-war Europe', in B. Eichengreen (ed.), *Europe's Post-war Recovery*, 3–35, Cambridge: Cambridge University Press.
Feuerbach, L. (2012), *The Fiery Brook: Selected Writings*, trans. Z. Hanfi, London: Verso.
Frayssé, O. (2017), 'Guy Debord, a Critique of Modernism and Fordism: What Lessons for Today?', in M. Briziarelli and E. Armano (eds), *The Spectacle 2.0: Reading Debord in the Context of Digital Capitalism*, 67–79, London: University of Westminster Press.
Gabel, J. (1975), *False Consciousness: An Essay on Reification*, trans. M. A. Thompson, Oxford: Basil Blackwell.
Gadamer, H. (1976), *Hegel's Dialectic: Five Hermeneutical Studies*, trans. P. C. Smith. New Haven, CT: Yale University Press.
Galbraith, J. K. (1999), *The Affluent Society*, London: Penguin.
Gilman-Opalsky, R. (2011), *Spectacular Capitalism: Guy Debord and the Practice of Radical Philosophy*, London: Minor Compositions.
Goldner, L. (1991), 'Amadeo Bordiga, the Agrarian Question and the International Revolutionary Movement', *Critique: Journal of Socialist Theory* 23: 73–100.
Hafner, K. (1993), 'Gebrauchswertfetischismus', in D. Behrens (ed.), *Gesellschaft und Erkenntnis: zur materialistischen Erkenntnis- und Ökonomiekritik*, 59–88, Freiburg: Ça ira-Verlag.
Harris, H. S. (1977), 'Introduction to Faith and Knowledge', in *Faith & Knowledge*, trans. W. Cerf and H. S. Harris, Albany, NY: State University of New York Press.

Harvey, D. (1990), *The Conditions of Postmodernity: An Enquiry into the Origins of Cultural Change*, Malden, MA: Blackwell.

Hayes, A. P. (2017), 'How the Situationist International became what it was', PhD diss., Australian National University, Canberra, Australia.

Hegel, G. W. F. (1969), *Science of Logic*, trans. A. V. Miller, Amherst, NY: Humanity Books.

Hegel, G. W. F. (1970), *Phänomenologie des Geistes*, Frankfurt am Main: Suhrkamp.

Hegel, G. W. F. (1975), *Aesthetics: Lectures on Fine Art*, vol. 1, trans. T. M. Knox. Oxford: Oxford University Press.

Hegel, G. W. F. (1977a), *The Difference Between Fichte's and Schelling's System of Philosophy*, trans. H. S. Harris and W. Cerf, Albany, NY: State University of New York Press.

Hegel, G. W. F. (1977b), *Faith and Knowledge*, trans. W. Cerf and H. S. Harris, Albany, NY: State University of New York Press.

Hegel, G. W. F. (1977c), *Phenomenology of Spirit*, trans. A. V. Miller, Oxford: Oxford University Press.

Hegel, G. W. F. (1984), *Hegel: The Letters*, trans. C. Butler and C. Seiler, Bloomington: Indiana University Press.

Hegel, G. W. F. (1985), *Introduction to the Lectures on the Philosophy of History*, trans. T. M. Knox and A. V. Miller, Oxford: Clarendon Press.

Hegel, G. W. F. (1991a), *Elements of the Philosophy of Right*, trans. H. B. Nisbet, Cambridge: Cambridge University Press.

Hegel, G. W. F. (1991b), *The Encyclopaedia Logic*, trans. T. F. Geraets, W. A. Suchting and H. S. Harris, Indianapolis, IN: Hackett.

Hegel, G. W. F. (2004), 'The German Constitution', in *Political Writings*, trans. H. B. Nisbet, 6–101, Cambridge: Cambridge University Press.

Hegel, G. W. F. (2007), *Hegel's Philosophy of Mind*, trans. W. Wallace and A. V. Miller, Oxford: Oxford University Press.

Hegel, G. W. F. (2010), *The Science of Logic*, trans. G. di Giovanni, Cambridge: Cambridge University Press.

Hegel, G. W. F. (2018), *Phenomenology of Spirit*, trans. T. Pinkard, Cambridge: Cambridge University Press.

Hesse, C. (2018), 'Virtual Experience', trans. E.J. Russell and V. Zhizhchenko, *Cured Quail* 1 (January).

Horkheimer, M. (2002), 'Traditional and Critical Theory', in *Critical Theory: Selected Essays*, trans. M. J. O'Connell et al., New York: Continuum.

Houlgate, S. (2011), 'Essence, Reflexion and Immediacy in Hegel's *Science of Logic*', in S. Houlgate and M. Baur (eds), *A Companion to Hegel*, 139–58, Malden, MA: Blackwell.

Huizinga, J. (2019), *In the Shadow of Tomorrow: A Diagnosis of the Modern Distemper*, trans. J. Huizinga, Providence, RI: Cluny Media.

Hussey, A. (2001), 'Requiem pour un con: Subversive Pop and the Society of the Spectacle', *Cercles* 3: 49–59.

Hyppolite, J. (1969), *Studies on Marx and Hegel*, trans. J. O'Neill, London: Basic Books.
Hyppolite, J. (1997), *Logic and Existence*, trans. L. Lawlor and A. Sen, Albany, NY: State University of New York Press.
Internationale Situationniste (1997), *Internationale situationniste: Édition augmentée*, Paris: Librairie Arthème Fayard.
Jappe, A. (1999a), *Guy Debord*, trans. D. Nicholson-Smith, Berkeley: University of California Press.
Jappe, A. (1999b), 'Sic Transit Gloria Artis: "The End of Art" for Theodor Adorno and Guy Debord', *SubStance* 28, no. 3; Issue 90, Special Issue: Guy Debord: 102–28.
Jappe, A. (2010), 'Baudrillard, détournement par excès', *Lignes* 31.
Jappe, A. (2018), 'The Spectacle and the Culture Industry, the Transcendence of Art and the Autonomy of Art: Some Parallels between Theodor Adorno's and Guy Debord's Critical Concepts', in B. Best, W. Bonefeld and C. O'Kane (eds), *The Sage Handbook of Frankfurt School Critical Theory*, vol. 1, trans. D. Nicholson-Smith, 1285–301, London: Sage.
Jorn, A. (2002), *Value and Economy: Critique of Political Economy and the Exploitation of the Unique*, trans. P. Shield, Farnham: Ashgate.
Knabb, K. (ed.) (2006), *Situationist International Anthology: Revised and Expanded Edition*, Berkeley, CA: Bureau of Public Secrets.
Krahl, H. (1971), 'Bemerkungen zur Akkumulation und Krisentendenz des Kapitals', in *Konstitution und Klassenkampf: Zur historischen Dialektik von bürgerlicher Emanzipation und proletarischer Revolution*, 84–99, Frankfurt am Main: Neue Kritik.
Kraus, K. (1986), *Half-Truths and One-and-a-Half Truths: Selected Aphorisms*, trans. H. Zohan, New York: Carcanet Press.
Le Bras, L. and E. Guy (eds) (2016), *Lire Debord: Avec des notes inédites de Guy Debord*, Paris: Éditions L'Échappée.
Lefebvre, H. (1968), *Dialectical Materialism*, trans. J. Sturrock, London: Cape Editions.
Lefebvre, H. (1982a), *Logique Formelle, Logique Dialectique*, Paris: Éditions Sociales.
Lefebvre, H. (1982b), *The Sociology of Marx*, trans. N. Guterman, New York: Columbia University Press.
Lefebvre, H. (1991a), *Critique of Everyday Life*, vol. 1, trans. J. Moore, London: Verso.
Lefebvre, H. (1991b), *The Production of Space*, trans. D. Nicholson-Smith, Malden, MA: Blackwell.
Lefebvre, H. (2002), *Critique of Everyday Life, Volume 2: Foundations for a Sociology of the Everyday*, trans. J. Moore, London: Verso.
Lefebvre, J. (2014), 'German', in B. Cassin (ed.), *Dictionary of Untranslatables: A Philosophical Lexicon*, Princeton, NJ: Princeton University Press.
Lenin, V. I. (1981), *Collected Works, Volume 38: Philosophical Notebooks*, trans. C. Dutt, Moscow: Progress Publishers.
Lowe, D. M. (1983), *History of Bourgeois Perception*, Chicago: University of Chicago Press.

Lukács, G. (1971a), *History and Class Consciousness: Studies in Marxist Dialectics*, trans. R. Livingstone, London: Merlin Press.

Lukács, G. (1971b), *The Theory of the Novel*, trans. A. Bostock, Cambridge, MA: MIT Press.

Lukács, G. (1978), *The Ontology of Social Being: Hegel's False and his Genuine Ontology*, trans. D. Fernbach, London: Merlin Press.

Lukács, G. (2000), *Tailism and the Dialectic: A Defense of History and Class Consciousness*, trans. E. Leslie, London: Verso.

Mannheim, K. (2015), *Ideology and Utopia: An Introduction to the Sociology of Knowledge*, trans. L. Wirth and E. Shils, London: Harcourt, Brace and Company.

Marcuse, H. (2009), 'The Concept of Essence', in *Negations: Essays in Critical Theory*, trans. J. J. Shapiro, London: MayFlyBooks.

Marx, K. (1962), 'Das Kapital: Kritik der politischen Oekonomie. Erster Band', in *Karl Marx Friedrich Engels Werke*, Band 23, Berlin: Dietz.

Marx, K. (1975a), 'Comments on James Mill, *Élémens d'économie politique*', in *Marx and Engels Collected Works*, vol. 3, 211–28, London: Progress Publishers.

Marx, K. (1975b), 'Contribution to the Critique of Hegel's Philosophy of Law, Introduction', in *Marx and Engels Collected Works*, vol. 3, 175–87, London: Progress Publishers.

Marx, K. (1975c), 'Economic and Philosophic Manuscripts of 1844', in *Marx and Engels Collected Works*, vol. 3, 229–349, London: Progress Publishers.

Marx, K. (1975d), 'The Holy Family', in *Marx and Engels Collected Works*, vol. 4, 5–211, London: Progress Publishers.

Marx, K. (1975e), 'Letter from Marx to his Father in Trier', in *Marx and Engels Collected Works*, vol. 1, 10–21, London: Progress Publishers.

Marx, K. (1975f), 'On the Jewish Question', in *Marx and Engels Collected Works*, vol. 3, 146–74, London: Progress Publishers.

Marx, K. (1976a), *The Commodity* [first chapter of the first German edition of *Capital*], trans. A. Dragstedt, https://www.marxists.org/archive/marx/works/1867-c1/commodity.htm.

Marx, K. (1976b), 'Manifesto of the Communist Party' in *Marx and Engels Collected Works*, vol. 6, 477–519, London: Progress Publishers.

Marx, K. (1976c), 'Moralising Criticism and Critical Morality', in *Marx and Engels Collected Works*, vol. 6, 312–40, London: Progress Publishers.

Marx, K. (1976d), 'The Poverty of Philosophy', in *Marx and Engels Collected Works*, vol. 6, 105–212, London: Progress Publishers.

Marx, K. (1978), 'The Value-Form. Appendix to the 1st German edition of Capital: Vol. 1, *1867*', trans. M. Roth and W. Suchting, *Capital and Class* 2, no. 1 (Spring): 134–50.

Marx, K. (1983), 'Marx to Engels. 1 February 1858', in *Marx and Engels Collected Works*, vol. 40, 258–60, London: Progress Publishers.

Marx, K. (1986), 'Economic Manuscripts of 1857–58', in *Marx and Engels Collected Works*, vol. 28, London: Progress Publishers.

Marx, K. (1987), 'A Contribution to the Critique of Political Economy', in *Marx and Engels Collected Works*, vol. 29, 257–420, London: Progress Publishers.

Marx, K. (1989), 'Theories of Surplus Value', in *Marx and Engels Collected Works*, vol. 32, London: Progress Publishers.

Marx, K. (1994), 'Economic Manuscript of 1861–64', in *Marx and Engels Collected Works*, vol. 34, London: Progress Publishers.

Marx, K. (1996), *Capital*, vol. 1, in *Marx and Engels Collected Works*, vol. 35, London: Progress Publishers.

Marx, K. (1998), *Capital*, vol. 3, in *Marx and Engels Collected Works*, vol. 37, London: Progress Publishers.

Mattick, P. (1969), *Marx and Keynes: The Limits of the Mixed Economy*, Boston: Extending Horizons Books.

Mattick Jr., P. (2018), 'Is there a Society of the Spectacle?', *Cured Quail* 1 (January).

Merrifield, A. (2005), *Guy Debord*, London: Reaktion Books.

Mudimbe, V. Y. and A. Bohm (1994), 'Hegel's Reception in France', *Journal of French and Francophone Philosophy* 6, no. 3: 5–33.

Murray, P. (1983), 'Hegel and the Logician of Capital: An Interpretation of Marx's Parisian Critique of Hegel', in *Hegel-Jahrbuch*, 187–93, Rome: Wilhelm R. Beyer.

Murray, P. (1988), *Marx's Theory of Scientific Knowledge*, Amherst, NY: Humanity Books.

Murray, P. (2015), 'The Secret of Capital's Self-Valorisation "Laid Bare": How Hegel Helped Marx to Overturn Ricardo's Theory of Profit', in F. Moseley and T. Smith (eds), *Marx's* Capital *and Hegel's* Logic: *A Reexamination*, 189–213, Chicago: Haymarket.

Nancy, J. (2000), *Being Singular Plural*, trans. R. D. Richardson and A. E. O'Byrne, Stanford, CA: Stanford University Press.

Nelson, A. (1999), *Marx's Concept of Money: The God of Commodities*, London: Routledge.

Ovid (2004), *Metamorpheses*, trans. D. Raeburn, London: Penguin Classics.

Pashukanis, E. B. (2002), *The General Theory of Law and Marxism*, trans. B. Einhorn, London: Transaction Publishers.

Perspectives (1975), *At Dusk: The Situationist Movement in Historical Perspective*, Berkeley: Perspectives.

Pinkard, T. (1996), *Hegel's* Phenomenology: *The Sociality of Reason*, Cambridge: Cambridge University Press.

Pohrt, W. (1976), *Zur Theorie des Gebrauchswerts oder über die Vergänglichkeit der historischen Voraussetzungen, unter denen das Kapital Gebrauchswert setzt*, Frankfurt am Main: Syndikat.

Postone, M. (1993), *Time, Labor and Social Domination: A Reinterpretation of Marx's Critical Theory*, Cambridge: Cambridge University Press.

Postone, M. (2009), 'The Subject and Social Theory: Marx and Lukács on Hegel', in A. Chitty and M. McIvor (eds), *Karl Marx and Contemporary Philosophy*, 205–20, New York: Palgrave Macmillan.

Rancière, J. (2009), *The Emancipated Spectator*, trans. G. Elliott, London: Verso.

Reichelt, H. (2001), *Zur logischen Struktur des Kapitalbegriffs bei Karl Marx*, Freiburg: ça ira- Verlag.

Reichelt, H. (2005), 'Social Reality as Appearance: Some Notes on Marx's Conception of Reality', in W. Bonefeld and K. Psychopedis (eds), *Human Dignity: Social Autonomy and the Critique of Capitalism*, 31–68, Aldershot: Ashgate.

Reichelt, H. (2007), 'Marx's Critique of Economic Categories: Reflections on the Problem of Validity in the Dialectical Method of Presentation in *Capital*', *Historical Materialism* 15, no. 4: 3–52.

Reinicke, H. (1975), *Revolte im bürgerlichen Erbe. Gebrauchswert und Mikrologie*, Giessen: Achenbach.

Rizzi, B. (1985), *The Bureaucratization of the World. The USSR: Bureaucratic Collectivism*, trans. A. Westoby, London: Tavistock Publications.

Roth, M. S. (1988), *Knowing and History: Appropriations of Hegel in Twentieth-Century France*, Ithaca, NY: Cornell University Press.

Rubin, I. I. (1973), *Essays on Marx's Theory of Value*, trans. M. Samardzija and F. Perlman, Detroit: Black & Red.

Russell, E.J. (2015), 'The Logic of Subsumption: An Elective Affinity between Hegel and Marx', *Revista Opinião Filosófica* 6, no. 2.

Russell, E.J. (2018), 'Georg Lukács: An Actually Existing Antinomy', in B. Best, W. Bonefeld and C. O'Kane (eds), *The Sage Handbook of Frankfurt School Critical Theory, Volume 1: Key Texts and Contributions to a Critical Theory of Society*, 216–33, London: Sage.

Schlick, M. (1974), *General Theory of Knowledge*, trans. A. E. Blumberg, New York: Springer.

Schmidt, A. (1972), 'Henri Lefèbvre and Contemporary Interpretations of Marx', in *The Unknown Dimension: European Marxism since Lenin*, New York: Basic Books.

Simon, R. (2001), *Fondements critiques d'une théorie de la révolution: Au-delà de l'affirmation du prolétariat*, Paris: Éditions Senonevero.

Sinnerbrink, R. (2007), *Understanding Hegelianism*, Stocksfield: Acumen Publishing.

Situationist International (2003), 'Appendix 5: Communiqué from the SI concerning Vaneigem', in *The Real Split in the International: Theses on the Situationist International and its Time, 1972*, trans. J. McHale, London: Pluto Press.

Smith, T. (2015), 'Hegel, Marx and the Comprehension of Capitalism', in F. Moseley and T. Smith, *Marx's Capital and Hegel's Logic: A Reexamination*, 17–40, Chicago: Haymarket.

Sohn-Rethel, A. (1983), *Intellectual and Manual Labour: A Critique of Epistemology*, trans. M. Sohn-Rethel, Atlantic Highlands, NJ: Humanities Press.

Sohn-Rethel, A. (2020), 'The Formal Characteristics of Second Nature', *Selva*, https://selvajournal.org/the-formal-characteristics-of-second-nature/.

Surplus Club (2015), 'Trapped at a Party Where No One Likes You', *Sic* 3, http://sicjournal.org/trapped-at-a-party-where-no-one-likes-you/.

Taylor, C. (1975), *Hegel*, Cambridge: Cambridge University Press.

Théorie Communiste (2010), 'Autoprésupposition du capital : essence/surface/fétichisme', *Théorie Communiste* 23 (May).

Vaneigem, R. (2012), *The Revolution of Everyday Life*, trans. D. Nicholson-Smith, Oakland, CA: PM Press.

Vaneigem, R. (2015), *Raoul Vaneigem: Self-Portraits and Caricatures of the Situationist International*, trans. W. J. Brown, New York: Colossal Books.

Verene, D. P. (1985), *Hegel's Recollection: A Study of Images in the* Phenomenology of Spirit, Albany, NY: State University of New York Press.

Villon, F. (1977), *The Poems of François Villon*, trans. G. Kinnell, London: University Press of New England.

Wark, M. (2013), *The Spectacle of Disintegration: Situationist Passages out of the 20th Century*, London: Verso.

Winfield, R. (1999), 'Concept, Individuality and Truth', *Bulletin of the Hegel Society of Great Britain* 20, no. 1–2 (39/40): 35–46.

Wright, K. (1983), 'Hegel: The Identity of Identity and Nonidentity', *Idealistic Studies* 13: 11–32.

Zamora, D. (2013), 'When Exclusion Replaces Exploitation: The Conditions of the Surplus- Population under Neoliberalism', *Nonsite.org* 10 (September).

Index

absolute idealism 32, 34, 112, 215n, 216n
abstract
    labour 5, 32–3, 66, 86–7, 89, 91, 96, 113, 156, 167, 216n, 217n
    space 176, 219n, 225n
abstraction 5, 32–4, 44, 61, 63, 65–6, 76, 78–81, 86–7, 96, 109, 119, 143, 156, 158, 176, 203, 207n, 215n, 216n
accident 91, 150–1
accumulation 2, 19, 37, 40, 68, 70, 95, 101, 103, 105, 107, 186, 193, 197, 202–3, 206n
acme of ideology 47
actuality 4, 11, 15, 18, 21, 31, 34–5, 47, 50, 75–6, 80, 82, 92, 94, 103, 122, 128–30, 137, 144–52, 156–8, 163, 167, 182–3, 186–9, 191–4, 196, 199, 212n, 216n, 223n
Adorno, Theodor W. xviii, xix, 4, 6, 14, 16, 20, 23–4, 30–9, 41–4, 46–7, 49, 54, 60, 66, 81–2, 95–6, 99, 143, 167–9, 176, 183, 188, 192, 195, 198–9, 206n, 209n, 210n, 211n, 212n, 220n
advertising xvi, 1, 6, 8, 23, 40, 44, 68, 88, 98, 100–1, 103–4, 192, 196, 208n, 220n
affluence 69, 97, 99, 202, 204, 228n
Agamben, Giorgio xiv, 1
Algeria 174
alienation xvii, 10, 45, 77, 79, 80, 83–4, 97, 99, 105, 119, 125, 131, 143, 165, 192, 202, 215n, 216n, 218n, 219n, 225n
Althusser, Louis 1, 202, 205n
Anarchism 202
Anders, Günther 177–8
anti-imperialism 214n
antinomy 4, 7, 10, 52, 110–18, 124–7, 200
antisemitism 96
appearance xvi–xviii, 2–3, 8, 11–13, 16, 18–19, 20–1, 25–8, 30, 35, 41–2, 46–50, 55–6, 58–67, 72, 75, 80–1, 84–5, 87–92, 94, 100, 103–8, 116, 119–20, 122–37, 142–3, 146, 149, 151, 153–60, 162–3, 178, 180–3, 187–9, 191, 193–5, 199, 208n, 213n, 214n, 215n, 218n, 219n, 221n, 222n, 225n
    see also Erscheinung
arch-ideology 47
Arguments xviii, 23, 201, 211n, 227n
Aristotle 55, 105, 223n
art xiv, xviii, 13, 62, 98, 169, 201, 210n
Arthur, Christopher J. 79, 87, 216n
assimilation 135, 165
austerity 18, 175, 192
automatic subject 21, 154–6
automobile 176, 193
autonomy xv, 2, 5, 11, 39, 42, 45, 47, 50, 77–8, 87–9, 94–5, 97, 101–7, 113, 118, 122, 124, 138, 156–7, 180, 195, 203, 215n
avant-garde xv, 1, 13, 201, 218n

Backhaus, Hans-Georg 66, 79, 215n
baroque 128, 193, 208n
Baudrillard, Jean xvi, 1, 40, 212n
Bauer brothers 77
becoming visible of capital 89, 103, 157
Begriffslogik 11, 18, 21, 127–8, 141, 150, 152–4, 156, 158–63, 165, 178, 183–9, 221n, 224n
Bellofiore, Riccardo 79–80, 211n
Benjamin, Walter xvii, 153
Berlin Wall 182
Black & Red 207n
Bolshevism 180, 201, 220n
Bonapartism 170
Bonefeld, Werner 6, 47, 96, 173
Boorstin, Daniel J. 7
bourgeois
    society 4, 10, 32–3, 42–4, 79, 109, 120, 165, 170, 172, 174, 177, 182–3, 198, 224n
    thought 42–4, 115–16
Boutroux, Émile 200
Breuer, Stefan 96

Bunyard, Tom 9–12, 211n
bureaucracy 68–9, 113, 170, 174, 179–82, 201–2, 224n, 225n, 226n

Caesar 194
Camatte, Jacques 106, 218n
capital xvii, 5, 16, 19, 43, 65, 68, 78–80, 83–8, 92, 101–7, 134, 138, 154–7, 170, 172, 174, 176–7, 193, 197, 202, 204, 207n, 211n, 215n, 216n, 218n, 225n, 227n
Capital
    Vol. 1 8, 14, 17, 65, 79, 83–4, 86–7, 89–91, 102, 107, 154, 172, 206n, 216n
    Vol. 2 102
    Vol. 3 102, 155
capitalism xv–xvii, 3–4, 17, 19, 22, 67–8, 84, 88–9, 92, 108, 113, 118–20, 164, 171, 179, 192, 197, 202, 204, 212n, 218n, 219n, 224n
capitalist 78, 155–6, 179
    mode of production 2–3, 5, 13, 43, 79, 84, 86–7, 90, 92, 104, 110, 173, 176, 206n, 217n
    society xix, 3, 17, 31, 33, 54, 62, 65, 80, 84–6, 105, 113, 124–5, 157, 162, 173, 183, 191, 218n
Castoriadis, Cornélius 201, 227n
Catholicism 46
celebrity 68–70, 103, 143
centralization 180
Chamfort, Nicolas 1
Chase, Robert 23
Châtelet, François 17
China 67, 174, 176, 214n
Christ 148
Christianity 74–5, 144, 148
Cieszkowski, August von 9, 211n
circulation 97, 102–5, 155–6, 176–7, 182, 193, 203
Clark, T.J. 206n, 208n
class xvi, 5, 32, 43–6, 49, 62, 100, 106, 109, 114–15, 125, 143, 148, 154, 156, 170, 172–4, 177, 179, 180–1, 192, 202–4, 208n, 219n
Clausewitz, Carl von 198, 207n, 208n, 209n
cliché 68, 169

coherence 3, 6, 8, 11, 15, 18, 21, 39, 68, 107, 110, 119, 127–31, 134, 137, 145–6, 154, 158–9, 183–4, 188, 191, 194, 223n, 225n
Cohn-Bendit, Daniel 202
Cold War 181
Collège de France 9, 127, 205n, 208n
colonialism 68
commensurability 3, 19, 33, 39–40, 42, 44, 58, 61, 63–4, 72, 77, 80, 92, 96, 128–30, 135–8, 140–2, 144, 157, 162, 175–6, 178, 181, 183, 188–9, 191–4
commodity xvi, xvii, 2–5, 17, 37, 40, 44, 46, 50, 64–6, 69–70, 83–95, 101–10, 113, 115, 118–25, 142, 154–5, 157, 170, 172–9, 182, 193, 199, 203, 207n, 212n, 217n, 220n, 224n, 225n, 227n
communication xvii, 1, 69–70, 107, 124, 169, 176, 193, 196, 203
comparison 140, 166
concentrated spectacle 69–70, 128, 154, 166, 171, 178–82
concept xv, 2–4, 6, 8, 10–11, 15–18, 27–8, 30–2, 34, 39, 44, 53–4, 97, 111, 120, 128, 153–4, 157–66, 174, 183–7, 189, 191–2, 194–5, 198–200, 208n, 223n, 224n
    see also Begriffslogik
concrete 17–18, 30–1, 45–7, 54, 65–6, 76–8, 80, 84–9, 94, 96–7, 100–1, 105, 117–19, 122, 125, 132–5, 145, 148, 150, 153–4, 156–8, 160–2, 166, 177, 183–4, 186, 193, 195, 205n, 213n, 215n, 217n, 225n
    activity 7, 66, 97
    labour 33, 66, 86, 89, 96, 156
concreteness 5, 47, 65, 86, 94, 96, 101, 118–19, 158, 160, 186
consciousness 7, 10, 18, 23, 25, 27–30, 35–7, 43, 45, 55–63, 75, 88, 112–13, 115, 118, 146, 148, 156, 200, 205n, 213n, 222n, 226n
consumer demand 98–9
consumerism 1, 6, 8, 18, 101, 104
consumption xiv, xvi, 19, 37, 40, 73, 86, 88, 95, 98–102, 105–6, 166, 169–70, 176–7, 181, 192, 203–4, 217n
contemplation 11, 45, 63, 97, 115–16, 118–19, 222n

content 6, 12, 18, 25, 28, 44, 51, 57, 63, 66, 72, 93, 108, 116–17, 122, 133, 135, 137, 147–50, 154, 158, 162, 178, 184, 187, 189, 216n
contingency 8, 15–18, 29, 119, 128, 142, 149–50, 153, 184, 187, 194, 197, 223n
contradiction xix, 4, 40, 52, 67, 76, 78, 115, 139, 189, 195, 227n
council-communism 218n, 227n
country 67, 128, 154, 165–6, 175–7, 183, 202–3, 214n, 224n
critical theory xvi, 1–2, 4–6, 13, 15–20, 22–4, 31–2, 96, 106, 113, 143, 154, 164, 166, 183, 188–9, 191–2, 196–7, 202, 208n, 210n, 211n, 220n, 221n
critique
   of political economy 1–2, 13–14, 16, 21–2, 64–5, 78–9, 82, 84–6, 104–5, 107–8, 113, 121, 138, 173, 192, 195, 215n, 216n, 217n
   of society 85, 113, 204
cult of the leader 180, 225n
culture xiv, 6–7, 19, 88, 97, 112, 117, 144, 165, 167–8, 170, 177, 193, 208n, 210n
   industry 6, 167–8, 170, 177, 210n
Czechoslovakia 181

Darstellung 16, 26–7, 79, 84
Dauvé, Gilles 84, 227n
deception 7, 26, 41, 48, 208n
decomposition 200
decompression 224n
deconstruction 199
deficit spending 68, 175
deindustrialization 177
dérive 208n
determinacy 16, 53, 74, 129, 136, 140, 158, 160–1, 163, 166, 186, 197, 204, 210n, 222n, 225n
determinate negation 25, 28, 30, 53, 87, 105, 221n
determination xviii, 8, 12, 14, 16–17, 19, 20–1, 25, 28, 30–2, 37, 44, 51–3, 57, 59, 63, 76, 84, 86–8, 91, 96, 101–2, 105–7, 110–11, 113, 116–17, 122, 125, 128–32, 137–41, 144–7, 149–50, 154, 156, 159–61, 163, 174, 185–8, 192–3, 203, 221n, 222n, 224n

dialectic xv, xviii, 4, 6, 10–12, 16–17, 19, 20, 21, 23, 25–6, 28, 30–5, 37, 49, 51–3, 67, 85, 115, 117, 127, 164, 185, 187, 198–200, 203, 207n, 209n, 211n, 213n, 215n, 219n, 221n, 226n
Dialectic of Enlightenment 23, 43, 143, 192, 220n
Diamat 115, 219n
differentiation 4, 11, 18, 21, 39, 52–4, 68–9, 72–3, 78, 80–1, 94, 127–9, 132, 138–42, 145, 147, 149–51, 153–6, 158, 160–3, 165–7, 170, 172, 174–5, 178–9, 181, 183, 194, 196, 220n, 225n
diffuse spectacle 69–71, 128, 154, 166, 171, 178–83
diversity 8, 46, 50, 56–7, 68, 77–8, 81, 108, 127, 130, 133–7, 139–40, 159–60, 165–6, 181, 189, 209n
division 4, 7, 12, 20, 43, 50, 62, 66–73, 81, 113, 116, 124–5, 160, 163, 166, 170, 174, 179, 222n
   of labour 3, 43, 71, 113, 201, 218n
domination 2–3, 5, 15, 20–1, 31, 34–5, 42, 44, 54, 80–1, 83, 87–8, 93, 95–6, 104, 110, 118, 123–4, 126, 130, 143, 149, 157, 164, 171, 174, 179–80, 202, 210n
dualism 4, 6, 40–1, 46, 55–7, 65, 85, 113, 115–16, 126, 151, 164, 166, 186, 188, 226n

Ebert, Friedrich 180
economic
   crisis 192, 224n, 225n
   growth 68, 202–4, 227n
   stagnation 202
economism 202
Éditions Champ Libre 179, 206n, 211n
Egypt 174
Eichendorff, Joseph von 214n
Ellul, Jacques 100
employment 169, 202–3
Encyclopedie des Nuisances 165
Engels, Friedrich 77, 115, 219n, 221n
Enlightenment 42
epistemology 29, 43–4, 55, 74–5, 80, 109, 112, 114–15, 199, 207n, 216n, 219n
equality 64, 83, 130, 136, 139–41, 165, 173–4
   see also commensurability

equalization 64, 86, 89, 155, 165, 194, 199, 216n
  see also commensurability
equivalent form of value 45, 90–1, 93–4, 97, 105, 138, 142, 173, 178, 220n
Erscheinung xvi, xvii, 4, 26–7, 35, 40, 50, 55, 58–9, 61–4, 80, 84–5, 90, 93, 100, 103–7, 121, 124, 130–7, 139, 141–7, 150, 152, 155–6, 222n
essence xv, xvii, 8, 16, 18–19, 21, 25–6, 28–9, 34–6, 39–42, 46–7, 56, 59–62, 64–6, 68, 75–8, 85, 93, 97, 103, 116–17, 122, 124–8, 130–4, 136–7, 139, 141, 145–6, 149–50, 153, 158–9, 165, 170, 175, 182, 215n, 218n, 221n, 222n
  see also Wesenslogik
everyday life 64, 142, 144, 151, 157, 166–7, 201, 206n, 210n, 217n, 223n
Excalibur 194
exchange
  process 5, 32, 63, 78, 86–9, 91, 96, 99, 102–3, 105, 113, 156, 215n, 216n, 218n
  -value xvii, 19, 21, 33, 39–40, 63–4, 78, 86–7, 89, 91–7, 99, 101–3, 105–6, 108, 130, 136, 138, 141–2, 144, 157, 169, 172–3, 175, 189, 195, 204, 207n, 210n, 216n, 217n, 221n
existence 26, 34, 62, 65–6, 77–9, 86, 88, 90, 92, 94–5, 102, 106, 113–16, 118, 120, 122, 124, 132–6, 139, 145, 148, 154–7, 161, 167, 169–70, 187–8, 207n, 222n
existentialism 1, 126, 162, 199
exploitation 5, 144, 164, 180, 196, 204, 214n, 225n
exposition 15–17, 22, 26, 36, 46, 84, 86, 88–90, 92, 124, 147, 149–50, 169, 187, 191, 195, 215n
  see also Darstellung
exteriority 38, 41, 59, 62, 74, 128, 132, 136–7, 141–2, 145–8, 153, 158, 164–5, 170, 174–5, 183, 186, 189
external relation xvii, 18, 29, 39, 41, 55, 92, 94, 111–12, 114–15, 125, 132–3, 139, 141, 151, 162, 166, 222n

facticity 17, 41, 114, 140, 145, 149, 151
Faith and Knowledge 19, 21, 110–12, 114, 125

falsehood 10, 19–21, 24, 30–1, 36, 41–2, 49, 53–5, 100, 121, 183, 191, 211n, 215n
falsification 36, 39–40, 46–7, 88–9, 95, 120, 124, 181–2, 199–200
fascism 200, 225n
fatalism 114–15
fetish xvii, 2, 5, 11, 45, 65, 87–90, 96, 104, 107, 109, 113–15, 119–20, 122, 155–7, 173, 207n
Feuerbach, Ludwig 2, 9, 11, 41, 45, 50, 73–7, 80, 82, 186, 211n, 215n
Fichte, Johann Gottlieb 52, 111–12, 220n
fictitious capital 104, 193
film 129, 167–8, 177, 204, 207n, 226n
finitude 76, 112, 134–6, 147–8, 188, 212n
First World War 203
Fontenelle, Bernard Le Bovier de 15
force 12, 20, 34, 50, 54–67, 69–70, 72, 81, 88, 93, 110, 124, 129–30, 135–6, 141, 145, 208n, 213n, 214n, 222n
Fordism 228n
formal rationalization 113, 118–19
formalism 6, 81
form of value 21, 84, 89–92, 94, 101–3, 157
fragmentation 3, 36–8, 43–4, 46, 62, 73, 113, 119–21, 125, 127, 144, 165, 199, 217n, 226n
France xviii, 9, 121, 127, 164, 197, 200, 202–3, 205n, 206n, 207n, 208n, 227n
Frankfurt School 4, 13, 16, 20, 22–3, 192
  see also Institut für Sozialforschung
French Communist Party (PCF) 200–2, 205n

Gabel, Joseph 35, 211n, 215n, 220n
Gadamer, Hans-Georg 54, 56
Galbraith, John Kenneth 86, 97–100, 217n
Galileo 55
Garnault, Jean 118
Gaulle, Charles de 201, 203
Gebrauchswertfetischismus 96–7
Gemeinwesen 92, 101, 157
generality 38, 42, 96, 101, 120, 129
German Idealism 13, 33, 36, 75
Goethe, Johann Wolfgang von 177
government spending 68, 98, 175
Goya, Francisco José de 49
Great Leap Forward 67

Grimm, William 214n
ground 2, 7, 55–7, 64, 67–8, 85, 122, 132, 134–6, 150, 162–3
Grundrisse 98, 100–2, 113, 138, 155, 160, 172, 176

Hafner, Kornelia 96
Hayes, Anthony 208n, 227n
Hegel reception 197–200, 227n
Hegelian Marxism 2, 11, 13, 197, 199, 200, 205n, 208n
Heterogeneity 6, 18–19, 32, 73, 81, 86, 89, 94, 119, 121, 128, 135, 140, 161, 184, 194, 198–9
Hilferding, Rudolf 150
historicism 199
Horkheimer, Max 23, 43, 60, 88, 143, 167, 192, 206n, 220n
Huizinga, Johan 191
humanism 77, 175, 199
Hungary 181
Hyppolite, Jean 8–9, 36, 127, 135–7, 141, 159, 163, 187, 199, 205n, 207n, 208n, 213n, 216n, 221n

idea xvi, xviii, 34, 159–60, 184–8, 226n
idealism 13, 32–4, 36, 41, 79–80, 111–12, 195, 207n, 211n, 215n, 216n
identification 6, 19–21, 31–3, 43, 52, 76, 96, 109, 117, 122–3, 125–6, 136, 138, 143–4, 169, 188–9, 192–3, 210n, 215n, 220n
 see also Identitätszswang
Identitätszswang 68, 109, 121, 138, 141, 143–4, 167–9, 182, 185, 192, 215n, 220n
identity 3–4, 18–20, 24, 28–9, 31–4, 39, 41, 44, 46–7, 49–55, 64, 66–7, 85, 88, 98–100, 102, 105, 111–12, 115–17, 121–2, 128, 130–2, 135–47, 149, 152–3, 155, 157–8, 161, 163–6, 170, 172, 174–5, 178, 182–3, 185, 188–9, 191, 199, 220n, 224n; *see also* Identitätzszwang
 of identity and non-identity 20, 32, 39, 49–50, 52, 67, 128, 137–8, 140, 146, 157, 183, 188–9
ideology xviii, 5, 20, 24, 38, 42–7, 88, 103, 164, 181–2, 205n, 212n, 214n

illumination 24, 145, 147, 150, 152, 184, 191
illusion xvii, 6–7, 27, 34, 40, 42, 44–6, 75, 80, 94–5, 120, 146, 162, 195, 225n
image xvii, 6–7, 34, 38, 50, 59–60, 62, 68–70, 75, 78–80, 85, 87–8, 93–4, 96–7, 101, 103–6, 115, 118, 120, 122, 124, 126, 129, 133–4, 136, 143, 145, 147–8, 157, 167, 180–1, 188, 192, 195, 201, 204, 207n, 208n, 225n
imitation 105, 168, 196, 206n, 220n
immediacy 17, 25–8, 30, 38, 47, 56–8, 85, 98, 111, 116–17, 125, 131, 137, 145, 168–9, 187, 200, 207n
immigrants 164–5
immiseration 18, 99, 204
indeterminacy 6, 8, 15
indifference 44, 112, 129, 133–4, 136, 138–9, 147, 207n, 221n, 222n
individuality 69, 79, 103, 121, 154–5, 161
 see also singularity
industrialization 67, 174, 177, 180, 202–3
inflation 202
Institut für Sozialforschung 4, 23, 210n
integrated spectacle 70, 72, 171–2, 178, 181–2
integration 40, 120, 143, 167, 171, 175–7, 197–9, 203–4, 225n
intellectual intuition 38, 200
interest-bearing capital 104
interiority 56–7, 59, 61, 65, 132, 136–7, 141–2, 145–7, 158, 166
internal relation 8, 16, 21, 43, 53–4, 61–2, 84, 94–5, 112, 114, 116, 130, 135–6, 141–2, 151–3, 163, 166, 170, 172–3, 222n
International Symposium on Marxian Theory (ISMT) 79, 211n
international trade 46
Internationale situationniste 17, 39, 49, 64, 70–1, 100, 118, 121–3, 140, 142, 168, 174, 179, 186, 210n, 214n, 217n, 224n
intuition 38, 200, 222n
inversion 5, 8, 20, 31, 46–50, 55–6, 60–2, 64–6, 72, 74–6, 80–1, 87–9, 94–5, 99, 103–4, 106, 113, 115, 120–1, 124, 130, 135–7, 141, 148, 156–7, 194, 213n

inverted world 20, 46, 48, 50, 55, 60–2, 64–6, 81, 89, 104, 120, 135, 137, 157, 213n
irrationality 6–7, 15, 49–50, 183
irreversible time 225n

Jacobi, Friedrich Heinrich 38, 111–12
Jappe, Anselm xvii, 11–12, 202, 210n, 212n, 219n, 225n
Jorn, Asger 140, 217n
juridical relations 113, 172–3, 202
justification 10–11, 40, 45, 54, 70, 88–9, 95, 99, 106, 157–8, 167, 169–70, 175, 193, 201
  see also legitimation

Kant, Immanuel 33, 55, 60, 111–12, 199–200, 207n, 216n, 219n, 220n
Keynesianism 174
Khayati, Mustapha 35, 210n, 224n
Khrushchev, Nikita Sergeyevich 72, 198
King Tut 194
kingdom of laws 59–60, 133–4
Kojéve, Alexandre 199
Korsch, Karl 2, 9–10
Krahl, Hans-Jürgen 96
Kraus, Karl 13, 23, 68

labour xvii, 3, 5, 32–3, 43, 66, 68–9, 71, 85–7, 89, 91–3, 96, 102, 113, 118, 144, 155–6, 167, 169, 180, 201, 203–4, 207n, 216n, 217n, 218n, 227n, 228n
  -power 5, 40, 102, 156, 166, 175–6, 180, 204
laissez-faire 174
Las Vegas 194
Lassalle, Ferdinand 221n
Lautréamont, Comte de 201
Le Monde 140, 198
Le Nouvel Observateur 17
Lebovici, Gérard 179
Lefebvre, Henri xviii, 5, 9, 107, 133, 142, 146–7, 161–2, 167, 176, 178, 185, 187, 200–2, 205n, 216n, 222n, 227n
Lefort, Claude 17
legitimation xviii, 44, 54, 95, 157, 169, 171, 175
Leibniz, Gottfried Wilhelm 55

leisure 88, 128, 154, 166–70, 175, 183
Lenin, V.I. xvii, 11, 115, 180, 201, 208n, 209n, 219n, 220n
liberalism 179
life xvii–xviii, 2–3, 6, 8, 16, 27, 35, 40–1, 47, 53, 68, 83, 88–90, 95, 100, 103–6, 111, 113, 118–20, 130, 139, 144, 152, 155, 157–9, 165–8, 172, 175, 186–8, 201–2, 206n, 207n, 210n, 217n, 218n, 223n, 226n
liquidity injection 175
looting 175, 202
Louis XIV 72
Lowe, Donald M. 101
Lukács, Georg xvii–xviii, 2, 9, 11–12, 21, 33, 109–11, 113–20, 124–7, 148, 179, 219n, 220n, 221n, 225n

Machiavelli, Niccolò 17
mafia 171–2
Mandela, Nelson 72
manifestation xvii, xix, 7, 26–7, 56, 61, 78, 95–6, 116, 130, 145, 147–8, 150–1, 158, 193
  see also Erscheinung
manipulation 6–7, 88, 93, 100, 152, 168, 172, 192
Mannheim, Karl 38, 44, 212n
Mao Zedong 67
Marcuse, Herbert 23, 128, 210n
marginal utility 98
Marx, Karl xv–xix, 1–5, 8–17, 21–2, 39–40, 44–5, 50, 54, 63–5, 73–4, 77–87, 89–94, 96, 98, 100–2, 104–8, 110, 113, 115, 118, 120–1, 138, 142, 146, 148, 154–7, 160, 162–3, 170, 172–3, 176, 188, 192, 195, 197, 199–202, 205n, 206n, 208n, 210n, 211n, 212n, 215n, 216n 217n, 218n 220n, 221n, 224n
Marxism 2, 11, 13, 106, 110, 115, 172, 197, 199–202, 205n, 208n, 210n, 218n
Marxist-Leninism 201, 220n
mass media xvi, 6–7, 148, 193
materialism xvii, 115, 205n
materialization of ideology 42, 45–7, 205n
media personalities 68, 96, 103, 152, 172, 180

mediation xix, 25, 28, 38, 47, 52, 62–3, 68, 76, 85, 114, 116–17, 125, 141, 159, 161, 168, 172, 175, 207n, 222n
mercantilism 170
metaphysics 66, 74, 76, 112, 150, 152, 214n, 215n 217n
Middle Ages 46
mimesis xv, 41, 44, 109, 114, 143, 168, 192, 194, 220n
Minima Moralia 14, 24, 30, 35
mirror xvii, 34, 56, 60, 75, 80, 85, 90–2, 106, 114–15, 122–4, 126, 145
misinformation 7
modernity 113
modernization 123, 182
Moinet, Jean-Louis 206n
monetary stimulus 68, 175, 203
money 21, 33, 43, 63, 65, 80, 84–7, 90–7, 101–5, 107, 120–1, 138, 154–7, 178, 207n, 212n, 223n
monopoly on use-value 86, 92–4, 97–8, 101
Mumford, Lewis 176
Murray, Patrick 79, 116, 215n, 216n
Musil, Robert 132
mystification xvi, 44, 50, 76, 88, 93–4, 104, 107, 121–2, 126, 173, 191
myth xiv, 43, 45, 96, 109, 123, 143, 225n

Nancy, Jean-Luc 6, 40–1
narcissism 169
Narcissus 109, 123
national liberation 96, 174
nationalism 68, 174
natural sciences 60, 111, 214n
necessity 6, 15, 30, 54, 64, 84–5, 104, 111, 114, 126, 130, 137, 145–6, 148–51, 158, 173, 176, 184, 222n, 223n
needs xvi, 33, 39–42, 64, 94–6, 98–101, 167, 176–7, 192, 203, 220n, 228n
negation xviii, 11, 25, 28, 30, 39, 53, 76, 86–7, 89, 97, 105, 139, 221n, 222n
Negative Dialectics xviii, 32, 42, 199
Neo-Kantianism 199–200
Neue Marx-Lektüre 79
Newton, Sir Isaac 55 214n
Nicholson-Smith, Donald 207n, 208n
Niethammer, Friedrich Immanuel 51
nominalism 5–8, 37, 93, 161, 208n

nouveau prolétariat 204
Novalis 38

objectivity xviii, 5, 15, 27, 29, 31–4, 43, 58, 63, 65–6, 75, 80, 87, 89, 107–9, 112, 116–17, 119, 156, 158–62, 184–6, 195
ontology xvii, 12, 24, 33, 41, 45, 66, 73, 75–6, 79–80, 84, 94, 116–17, 123, 126, 153, 199–200
opacity 13, 55, 105, 146
opposition 7, 28, 35–6, 43, 51–3, 59, 61, 66, 97, 112, 135, 141, 145, 154, 160, 163–6, 175, 181, 185, 189, 213n, 224n
opticality 75, 91, 94, 124, 130, 144–5
organization of appearance 41, 73, 106, 119, 123, 178
otherness 125, 130–1, 138–9, 141, 184–5, 224n
Ovid 109

pan-logicism 199–200
Papaïoannou, Kostas 9, 160–1, 224n, 226n
parataxis 209n
participation 5, 169, 193, 195, 219n, 220n, 225n
particularity 5, 8, 40, 65, 86, 89, 121, 129, 154–5, 158–62, 185
Pascal, Blaise 144
Pashukanis, E.B. 172–3
passivity 27, 57, 116, 119, 151, 192, 207n, 209n, 220n
pathological identification 167, 169, 215n *see also Identitätszwang*
Pericles 72
personification 5, 69, 78, 96, 106, 143, 155–6
petrification 32, 54, 73, 115–16
phenomenology xvii, 25, 27, 30, 93, 107–8, 199
Phenomenology of Spirit xvii, xix, 2–3, 8–9, 19–20, 24–30, 35–7, 48, 50, 55–6, 62, 108, 135, 141–2, 148, 188, 198, 200, 207n, 212n, 213n, 222n,
philosophies of reflection 110–17, 125, 219n, 220n; *see also Reflexionskategorien*

philosophy of identity 24, 32–3, 39, 46–7, 49, 52–3, 111–12, 116–17, 138
photography 105, 115, 143, 167, 169, 208n
Pinkard, Terry 58, 214n
planned economy 69, 177, 179
Plato 15, 41, 55, 115, 128
play of forces 57–60, 63–4, 72, 145
Pohrt, Wolfgang 96
Poland 181
police 68, 71, 143, 164, 174–5, 179–80, 182
political economy xvii, 1–2, 13–14, 16–17, 21–2, 64–5, 69, 78–80, 82–6, 104–5, 107–8, 113, 121, 138, 173, 192, 195, 210n, 215n, 216n, 217n, 224n, positivity
positivism 27, 41, 44, 80
possibility 31, 72–3, 87, 121, 149, 159, 195, 223n
postmodernism 1
Postone, Moishe 113, 201
postwar property 14, 17–18, 70, 84, 110, 167, 169, 193, 197, 202–4
see Trente glorieuses years
Potlatch 130, 226n
practicism 186
praxis xvi, 5, 9–10, 12, 146, 179, 211n
presentation 17, 25–6, 77, 79 84, 93, 103, 167, 186, 221n
see Darstellung
private property 173
production xvi, 2–3, 5, 13, 33, 36–7, 40, 43, 45, 50, 66, 68, 70, 79, 84, 86–8, 90, 92, 94, 98–106, 110, 113, 122, 129, 146, 152, 166–7, 169–73, 176–7, 181, 186, 201, 203–4, 206n, 208n, 217n, 218n, 220n, 224n, 227n, 228n
productive investment 193
productivism 227n
productivity 97–9, 169, 180, 202, 204
profit 85, 94, 155, 202
proletariat xvii, 18, 78, 103, 109, 124, 144, 169, 180–1, 192–3, 198, 203–4, 209n, 225n, 228n
protectionism 68, 173–4
pseudo-cyclical time 217n
psychoanalysis 201, 210n, 226n
psychogeography 208n

publicity 47, 101, 106, 150, 175, 177, 191, 209n
purchasing power 18, 92–3, 138, 169, 204

quantification 43, 63, 118, 219n, 225n
Quillet, Juvenal 1, 220n

Rancière, Jacques xiv, 6, 41
rationality xv–xvi, 3, 6, 18, 22, 33, 39, 49–50, 53, 73, 76, 167, 183–4, 188–9, 192, 195, 217n
rationalization 43, 49, 113, 118–19, 179, 192, 220n
real
 abstraction 216n
 subsumption 39, 95, 102, 203
Realphilosophie xviii, 188–9, 223n
reason 18, 49–53, 58–9, 76–8, 88, 106, 112, 117, 150, 185, 196, 198, 219n, 224n, 226n
 see also Vernunft
recognition 27, 39, 66, 69, 72, 112, 140, 167, 170, 173, 182, 185, 192, 194
reconciliation 4, 10, 18–20, 22, 31–3, 47, 52–3, 68, 76, 82, 121, 128, 141, 169, 178, 182, 189, 192–3, 199–200, 226n
recuperation 164, 209n
reflection xvi, 21, 26, 36, 46, 75, 90–2, 94, 109–17, 119, 122, 125, 131–2, 134–5, 137, 139–40, 143, 145, 149, 151, 153, 159, 166, 187–8, 211n, 219n, 220n, 222n
 see also Reflexionskategorien
Reflexionbestimmung 91, 114, 131–2, 138–41, 144–5
Reflexionskategorien 75, 80, 114
Reichelt, Helmut 65–6, 79, 88, 106
reification xvii–xviii, 2, 5, 11–13, 21, 32, 54, 63, 87, 109–11, 113–21, 124–7, 144, 167, 169, 192, 196, 215n, 219n, 221n, 225n
Reinicke, Helmut 96
relationality xvii, 25, 94, 111, 116, 122, 130, 132, 137, 139, 145, 222n
religion xvii, xviii, 45–6, 62, 74–5, 79, 120–1, 138, 143, 148, 215n, 217n
Renaissance 218n

representation xvii, 2, 6, 26, 66, 68, 75,
    88–9, 92–3, 97, 101, 103, 106, 124–5,
    146, 148–9, 158, 168–9, 181, 184,
    194, 207n, 210n, 213n, 218n, 225n
    see also Vorstellung
reproduction 3–5, 16–17, 41, 46–7, 76, 84,
    102, 106, 134, 143, 152, 155–7, 167,
    170, 204
revelation 27–8, 53, 136–7, 146, 152, 169,
    183, 187
Rickert, Heinrich 115
riots 174, 202
Rizzi, Bruno 170–81
Roman Holiday 178
Rubin, Isaak Illich 221n
Russia 174, 180, 182, 208n, 209n

Sanguinetti, Gianfranco 43
Sartre, Jean-Paul 198, 202
satisfaction 8, 15, 20, 30, 37, 40–2, 47, 81,
    94–6, 98–100, 119, 121, 167, 170,
    196, 200, 203–4, 226n, 227n, 228n
Schein xvii, 26–7, 40–1, 44, 58–9, 61–2, 75,
    78, 131–2, 145, 147
Schelling, Friedrich Wilhelm Joseph 52,
    111, 220n
schizophrenia 72, 194, 215n
Schlegel, Karl Wilhelm Friedrich 38, 214n
Schleiermacher, Friedrich 214n
Schlick, Moritz 41
Schmidt, Alfred 201
Science of Logic xv, 3, 8, 16, 19, 21, 28, 51,
    74, 110, 115–16, 127, 129, 131, 139,
    158, 185, 188, 208n, 215n, 219n,
    221n, 222n, 223n
Second International 115, 220n
Second World War 203
Seinslogik 129, 131–2, 138–9, 141, 149,
    158–9, 222n, 224n
self-consciousness 29, 55, 62, 213n
self-management 201, 227n
semblance 26, 44–5, 58, 68, 77–8, 95
    see also Schein
semiotics xvi, 1, 194, 208n
sensuous supersensible 20, 50, 58, 61–2,
    65–6, 86–7, 89, 96, 135
Silicon Valley 169
Simmel, Georg 113
Simon, Roland 227n

simple form of relative value 90
simulacra 1
singularity 8, 154, 160–2
Situationist International 15, 17, 23, 39–40,
    49, 64, 100, 118, 138, 140, 142, 152,
    164, 166–7, 169, 174, 181, 183–4,
    186–7, 194, 196, 198, 201–2, 207n,
    208n, 210n, 214n, 217n, 218n, 224n,
    226n, 227n
Six Day War 214n
Smith, Tony 79, 215n
social
    democracy 175, 193, 220n
    form 2, 5, 19, 31, 38, 84, 88, 105, 109,
        113, 115, 119, 124, 171, 173, 179
    housing 176
    media 1, 169, 193
    organization of appearances 11–12,
        137, 159, 189, 208n
    synthesis 4, 17, 44, 87, 103, 207n, 216n
Socialisme ou Barbarie 179, 201, 218n,
    219n, 227n
Sohn-Rethel, Alfred 4, 44, 105, 207n, 216n
solicitation 20, 40, 50, 57–8, 61, 63–4, 67,
    69, 81, 104, 135, 141, 145
Soviet Union 171, 179, 181, 201, 219n
spatialization 176–8, 219n, 225n
spectator 35, 37–8, 121, 125, 140, 168, 182,
    185–6, 188, 209n
speculative xv, xvi, xix, 1–4, 10–11, 13,
    15–16, 19–22, 32–4, 39–40, 47,
    49–55, 61–3, 65–8, 70–82, 99,
    110–12, 117, 119–22, 124–8, 138,
    141–3, 148, 150, 153–4, 162–3,
    165–6, 170, 175, 178, 183–5, 187–9,
    191–2, 194–6, 200, 205n, 213n,
    215n, 216n, 221n, 222n
speculation xvii, xviii, 8, 11, 20, 39, 50,
    52–3, 74, 77–80, 97, 124, 127, 187,
    210n, 213n, 216n
    see also speculative
speculative identity 4, 19–20, 47, 50–5, 99,
    112, 128, 163, 170, 175, 183, 185, 191
Spencer, Herbert 198
spirit 14–15, 18, 20, 28–30, 32, 34–5, 46,
    51–2, 54, 75–6, 79, 99, 148, 154, 159,
    187–9, 200, 209n, 212n, 226n, 227n;
    see also Phenomenology of Spirit
Stalinism 197, 200–1, 208n, 220n

state xvii, xviii, 19, 68, 70, 72, 88, 119–21, 128, 154, 166, 170–5, 179–83, 193, 201, 203, 224n
  infrastructure 203
  intervention 195, 224n
  socialism xvii, 179–80, 201
Straram, Patrick 227n
strategy xiv, xvii, 6, 13–14, 198, 207n, 209n, 226n
structuralism 199
subjectivism 29, 42, 98, 126
subjectivity 33, 42, 54, 74, 111–12, 114, 119, 125, 158–9, 173, 185–6, 198, 209n, 220n
substance 25, 27–9, 40, 44, 47, 55, 57, 59–60, 77, 80–1, 86, 89, 104, 106, 108–9, 112, 149–51, 153–5, 161, 185
Sue, Eugène 77
Sun Tzu 198
supersensible
  beyond 55, 61–2, 80, 112; *see also* *übersinnliche Jenseits*
  world 27, 50, 56, 58–62, 65–6, 96, 135–6
superstructure 173
surplus value 5, 155–6, 180, 203
Surrealists 201, 209n
syllogism xvi, 7, 154, 160–1
system xv, xvii, xviii, 6, 10–11, 14–16, 19, 25, 30–1, 33–5, 37, 39–40, 44–6, 51, 67–9, 83–4, 95, 111–12, 118, 124, 146, 149, 151, 154, 158, 164, 169–70, 173, 180, 186, 192, 194, 196, 199–200, 203, 206n, 207n, 211n, 213n, 217n, 221n, 224n, 226n
systematic dialectics 211n

Tacitus 14
Tauschen 58, 62, 214n
  see also exchange
tautology 39, 122, 157, 170, 220n
technology 6, 69–70, 88, 93, 129, 177, 202, 208n, 212n, 225n
television 1, 143, 182, 208n
the absolute xvi, xvii, xix, 5, 25, 29, 34, 37, 39, 75, 112, 144, 147, 149–52, 188, 213n, 215n, 216n
thinghood 5, 8, 10, 27–9, 34, 36, 44–5, 55–9, 61, 65, 75, 86–7, 91, 107, 116, 120, 122, 131–3, 135, 139, 141, 143, 145, 150, 168, 181, 192, 219n, 222n, 225n
Third International 220n
Tieck, Ludwig 49, 213n, 214n
total
  commodity 88, 108, 203, 216n, 217n
  ideology 44
totalitarianism 44, 68–9, 80, 118, 180, 225n
totality xviii, xix, 3, 5–8, 12, 15–19, 21, 25, 27, 30–40, 49, 52–5, 58–9, 61–4, 78, 81, 84, 88, 91, 93, 97, 101–3, 106–8, 118–19, 124, 127–30, 132–5, 137–8, 141–3, 145, 149–51, 153–5, 157–8, 160, 162–4, 170, 175, 177, 181, 183–4, 186, 191–2, 195–6, 198–9
  of appearances 63, 128
tourism 176, 178
town 128, 154, 165–6, 175–7, 183–4, 224n
transcendental idealism 207n, 220n
transparency 105, 130, 140, 145–7, 149–50, 152, 154, 157, 161, 175, 182, 187, 195–6
Trente glorieuses years 197, 202
Trotsky, Leon 220n
Trump, Donald 72
truth xvi, xix, 4–5, 10, 14, 19–20, 23–32, 34, 36–7, 39, 41–7, 49, 53, 55, 57, 59–61, 66, 72, 74–5, 89, 110, 116, 118, 121–2, 128, 132, 136–7, 155, 158–60, 166, 184, 189, 196, 208n, 211n, 213n, 215n, 219n

übersinnliche Jenseits 55, 112, 122, 126, 131, 133
understanding 20, 50–2, 54–6, 61–3, 66, 72, 81, 127, 141, 213n, 214n, 219n, 222n
  see also *Verstand*
unification 7, 31, 62, 70, 106, 117, 122, 125, 162, 182, 206n
unitary critique 8
unity-in-separation 3, 12, 50, 53, 60, 67, 69, 72, 81, 125–6, 174
universal
  equivalent 33, 45, 91, 93–4, 97, 101, 138, 142, 173
  relative form of value 91
universality 16, 21, 44–5, 56–7, 93, 101, 120–1, 128, 137, 154–6, 158–62, 173, 199

untruth 26, 28, 31–2, 34, 39, 47, 196
urbanism xiv, xviii, 19, 77, 103, 176–7, 203, 209n
use-value 19, 21, 33, 65, 86–7, 89–103, 105–6, 138, 142, 169, 217n
   fetishism 96; *see also* *Gebrauchswertfetischismus*

valorization 5, 102, 140, 155–7, 204
value xv, xvi, xvii, 3, 5, 19, 21, 63, 65, 71, 78, 80, 83–97, 101–8, 120–1, 124, 130, 138, 144, 154–7, 172–3, 180, 201, 203–4, 207n, 212n, 216n, 217n, 221n
Vaneigem, Raoul 64, 76, 99, 138, 142–4, 151–2, 180–1, 206n, 207n, 210n, 224n
Vanguardism 180, 201
Vaugelas, Claude Favre de 209n
Verdoppelung 72–3, 165–6, 178
Verene, Donald Phillip 214n
Vernunft 18, 51–2, 58, 66, 81, 117, 187, 199, 200
Verstand 51–3, 55–60, 62–6, 81, 111, 117, 187, 200, 213n, 219n
Vietnam 214n
violence 69–70, 151, 174–5
visibility 104, 133, 137, 145–6, 150, 195
visualization of value 90, 92, 97, 105
Vorstellung 26–7, 62–3, 75, 142, 148, 196, 207n, 210n, 211n, 222n

wages 78, 169, 180, 204
Watts 174
Weber, Max 113
Wechsel 63, 141, 214n
   see also exchange
Weltanschauung 46–7, 88, 93, 124, 129, 130, 133, 144, 222n
Wesenslogik 9, 21, 85, 91, 110–11, 115–17, 121–2, 124–30, 133, 136–42, 144–7, 150–4, 157–9, 161–3, 165, 182, 186, 221n, 222n, 224n
whole xix, 4, 16, 24–5, 27, 29, 30, 32–9, 43–5, 47, 49, 51–2, 54, 57–8, 61, 73, 97, 100–1, 103, 107, 112–13, 120, 136, 146, 149, 153–4, 159–61, 163, 165–7, 183, 186, 191, 193, 213n
Wirth, Louis 38, 212n
work 2, 10, 39, 78, 88, 124, 128, 154, 165–70, 174–5, 179–81, 183, 201–4, 218n, 222n, 227n
workerism 227n
workers' movement 2, 10, 39, 78, 179, 181, 202, 218n, 227n
world
   of appearance 58–9, 64, 66, 134–6
   market xvii, 69, 173, 181

Young Hegelian 9, 12, 77, 80, 211n, 216n

www.ingramcontent.com/pod-product-compliance
Lightning Source LLC
Chambersburg PA
CBHW072136290426
44111CB00012B/1883